Fraudulent
Lives

States, People, and the History of Social Change
Series editors Rosalind Crone and Heather Shore

The States, People, and the History of Social Change series brings together cutting-edge books written by academic historians on criminal justice, welfare, education, health, and other areas of social change and social policy. The ways in which states, governments, and local communities have responded to "social problems" can be seen across many different temporal and geographical contexts. From the early modern period to contemporary times, states have attempted to shape the lives of their inhabitants in important ways. Books in this series explore how groups and individuals have negotiated the use of state power and policy to regulate, change, control, or improve people's lives and the consequences of these processes. The series welcomes international scholars whose research explores social policy (and its earlier equivalents) as well as other responses to social need, in historical perspective.

Fraudulent
Lives

IMAGINING WELFARE CHEATS

from the Poor Law to the Present

STEVEN KING

McGill-Queen's University Press

Montreal & Kingston · London · Chicago

ISBN 978-0-2280-2279-4 (cloth)
ISBN 978-0-2280-2280-0 (paper)
ISBN 978-0-2280-2318-0 (ePDF)
ISBN 978-0-2280-2319-7 (ePUB)

Legal deposit fourth quarter 2024
Bibliothèque nationale du Québec

McGill-Queen's University Press in Montreal is on land which long served as a site of meeting and exchange amongst Indigenous Peoples, including the Haudenosaunee and Anishinabeg nations. In Kingston it is situated on the territory of the Haudenosaunee and Anishinaabek. We acknowledge and thank the diverse Indigenous Peoples whose footsteps have marked these territories on which peoples of the world now gather.

LIBRARY AND ARCHIVES CANADA CATALOGUING IN PUBLICATION
Title: Fraudulent lives : imagining welfare cheats from the Poor Law to the present
  / Steven King.
Names: King, Steven, 1966- author.
Series: States, people, and the history of social change ; 9.
Description: Series statement: States, people, and the history of social change ;
  9 | Includes bibliographical references and index.
Identifiers: Canadiana (print) 2024040078X | Canadiana (ebook) 2024040081X |
  ISBN 9780228022800 (paper) | ISBN 9780228022794 (cloth) | ISBN 9780228023180
  (ePDF) | ISBN 9780228023197 (ePUB)
Subjects: LCSH: Welfare fraud—Great Britain—History.
CLASSIFICATION: LCC HV248 .K56 2024 | DDC 364.16/3—DC23

This book was designed and typeset by pata in Minion Pro 11/14

CONTENTS

FIGURES

PREFACE

In 2020–21 the British government developed schemes to support the incomes and employment of those affected by COVID lockdown. These included extensions to existing benefit levels and the appropriation of new welfare models (especially "furlough") from other countries and contexts. As lockdowns subsided, attention moved to the question of how much money had been lost to systemic gaming of government schemes. Estimates vary wildly. We will never know the true magnitude, but reporting of suspected fraud has been substantial and concern over "wasted" money sustained.[1] While His Majesty's Revenue and Customs has thus far approached the recouping of incorrectly claimed income support with a light brush, high-profile court cases are underway.[2] An official inquiry has begun, though whether it will truly capture the meltdown of the benefit system and the wider welfare landscape of the National Health Service and mental health services remains to be seen. In the longer term, British government responses to the crisis have focussed on revenue-raising to fund catch-up and level-up, but a wider conversation will also be needed regarding the purpose and funding of the welfare system broadly defined – about what it means to be a "welfare citizen." The 2023/24 cost-of-living crisis merely exacerbates the need for this wider conversation.

Moral outrage over the gaming of the welfare state and the underlying benefits system is not, of course, new. In 2019 the *Daily Mail* reported the case of Elise David, signed off sick with back problems but still competitively show-jumping.[3] To most of those commenting on the article, this was a case of someone "swindling" the state without meaningful consequence. Whether welfare fraud had increased in the run-up to COVID is moot, but reporting of it was certainly prominent. Who, for instance, could forget Mark Hetherington, aka "The Stripping Ninja," convicted of faking benefit claims for chronic anxiety and agoraphobia after he was caught doing erotic dancing and nude modelling for art students?[4] More widely, it is possible to trace a strong and consistent seam of contemporary public scepticism over the moral worth of some welfare recipients.[5] Marie Buchan, for instance, received widespread attention in December 2014 because she was planning a "lavish" Christmas for her eight children funded by debt and £2,227 per month in benefits. Indeed, as objected in the

Daily Mail: "the unemployed single parent hasn't paid for any of it. Their lavish Christmas and new home is all thanks to the British taxpayers."[6] Right-leaning newspapers have rich traditions of publicising "abuse" of the welfare system, but even journalists of a different political persuasion have not been absent from this arena.[7] Commentary regarding Buchan and the wider canvas of issues raised by reality television programmes such as *Benefits Street* was scathing.[8] Contributors to online discussion forums across several platforms noted variously that: such benefits equated to a salary of c.£40,000; Buchan was "selfish"; the situation was "unbelievable"; "something dodgy [is] going on"; and that Buchan "lacked all moral fibre and self-respect."[9] Recent times of crisis have exacerbated public and press commentary about the supposed ease with which the welfare state is defrauded, but they do not *cause* such concerns. Indeed, and as we shall see in this book, the roots of fear about fraudulent claims and their impact on the finances and standing of the welfare state were established in the founding documents of our national welfare system. Public and policy rhetoric about fraud risk and prevention has been a continuous aspect of the framing of the British welfare experience ever since.

In practice (and a theme developed in chapter 3), the extent of fraud, as measured, seems modest. Modern longitudinal studies of the welfare system in its broadest sense show that over a life-course relatively few people gain real advantage in terms of "their" share of state resources.[10] Indeed, it could hardly be otherwise, given the realities that, *inter alia*: the British welfare system is amongst the least "generous" in the OECD;[11] welfare resources are skewed fundamentally to pensions; and record employment levels have coexisted with a systematic reduction in the real value of working age benefits.[12] In 2013 around 0.7% of the total welfare bill was reportedly lost to fraud.[13] By June 2017 the BBC was reporting for the 2015/16 tax year that only around £1.10 of every £100 paid was lost to fraud,[14] while *The Independent* noted that for the 2016/17 tax year the scale of fraud (around £3bn) was only 2% of the entire budget and was dwarfed by the scale of tax avoidance. *The Times* commentator Caitlin Moran raged over this same elision of welfare fraud and tax avoidance in December 2023.[15] Yet, the disjuncture between such headlines and recent popular perceptions – which tend to identify fraud as rife – is striking.

This disjuncture partly reflects the rhetoric and action of recent politicians. The post-2010 crackdown on welfare by the LibCon coalition, allied with the later introduction of Universal Credit, focussed attention on the supposed generosity of welfare packages in the round.[16] Before this, Tony Blair and Gordon Brown had mounted a moral crusade to get people off welfare and into work, generating extended press coverage of a supposed residuum who could not or would not work.[17] And before this, Margaret Thatcher's different administrations had systematically disguised structural and endemic later life-cycle unemployment by reclassifying those without hope of work as disabled, leading to a lasting and irremovable popular association of disability and fraud.[18] Yet to take this presentist view – to blame perceptions of endemic welfare fraud on an ignorant general public, stoked up by the popular press and the actions of modern politicians – is misleading. As we shall see, not only was fear of fraud written into the linguistic and policy framing of the earliest incarnations of our national welfare regime, but popular perceptions of the systemic abuse of welfare arrangements were everywhere and substantial.

Locating modern concerns, dilemmas, and perceptions of welfare fraud in a proper and effective historical context is one aim of this study. Focussing on the period from 1601 (the founding of the Old Poor Law, the world's first sustained national state welfare system[19]) and the present, part 2 considers the ways in which welfare fraud might arise or be constructed, ranging across a spectrum from intentional through to accidental. This complex "architecture" of fraud matters both for the way welfare has been constructed in the popular imagination and for the issues of fraud reporting and detection. Taking the four chapters together, we shall see that fraud by intent has always played a central role in popular perceptions of welfare recipients, irrespective of the fact that the welfare system moves (after 1905/06) from being focussed on discretion to being governed by universalising rules.[20] This is not necessarily negative – many people across this long period recognised that intense need could with justice foster welfare fraud – but it *is* pervasive. Other significant highlights from this section include the persistent association of fraudulent intent with single motherhood; the relationship between migration or immigration and popular perceptions of fraud;[21] and the remarkable historical and current vulnerability of welfare recipients and claimants to the redefinition of relationships, income streams, work activities, and so forth, all of which shift the ground for "genuine" claims.

Ranging over the same chronological period, the chapters in part 3 explore the questions of how and why welfare fraud – both its "real" and its perceived incidence – persists across the different incarnations of the welfare system. Each chapter explores a paradox emerging from the data: popular perception of substantial welfare fraud has strong historical longevity and yet, apart from short-term crisis moments, reporting of alleged welfare fraudsters and their activities is remarkably slim across the whole period;[22] local and national officials have and accrue considerable powers to seek out welfare fraudsters but rarely use them to the fullest extent; and those who frame policy have the power to crack down – and be seen to crack down – on welfare fraud and yet that power is used episodically at best. The essential sense of part 3 is that real or imagined welfare fraud persists because the public, officials, and policymakers of all periods want or need it to. Given the historical traction of this observation, in order to understand such welfare fraud we need to delve into the basic philosophies of those who claim, fund, and organise welfare, and into the wider question of how we interpret stratified welfare citizenship.

These themes are taken up in part 4, which investigates three key issues. The first is the relationship between actual or perceived welfare fraud and the consistently residualist role of the British welfare system. I argue that residualism both fosters and embodies low expectations of the system, its clients, and its moral basis across the full chronological sweep of the welfare state. The second issue relates to the intersecting interests of welfare recipients, the public, taxpayers, officials, and policymakers. I maintain that for the whole period 1601 to the present it has served no one's interests to systematically attack or detect fraud. And finally, I explore the future of the welfare state and underlying concepts of welfare citizenship. We shall see that from the 1880s to 1914 Britain was part of an international conversation about the rights and duties of the state and of its actual or future welfare citizens. Historians were at the forefront of that conversation.[23] The singular long-term impact of COVID will be the need for a new national and international conversation about what the rights and expectations of a future welfare citizen should look like and how the resulting welfare structures should be paid for.[24] Chapter 11 addresses this question in particular, arguing that historical perspective is important for future policymaking, and that unpicking the competing philosophies and perceptions around welfare fraud is vital to the future welfare-citizen project.

Undertaking a work of this chronological and thematic reach requires an exceptional dataset. The corpus consulted is described at length in the second chapter. Broadly the book relies on nine core sets of evidence:

1 Pauper letters, official and advocate correspondence, and administrative records (including minutes) relating to the Old and New Poor Laws, 1601–1929, and collected as part of two Arts and Humanities Research Council Project Grants and a Wellcome Trust Project Grant between 2008 and 2021.[25] The letter sets alone amount to over five million words;

2 Focus group perspectives arising from a jointly led and EU-funded multi-partner project on the rise of the Far Right in Britain and Europe, 1990–2017;[26]

3 Oral histories collected for other purposes but which touch on the welfare system by accident, including the Elizabeth Roberts Working Class Oral History Archive at Lancaster University;

4 Twenty-four oral histories and six focus group sessions (including claimants, self-identified fraudsters, non-claimants, and former administrators/policymakers) conducted between 1989 and 2016, all of which concentrated directly on the question of welfare fraud;

5 Field notes documenting *ad hoc* everyday encounters with attitudes to welfare fraud;

6 Existing datasets or reports from the Office for National Statistics, the British Social Attitudes Survey, the OECD, government departments, parliamentary committees, *Hansard*, political parties, politicians, think-tanks, and advocacy organisations;

7 A substantial collection of newspaper and news organisation articles (including comments adhered to them by the general public where possible), pamphlets, blogs, and social investigation materials spanning the period from the early 1700s to the present;

8 A collection of sixty-six memoirs, autobiographies, or diaries of people who reflect in passing or deliberatively on questions of welfare fraud broadly defined, and which cover the period 1690–1990; and

9 A diverse collection of ephemera, including instructional texts, films, photographs, justicing notebooks, and court records, which covers to varying degrees the whole period considered here.

This is the largest corpus ever interrogated to look at the longitudinal history of welfare. Even so, there are some forms of evidence that I do not consider, most notably court cases relating to welfare fraud. While I cover (as we see above) reporting of such cases, one of the contentions of this book is that detection and prosecution have been so rare that particular instances may not yield generalisable perspectives.

My focus is often on England and Wales. These were the two countries encompassed by the Old Poor Law and they were also joined together for the administrative purposes of the New Poor Law in 1834.[27] Scotland had, until 1845, an entirely separate welfare system more akin to the voluntary, religious, and municipal systems of continental Europe.[28] Even thereafter the Scottish system differed in key respects to that in force south of the border. Peter Jones and I have shown that it was not until the 1870s that Scotland was united with the rest of the mainland in a single welfare conversation.[29] Indeed, the country arguably became part of the national system only with the Liberal welfare reforms of the early 1900s. Nonetheless, Scotland is part of the analysis throughout, not least because we can find some elision of Scottishness with an inherent tendency to welfare fraud. The latter term is not (here or hereafter) used in a pejorative sense. As you will see from the story that ends this preface, I believe that much so-called fraud arises from the failings and philosophies of the system, its officials, and policymakers rather than from claimants themselves. However, in the linguistic architecture of the written sources used here – and even more in the oral histories and focus groups – rhetoric of fraud, cheating, and deception has a powerful hold and hence I use "fraud" as an encompassing reflection of that reality. I also repeatedly refer here to the term "welfare fraud" as opposed to "benefit fraud." This is because the term "benefit" (like the term "allowance") historically implies a right to support, whereas for the whole period from 1601 to 1908 and for many welfare recipients up to the 1940s, no such rights existed.[30] In turn, the term "welfare" captures payment in cash or kind to the unemployed, disabled, families (as in family allowances), the aged, carers, and immigrants/migrants.[31] It also encompasses support for the sick, though I do not deal in a sustained way with the post-1948 National Health Service. This decision reflects in part the difficulty of stitching together reliable historical evidence on the particularities of medical fraud over the long term, but more significantly it captures the fact that most people in my datasets who were commenting on welfare in the postwar era do not consider the NHS as part of "the welfare state," however incongruously this sits with modern policy understandings.[32] This is not to say the subject is absent – the issue of immigrants supposedly defrauding the NHS recurs in oral histories, for instance – but it is not central at the conceptual or document level. At the same time this book is *not* a long history of the development of the welfare state; nor does it follow the intricate twists and turns in the level of inequality in British society – both matters already executed in capable hands.[33] It is also important to understand that this is *not* a history of welfare fraudsters and their individual and collective motivations. I capture their views and experiences – sometimes deliberately, often accidentally – but my book is essentially about how those looking in on the issue of fraud conceptualise the act, the people involved, the reasons for it, and the consequences.

In planning the book, two intertwining logistical questions had to be played out. Would I adopt a chronological narrative, working through the different incarnations of the welfare state from 1601 to the present, adopting an approach familiar from other historical work on welfare? Or would I adopt thematic drivers and try to capture chronological change within the resulting thematic chapters, such that (to quote from one of the excellent anonymous referees for this book) "history serves as a kind of resource" but with the danger that the historical narrative becomes fractured or even disembodied? In the end, what struck me when analysing millions of words of evidence and thousands of stories as I prepared to put the book together was just how easy it would have been to simply cross out the dates on those sources. Linguistic registers, referential infrastructures, attitudinal trends, and other variables display remarkable historical continuities. I thus turned strongly towards a thematic approach. Doing so raised a further logistical problem: how to ensure that a book which starts with modern dilemmas does not simply use historical sources in an *ad hoc* or scattergun way? In one sense, the absence of meaningful historical evidence from the arena of debate over welfare fraud means that the addition of *any* historical sources is an advance. More seriously, however, I have in what follows tried to quantify the evidence drawn from different source types in different periods. While I often use a single story to emblematise or capture a particular point, or a series of stories drawn from different source types to illustrate continuity over time, these are not randomly chosen. They emerge from wider process of counting, classification, close reading, and ranking. The result still does not add up to a conventional narrative history but, for this theme in this policy and citizenship moment, that is (for me) alright.

The agendas driving this work will be clear from the discussion above. Nonetheless, they are encapsulated by a very personal story. My father, whose own parents were illiterate, still has only limited literacy himself, having left school before he was a teenager. When asked to fill in a (long) form dealing with pension credits, he simply guessed what ought to go in each box and filled them in with random words and figures that he knew. The pension credits duly rolled in for years until he received a letter demanding attendance at an interview on suspicion of his defrauding the system. I had known none of this, but the letter prompted my new involvement. We attended the interview suited and booted, with my father instructed to keep his mouth shut (no easy task), and I duly announced myself as the son, Professor Steven King. Within minutes of my beginning to speak and pick apart their process and assumptions, the case was dismissed. My father's payments continue to this day. For any campaigner dealing with the welfare state these will be depressingly familiar circumstances. But let us reflect on some navigation points in the story. My father was suspected of fraud because he had incorrectly filled out the form (cheating by accident) and because there had been a change in the rules that he had no knowledge of (cheating by definition and redefinition). But why that moment? Had someone "dobbed me in?" my father asked. The answer was clearly no because council estate people are not known for doing that sort of thing, as borne out strongly in my oral history sample. But something *had* changed. After all, it would have been obvious from my father's "scrawl" (his word) that the form was incorrectly completed when it arrived, and the HMRC super-database allowing them to look at the income and outgoings of every adult in the UK was by then operational. Officials *could* have known that there was something wrong with his payments.[34] By chance, and having moved on from a job he considered worthless, one of the officials I met that day signed up for a focus group. He quite properly did not talk about particular cases but made two important points: first, that welfare officials do not generally want to seek, and even less to find, welfare fraudsters (I revisit his reasoning in part 3); second, that often a change in personnel, a new minister, or the need to react to a particular scandal or newspaper headline was the trigger for a casual trawl of welfare payments they already knew or suspected to be wrong: "Examples had to be found."[35] My father was just such an example until the case officers were faced by someone with much superior knowledge and experience. In retrospect what strikes me most about these experiences – from the question of how illiterate or poorly educated people navigate the welfare system, through the role of advocates in short-circuiting the welfare process, and to the complete failure of those charged with running the system to seek and find welfare fraud in "normal" times – are the remarkable historical parallels and roots of my father's experience. Indeed, our sojourn at the benefits office is only truly explicable when set in an historical context. It follows, then, that history must be part of the process through which people like my father become future welfare citizens.

ACKNOWLEDGEMENTS

This book captures three decades of work on welfare fraud. In that time, I have incurred numerous debts to funders, including the Arts and Humanities Research Council, Wellcome Trust, Leverhulme Trust, and British Academy, though the book itself is not the product of any single grant. Colleagues who have worked as research associates on those grants – Carol Beardmore, Natalie Carter, Margaret Hanly, Alice Haydock, Peter Jones, Catherine Roberston, Jane Rowling, Alison Stringer, Steven Taylor – will recognise the data used here, and I am grateful for their efforts. Numerous others have given me material, and those sources – especially vestry minutes from Richard Dyson and Peter Jones – have been important to the argument of the book. More widely I am grateful to participants in the focus groups, perspectives from which are important to my argument here, and to those who have provided oral histories and family-interest material. Without these contributions, *Fraudulent Lives* would not "be."

There are also of course personal acknowledgements. Richard Baggaley and the team at McGill-Queen's University Press "went" for the original proposal of a book with roots in the discipline of history but ranging across so many other subject areas from anthropology and economics to media studies and sociology. I also owe a debt to my father, who appears often here. He is both a primary source and a man with strong views on welfare that have informed my own. Our joint journey through the British welfare system has been an eventful one. Finally in terms of acknowledgements, Professor Elizabeth Hurren has lived with this book in the background for many years and provided its title, for which I am truly grateful.

Steven King, Lyddington

CONVENTIONS

Paupers: Those receiving welfare in the pre-1929 incarnations of the welfare state, in distinction to applicants or those on the margins of welfare not *yet* in receipt of payments.

Select Vestries: Vestries constitute the ratepayers of a parish or other administrative or tax–raising unit with ultimate say over local tax-and-spend policy, including approving annual accounts. Select Vestries were (elected or appointed) subsets of this broader group, usually actively involved in day-to-day decision-making over who got what and how much. This body had powers to direct officials such as the overseer of the poor. Until 1834 only approximately 32 per cent of parishes had or had experimented with Select Vestries.

Pension: Prior to 1929 this term referred to regular allowances given (on a discretionary basis) to the aged or other long-term welfare-dependent groups such as the disabled. From 1908 and thereafter it also referred to what we now know as the state pension.

Quoted text from primary materials retains original spelling, punctuation, and emphasis unless stated.

ABBREVIATIONS

AHRC Arts and Humanities Research Council
BBC British Broadcasting Corporation
BRO Berkshire Record Office
BSA British Social Attitudes Survey
CORO Cornwall Record Office
COWAC City of Westminster Archive Centre
CRO Cumbria Record Office
DGAC Dumfries and Galloway Archive Centre
DRO Devon Record Office
DWP Department for Work and Pensions
EYRO East Yorkshire Record Office
GRO Gloucestershire Record Office
HAC Highlands Archive Centre
HMRC His Majesty's Revenue and Customs
HRO Hampshire Record Office
LERO Leicestershire Record Office
LGB Local Government Board
LIRO Lincolnshire Record Office
LRO Lancashire Record Office
NAO National Audit Office
NDRO Northumberland Record Office
NHS National Health Service
NORO Norfolk Record Office
NRO Northamptonshire Record Office
OECD Organisation for Economic Co-operation and Development
ORO Oxfordshire Record Office
PLB Poor Law Board
PLC Poor Law Commission
SLAC Sutherland Local Archive Centre
SORO Somerset Record Office
SURO Surrey Record Office
TNA The National Archives
WYRO West Yorkshire Record Office

part one
Frameworks

CHAPTER 1

Fraud, Fraudsters, and Doubt

The 1601 Elizabethan Old Poor Law established four broad principles that were, with superficial modification, to shape the national welfare scene for nearly 350 years.[1] First, relief of the needy was placed in the hands of local ecclesiastical parishes. To meet these obligations, newly created "overseers of the poor" were to raise money from a local tax on property. This principle of aligning local poverty with local relief was modified (especially in 1723 and 1782 by enabling acts which allowed for combinations of parishes to administer welfare or build workhouses), but in most places and at most times the single parish remained the core focus of the Old Poor Law. Localized control was both necessary – the Elizabethan state lacked the reach to introduce national uniformity or central direction – and prudent; it was assumed that those who bore the brunt of paying for welfare would be diligent in controlling costs. The Poor Law Amendment Act of 1834 changed the locus of welfare administration in England and Wales, with parishes becoming systematically organized into larger "unions." A core of localism was maintained by the fact that these new administrative units were governed by "guardians" who were still elected at parish level.[2] Continued local involvement and control after 1834 had fundamental consequences for the reach of the newly established central authorities. Such localism also stood at the heart of the Scottish poor law pre- and post-1845.[3] The Liberal welfare reforms, which sat alongside the New Poor Law for almost a quarter of a century from 1906, further threatened the localism of the English and Welsh (and by then, Scottish) welfare system. Even so, substantial numbers of the dependent poor were tied into essentially local arrangements up until the 1940s.[4] The centralised and directed system that developed gradually post-1948 can thus be understood as a brief historical version of the welfare state.

The second broad principle established in 1601 was that of deservingness and not. Located in older duties and obligations associated with the gift relationship,[5] the category of "deserving" was simultaneously both elastic and circumscribed; corporate and individualised; moral as well as economic.[6] Under the Old and New Poor Laws (that is, 1601–1929), children and the sick claimed a broadly constructed "deserving" status, but even elements of the Liberal reforms such as the state pension were also shaped by questions of deservingness.[7] Being deserving was in turn reversible at both the group and individual level, and susceptible to moral panics, economic downturns, and changing political will. While the advent of the postwar welfare state began to remove such fragilities,[8] we shall see that the conceptual infrastructure of deservingness – moral duties to work, prior contribution, gratitude, sexual restraint – is arguably little different in the 2000s from what it was in the early 1600s.[9] It is all too easy to regard current questions about entitlement – Has someone made enough national insurance contributions to gain a state pension? Should immigrants with no record of financial contribution be entitled to welfare? Should the state pay for the support of women with multiple illegitimate children? – as reflections of the modern welfare state when they actually speak keenly to philosophies of deservingness first codified by law in 1601.

A third broad principle was that of local discretion. Crudely, under the Old or New Poor Laws no one had an entitlement to *receive*, as opposed to *apply for* welfare. In this framework, eligibility for relief could be compromised or rescinded on the basis of local moral judgements and unsubstantiated rumour. As I have shown elsewhere, two people with exactly the same circumstances could be treated very differently in terms of relief eligibility within the same parish, let alone between adjacent or proximate places.[10] Yet, the theoretical power of arbitrary local officials was tempered by a right of appeal to magistrates who, much like judges seeking to control the political abuse of "welfare power" in the 2020s, could do much to establish precedent.[11] Moreover, I and others have argued that paupers and poor applicants equated local discretion with a right to contest and negotiate welfare.[12] Indeed, the existence of local discretion remained a cornerstone of welfare practice during the interwar period, and its role or potential role in the overall welfare framework remains a subject of heated discussion even today.[13] Certainly we should beware of assuming that local discretion as fact or rhetorical artefact inevitably retreats in the face of the centralising and universalising tendencies of the state in the later twentieth century.[14] In this sense, the absence of any historical perspective in much of the literature on modern iterations of local discretion is especially regrettable.

The final principle embedded in the 1601 law was that of residuality. Its essence in that law is that English and Welsh (and even more, Scottish[15]) welfare was never *meant* to provide comprehensive support to claimants. This is ultimately true of all national European systems but the British commitment to residuality has unusual longevity and intensity.[16] The exact "generosity" of different elements of welfare varies according to a recipient's life-cycle stage, exogenous circumstances, region, and cause of poverty. Nonetheless, many welfare historians have pointed out that very limited income replacement rates emerged from the British welfare system before the 1940s.[17] While the postwar welfare state may have pushed back against residuality with its "cradle to grave" philosophy, the interlude was a brief one. Many modern commentators now reflect on the absolute insufficiency of British welfare payments as well as their relative inadequacy on the international stage.[18]

A Changing Canvas

These persistent conceptual frameworks are important for my argument that welfare fraud as practice and as a construct of the public and policy imagination can *only* be understood through analysis of the deep historical roots of the national welfare system. Their imprint on modern welfare debates and problems is profound if often unremarked.[19] However, particularly from the mid-nineteenth century forwards, significant changes gathered pace which constitute important framing factors for understanding the milieu on which the public, policymakers, and advocates or opinion-shapers came to draw. Thus, while I note above that discretionary welfare as a process has greater longevity than is usually acknowledged, the rise since 1908 of formulaic, rules-based and increasingly universalising welfare practices and entitlements has complex consequences for my argument. Rules and entitlements make it (theoretically) easier to define what fraud is and is not.[20] Because they are "national" and can be "known," rules may also be weaponized to encourage the "general public" to report transgression. Moreover, rigid entitlements that are flexible only at the very edges make the post–1948 welfare system in particular less elastic and responsive, potentially incentivising dishonesty. These issues are explored at much greater length in part 2.

Alongside, and partly related to these changes in the critical mass of local discretion, we can observe increasing central knowledge, and later central control of the welfare system. The British state began collecting welfare expenditure information in unplanned and superficial ways in the 1750s, but not regularly until after 1813.[21] The 1834 New Poor Law was in turn a deliberate intervention to extend central control of welfare practice in English and Welsh regions, and even more to extend central knowledge.[22] Annual published returns of spending categories allowed the different iterations of the Central Authority, politicians, individuals, and communities to understand how their own practice was and might be calibrated to the national "average" or to comparable place-based peer groups.[23] The supplementary and overlapping information-gathering required by the Liberal welfare reforms marked a step-change in both information flows and central controls, themes which have continued unabated into the 2020s, when no fewer than nineteen different arms of parliament or government (plus private and semi-public data collectors and handlers) provide summative reporting on aspects of the non–NHS welfare state.[24] Yet, we should also understand that complex information garnered by the general public through multiple and often partial or contradictory channels usually becomes distant information, creating a significant gap between what "the public" can know about both welfare and welfare fraud and what they do or can be bothered to know. In this gap sits the fertiliser for radical popular imagination.

Another gap – the "familiarity gap" between those who pay for welfare and those who benefit – is also a product of the post-1850 period. Under the Old Poor Law the socioeconomic distance between marginal local taxpayers and recipients was slim. As Derek Fraser and others have noted, the New Poor Law in its initial period did surprisingly little to disrupt this picture, and many local ratepayers complained (with justice) that they were little more than paupers themselves.[25] The risks of the lower-middle orders falling into poverty were ever-present and there was also a surprising lack of physical distance between "solid" ratepayers and those they funded.[26] From the later nineteenth century, however, a number of coalescing processes that occur repetitively in different guises drove conceptual, experiential, and physical wedges between taxpayers and welfare recipients. Amongst them were urban renewal, including slum clearance and council-house construction; the decline of pauperism as living standards improved;

institutionalisation of people with sensory, physical, and mental impairments; post-1908 welfare reforms which gradually left the anonymous job centre as the visible manifestation of need; taxation structures which broke apart welfare payments from local revenue raising; and, above all, structural income inequalities. Recent policy changes such as the income cap above which child benefit is withdrawn have substantially increased the impact of this "familiarity gap." At the bottom end of the income distribution, the 2020s have seen rising minimum-wage thresholds and frozen tax-free allowances, such that there is no meaningful difference between those in low-paid jobs paying taxes and those largely or wholly dependent upon welfare. This situation exactly replicates the 1660s. For the bulk of taxpayers, and even more so the very small percentage of payers who disproportionately fund British public services, the familiarity gap has widened inexorably post-1948 and in accelerated fashion from the later 1980s. Pressure groups, some think-tanks, and left-leaning Liberal elites have consistently tried to keep the poor and the residuality of the welfare system in the public spotlight. However, the inevitable tri-partite effect of the familiarity gap – not caring "enough" to demand remedial action; the de-legitimisation of particular groups and welfare recipients as a whole; and the idea that there "must" be fraud and inveterate scroungers – has had an insistent place in public commentary.[27] As Katherine Curchin has argued, the development of a passive welfare economy where welfare entitlements are cut adrift from contributions, has undermined the moral status of claimants.[28] Seen collectively, the familiarity gap does much to explain recent observations of low and weakening public support for redistribution through the welfare state.[29]

A final important contextual development gathering pace from the nineteenth century has been the rapid and significant change in how ordinary people obtain their information about welfare bills, rules, and recipients. Eighteenth- and nineteenth-century newspapers carried significant coverage of general poor law matters and specific events and incidents, including riots and opinion pieces on workhouses.[30] By the 1840s, journalists were covering and reporting discussions in Board of Guardian meetings at union level, as well as all manner of other information about poverty and welfare.[31] Indeed, a sense that newspaper reporting (editorials, local and national news, letters, and spin-off investigations and activities) fundamentally shaped public perceptions of the post-1834 welfare system has been a historiographical mainstay.[32] Certainly from the 1750s newspaper reporting was supplemented by extensive pamphlet writing, records of local inquiries, and (notably from the 1840s) independent journalistic investigation that might fuse into or overlap with the social investigation movement which became prominent from the 1850s and continues today.[33] Moreover, "how to" guides for officials were widely available. There is substantial evidence that the poor and their advocates read them. And reporting of expenditure trends was both normative and enhanced during times of national economic stress or periods of welfare reform.[34] The public ecology of knowledge about the Old and New Poor Laws was thus diverse and remained rooted in the local, knowable, and see-able. In the course of the twentieth and twenty-first centuries, this ecology narrowed decisively, and a modern imperative to understand how the welfare system and its claimants (and fraudsters) are constructed in the newspapers, on TV, and over the internet reflects these realities. Such narrowing has profound consequences which become apparent if we ask: "*where* does the welfare state exist?" For the eighteenth, nineteenth, and even the first part of the twentieth century, the answer to this question was found in the everyday realities of taxpayers and claimants, and secondarily in newspapers, pamphlets, the courts, halls of central government, and images. As the West Country farmer Samuel Kendall noted: "What is simply '*news*' in the ordinary way to the individual or the public often spells tragedy in any of our family private circles," tragedy that required action and empathy.[35] By the 1970s, or indeed arguably even the 1960s given the profound shock over poverty and welfare that the film *Cathy Come Home* is said to have had on the public psyche, the welfare state had come to exist largely in the imagination.[36] Welfare became less something that was experienced and more something that was constructed. Such change has had fundamental consequences for the value placed on different welfare strands, the locus of perceived responsibility for the poor (central government rather than communities and individuals[37]), and the power of high-profile cases to shape the way that fraud was suspected, rhetoricised, and acted upon.[38]

Writing about Fraud

Set against these backdrops, the historiography of welfare *fraudsters* is surprisingly shallow. Writing in 2002, Keleigh-Ann Groves argued that there was "a small but growing body of research which seeks to explore why people engage in benefit fraud." One of her own central contributions was to identify a template of motivations that focussed on the agency of fraudsters – proper beginnings, fall from grace, and supplementary explanation including need, benefit complexity, and above all people's ability to fill their normative roles, including motherhood and fatherhood.[39] Subsequent British and international research projects have done something to enrich this understanding. In terms largely of the experiences of the last two decades we now understand that fraud is motivated by complex intersections of organised and directed crime, ignorance, economic desperation, a desire to buck the system, senses of natural right to certain necessities and lifestyles, bad luck, free-riding,[40] greed,[41] wider stigmatisation of welfare including endemic scrounger labelling,[42] and the self-reinforcing complexity of welfare processes which push certain sub-groups of welfare recipients inexorably to the margins of complete destitution. There is no equivalent body of material on the motivations and attitudes of fraudsters in the variously constituted welfare systems of the period from 1601 to the later 1970s. While the literature on vagrants, beggars, and thieves is rich, surprisingly little of it touches upon the claiming and defrauding of welfare.[43] Rather, for both contemporaries and subsequent historians, the issue of welfare fraud becomes intricately entwined with discussions of the presence and activities of so-called scroungers and malingerers. In the wider and more general histories of welfare, the fraudster and his or her motivations have the most fleeting of presences.[44]

As I mentioned in the preface, this book is *not* about welfare fraudsters as such; it focusses rather on public and policy constructions of welfare fraud. In this area, the recent and historical literature has a more determined imprint and sits at the intersection of multiple disciplines – economics, philosophy, sociology, anthropology, media, management, English literature – rather than being rooted *solely* in history and social policy. No single review of that literature can do justice to its intellectual, methodological, and substantive range, though Peter Golding and Sue Middleton's analysis of 1976 as a turning point for public anxiety – an anxiety variously focussing on welfare recipients living in luxury, the existence of professional and skilled fraudsters, administrative failure to confront fraud, and perceptions of endemic fraud – is a foundation point.[45] Five features are, however, important for the wider agenda of this book over and above writing about the scale of fraud (dealt with at length in chapter 3). First, while fraud and fraudsters as specific categories of analysis are missing from most historical studies as I suggest, proxy categories, including research on the workshy, "inadequate" parents, single mothers, fractured families, the non-working "disabled," and "dossers," are a rich linguistic and actual presence. Some – single mothers, for instance – have a consistent place in narratives of dishonesty right up to the present and across the disciplinary spectrum.[46] Other groups – the disabled, for instance – hove into and out of view as potential fraudsters in the public and policy imagination.[47] This picture is complicated by the fact that attitudes towards welfare fraud and fraudsters are simultaneously an independent variable (generated by personal experience, suspicion, and knowledge) and a dependent one (that is, arising from the measurable and knowable). Thus, significant numbers of those who give written or oral testimony reflecting on the issue do so not on the basis of first-hand experience but from gossip. The way they remembered and linguistically constructed fraud depended on who and what they heard, not just on wider thinking about codified groups of the poor. Seventeenth-century rumour about vagrants and underemployed migrant workers descending on towns and posing a threat to socioeconomic and cultural order have a twenty-first-century analogue in a core fixation of the Brexit debate: that immigrants hoovered up benefits to which they were not entitled and thus were somehow treated more generously than the native population.[48] This book employs focussed case studies of particular types of welfare recipients precisely for these reasons, and a wider suite of relevant literature is contextualised in subsequent chapters.

Meanwhile, a second and related feature of the wider debate is about public construction of an underclass, a "residuum," broadly understood. This matter has gained enhanced piquancy in the aftermath of COVID as workforce shortages coincide with record numbers of people on long-term welfare dependency,[49] but the concept of a residuum has consistently been of interest to historians and others.[50] There is little agreement on the historical definition of this group; writers variously construct it as an economic, social, moral, locational, group-based, behavioural, or even inherited category.[51] Though often seen as rooted in the social investigation movements of the nineteenth century,[52] linguistic and rhetorical registers referring to underclasses can in fact be traced back to the social protest movements of the early nineteenth century or even to the episodic vagrancy crises of the early modern period. Such underclasses (like their modern counterparts) were not just potential welfare fraudsters but potential criminals, vandals, social outcasts, disease vectors, and moral vacuums as well.[53] The imputed size of the underclass varies according to background socioeconomic conditions,[54] chosen definitions, or thinking about the meaning of poverty,[55] and the group is always imagined as (sometimes simultaneously) receding and advancing, hopeless and shifty, and beyond help or crying out for it. Crudely, the size of the underclass has generally been estimated at between 3 per cent and 7 per cent of the national population. Some groups have a consistent place in the popular understanding of this term, but in broad terms its perceived membership has usually had more to do with personal and moral failings than with simply being part of a certain life-cycle or economic stratum.[56] In turn, models of the underclass shape the way welfare is understood and how members of the public prioritise action on welfare fraud and welfare fraudsters.[57] Thus, it matters historically and presently whether tales and gossip about fraud are grasped and retold as instances of bad people with bad upbringing and bad attitudes, or as examples of a systemic problem relating to an active, large-scale, and suspectable underclass.[58]

Ultimately this distinction is shaped by the particularities of the storyteller and the stories they tell. Nonetheless, a focus on the underclass leads us to a third central feature of the literature important for this book: the tension between seeing the poor in general as essentially untrustworthy and, alternatively, constructing them as possessing natural, logical, or human rights. Though largely understood in presentist terms and from the disciplines of law, social policy, economics, and sociology,[59] this tension was in fact deeply inscribed into the founding act of the British welfare system. A moral and theological duty to help the poor was firmly established before 1601. These were not exactly human rights, but perhaps close enough. The Old Poor Law changed the complexion of the issue, moving the expectation of action away from voluntary or co-opted giving with an element of moral force, towards the imposition of a redistributive tax on property owners.[60] This change gave rhetorical and moral force to categories of deservingness which (as we have seen) gained sustained and persistent traction on the British welfare state.[61] Even so, the philosophical commitment of the English and Welsh population to welfare was concrete. At times of what we might construct as "crises of the welfare state" – the 1790s, 1820s, 1920s, early 1950s, and the 2010s – this commitment appears to have been largely unshaken. Yet it is quite another thing to argue that there was widespread support for the claims and rights of the poor, let alone human rights to social justice.[62] As I shall argue in chapter 3, the establishment of the world's first national welfare system created a powerful accompanying scepticism about the honesty of the poor as a whole, one that we generally do not see in states that came later (sometimes centuries later) to formulating national systems and with a very different mix of insurance or contribution elements and wholly different political complexions.[63]

A fourth strand of the broader literature on constructions of welfare fraud has focussed on questions of surveillance infrastructures and the related administrative and financial costs of action and inaction. In a modern sense, we know both that the possibilities of surveillance have grown substantially over the last twenty years,[64] and also that the reality of finite financial and human resources induces those charged with completing such surveillance to make fine judgements about value-for-money.[65] The deeply presentist construction of this issue is misleading; from the very earliest days of the British welfare system, Kirk elders in Scotland and overseers of the poor in England and Wales were specifically enjoined to "know" their poor and employ continual engagement lest circumstances change. At times of stiff welfare reform such inspection and surveillance could be shared by charities and even private agencies, prefiguring modern trends for the outsourcing of welfare-related administration, including fraud control.[66] Yet joining the modern with the historical records encourages us to consider wider agendas that have a persistent if fractured place in the welfare literature: Should the poor have agency? Did they? Who "owns" the information that circulates in the administrative processes of the state? Who can and should hold the control points of the welfare system? How can the state legitimately get information on fraudsters and their activities? And what should the limits on state knowledge be? When considered on the long historical canvas, welfare fraud offers a lens through which to explore these basic questions.

This observation takes us in turn to a final important feature of the literature used to frame this book, that of *welfare citizenship*. From 1601 to the present, spending on welfare (especially where we include the sick pre- and post-1948) constitutes the single most significant strand of government intervention. Exactly how much has been spent at different times is opaque.[67] Well into the twentieth century, elements of spending were included in the "welfare budget" even though they had little, or at best tenuous connection with the needs of the poor.[68] Efforts to assess spending levels more generally are complicated by the episodic presence of charities and arm's-length organisations, fractured central record-keeping, and "hidden" spending on particular groups of claimants.[69] At its least generous (and ignoring the tiny payments made to encourage people to move on or to address fleeting incapacities), the Old Poor Law would make small cash payments and expect the poor to meet their wider needs by allocating the cash to their most urgent priority. At its most supportive, by contrast, the parochial state would meet housing,[70] fuel, food, and clothing needs in a single package. Brodie Waddell, using an intricate matrix of hypothecation from knowable parish spending, suggests that in 1600 only 0.06 per cent of GDP was spent on welfare but that by 1800 the percentage had risen to 1.84 per cent, indicating a decided tilt towards the more comprehensive end of the spectrum in most parishes.[71] Surprisingly little changed post-1834. The fearsome reputation of the New Poor Law workhouse may or may not be deserved[72] but for most people and at most times welfare was dispensed in the form of payments in their homes. Even restrictions placed on guardians by law and mandate preventing them from paying rents, buying tools, or providing other elements of the comprehensive package offered by the Old Poor Law at its best seem often to have been honoured in the breach. The proportion of state resources absorbed by social welfare spending in the nineteenth century is not straightforward, given the apportionment of the costs of administering the New Poor Law, the accounting mechanisms used for arm's-length institutions such as cottage homes, and the sometimes murky overlap between "state" and "charitable" funding.[73] But George Boyer suggests that by 1907 spending was just 0.8 per cent of GDP, a substantial fall from Waddell's estimates for 1800.[74] The gradual extension of rights-based and universalist payments post-1908 increased the absolute amounts spent by the local and national state on social welfare broadly defined, but the proportionate change is flattened by wider increases in and extensions of the remit to government spending outside of wartime conflict.[75] Even so, Boyer posits that welfare broadly defined was absorbing 9 per cent of GDP in 1960.[76] By the accounting year 2020/21 Britain was spending 11.8 per cent of GDP on non-NHS welfare (more than doubling since 2000/01), with this figure then increasing substantially during COVID and the recent cost-of-living crisis.[77]

This extensive role of welfare in public spending has always been accompanied by a complex matrix of expectations, including: expectations of the welfare system held by claimants and potential claimants; expectations of claimants by themselves, politicians, taxpayers, and the "public"; and expectations fostered by what we might understand as opinion mediators such as newspapers or (more recently) blog sites. These overlapping, complementary, and sometimes competing expectations have in effect defined what it meant and means to be a "welfare citizen." This status, so defined, strays well beyond the written rules that shape the processes of applying for, receiving, and keeping welfare payments. It features prominently in the popular imagination at times of crisis or stress, or in response to exogenous factors that prompt "people" to think about the causes or consequences of poverty and the meaning and function of the welfare system, as the relative balance of the obligations and duties of state, individual, and family comes under scrutiny. Extensive and extended "rights" to welfare were, as I began to argue earlier in this chapter, a product of the postwar era, and there has been much debate about the dilution of those rights (and thus on the meaning of welfare citizenship) from almost as soon as they were granted.[78] For the purposes of this chapter, however, the key point is how the status and obligations of claimants have been understood at different points. This is important for a sense of how and why people form their opinions about the scale and depth of welfare fraud and (crucially) whether the public feel strongly enough to shape the agendas of policymakers.

The legislation of the Old Poor Law had little to say on the obligations and status of welfare citizens beyond establishing the broad and elastic categories of deserving and undeserving poor. Still, historians of the early Old Poor Law have set out some important markers, most obviously a sense that welfare recipients should be grateful, deferential, cautious, and self-reliant, drawing on the resources of taxpayers for the shortest possible time and in the shallowest way possible.[79] Assessing how far these characterisations applied to the claimant population in the seventeenth and early eighteenth centuries requires further research. More clearly, by the early nineteenth century parishes had proven themselves chronically unable to get rid of charlatans, fraudsters, and serial claimants. These people joined other poor applicants and recipients in actively negotiating their relief, often without even the veil of deference. Arguably, the typical welfare citizen had, over two hundred years, become rather less grateful and rather more entrepreneurial, a change that was widely regretted in public commentary founded on a much more limited and backward-looking conceptual model. Such models were further undermined over time. Welfare citizenship became a substantial issue from the 1790s, as inflation and rising poverty drove massive increases in nominal poor-relief bills at the same time as growing public commentary on the demography of the poor raised fears of a perpetual underclass of the chronically poor reproducing themselves at will under the auspices of state welfare.[80] At least in the public imagination of the elite, the acceptable welfare citizen was one who did not breed – and certainly not outside marriage.[81]

Discussions about the broad concept of welfare citizenship (even if not officially so-called, as we shall see in chapter 11) were of course continuous. Nonetheless, and as I suggest above, several "fracture" points stand out.[82] The 1834 New Poor Law was *not* one of them. Although it marked a significant organisational and procedural change, altering the balance of power between centre and locality and pauper and taxpayer, the New Poor Law was not underpinned by a radical change in the definition of welfare citizenship.[83] By contrast, it was the 1880s and early 1890s that marked a decisive break in the conceptual infrastructure, ushering in foundational changes that were to persist until the first New Labour Government of the later 1990s. It was at this time that the emergence of poverty lines and detailed research on the lives of poor people in London and the provinces challenged the idea that poverty largely reflected individual failings.[84] For Marjorie Levine-Clark, these influences coalesced to give weight to narratives and concepts of "honest poverty," or a sense that exogenous circumstances constrained the ability of men and women to plan substantial self-help routes and could catapult respectable people with a record of prior contribution into dependency despite their best efforts.[85] Sickness, trade downturn, and structural imbalances in the economy or labour market and in wage earning were all features that created a grasping underlay of poverty which the state had an obligation to recognise and ameliorate. This was a matter of "civic and economic agency for honest poor men" but it would also signal their "incorporation into the nation."[86]

In practice, the challenge to long-established models of welfare citizenship was greater than this focus allows. Deeply rooted linguistic reference points of shame-faced poverty – the idea that respectable people could be drawn into shameful dependence[87] – alongside wider notions of contributory citizenship with roots in the obligations of a state to those providing military service, became juxtaposed with wider European concerns over the meaning, unity, and purpose of the state as an entity to fundamentally change the public conversation about both poverty and welfare.[88] In Britain at least, the growing importance of female involvement in welfare practice and the democratisation of elections for Boards of Guardians added urgency to an increasingly international feeling that existing models of welfare citizenship were failing.[89] By the later 1890s the status of welfare citizenship was fast becoming established in the policy (and indeed public) mind. We see state duties, contributory and non-contributory entitlement, a dilution of individual and familial obligation, and the replacement of expectations of deference and gratitude with expectations of administrative probity, accumulating contribution, and honest dependency. The Liberal welfare reforms, so often understood as a matrix of measures that after 1906 provided the foundations for the later welfare state, were merely an extension of this thinking and a response to the changing model of welfare citizenship that it embodied.

Whether the poverty and welfare consequences of the Great Depression did as much to change the basis of welfare citizenship as they did to etch the residual nature of welfare on the public imagination is moot.[90] More certainly, the period from the early 1940s through to the 1952 Conservative administration represented a further period of evolution in the expectations of the marginal and taxpaying populations and the understandings of the nature of, and obligations attached to, welfare citizenship.[91] Even so, many commentators have overstated the degree to which post-1948 developments in particular changed the basis of welfare citizenship.[92] Clearly, the linguistic register of "clientage" and an enhanced understanding and rhetoricisation of rights to and expectations of support are firmly rooted in this period. The financing and scope of the welfare system also changed markedly even outside the National Health Service. Yet the vision of William Beveridge – a comprehensive system of rights that guaranteed more than basic living and contributed strongly to social cohesion – was not realised.[93] Residualism still stalked a system that was persistently vulnerable to competing models of the "proper" place of state welfare. More elastic incarnations of welfare citizenship were subject to reversal in the face of changed ideologies, cost, and the resurgence of normative worries that state involvement created underclasses unwilling or unable to look after themselves.[94]

By contrast, two periods in the later twentieth century offer more fundamental disjunctures which are important to the agenda for this book. The first was in 1986 and more generally the latter half of the 1980s.[95] Financial deregulation, the initial consequences for citizenship arising out of council house sales, tax reform, and sustained efforts to rationalise (and arguably ration) benefits came together to lay the foundations for changed attitudes towards wealth and income inequality and the value of self-reliance vis-à-vis the welfare system.[96] Tony Blair and Gordon Brown took up those multiple agendas in 1997, the year that marks the second major disjuncture.[97] By the early 2000s the nature of welfare citizenship had changed, arguably even reverted to the much older models of the Old Poor Law.[98] The ideal welfare citizen was self-reliant, in work for most of the time or in some form of part-time work, and had obligations as well as rights. Hard-working taxpayers were the analogue to the welfare citizen, and the effective cap on rates of direct taxation for this group that has done so much to constrain the actions of subsequent chancellors was established in this period. Certainly the "New Deals" for welfare recipients implemented from 1997 improved skills, bolstered work participation (not least through the provision of childcare support), and reduced underlying levels of poverty through a combination of welfare support and a new minimum wage. On the other hand, the language of duty and reciprocation that accompanied these changes under the Blair-Brown administration was a direct reflection of their joint conception of the nature and meaning of welfare citizenship.[99] While the post-2010 LibCon coalition rhetorically extended this attempt to redefine welfare citizenship – an ever-keener focus on individual rather than state responsibility and the need for rights to be balanced by contribution and fairness to taxpayers[100] – the citizenship model at the first outbreak of COVID did not reflect this or subsequent Conservative engineering.

Arguably, then, record welfare spending was by 2020 perched on top of a model of welfare citizenship that had come full circle since 1601.[101] As I began to argue in the preface, however, COVID has wrought intricate changes in public attitudes to the role of the state, the definition of welfare, and the palette of rights and obligations that define citizenship. The period from

2020 to early 2022 encompassed the biggest real-terms welfare "splurge" since 1601. At peak COVID, a remarkable 54 per cent of the population had some connection with the welfare system, not including the NHS. These figures eclipse those that can be imputed for the later 1790s. The impact on state finances has been catastrophic as fiscally incontinent governing and opposition parties competed to argue for the permanent uprating of welfare payments and the inexorable transfer of taxation resources to state pensioners.[102] In turn, the 2023 cost-of-living crisis fuelled insistent calls for "government help," resulting in an energy price cap which made the entire population into welfare citizens against the backdrop of record postwar tax rates. For these reasons, chapter 11 reflects on where the welfare state (and with it, welfare fraud) might go in the 2020s.

Finding a Place

The foregoing discussion shows that public and policy understandings of welfare fraud emerge from a complex matrix of continuity and change in variables including: information gathering and giving, concepts of citizenship, mediatisation of public life, personal belief systems, fluid concepts of the underclass, and the tension between popular support for a welfare state and an ingrained suspicion of the claims of the poor. Yet, a literature that spans multiple disciplines and approaches remains fractured, and the lack of historical perspective on fraud and fraudsters is notable.[103] Large and important questions about fraud – its incidence, ecology, and persistence – are thus neglected, and current issues that should be understood as having deep historical roots (and hence potentially solutions that draw on historical research) are disembodied from their proper context. Thus, on 26 August 2021 a *Daily Mirror* report covering how the Department for Work and Pensions (DWP) investigated fraud cases attracted eight online comments, one of which suggested: "Most are probably spending it [defrauded welfare payments] on pot."[104] On the day I read this comment I happened to be going for a medical test. The same article came up in conversation (at her instigation once she knew I was writing this book) with the nurse taking blood. Her feeling, strongly expressed, was that fraud was written into the very DNA of claimants, who would rather confect stories (and thus be reliant on taxpayers such as herself) than use the same energies to better their lot.[105] Framed and understood in a modern sense, such attitudes reflect the particularities of media coverage, the demonisation of welfare recipients at a time of emerging labour shortages, or even a sneaking suspicion that people were just being "allowed" to be dependent by a useless state. Yet, if we track backwards 193 years to 29 January 1828, we find the Somerset diarist John Skinner starting a long and winding story about "old Rossiter" and his wife who claimed to be housebound because of illness and infirmity. In the course of four further diary entries about the couple, he came to the conclusion that their need was feigned. By 17 July 1828 he was writing: "At length I began to perceive the imposition … I have observed among the lower orders that this kind of cunning is frequently considered *the acme of wisdom*."[106] This anecdote is not merely a random incident; we will encounter many other historic stories of this sort. Taken together, they provide a conceptual, narrative, and analytical thread that runs seamlessly to the attitudes of modern online commentators.

This story should encourage us to seek a different explanatory framework for public constructions of fraud, as well as prompt questions about why fraud persists and how its persistence impacts the long-term health of the welfare system. Doing this requires a cross-disciplinary approach, a very large and complex dataset stretching over 420 years, and a detailed sense of how we can and should define welfare fraud. It is to these issues that the following chapter turns.

CHAPTER 2

Finding and Doing

In May 2012 the *Sunday Times* reported on a "Benefit Cheat [who] Hangs on to Chelsea Flat":

> An illegal immigrant has used human rights legislation to allow her to continue living in a council flat in one of London's most desirable areas despite being a convicted benefits cheat. Joy Chishimba is still receiving welfare payments on a property in Chelsea even though she used a false British passport [she was a Zambian national outstaying a visa] to defraud the taxpayer of more than £30,000 … Chishimba admitted she was wrong to carry out the fraud, but claimed she had been forced to take "desperate" action after accidentally becoming pregnant and being kicked out by her ex-boyfriend. "I didn't just wake up one day and decide to do this, I had to protect my daughter" she said.[1]

Most newspapers reported on the case around the same time, the *Daily Mail* noting that "The Royal Borough of Kensington and Chelsea council … received a tip-off that Chishimba was an illegal immigrant."[2] The outrage in online forums was widespread and predictable. In structures of civic and moral stratification, immigrants, and particularly illegal immigrants, have a determined place for both policymakers and the general public.[3] For commentators the case embodied a toxic combination of unworthiness: illegal immigrant (and, largely an unspoken issue, Black[4]), single mother, benefit fraudster, feckless client of the state, and someone with a shameless lack of gratitude.[5] There was rather less reporting of the subsequent legal battle over the right to "hang on" to the accommodation and Chishimba's ultimate eviction. The website *Zambia Watchdog* reported the outcome on 15 October 2012, quoting a local newspaper:

"At the heart of this case is fairness," said the Royal Borough's Cabinet Member for Housing, Cllr Tim Coleridge. He continued: "Should someone who has obtained a scarce council resource through deception be allowed to hold onto it thereby denying someone else? We do not think so and I am pleased and relieved to see the County Court agreeing with us so firmly."[6]

We return to many of the issues raised by this case in subsequent chapters. Here the key question is one of *definition*. Superficially, Chishimba is caught squarely by the definitional wording on the government's own fraud website landing page: "You commit benefit fraud by claiming benefits you're not entitled to on purpose. For example by: not reporting a change in your circumstances [or by] providing false information."[7] Yet she had also defended herself with a subtle argument centring around natural justice *in extremis*. I began to explore this theme in chapter 1, but it needs further attention here as we unpick the intricacies of public understanding: Chishimba had not woken up intent on defrauding the system; she had no choice, being a single woman with a vulnerable daughter. Claims of this sort are rooted in perspectives such as those of Raymond Plant, who argued in 1988 that citizenship, however tenuous or fleeting, meant that "the right to the means to life has priority over the unfettered right to property."[8] It would be easy to couch this example in terms of the modern linguistic register of human rights.[9] In fact the ego-documents that throw light on the English and Welsh (later British) welfare system from its inception are replete with similar rhetoric of natural justice or, as it might be conceived, "fraud by necessity." The oral histories informing this book make exactly the same point. "RK" in his reflections on council estate life in 1980s Northamptonshire noted: "They had to do it; there was nothing to do or to get, they had families to feed."[10] Further back, Stephen Reynolds in his account of living in the poor fishing community of Sidmouth (Devon) in the early 1900s noted that the poor man "knows vaguely ... that only by a succession of miracles, a long series of hair's-breadth escapes and lucky chances, does he stand at any moment where he is."[11] Almost a century earlier (25 February 1823), John Pearson had asserted his natural rights. Having badly injured his leg, Pearson suggested that his not having had a reply to an earlier request "inducies me to think that you supose me to be imposing." He set out the likelihood of permanent weakness in his leg and ended the letter with an appeal to *both* humanity and natural rights, asserting:

now Sir you may judg of my situation whether I am in Necesity or not but I have don as long as I Can so that without your asistance I must be obliged to apply to this township for Relief which I should be very sory to do if it was not Real necesity but I hope you will not put me to that.[12]

Pearson's was not an isolated case. There are more than a thousand letters in my data spanning the period from the early 1700s to early 1900s in which welfare payments were *in extremis* constructed as an inevitable right for the individual and an obligation for the state.[13] Such views affect both how fraudsters justify their actions (as with Chishimba) and how far ordinary people characterise, sympathise with, or are even complicit in welfare fraud.

Yet these examples also suggest the complexity of *defining* welfare fraud both in the present and historically. What might the current government definition of "on purpose" look like? How should we understand the very notion of "fraud" in looking back to the essentially discretionary welfare systems of the pre-1929 period where the intent of claimants could be subjectively (and indeed morally) defined by the person receiving the claim? And how does the definition of intent vary across the three categories of engagement with the welfare system – applying, getting, and renewing – at different points in time? The next section of the chapter explores these basic linguistic and definitional issues. It proposes that we can identify five broad types of welfare fraud – an "architecture of fraud" – which chapters 3 to 6 examine closely. In subsequent sections we deal with the scale, strengths, weakness, and coverage of the core source sets that allow this book to consider fraudulent lives over the very long term and at a truly national level, and with the conceptual and interdisciplinary methodologies that are required in order to analyse and pin together that diverse and voluminous set of data and challenge the presentism which frames so much of the current literature.

Defining and Locating

At the heart of modern concerns about welfare fraud stand the concepts of intent and deliberation. The preface gave some examples of newspaper articles which point definitively (if often hysterically) to people wrongly claiming benefits "on purpose." We can extend this approach for the post-1990 period. A suite of searches for the terms "benefit fraud" or "welfare fraud" (and their linguistic equivalents, such as "scrounger") across the newspapers analysed for this book generates some four thousand hits relating to Britain or the devolved administrations.[14] Many pattern seamlessly onto the examples we have already encountered: a man who "pocketed 26,000 in disability benefit" despite being an avid golfer and using his taxpayer-provided car to get to the golf club; a refugee who, "scarcely able to believe her luck at the mass of benefits that flowed her way after her family arrived in Britain … was greedily building up savings and hiding a private income of £16,000 a year, and keeping them secret from the authorities";[15] and the "five biggest cheats who between them stole £750,000" shamed by the government in 2014.[16] By 2024 there was widespread worry about fraudsters simply "making up" children to gain a range of welfare payments. Some cases garnered particular notoriety because they involved famous or once-famous people: P.J. Proby was accused of fraud in 2011 and responded by suggesting: "The Government's always been against me. They come after me when they are bored";[17] Kevin Glancy, the former Bronski Beat singer, who "avoids prison after fiddling more than £30,000 in benefit fraud scam";[18] and David Lyttleton, who was prosecuted after he failed to declare a legacy from his father, Humphrey Lyttleton.[19] While reported mitigation in the thousands of cases might point to depression and mental illness, marriage break-up, intermittent and episodic illness, or supposed lack of knowledge, the original intent to defraud was often apparent. Modern ego-type sources used for this book – letters, oral histories, focus groups – also suggest that individuals and communities were keenly aware of an undercurrent of deliberate fraud. Over half of those who offered oral histories identified serial offenders, and a significant minority felt they could identify fraud running in families, within and between generations. For these reasons, part 2 of this book starts with a chapter on fraud by intent.

Yet, we should not be deceived by modern media coverage or particularly notable scandals, however much such coverage captures the popular headlines.[20] Most cases of suspected fraud either proceed no further than the inquiry stage – because intent cannot be proven, evidence is wrong or contradictory, or cases lapse for other reasons, including being timed out – or because they are resolved prior to prosecution through sanction, warning, or other mechanisms of control and coercion.[21] The pension credits "case" against my father was dropped simply because he had an articulate and powerful advocate who could ensure that the assumptions of modern case officers – that you as a claimant must prove your innocence – were challenged and re-instated in the proper order, with the state having to prove intent and purpose. These observations are not of course "new" in the sense of accumulated social policy literature; nor is evidence that, given limited resources and the consequences of losing too many court encounters, the welfare authorities tend to prosecute only the clearest and most high-profile or egregious cases.[22] In this sense we might subtly amend the government definition encountered above: "~~You~~ *Some people* commit benefit fraud *that we can seek to prosecute* by claiming benefits ~~you're~~ *they're* not entitled to on purpose. For example by: not reporting a change in your circumstances [or by] providing *ambiguous* information."

To some extent, however, these matters of intent are illusory. As well as identifying fraudsters in their communities, those who have provided testimony for the post-1945 elements of this book identify considerable ambiguity. They speak of people being "caught out" by intricate forms, rule changes they were not aware of, or changes to customary practice and interpretation. Thus, in oral testimonies and focus groups, there was a palpable sense of anger from those caught out (and in effect demonised as fraudsters) when politicians put a return to work for the structurally unemployed in decayed northern and midland towns back on the political agenda.[23] Almost all the ego-material dwells also on genuine uncertainty over how to interpret known rules. When does (and should) a live-out boyfriend get classed as a regular enough fixture to affect welfare payments? If a divorced partner makes intermittent child support payments, when does intermittent become regular enough to be classed as "income" for welfare purposes? If disabling pain comes and goes during the course of a day, week, or month, at what point do you become able-bodied *enough* to have to inform the welfare authorities? If you sell things on auction sites, does this count as income for welfare purposes, given the existence of a tax-free allowance for such activity if you are not in receipt of welfare support? These everyday ambiguities inflect the attitudes of communities and individuals to welfare fraud and generate a real sense that it is possible to cheat by accident or to be "caught" by changes to rules, thresholds, and definitions. Many of these modern commentators – those looking in on welfare fraud and those accused of committing it – also highlight a further group of fraudsters: people who are constructed as "shifty" or inherently dishonest by association. As we might expect from the discussion of deservingness, welfare citizenship, and the underclass in our first chapter, single mothers are a prominent sub-category of this group, as are immigrants such as Joy Chishimba and the children of disabled adults, who are sometimes seen as helping those adults "put on" their disabilities whenever they go into the public arena.[24] Few of those providing direct testimony for this book could (as opposed to would) name names, but most had "heard stuff," in effect identifying a further definitional category of "cheating by rumour."[25]

Against this backdrop, the four chapters of part 2 encompass explorations of fraud by intent, by association (including rumour), by definition or redefinition, and by accident, with fraud by necessity a cross-cutting theme. At the heart of the argument is the idea that these categories are wrongly constructed in presentist terms and yoked systematically to the rise of national rule-based welfare systems underpinned by universalist principles. Rather, they transcend historical chronology and the organisational constellation of welfare services and payments. This long continuity matters both for how we should think about fraud and the mechanisms for confronting it, and for the meaning and purpose of the wider welfare state.

Sources and Approaches

Yet, writing about perceptions of welfare fraud over the very long term presents considerable challenges. While I argue that there are remarkable long-term continuities to fears and perceptions of welfare fraud, measuring it in any precise *comparable* way over this period for all three stages of welfare engagement – application, receipt, and renewal – is impossible. On 13 May 2021 the *Guardian* reported that the Department for Work and Pensions (DWP) had traced "Record levels of benefit fraud in first year of [the] pandemic in Britain."[26] The document to which this article referred was clear in its terms of reference and definitional framework, but at its heart were multi-layered assumptions, projections, interpolations, and caveats.[27] Even with all the modern apparatus available in 2021, the precise figures reported by the *Guardian* were little more than guesswork or, worse, illusory. We return to this 2021 report in chapter 3. For now, it follows that historic levels of welfare fraud can only be estimated or inferred. This is not to say that precision must be entirely sacrificed – we will see that there are in fact some very convincing figures – but that any definitive time-series must be foregone.

Even dealing with public and policy *constructions* of fraud, however, requires caution. The linguistic registers used to talk about, infer, or allege fraud of all sorts changes over time and varies according to whether writers, speakers, and commentators deal with personal acquaintances and kin as opposed to groups of "the other" such as immigrants, migrants, and single mothers.[28] To some extent such registers are inter-correlated with the changing means though which fraud is or can be identified. The absence of Civil Registration prior to 1837 meant that establishing the identity of an individual, let alone their accumulated contribution or deservingness, was problematic. Analyses of the nineteenth-century censuses point to a stock of people whose names, ages, and place of birth varied between statements, and the enduring problems of establishing who someone "was" inflect much welfare decision-making prior to the 1920s. Detecting fraud prior to this was, therefore, a matter of observation, speculation, rumour, or individual past history, and the linguistic register to describe and have an opinion about fraud was similarly personalized across all the pre-1900 sources: X is not to be trusted; I have heard something about Y; you/we have been misled by Z. This situation changed progressively across the twentieth century, as rule-based systems and formalised reporting and detection systems lead to a parroting of official or schematic language (reporting, rule-breaking, deliberation, entitlement, detection, dishonesty, withholding information) in newspapers, blogs, comments, and oral histories. It is striking how often focus groups just cited information that was "out there." On the other hand, and as I began to argue in the preface, assembling a set of core sources that can collectively reveal linguistic and attitudinal complexity and dynamism both at national level and more locally or individually can do much to mitigate potential problems.

This book thus deploys a very considerable and diverse dataset covering the period from 1601 to 2024. Foremost are letters written by, for, or about the dependent poor (including advocate letters), along with associated correspondence by officials charged with making decisions on welfare cases. Drawn from every county in England and Wales and five in Scotland, the core letter set covers the period from 1711 until the early

1900s.[29] Together, these and related documents (including the minutes of poor law guardians in selected locations for the period 1834–1900 and parochial vestry minutes prior to 1834[30]) amount to some five million words. Such sources privilege the voices and experiences of the noisy and combative, and of course we must be alive to questions of truthfulness and representativeness.[31] Yet, given that they cover most mainland counties and encompass the whole spectrum of socioeconomic community type and literacy (from those with basic orthographic skills to people of standing and education slipping down the social scale), such letters constitute a formidable untapped core for a study of welfare fraud over the long term.

These ego-type materials are supplemented and extended by other source sets of the same genre. Over more than thirty years I have read, categorised, and analysed sixty-six diaries, autobiographies, and (especially) broadly construed memoirs and "memorial" books. The strengths and weaknesses of diaries and autobiographies are extensively considered in the broader literature.[32] Memoirs and memorials are less commonly used and in one sense the labels are misleading. Thus, my material runs from the three volumes of Cecil Torr's *Small Talk at Wreyland*, which combines personal memories and reflections with material drawn from the extensive letters and diaries of family members and some anecdotes but offers little by way of thematic ordering or logical sequencing, through to the stilted and ordered West-Country farming memoirs of Samuel Kendall already encountered in chapter 1.[33] These books are neither a record of particular lives nor a comprehensive rendering of the life, character, and culture of individual places. But in some respects this is the point; we are interested in finding where welfare and welfare fraud appears as part of the casual and everyday observation of authors. Against this backdrop, while the diaries, autobiographies, and memoirs (amounting to just under three million words for close reading) have a variable yield when it comes to perspectives on welfare fraud, few fail to mention the issue directly or indirectly. Since I have simply read what came to hand rather than assemble a structured sample, this level of concentration is remarkable. When I draw on individual examples, then, the findings are more than anecdote, and capture something systemic in the sources themselves. The ego-set covers the period from the 1690s to the 1980s, though it is strongest for the period from the early 1800s to the 1950s.

Manuscript and printed sources like these are reinforced with three strands of oral history or written testimony. First, I have analysed a number of pre-existing publicly available oral history collections for perspectives on welfare in general and welfare fraud in particular. These range in scale from the four million words transcribed by the Hertford and Ware Oral History Group, through to 104 relevant interviews available in the Elizabeth Roberts collection and the two dozen life histories written by people with connections to Old Headington (Oxford), and their contents cover the period from the early twentieth century to the early 2000s. Repurposing oral and written testimony in this way is not of course unproblematic.[34] The Hertford and Ware oral histories, for instance, concentrate on education, war, and the built fabric of the area, and on these matters they provide a singularly comprehensive account. As with memoirs and other book-form ego-documents, however, a project focussing on perceptions, as this one does, can find as much value in fleeting and accidental references and inferences as in sustained commentary. The pre-existing oral histories have both. Second, I have conducted twenty four oral histories (fourteen with men and ten with women) which focus specifically on the question of welfare. The earliest dates from 1989, and the latest one used here was taken in 2016. The remembered events stretch broadly from the 1920s to the 2020s, with a particular emphasis on the period between 1936 and the early 2000s. All interviews were in semi-structured format, with the same eight core questions about welfare and attitudes towards welfare fraud asked of each respondent as a starting point. Interviewees were drawn across ages ranging from nineteen to eighty-four, and amongst them were current and former welfare recipients, those who had never "gone to the state," a core of middle-class individuals, and a small selection of *former* officials. Five participants had been convicted of welfare fraud and 35 per cent had been accused of it at some point. People were disproportionately drawn at the time of interview from council or social housing estates in Northamptonshire, Oxfordshire, Shropshire, Rutland, and Lancashire, though, as I observe, the middle-class and higher-income brackets were not absent. Since 31 per cent of all interviewees had relatively recently moved into the areas where they were interviewed, I inevitably gathered perspectives from a wider spatial and community-type range. I did not in constructing my sample encounter the reluctance, suspicion, and hostility elaborated by Keleigh-Ann Groves.[35] Focussed oral histories such as these generate very particular perspectives, but in a reverse of the pre-existing oral history resources it is striking how often issues such as education, literacy, shopping, the built environment, national politics, family, and transport occur as incidental discussion items.[36] Four people who provided family letter sets or photographs, authored their own material, or wrote "late" unpublished memoirs and autobiographies were *also* part of the oral history or focus group samples, thereby yielding an important bridge for, and grounding to, their written observations. In some ways they serve as a control group for the wider set of interviewees. Finally, the book uses perspectives (embodied in field notes and summative records) drawn from focus groups: one established in 2014 as part of an EU project investigating growing Far Right influence on the web, and two convened specifically to consider welfare fraud. The groups met a collective six times between 2014 and 2016. I also use *ad hoc* encounters (familiar from disciplines such as anthropology) with individuals who, completely unprompted, conveyed their views on welfare fraudsters as part of conversations that developed once they knew I was writing this book.[37]

Inevitably for a project of this sort, it has also been necessary to include pamphlet and newspaper sources, as we have already begun to see. These include the British Library Newspaper Collection (and Welsh and Scottish equivalents), individual newspaper archives, Nineteenth-Century Pamphlets Online, Gale Digital Resources, Adam Matthew Digital Resources, Wellcome Trust, and Hathi Trust, as well as modern think-tank and pressure-group archives. In total 159 discrete pamphlets, opinion pieces, manuals, and reports stretching from 1654 to 2023 were analysed. While a focus solely on welfare fraud in these materials is rare on the historical front (eight hits across all of the digitised pamphlet resource platforms and multiple search terms[38]) many of those dealing with the organisation of the poor laws, the scale and causation of poverty, vagrancy, begging, and questions of demography or taxation contain material ranging from the honesty and dishonesty of the poor as a class through to discussion of individual cases of need on the one hand and fraud on the other. In terms of online newspapers for the pre-1930 period, the well-known problem of defining search terms and filtering results has particular purchase. Thus, the search term "welfare fraud" yields just twenty-two results, while combinations of phrases such as "Old Poor Law," "New Poor Law," "scrounger," "charlatan," "beggar," "imposter" or "imposing," and "poor relief" yield many hundreds of thousands, including a good number of articles that deal indirectly with welfare fraud. It was therefore necessary to devise a series of search terms and filters to identify five types of reporting: technical and procedural; editorial intervention; investigative journalism; external writing (that is, commissioned articles); and incidental mentions. Since a significant number of officials, advocates, and even the poor themselves wrote to newspapers and kept cuttings of their efforts, it was possible to tailor the search terms to functional contemporary linguistic registers and lexis. Thus, incidental mentions could be pinpointed by applying secondary filters such as "tyranny" (as in the tyranny of withdrawing an allowance for an accidental oversight), "charlatan," "malingering," "scrounging," "loafing," or "determined" (as in "a determined attempt to deceive"). Such terms are particularly effective when combined with mention of specific welfare schemes (the "dole" for instance) that were in force for periods interrogated. These indicative search terms point both to the complexity of finding case material in the online press resources and to the variety of linguistic registers in which positive or negative commentary on welfare fraud was constructed.

For the post-1930 and notably the post-1950 period, British Library resources were supplemented with the particular archives of four newspapers – *The Times*, *Telegraph*, *Daily Mail*, and *Guardian* – as well as BBC reporting across all its platforms. Primary and secondary search terms were adapted to reflect the evolution of the official language of the welfare state as outlined earlier, and also the evolution of welfare schemes themselves. Any individual cases from the 2000s in this book were reconstructed across multiple news outlets, and all post-2000 online comment functions attached to individual stories were analysed and categorised. As far as possible I have drawn on sources generated by organisations and outlets from across the spectrum of political persuasion, both to avoid a sense that quoted examples add up to "well, they *would* say that" and (relatedly) to show that welfare fraud as a concern bisects the political spectrum. In total, the book draws on 46,000 comments attached to individual articles, blogs, and analytical interventions. The latter do not constitute a unified body. It is not the case, for instance, that comments on newspaper articles in right-leaning newspapers were wholly or even overwhelmingly rabidly right wing. The same is true of articles in left-leaning newspapers or blog sites, though the bias in comments on such material is in fact more pronounced than in right-wing equivalents. This world is populated by some determined characters who appear across different threads and sometimes multiple times in the same thread, but the nature of commentary is more often shaped by the content of the article and who is "around" at the time of publication. The essential randomness of much commentary is precisely the point for this analysis. When using such material, I try to give a sense of the overall tone of the threads in which individual commentaries are located, and also sometimes to convey the dynamic development of threads frozen at the point of capture.

Framing data for parts 2 and 3 of the book is drawn from statistical and policy reports published by the Office for National Statistics, government departments, parliamentary committees, political parties, politicians, pressure groups, and membership organisations, which together have been producing broad estimates of welfare fraud since the 1980s. This material is supplemented with comparative statistical analyses from the OECD, articles and analysis from think-tanks or policy/stakeholder groups, and broad survey resources such as the British Social Attitudes Survey. For earlier periods, perspective is also provided by Parliamentary Inquiries and Royal Commissions, which often dealt tangentially with welfare fraud, and multiple keyword searching of parliamentary debate reported in *Hansard*.

A brief reflection on this source matrix shows that its chronological coverage is strongest from the eighteenth century onwards. This is inevitable, but for the pre-1700 period I also draw on key legislation in welfare and vagrancy law, pamphlet resources, locally generated petitions,[39] and (following Jonathan Healey and Peter King[40]) some magistracy documents. Moreover, while my final source category – ephemera – includes films and documentaries from the post-1960 period, some of the material collected here is focussed on the earlier dates of this study. Ultimately it is difficult to pin down the scale of this source base, but it amounts to the equivalent of at least twelve million words across the period 1601 to the present. With it, we can thus consider the construction of welfare fraud on a canvas much broader than the perspective that dominates the current literature. In turn the key point about this material is that views on such fraud – factual, emotional, judgemental, understanding, sympathetic, condemnatory, angry, or resigned – are absolutely everywhere. It could hardly be otherwise. As the twenty-one-year-old Samuel Kendall was told by other members of the "lower mighty" New Poor Law Guardians of

Bradford-on-Avon (Wiltshire) in 1878: "It is our duty and our privilege not only to help the poor, very correctly our first charge, but also to consider the interest of the ratepayers, already too heavily burdened!" This dual duty required the confrontation and punishment of fraud as defined by the law which "as a general rule … was as inexorable and inflexible as the Law of the Medes and Persians which altered not."[41]

Making sense of these sources – joining them together, identifying dominant themes and narratives – is at one level a complex task demanding a fusion of methodological approaches from different disciplines. At another level, however, this book is *merely* about stories: personal, familial, recycled, sensationalised, constructed, and reconstructed in the personal and popular imagination. As "VC" noted in an interview of 17 January 1989: "everyone's got one [a story] it's just that some people have better ones than others."[42] Whether she was right about a hierarchy of stories is a matter for part 2. For now, each account, each story, combines to a varying degree not only the genres of recount, anecdote, exemplum, illusion, and observation (to adopt and adapt the classificatory tools of Jim Martin and David Rose), but also frequently the additional imperatives of advocacy, sympathy, and judgement.[43] A central interpretive motif is of course that most of the stories are selective, edited, or censored. They have an agenda. Some are directed and others can only be reconstructed through detailed record linkage, with all the dangers of omission and false linkage that this process implies. Even then, some of the perspectives on which I can draw are not simply unwitting but downright fleeting and accidental. Yet they can also be remarkably rich, as for instance with John Rutherford, who acted as an advocate for the poor of Poplar workhouse whilst an inmate there in the 1880s and who defrauded the poor law under the very eyes of workhouse staff by securing an advance for his polemical book on workhouse life.[44]

If we are to avoid a sense of cherry picking *ad hoc* or sensational examples, however, stories still need to be curated. This is even more important in the sense that (as outlined in the preface) I adopt a thematic rather than a linear chronological approach to the topic and the evidence. For this reason, over and above the obvious quantitative nature of statistics on welfare fraud, I count within and across source types, including *inter alia*: frequencies of words and phrases (fraud, cheats, benefit cheats, fibbing, and so forth) in and between source genres; the gap between official estimates of welfare fraud and its *perceived* scale in different sources; the contested numbers of fraud investigators; mentions of welfare fraud in all sixty-six ego-documents; and the seasonality of fraud across all source types. Such approaches can be seen in chapters 3 to 9, where these broad cross-source and cross-period measures provide some sense of the representativeness of individual cited examples. I also look for similarities and discontinuities of language and attitude in different source types and different periods, as for instance when I discuss the remarkable continuities across letters, newspaper articles, films, comments, ego-documents, and oral histories in sympathy for those caught out by complex bureaucratic forms. Particularly in parts 2 and 3, the categorisation and ranking of features of the primary material provide a corpus-level overview that then drives the choice of emblematic examples. We see this, for instance, in rankings of reasons for not informing on welfare fraudsters, which show remarkable continuity across the chronological dimensions of this work. In the end, welfare fraud has a determined imprint across the source base, either because it was meant to be thus or because the sources pick up much wider concerns by accident. This in itself is an important backdrop to the curation of stories, and it makes it imperative that I also dwell at length on examples that disrupt what is otherwise a story of strong historical continuity. For this reason, we see an extended discussion of thematic areas such as disabled people as welfare fraudsters, on the subject of which the later twentieth century does indeed represent a watershed in universal attitudes.

These are important methodological checking mechanisms. Yet, if this is not an anthropological study, it *is* concerned with a matrix of human relationships requiring intensive observation recorded in informal field notes, including: of the body language of interviewees; of the emotional canvas that talking and writing about welfare fraud seems to foster and feed from; of the fear that can still be read on the faces of those previously accused of welfare fraud; and of the desperation that writers and speakers convey in various subtle ways and which filmic representations of traps set by the welfare state for the unwary – *Cathy Come Home, I, Daniel Blake*, and *Skint* – pick up very successfully. This book is punctuated with such observations. They bring welfare fraud to life – an exercise in deep cultural history where the individual example is as important as the wider dataset. Standing on the juncture between sociology and anthropology, I also trace and use what might be termed an *ecology of comment*; I am interested in the way that those leaving online comment to newspaper articles or blogs express themselves, and how that language changes according to the responses of others, how it moderates or becomes more extreme depending on the rapidity of incoming comments, and whether commentary changes as contextual "facts" enter the public domain; in the way that interviewees sometimes follow up their sessions to clarify points; and in the way that certain writers in my different source genres seem to have had particular power in shaping subsequent constructions of welfare fraud by those around them. The advocate Joseph Rowntree, for instance, wrote over 112,000 words to the central authorities of the New Poor Law and enclosed an equal number in the form of press cuttings of his letters to editors. His subjects and arguments were multi-layered, but the single central motif was to contest the idea that the poor were dishonest simply because of their poverty. Rather, he argued, it was the system itself and its degrading structures and processes that fostered dishonesty.[45]

This is not of course an exhaustive review of the methods brought to bear on the data. Yet it gives a sense of the approach to the book as a whole, which is that I alternate broad overview and perspective with intense, sometimes personal and often micro-detail which is something more than random example. This is deliberate and indeed necessary for a study adopting a thematic approach over such a long time period, and a topic on which everyone has and always has had an opinion.

Such approaches also allow me to situate the specific issue of fraudulent lives in wider models and debates, especially questions about the meaning of citizenship; the relationship between the state and its citizens, or perhaps more accurately the question of what the state is "for"; and understandings of power and resistance. Over the long time span that I am interested in, the meaning, function, and character of citizenship has changed fundamentally with the incremental extension of the local and national franchise, the changing capacities of the central information state, and wider societal changes which speak (perhaps temporarily) to inclusive rather than exclusive citizenship rights. On the other hand, few of those providing ego-material for this book effectively constructed themselves as active citizens. The chapters also deal centrally and repeatedly with models of power, control, resistance, and community. For many oral history respondents, the power of "they" in conversations (that is, politicians, civil servants, and officials[46]) was to be resisted by unbelief and disengagement on the one hand and an alternative location of the self in the local, knowable, and observable on the other. This is a theme across my data and I use the conceptual approaches of James Scott – in essence that resistance to power manifests and builds in the accumulation of small, and sometimes not so small acts of disobedience, disbelief, and symbolic action – to try and disentangle the multiple ways in which "my" storytellers make sense of the powerful and the stories of the powerful.[47]

In this sense, the graffiti etched onto the windows and walls of the Southwell workhouse by pauper inmates from the 1820s onwards is no different in conceptual models of resistance to the graffiti noted by Carl Richards of Eastwood (Nottinghamshire) when he first went to the "Dole Office" in the 1980s: "It was very common to see graffiti scribbled by bored people on the walls, notice boards and window panes."[48] Eliding the two instances is not random or *ad hoc*; it gets to the heart of how we must understand systems of power over the very long term. I go on to supplement the analysis with an implicit grounding in the concept of emotional communities; officials, advocates, observers, and most of the poor whose direct testimony I use had a grudging respect for *some* welfare fraudsters and even more those who were wrongly accused. These people were not (or in most cases not just) part of the same physical community, but they were part of a wider emotional community of poverty and its alleviation.[49] Stephen Reynolds locates this very precisely, arguing way beyond his intimate Sidmouth experiences, that enforced and extreme thrift, "like extreme cleanliness, has often a singularly dehumanising effect. It hardens to the nature of its votaries, just as gaining what they have not earned most frequently makes men flabby … It is all right as a means of living, but lamentable as an end of life."[50] The 46,000 comments on welfare fraud cases that I was able to harvest tended towards the judgemental and certain, but the deeper stories that I reconstruct speak much more of cohesive community identities.

Conclusion

Perceptions of welfare fraud are multi-layered, dynamic, contradictory, and (because they are rooted in the particular experience of individuals) unstable. Addressing the issue on a national scale and across the long period covered here amplifies these complexities. Diverse sources, methods, and conceptual framing can cut through the noise and underpin a focus on regularity and trend rather than particularity and reaction. Individual stories, rhetoric, and even body language can be contextualised with corpus statistics, place, and community to provide a framework of analysis. Yet in the end this is a book in which stories embody and drive the agenda, and nowhere more so than in consideration of the issue of deliberate fraud, to which we turn in chapter 3. By necessity, such stories are incomplete, messy, contradictory, and partial, but in some senses this is a methodological asset. Welfare fraud is a messy business; it is the ground on which the notionally powerful constellate action and inaction, and on which the notionally powerless evade or seek to confront deeply embedded elite privilege. Contestation might take the form of a surly nod or the folding of arms, or it might extend to fighting a court case and invoking the power of community, advocacy, and rationality. But it *is* messy; and it can also be heart-breaking, as for instance when we read the November 2021 BBC report that "Around 100 people denied fast-tracked disability benefits for terminal illness died challenging the decision." The claims of these people had been categorised as premature at best and fraudulent at worst. Even here, however, things are more complex than they seem: a spokesperson for Marie Curie, for instance, "had 'serious concerns about the DWP's ability to recognise when a claimant was approaching the end of life and was in desperate need of support.'"

But this concern misses the point about the British welfare system. Its very rationale from 1601 onwards, as we have already seen, was to be residual, to set a high bar for deservingness and (at least in terms of practical operations) to delay decisions and payments as a way of managing and rationing demand. A DWP spokesperson claimed that "Our priority is dealing with people's claims quickly and compassionately" while patients, patient groups and charities, on the other hand, "said the current process was overly complex and stressful."[51] These are two different languages and conceptual registers. They speak to completely opposite constructions of the nature and meaning of the welfare state, and of welfare citizenship. We see them played out in powerful modern films and dramas where the fixity and irrationality of modern welfare rules drive reasonable people to unreasonable ends, and in the ChatGPT exercise that opens chapter 11.[52] But these would have been familiar dilemmas to welfare claimants and decision-makers in the past. In exploring that past I do not seek to provide equal analytical weight to each century, half-century, or incarnation of the British welfare state. This decision partly reflects the reach and density of sources, and the thematic structuring of the book. It also reflects a conscious sense that my starting point – modern dilemmas about welfare fraud – must be understood as part of a historical process marked out by continuity, where history is a resource that largely determines the present.

part two
Honesty and Dishonesty

CHAPTER 3

Cheating by Intent

In 2019 Judge Angela Neild passed sentence in the case of Joanne Mole, who had been convicted of fraudulently claiming £74,000, having lied about being a single mother. Neild suggested that, although the British welfare system was "overrun and creaking," it had a "unique" status in the world. Its stability, she argued, was heavily reliant on the honesty of claimants because, "It is not easy to detect claims of this nature which are made fraudulently."[1] Whether the latter claim is true is a matter for part 3. For now, the judgement evidences a striking lack of historical perspective. Rather than see the welfare system as relying on the honesty and probity of claimants, it is possible to argue that its framing has always assumed that the poor (applicants, claimants, and renewers) *will* be dishonest. By extension, its mechanisms (forms, welfare levels, monitoring processes) have always been about containing dishonesty and moral failings. Neither the commitment to a residualist welfare system nor repeated discussion of the nature and meaning of welfare citizenship outlined in my first chapter is incompatible with this perspective.

The 1601 act that instituted the Old Poor Law was (in terms of word-age and clauses) almost wholly concerned with the tri-partite tasks of raising money, accounting for that money, and establishing systems of control and monitoring. It had four guiding principles for the welfare of the poor: that parents and grandparents should (if able) provide welfare for their children and vice versa; children could be apprenticed (with or without parental consent) until the ages of twenty-four for boys and twenty-one for girls; that the local ecclesiastical parish was to find or make work for those who "use no ordinary and daily Trade of Life to get their living by"; and that the parish was to raise "competent sums of money for and towards the necessary Relief of the Lame, Impotent, Old, Blind, and such other among them being Poor and not able to work."[2]

As becomes apparent if these words are turned on their head, they are infused with both the fear and expectation of *systematic* intentional fraud. It was *expected* that families would avoid their "duty" to support poor relatives; children *had* to be apprenticed to make sure that they did not fall into the moral degradation of dependency; and able-bodied people were *expected* to fail in their moral duty to work and avoid dependence. Even the final clause relating to the groups that would later come to be understood as the "deserving poor" can be read as enfolding low expectations of honesty: parish rates were to contribute *towards* the welfare of these groups not meet their whole welfare needs; relief was only to be given where *necessary*, in effect highlighting a borderland of interpretation where relief was not strictly necessary; and some amongst these groups were expected to make fraudulent claims, *not* being strictly poor or unable to work.[3]

While some historians have focussed on the communal duties imposed by this act and subsequent amending or augmenting legislation,[4] a closer reading suggests both that relief was supposed to be highly residual *and* that the moral worth of the poor was strongly open to question. Indeed, almost all the sixty-six examples of life-writing used for this study contain symbolic accounts of subtle and not so subtle attempts to "play" the law. The story recounted by Reverend John Skinner of Camerton (near Bath, Gloucestershire) offers a pointed example. After being widowed, Rebecca West had married Samuel West. Her two children from the first marriage worked with him in the local coal pit. The children retained the settlement of their dead father in the nearby village of Sodbury and so in 1805 West "dressed himself in his Sunday clothes, and assuming a deal of consequence went to Sodbury, pretending he was a farmer living at Camerton and had seen the boys, and would, if approved of, take them both as apprentices at £5 per head." The overseer of Sodbury, suspicious, wrote to Skinner asking if such a farmer existed and he revealed the fraud, noting in a pointed exemplum that West "was a tricking fellow."[5]

Official and pauper correspondence is equally replete with tales of deliberate fraud. Thus, when Henry Roper, the overseer of Oundle (Northamptonshire) wrote to his counterpart in Peterborough (Cambridgeshire) on 23 May 1835 in response to being asked for authority to give Elizabeth Brownlow relief, he said that Brownlow had been:

in our workhouse some short time ago & derived great benefit from the treatment. Indeed got as she herself said quite well
& left it. She has been for some years constantly on our Parish
Books & we were much astonished at her <u>very</u> quick <u>recovery</u>
from her treatment at the workhouse

Roper added a mournful postscript: "We considered that she came the
old soldier over us to use a Common phrase for the last year or more."
Brownlow, like Joy Chishimba and others encountered so far in this book,
was constructed as duplicitous, the epitome of moral hazard, and operating
in a liminal space where the powerless evaded the powerful.[6] Individual
cases like this – more than two hundred in the pre-1834 data – are overlain
for the Old Poor Law period by a broader and deeper sense that the poor in
receipt of or applying for relief were inherently untruthful and dishonest.
This attitude is well captured in correspondence from Benjamin Nathall,
Charles Bagge, Thomas Hawkins, and William Clarke – respectively
mayor, minister, and churchwardens of King's Lynn (Norfolk) – who
wrote on behalf of the widow Sarah Doe on 13 February 1758. The men,
rhetorically melding together sympathy, judgement, and recount, found
it necessary to argue in her defence that Doe had:

> in some part of her time lived well & in reputation, and even to
> the present day ... done every thing in her power, to make her-
> self as little troublesome as possible, but is now become too old
> and infirm to provide any thing towards her support ... At the
> request of Mrs Doe I [Charles Bagge] have drawn up ye above
> Certificate, in order to assure you and Others concerned, that
> she really is an Object of Compassion. I have done This, with
> design to obviate the Objection in your Letter ...[7]

On what basis the overseers of Oxford had earlier objected to relieving Doe
is unclear, but the assumption that she could work, might have resources
and friends, or had brought the poverty on herself is framed by the reply
from these key officers of King's Lynn.

At a broader level, Malthus also constructed the poor as untrustworthy
and governed by animal instincts, and argued (albeit briefly) that the children of early nineteenth-century paupers should lose their right to apply

for poor relief.[8] If we jump forward to the early twenty-first century, over half of the comments about welfare fraud harvested for this book were categorised by me as being centrally rooted in beliefs about the dishonesty of welfare recipients. This categorisation is broadly exemplified by the sentiment of "sensiblegirl" in a 2016 comment:

> It's ever so easy to con the benefits system. Just lie. They never check. I know so many women who do that and have never been found out. And they've been kept by us for years. Decades in some cases. Some with kids at private school. I kid you not.[9]

The New Poor Law of 1834 apparently codified this essential connection between poverty, permanent or episodic welfare dependence, and intentional dishonesty through its implementation of the principles of less eligibility and the deterrent workhouse.[10] It was not until the 1870s and the emergence of practical and rhetorical models of "honest poverty" that a counter-narrative to the "tricking fellow" can be seen.[11] Even then it was shallow and fragile. The Liberal welfare reforms were played out against the backdrop of a latent (and sometimes active) concern not just about deservingness but also about the potential scale of intentional fraud that might still require control by the use of institutional welfare.[12] Jumping forward to 1942, the initial Beveridge Report contained thirty-five passages that can be read as reflecting concern about the potential for fraud and malingering in a universalist welfare system. These start at clause 9 (which argues that "The State should offer security for service and contribution," of which work was the central pillar) and end at clauses 417–19.[13] Such implicit doubts help to explain the numerous competing models for social welfare reform at that time, and then the only partial implementation of the report itself.[14] The ongoing power of an expectation of dishonesty is framed with searing clarity in the filmic treatment of Cathy and Reg in *Cathy Come Home* and Daniel in *I, Daniel Blake*.[15]

The case of Joanne Mole reveals a significant elite misconception of the philosophical and pragmatic underpinnings of the British welfare state, but the question of how far the fears of its policymakers were realised remains. This is the major focus of the current chapter, which turns first to the measured scale of intentional welfare fraud in the present day and then undertakes a complex reconstruction of the dimensions of intended and planned dishonesty in and through the fractured historical sources. Developing a theme initiated in the preface, I argue that, as officially measured, the scale of deliberate fraud is and always has been slim. The chapter then tensions this observation against popular perceptions, beginning in the early 1600s and continuing today, that fraudulent activity is rife and sustained. Part of this disjuncture reflects the fact that official statistics are hopelessly flawed. More is explained by the complex architecture of fraud – a sense that much fraud is accidental or engineered into and by the system – which is the subject of the remaining chapters of this section. There are also, as we shall see, compelling historical reasons for the persistence of popular views of the scale of fraud.

Dimensions

In November 2021, and following up the Department of Works and Pensions' own reporting as set out in chapter 2, the House of Commons Committee of Public Accounts delivered a scathing assessment of the performance of the DWP in tackling fraud *and* error. It noted that COVID had driven a doubling of the amount lost up to "an eye watering £8.3 billion" or 7.5% of entire departmental spending apart from pensions. In the 2020/21 accounting year this figure was an increase "from what was already the highest rate since records began." In a striking aside, the committee noted that the comptroller and auditor general had qualified the accounts of the DWP (and predecessor bodies) every single year since 1988 because of its failure to get to grips with under- and over-payments.[16] Universal Credit, the basket of welfare support, including housing, employment, and disability benefits given to the poor, was singled out as being used by "organised criminals and dishonest opportunistic individuals" during COVID "to steal from the taxpayer," such that some 14.5% of the Universal Credit budget was lost to fraud and error.[17] The picture is of course more complex and nuanced than these headlines allow, as we can see by moving back to the 2019/20 DWP fraud report, which also contained restated figures for 2018/19, so that it covered a two-year observation window. Published on 4 May 2020, this consolidated report, methodological appendices, and data tables suggested that 2.4% of all benefit expenditure was overpaid in 2019/20 (2.1% in 2018/19) and that a further 1.1% was underpaid. The overpayment rate was the *cumulative* figure for official errors, claimant errors (i.e., innocently misstated information) and intentional fraud. Around 1.4% of the budget was lost to active fraud, a slight increase from the 1.1% of 2018/19.[18] The latter figure masked radically different fraud records for individual benefit types. Thus, 7.6% of all Universal Credit applications and 3.7% and 3.1% respectively of Housing Benefit and Jobseeker Allowance claims were deemed fraudulent as opposed to just 0.3% of Incapacity Benefit and 0.5% of Disability Living Allowance claims.[19] Multiple methodological changes (the 2019/20 report recorded ten A4 pages of changes to methods since 2005[20]) and the fact that the fraud reports consider a different basket of benefits each year, mean that a strict longitudinal comparison of figures is impossible. Even so, a broadly similar approach has been taken since 2004/05, and consideration of historic reports suggests that intentional fraud was also "low" at this date, with 2.9% of all spending lost to fraud (2%) and error (0.9%).[21] Further statistical evidence is available from National Benefit Reviews carried out annually by the DWP and predecessors from 1994/95 for changing subsets of benefit types, and (at a less specific level) in National Audit Office and Comptroller General reports and answers to parliamentary questions back to the late 1980s. The central message is crystallized in figures from 1995 and 1998 respectively which suggest that 2.7% and 2% of the non-pension welfare budget was lost to intentional fraud in those years.[22]

Ambiguities over the definition of fraud, the fact that estimates were generated episodically by different arms of government and parliament, early think-tanks, and charities – and the effect of different methods being used to calculate how much was spent on welfare in the first place – together mean that gaining a longer-term perspective on intentional fraud at the time-series level is deeply problematic. In a 1989 parliamentary debate Peter Lloyd was asked how much fraud had cost the Department for Social Security in every year since 1979. He replied: "No reliable estimate is available of the cost of social security benefit fraud."[23] In fact we have relatively reliable figures for 1979 and again for the period from 1968 to 1973 (the latter arising from Henry Fisher's enquiry into welfare fraud[24]) which suggest that around 4% of the broadly defined welfare budget was lost to fraud, both intentional and unintentional. These estimates fit seamlessly with 1969 claims in a parliamentary debate that between 1% and 5% of Supplementary Benefit claims were fraudulent.[25] While no reliable measurements for welfare fraud in the round exist for the 1950s – though figures tracing prosecutions for defrauding particular types of benefit all suggest low levels – estimates for 1958 and 1952 confirm the range as 1–5% of welfare budgets.[26] Interwar perspectives are harder to obtain, given the disproportionate focus on unemployment in this period. Still, a 1936 Cabinet discussion capturing reportage on the complexity of tweaking unemployment assistance inferred that around 4% of all claims were fraudulent.[27] This is much less than the percentage of claims for unemployment and sickness payments that were disallowed in the early 1930s, but the disallowance process conflated intentional fraud with cases where the rules of the different schemes made young people and others ineligible.[28]

For the period of the New Poor Law, 1834–1929, attempts to calculate the scale of intentional fraud get no easier. The variously constituted central regulatory authorities (equivalent to the DWP) did not collect specific statistics on fraud. We can, however, glean something from their published annual reports. Almost all of them had something to say about vagrants, who were considered the archetype of dishonesty. To take just one example of the seventy-plus volumes, the fifth annual report of the Local Government Board, covering the period 1875/76, noted that, by recommending accommodation of vagrants in isolation cells, the board had curtailed opportunities for "evading the operation of the law" and significantly reduced the numbers relieved nationally. Elsewhere in this volume the LGB set out new forms and claim tickets for those seeking relief in kind (bread, clothing, and so on) as a way of confronting dishonesty. The potential for fraud was thus clearly in the minds of central administrators even if they did not measure it. Most annual reports, however, also carried case studies of particular places or classes of paupers. The study for 1875/76 dealt with Manchester, where the guardians noted a sharp decline in the numbers of people on outdoor relief after they had increased conditionality in 1874. Thus, the 2,319 recipients of September 1874 had dwindled to 1,429 by September 1875, a decline of 62 per cent. The board had, it argued, "by compulsory education … shown 890 individuals that if they would only make an attempt they might maintain themselves without having recourse to the rates." This did not equate to identifying 890 fraudsters because the general rate of dependence had also fallen in the same period, but Mr Rooke, the report's author, used the statistics of the LGB to argue that only 178 of the 890 would have left anyway, thereby identifying a substantial seam of people who had been intentionally defrauding the system.[29] We should beware of drawing more general conclusions, given that this report was written during the crusade against outdoor relief when the sharp curtailment of welfare led to significant suffering.[30] To obviate these temporal issues, I have analysed all published *Annual Reports* and collated every case study of place, pauper "class," or scandal where some quantitative dimension to welfare fraud could be found or imputed.[31] This exercise suggests that in the period after 1847 an average of 10% of all *claimants* were suspected of being fraudsters. Given that most were on outdoor relief and that *per capita* workhouse costs were invariably much higher, the proportion of total welfare resources lost to fraud can be broadly estimated at 4–6 per cent between 1847 and 1929.

This range is somewhat below the level that can be implied from the 1832 Royal Commission establishing the philosophical base for the New Poor Law. Ratepayers and officials giving evidence suggested that fraud and the opportunity for fraud was systemic. George Huish, assistant overseer of the parish of Saint George's Southwark, typifies this view.[32] He argued that: "unless you have a considerable number of men to watch every pauper every day, you are sure to be cheated. Some of the Out-door paupers are children, others are women; but, taking one with another, I think it would require one man's whole time to watch every twenty paupers." Huish went on to argue that the "greater number of our out-door paupers are worthless[33] people" and he saw the *intention* of fraud as endemic, a presumption encapsulated in a cautionary anecdote:

> Not long since a very young woman, a widow, named Cope, who is not more than 20 years of age, applied for relief; she had only one child … I spoke to her, and pressed her to tell me the real truth as to how so decent a young woman as herself came to us for relief: she replied that she was "gored" into it. That was her expression. I asked her what she meant by being gored into it. She stated, that where she was living there were only five cottages, and that the inhabitants of four out of five of these cottages were receiving relief … They had told her that she was not worthy of living in the same place unless she obtained relief too.[34]

Exactly the same logic has been traced for modern fraudsters by Martin Tunley.[35] The 1832 commission has been repeatedly criticised by historians for manipulating evidence to support fundamental reform, and so we should be wary of perspectives like that of Huish.[36] Even so, there were few dissenting voices to the shared elite discourse that the poor under the Old Poor Law had come to regard a little parish welfare as their right, whether they were *in extremis* or not.

The lack of dissenting voices is unsurprising. It is impossible to measure the scale of fraud in the more than fifteen thousand parishes that were responsible for funding and dispensing welfare from 1601 to 1834; officials kept no systematic records on this matter.[37] We can, however, exploit three record sets to gain broad perspective. The first is a collection of vestry minutes encompassing communities from Lancashire in the north to Dorset and Hampshire in the south and mostly dating to the period from the early 1800s. Such minutes detail individual discretionary relief decisions, but many of those decisions were prefaced by injunctions to parish officers to further investigate the cases before money was dispensed. Equally, in most places officials revisited the whole cohort of paupers on relief at least once during this period with a view to understanding whether recipients' circumstances had changed because of exogenous factors (food becoming cheaper for instance) or familial/work reasons, and removed people from the relief lists where such (undeclared) changes were suspected.[38] During both processes, the low level of suspected or detected fraud is remarkable. In the 1,762 cases where officials were asked to make further investigation just thirty-one had misstated their circumstances. Episodic review of relief cohorts sometimes saw 40 per cent of all people having their allowances downgraded or removed but, since we do not understand the political and philosophical background to most of these exercises, this figure is not a reliable indicator of substantial fraud. The fact that the vast majority of people affected by swingeing reviews rapidly returned to welfare or had their allowances restored suggests that the low figures for fraud highlighted by ongoing case investigations were likely representative.[39]

Attempts to understand how much money was lost to *intentional* fraud using this evidence are fraught with methodological difficulty. For four of the most comprehensive sets of vestry minutes it is possible to count the value of awards made each year and compare this total with the numbers of original requests – a process that gives a sense of how many of the claims received were seen as excessive if not fraudulent.[40] Undertaking this exercise suggests that less than 2 per cent of the entire welfare spend was lost to fraud. Moving back into the eighteenth century, we can use a second record set – pauper and advocate letters – to understand the broad scale of suspected and detected fraud. Thus, while some officials receiving requests for relief simply paid up, many others always or episodically explored whether the circumstances conveyed in a letter were "true." This they might do by visiting the applicant or asking fellow officials in the place of residence to carry out an assessment. In only 264 cases (from more than 3,000 letters) did investigation result in substantive contradiction of the stories told. Indeed, officials in host parishes often argued that poor applicants had not recounted even half of their suffering, while some overseers recognized that the attested needs demanded more resources than they could momentarily offer and regretted the fact.[41]

The mere handful of pauper letters available before 1755 reveal little by way of information about the scale of fraud. There is no alternative national dataset, but a third set of records can provide at least an outline. As Peter King has suggested, petty session decisions[42] and a handful of notebooks kept by justices of the peace can show the outcomes of contested local relief decisions. Not all or even many such cases point to fraud as opposed to parochial decisions on the acceptable level of spending or moral considerations of applicants and recipients. In these contexts, King argues that justices tended to favour the claims of the poor (and thus to prioritise their assertion of honesty), though with strict limits. Larger-scale (and earlier) perspectives can be obtained through similar disputes heard at Quarter Sessions, as Jonathan Healey has shown for Lancashire.[43] Thus, the eight transcribed volumes for the Buckinghamshire Quarter Sessions 1678–1733 detail 120 disputed relief claims and 51 prosecutions for fraudulent activity.[44] Such listings deal only with positive orders, such that we do not see the underbelly of cases where pauper claims were dismissed or settled. Even so these instances equate to less than 0.3 per cent of the Sessions' business, suggesting that the scale of welfare fraud was slim when looked for. This view is reinforced by seventeenth-century pamphlets such as *England's Weal & Prosperity*, which in 1681 proposed that public workhouses be built to "bring all Idle, poor People, beggars, vagrants &c. into such Habit of industry" that they would no longer be a burden to ratepayers. The elision of poverty in general with dishonesty was much as we might expect from the discussion above, but even the pamphlet's

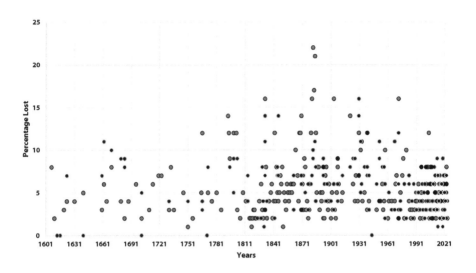

3.1 Official estimates of fraud, 1601–2023.

Notes: Where figures apply to a range of years, I have allocated the value to the last year in the range. *Source:* 404 observations. Formally measured or estimated figures for the proportion of resources lost to fraud of all types across all sources used for this volume. Descriptive measures – "significant," "lots" – are rejected.

author could not ignore the impotent poor and speculated that only one to two hundred thousand people might be caught by his new proposals.[45]

With all the caveats encountered above, figure 3.1 gives a broad representation of the total scale of fraud of all types as measured, implied, or hypothecated – and thus as it were "official" – from the different sources available. While the actual sums involved in fraud have spiralled since the late twentieth century, the "official" percentages of the welfare budget considered "lost" seem to have moved little over the time frame considered here. Varying methodologies, definitions, source types, spatial foci, and such like mean that the apparent precision in this graph is spurious. But in terms of orders of magnitude the results are intriguing. This sort of continuity over the very long term is missing from modern historical studies, media representations, and social policy concerns, and helps to contextualise the more recent continuities that I first highlighted in the preface and chapter 2. The figures also add weight to the idea that welfare fraud is and always has been dwarfed by tax fraud.[46] After all, the same sources that underpin figure 3.1 also carry extensive evidence of disputation and avoidance of local rate assessments. What these broad figures cannot do, of course, is distinguish in quantitative terms between definitive deliberate fraud and fraud that arises for other reasons, or between fraud at application, during receipt of benefits, or when trying to renew them. Here, we can deal only in impressionistic and qualitative perspectives. The remaining chapters of this section thus analyse other "types" of fraud. In the meantime, these observations have consequences: if the measurable scale of fraud exhibits substantial long-term continuity – if it is largely impervious to changes in the scale of welfare payments, organisation of the welfare system, changing models of welfare citizenship, and changing means of fraud detection – then the way we understand fraud as a process and its construction by ordinary people must also shift from presentist perspectives.

Constructing and Worrying about Fraud

A similar message emerges if we acknowledge that there is a fundamental disjuncture between comparatively and consistently low levels of officially measured (and thus "public") welfare fraud and modern popular (and largely "private") perceptions of the issue. My interviewees were all asked what proportion of welfare payments they thought were lost to deliberate fraud. Respondents felt that the "true" figure was around 36%, with remarkably little variation over time or place. There was a corresponding resistance to taxation to fund the welfare system.[47] Focus group estimates were higher (42%), but this is explained by the particular interest of participants in the welfare claims of immigrants. Even ex-officials estimated the "real" level of fraud to be around 17%, with a shifting proportion of claims above this amount also constructed as (to use the phrase of "TY," interviewed in 1994) "dodgy."[48] Figure 3.2 plots estimates of the scale of welfare resources lost to fraud from all comments in oral histories, focus groups, responses to newspaper articles and TV programmes, blog posts, and other "popular" sources collected for this project, and spanning the period from 1990 to 2023. Fewer than 5% of all estimates roughly matched official figures, whereas 29% of all commentators believed that more than 45% of welfare expenditure was paid to fraudsters. There is likely no consistency in the

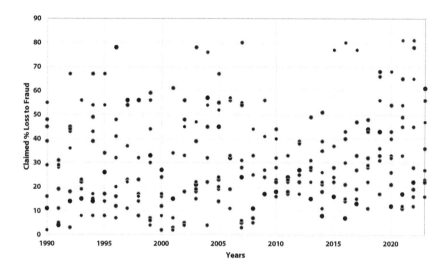

3.2 Popular estimates of welfare fraud, 1990–2023.

Notes: 489 observations. Cases where people claimed "a lot," most, the majority, etc., were discarded. I make no attempts to control for temporal lags in welfare stigma in the way adopted by Lindbeck et al., "Social Norms," 536, 540. *Source:* Views expressed in oral histories, focus groups, blogs, comments, and the media.

sorts of welfare encompassed by these sources, and I have deliberately not disentangled the definitions of fraud that underpin the different assertions. The yawning gap between a broad popular perspective and official measurements is nonetheless clear.[49]

As I have suggested, it is easy to think that these high modern figures are constructed through popular print, broadcast, and internet media as part of an exercise in rabble-rousing, xenophobia, or politically inspired hostility to welfare recipients, and then seep into the popular imagination.[50] Certainly focus group participants repeatedly returned to linguistic registers ("well, you read"; "I saw that"; "it is well known"), which suggest seepage. This pattern reflects the changing architecture of knowledge that I outlined in chapter 1. If, however, we return to the micro-perspective, then almost every time I asked individuals or focus groups questions about the scale of fraud, arm-folding and general toughening expressions and body language were the norm. Participants assumed they were being set up by an educated observer to give the *wrong* answer and so perhaps overstated rather than understated the figures. But more than this, the body language conveyed and encapsulated low levels of public trust in officialdom. I asked "KR" why he had folded his arms. He laughed: "They don't know half of what we do. It's shit these figures. They want us to think like that but we know; who d'they think we are?'[51] Such actions identify a complex hierarchy of attitudes towards fraud in the ordinary population, one in which deliberate misunderstanding can be seen as a tool of resistance to official narratives.[52]

These issues are revisited in subsequent chapters, but a presentist attitude that equates disjuncture between measured and imagined fraud with modern media and political attitudes does not serve well here. While it is impossible for earlier periods to construct the precise time series of figure 3.2, we have seen that those seeking to extinguish the Old Poor Law collected extensive testimony on real and imagined fraud. They were sufficiently in tune with broader public and political attitudes to generate systematic reform of the whole welfare system. Indeed, the sense that ordinary people constructed fraud as endemic *and* actively worried about it emerges most clearly from the early nineteenth century, as the expanding scale, reach, and depth of life-writing created a rich pool of evidence to match that of modern oral histories.[53] Of the life-writing or memoirs analysed for this book and covering the period from 1800 to the 1970s, 70 per cent deal directly with the issue, some in a sustained fashion. Thus, the Reverend John Coker Egerton of Burwash (Sussex) noted forty-eight instances or inferences of welfare fraud in his diaries between 1857 and 1888, including (on 30 March 1874) a "Long discussion" at the vestry meeting regarding cases "of chronic invalids who are supposed to be able to do some work. It is very difficult to do justice in these cases."[54] Even Beatrice Webb in an autobiography tracing her journey into socialism in the 1890s acknowledged that the "memory of the low cunning, brutal faces of the loafers and cadgers who hang about the [Royal] Mint haunt me."[55] Endemic beliefs that fraud was common and substantial are thus not necessarily centrally attributable to media narratives.

Within this broad framework, certain types of welfare are and were consistently constructed as vulnerable to fraud. In a modern sense, as we have seen, Universal Credit falls into particular disrepute. Single mothers also attract notable scepticism, as we saw with Joanne Mole, whose story initiated this chapter.[56] Yet suspicion of groups like absent or supposedly absent fathers and single mothers have much deeper chronological roots. They were core parts of the residuum and undeserving poor in the nineteenth century and tested the tolerance of communities from the very earliest days of the Old Poor Law. Even more keenly, people worried that those who claimed to be sick were in fact capable of doing much more towards supporting themselves. For this reason, those applying by letter or in person to access welfare resources usually spoke about degrees of ability and inability (as in "I am capable of doing some work if I can get it") or wrote about the inevitability of welfare dependence associated with certain medical conditions. In particular, those who sought to justify long-term claims on communities due to their old age emphasised their ability to do *some* work, setting the scene very directly for the modest income replacement rates associated with the British Old Age Pension from 1908. When beyond remunerative work, and well aware that simply being old was insufficient justification for dependence, they would argue that all other routes had by then been exhausted. Mary Harte, writing from Arlesford to Winchester (Sussex and Hampshire) on 1 February 1728, for instance, framed her letter with a cloak of desperation – borrowing and relying on in-kind support from her friends during the "long and Cold winter" – but now asked: "for ye love of God to considdor me" and "I beg & pray you to lend an Eare to my Complaints pitty my Case." As with others encountered so far in this book, Harte invoked structures of honesty, honest need, and natural rights to justify a claim that she must have known would be viewed with scepticism.[57] Such scepticism is given powerful embodiment in the reported motives for setting up the Shrewsbury (Shropshire) workhouse, where combatting the ingrained fraudulent intent of those claiming to be unemployed or beyond work was a major imperative.[58]

To an extent, disjuncture between the official, measured, scale of fraud and the level at which it manifests in the current and historic popular imagination is unsurprising, given the observation that the honesty of the poor as a whole was called into question in the founding statute of the British welfare system. Nor should we completely dismiss the sense that the variance reflects the role of the media in demonising welfare recipients and disseminating doubt about the accuracy of official measurements. Much has been written on this issue in a modern sense, as we have seen,[59] but there is also a consistent historical picture. Of the articles directly on fraud at my disposal for the period between 1800 and 1939, one (a letter to the editor) in the *Northampton Mercury* on 28 January 1824 strongly encapsulates such media demonisation. It is worth quoting at length. Written by a correspondent from the Northamptonshire village of Spratton, the letter parodied a local "beggar's marriage" in the following terms:

This curious and extraordinary wedding took place between Robert Colson and Margaret Wilson he was formerly a labouring man and she a servant girl, but latterly of the above profession [beggar]. Upon this occasion they invited all their friends, which consisted [of] the following highly distinguished personages: six good looking women, four wholesale timber merchants, three with wooden legs, six blind fiddlers, three jolly sandmen, five bouncing fish girls, and several others, whom I shall decline mentioning as I am indebted to them for this piece of information. At the wedding … [t]here was one man apparently blind would dance also; his wife became jealous, and not without a cause for he said he could see a pretty girl though he was blind, and one more handsome than his own wife. His wife then got him by the ear to whisper in it but loud enough for everyone to hear "You shall have hot tongue for supper my dear, you cannot say that black's white in my eye, but you are a deceitful old rogue" … After dinner was over, it was agreed by the party that there should be a three handed reel danced by the three men with wooden legs which afforded great amusement, for in turn they wet their wooden pins [legs] as mowers do their sickles, but unfortunately in repeating this wooden-legged reel one of the pins broke and broke the shins of the bridegroom. It was now become a late hour at night and the bride and bridegroom were put to bed, he being so drunk one of the party blackened his face with soot and grease so that in the morning the bride exhibited a droll appearance, with a mouth like a persons that is black with swearing.[60]

Here, then, the dishonest poor – the non-citizens of Spratton – were confected and laid bare for the readership in a semi-fictional exemplum. In the letter we find reason for people to worry about the capacity for pauper marriages to beget more paupers, a dishonest assembly of rogues (including a blind man who can see a pretty woman), moral bankruptcy, an absence of self-control, licentiousness and (the bride's mouth black with swearing) foul language. The beggarly couple and their ceremony appear ridiculous but also threatening to and cautionary for a ratepaying population. These perspectives have their counterpart in rabble-rousing public commentators who, like their modern counterparts, stirred up "otherness" at times of political advantage or economic disadvantage.[61] The mechanisms and structures of imagined fraud traced by Peter Golding and Sue Middleton in their 1982 work on attitudes to poverty in the press and amongst the public thus have deep historical roots as well as many more modern manifestations.[62]

Explanatory Structures

Yet, a disjuncture between official measurement of fraud and its alternative construction in the public imagination that has stood the test of more than four hundred years also requires a more subtle and encompassing explanatory structure than is currently available. In this sense a close qualitative and quantitative analysis of the data links the formation of popular attitudes to some of the themes first visited in chapter 1: the changing contours of welfare citizenship, growing physical and conceptual distance between taxpayers and welfare recipients, and the shifting traction of assigned identities such as the underclass and deserving or undeserving poor. There are many signals in the different sources, but the linkage is perhaps encapsulated in a letter (one of more than two hundred in the sample for nineteenth-century Scotland) from Dr Gregor MacDonald of Thurso (Caithness) on 24 August 1899. Visiting Johan MacKay, he "found her busily sewing at the fireside apparently in her usual health." Asked why he had been summoned, she told MacDonald that a nurse was required because MacKay was sick. The seemingly frivolous and unwarranted request for him to attend generated sustained epistolary invective on the part of MacDonald. He noted that on prior visits she had been out and about when he had arrived and that she was constantly demanding help that she did not need. For MacDonald, "This is really too bad & I do not know what remedy to apply" because she was now part of an underclass of fraudulent claimants.[63]

Other variables are also important, however, and form a complex matrix of overlapping explanations that underpin the rest of this section.

Foremost is a scepticism, both at a technical level and in terms of gut instinct, about the statistical and other processes that inform official measures of welfare fraud. The methodologies, assumptions, and bene-fit-type focus of modern official fraud measurement change from year to year, not to mention in the longer term. When I started my interviews for this project, official reports either did not exist or had not been accessed and read. For the people I interviewed post-2014, some had indeed read official publications after being prompted by newspaper reporting or be-cause of my upcoming interview. "KP" was interviewed twice, noting in his second (2016) encounter that he had been to the library after our first meeting and "been reading up" on the matter. The situation was, he said, "worse than I thought; these people are not serious about catching them [fraudsters] are they?" This was not a rhetorical question, but one posed in genuine disbelief.[64] "KP" had read that fraud statistics were based on hypothecations from active investigation of only a minute proportion of welfare claimants, generally less than 0.2 per cent. Five interviewees or focus group members also pointed out something that they knew from personal or community experience and that I had not initially appreciated from my reading of DWP, National Audit Office, and other official reporting: that in estimating fraud not only is the base sample tiny, but people who when contacted sign off as claimants or simply prove uncontactable are ignored in the subsequent statistics rather than being classed as fraudsters. Moreover, focus group participants recounted, and exemplified via stories of individual encounters, a basic ecology of community or familial know-ledge about what to do if contacted by investigators, measures bolstered by extensive online advice literature from a variety of law firms, interest groups, and charities.[65] Others had picked up doubts about the statistical methods from newspapers. It is for this reason that so much modern advocacy work focusses on dispelling popular statistical as well as attitudinal myths.[66] One interviewee, for instance, alerted me to hundreds of comments attached to a 2013 article on welfare dependency by the journalist John Humphreys, a significant number of which dealt directly or indirectly with questions of official measurement and definition.[67] *Hansard* also provides clues as to how mistrust of fraud statistics percolates and magnifies. Online searches for references to measuring welfare fraud in parliamentary debates and answers to parliamentary questions identify some fifty substantial instances between the 1960s and the present.

I am struck by how often government ministers and others claim that figures on fraud are not available or that getting them would take more resources than could be justified. Indeed, Peter Lilley claimed in 2001 that officials invariably answered the question, "how much fraud was there in the system?" with the retort, "No Government[s] in this or any other country, I was told, have ever been able to measure the level of fraud."[68] None of those providing personal testimony had read *Hansard*, of course, but, since many of the questions posed had originally come from constituents, it is unthinkable that the message – "this information is too difficult to get" – did not filter back and percolate into popular conceptions and estimations. Thus "EppingBlogger," in their response to the 2013 John Humphreys article noted above, confronted the idea of political connivance in failures to tackle fraud, arguing that Beveridge may have envisaged time-limited benefits, but: "Who was it that introduced it wrong? Who developed it in perverse ways? … it was the politicians who got it wrong."[69] Further back, interviewee "RK" had read Robin Page's 1971 *The Benefits Racket* and talked candidly about how the lessons of the book translated to his personal knowledge, and how perspectives from that book – chiefly that politicians were deliberately understating the extent of fraud – made it into the ecology of community knowledge.[70]

Capturing scepticism of official statistics in the deeper historical record is a more complex matter. In repurposed oral histories, we can detect a subtle but clear sense of the importance of particular individuals – information-brokers – to the emergence or perpetuation of doubt. This is embodied in the case of Mr B.1.P. of Barrow-in-Furness, who in an interview recorded in the Elizabeth Roberts collection recounted his attempts to educate interwar dole applicants.[71] Information-brokers also appear prominently as we move back from the 1930s. Regional and city-based statistical and other societies commissioned papers on many aspects of British social, economic, and cultural life, but poverty and welfare had a particular hold on their imagination. Attendees were treated to sustained dissection of and doubt over official statistics, and the published reports of such meetings ensured that complexities reached the public domain. Through these fora and a variety of other collective meetings of poor law guardians under the New Poor Law or at Petty and Quarter sessions under the Old Poor Law, doubt was sown. Particularly during the nineteenth century and interwar periods, the sampling and aggregation methods of central government, the reliability of evidence, and the processes for initial data collection were juxtaposed (in spoken and written papers) with experience of individuals and individual places. Government statistics often came off badly in the encounter. Thus, articles in the twenty-six extant volumes of the *Transactions of the National Association for the Promotion of Social Science* came back repeatedly to questions of welfare and the underclass, either directly or (indirectly) through discussions over penal policy. The regional meeting at York in 1864, for instance, considered a paper from the Reverend J.L. Foster on the settlement and removal laws. He explicitly eschewed freely available national statistics, claiming that "our own knowledge must satisfy us." He then went on to detail multiple instances of fraud in the York union where he was a guardian, noting one case in which a fraudster had said to him: "if the York guardians were such fools as to send his brass, he was not such a fool as to refuse it." The two thousand people "of the weekly wage class" who attended the meeting could have been in no doubt about the relative value of local *versus* official statistics.[72]

Various forms of life-writing for the pre-1945 period illustrate the reach and depth of the scepticism of government data and methods. Scepticism was sometimes associated with wider mistrust of the extension of government after the first flush of enthusiasm for the development of the information state.[73] More often, it was associated with a sense that the state was ill equipped to collect the nuanced data that the public ought to know. Thus, the hundreds of letters sent in response to the investigations of a "Special Commissioner" into the social, moral, and economic life of rural England on behalf of the *Daily News* in 1891 can be read as an outpouring of worry about the future of the countryside. They can – and should – also be understood as a reflection of the sense that the British government and its statistical operata simply did not capture or understand the crisis.[74] Of course the lack of central government data collection prior to the early 1800s means that we do not find similar scepticism about methods in the eighteenth century. Nevertheless, through injunctions in vestry minutes for officials to properly investigate cases, we see exactly the same pattern of doubt emerging even about local statistics. Ordinary ratepayers sometimes simply did not believe the summative financial reports with which they were presented. Thus, on 7 October 1819 the select vestry of Eling (Hampshire) issued a long defence of its record for the prior financial year, observing that it did so because "Insinuations have been thrown out of a <u>lavish</u> and most <u>careless</u> expenditure of the Parish money." In just over a thousand words, members assured readers of the accuracy of their accounts, a record of strong financial management, and above all the exertions of their assistant overseer in "discovering" a great many fraudsters who had "long been a burthen on the Parish."[75]

A further important variable for understanding distance between official measures and popular perceptions is what one interviewee called "knowing stuff." In chapter 1, I traced a strand of literature which argues that as information flows become larger and more complex, so those who finance welfare become more distant from recipients. Another dimension of this point is that, however data is collected and statisticalised, taxpayers simply do not believe it. Interviewees "just knew" that there was more welfare fraud than was acknowledged or they were told about. Mandated reporting of figures in newspapers or government publicity were juxta-posed with and placed lower in the hierarchy than stories that people had heard themselves. This prioritisation operates both at the elite level and amongst the poor, underpinning the long-term doubt about state statistics traced earlier in the chapter. Elite scepticism is often anchored in personal experience, as is elegantly captured in two similar stories located centuries apart. On 20 October 1969, during a debate about Supplementary Benefit, the MP for Twickenham, Roger Gresham Cooke, revealed that he had long harboured "doubts about the control exercised over supplementary benefits which are paid out":

> One or two cases have come to notice in my constituency in which people as well as receiving supplementary benefits have been found to have jobs on the side. My doubts were brought to a head earlier this year when a well-spoken man with an Irish brogue went to my constituency office and produced a hard luck story about not having fair treatment from the social security office. I put forward his case for sympathetic treatment, as a result of which he was paid £39 over 14 days. Further inquir-ies were made into his position, and it was found that he did not live in my constituency at all. He purported to come from a respectable address, but in fact he had only an accommoda-tion address for which he paid a pound or two. I arranged for

him to be interviewed by the social security office. When he turned up at my office in a van, he must have smelt a rat that something was to happen because he disappeared and has not been seen from that day to this. The doubts raised in my mind over this matter were confirmed by a startling article in the Spectator on 6 September by an official of the Supplementary Benefits Commission, an article which, I hope, was read by the Minister.[76] It told a horrifying story of widespread frauds and "fiddling" and such abuse of the system to make it almost a mockery.[77]

In an extended intervention, Gresham Cooke cited numerous examples of fraud and noted that, "One civil servant said on the radio that he believed that frauds were not 1 per cent., as the Government said, but possibly 5 per cent of the amount paid out." The minister of state did his best to assure the House that all was well: "The public ought to know what is being done to try to deal with the whole area of abuse, but I think that we ought to advise against the sort of rumour-mongering which is going on at present." His injunction failed. My own father recalls the 1969 "scandal" over Supplementary Benefit fraud and told me that one in three people on that welfare payment was a fraudster in his view.

A second story of exactly the same ilk shows the long-term reach of elite scepticism. Reverend John Skinner noted almost at the very opening of his diary in 1803 the case of "a stranger" called Holford, a sailor who, to avoid the press gangs, came to work in the Camerton coal mines. Quickly falling ill, he was cared for by the collier Robert Paine, who had applied without success to the overseer for a little help, given the terminal condition of his charge. Skinner remonstrated with the overseer: "He replied he could not give the parish money to strangers; that the man did not belong to Camerton, therefore he had no business to relieve him." Skinner knew the law as it stood after Rose's Act of 1795 rather better than the overseer and replied: "it was our business to relieve actual distress in a pauper who was too ill to be removed to his own parish; but I could effect nothing either by threats or by persuasions." When Holford died, the parish refused to bury him, leaving Paine to pick up the bill. Skinner's outrage was clear, but a wider nested story then unfolded, whereby Paine had sequestered Holford's earnings and sought to transfer the costs of illness and burial to the parish purse, keeping the substantial earnings he had retained from a man "whom he [the sailor] considered as his benefactor in the first instance because he had received him into his home." Skinner, like Gresham Cooke in 1969, had been taken in by a fraudster.[78] These are not random examples, but they reflect a wider and insistent underlay of elite scepticism in the life-writing and other ego-documents that make up my sample.

The non-elite also formed their views on the scale of welfare fraud from personal experience and across my sample were sceptical of anything in this area conveyed to them by elites. Those giving oral testimony in the later 1980s, 1990s, and even the early 2000s were more likely to claim that fraud was (much) higher than official statistics captured because they knew fraudsters and saw fraud being practised in the everyday. Later contributors and most of those who participated in focus groups were more likely to intersperse "knowing stuff" with the presumed instances of fraud collated from rumour and suspicion. At first I attributed this to media coverage of welfare fraud,[79] but in a focus group of 2016 I was struck by the views of one speaker (which gained wholesale acceptance) who suggested that the more complex intersection between the labour market and welfare during New Labour reforms had made it much more difficult to definitively locate fraud as opposed to (the speaker's words) "the stuff that *must* be, otherwise these people could not have the life they do."[80] In an interesting aside to these encounters, I asked everyone whether they tended to look more closely at those they assumed were on benefits during times of economic stress or perceived higher tax burdens for the working population. Almost all respondents agreed that they did.

Moving beyond these oral sources, most of the "ordinary" life-writers in my sample knew undetected fraudsters, as, for instance, in the case of Joy James of Nottingham across several autobiographical works focussing on poor working-class neighbourhoods in the postwar City.[81] Other sources support this sense that people "knew" or encountered significant undetected fraud. The vestry at Botley (Hampshire), for instance, worried in the 1810s about vagrants, gypsies, men who failed to apply for work when they could, and people who claimed relief even though they were known to possess property assets.[82] Their counterparts in Sutton (Surrey) episodically turned down the claims of suspected fraudsters and "suffered themselves to be summoned before the Bench of Magistrates" if these people complained.[83] The vestry of Ringwood went further, codifying their belief in endemic fraud through expectations that the assistant overseer would "in order to prevent impositions" through "enquiries or personal inspection … find out the real state of the persons who receive or apply for relief, and make himself acquainted as far as possible with the different characters and habits."[84] It is not, then, simply that people have always doubted government statistics and methodologies, but also that fraud is and always has been higher than such measures allow.

A third and final explanatory variable shaping unbelief in official fraud measures adds complexity to this framework. Setting aside the truly visceral anti-welfare material in my sample, most people do not construct fraud as a uniform "lump." Some 168 people responded to a *Daily Mail* story covering another Angela Neild welfare fraud judgement in 2019.[85] The commentator "Alan Rodgers5555" captured the broad tone of these contributions, arguing that: "Not only does crime pay in the UK, it pays very well. But come on, a free money (aka benefits) system that operates on honesty? The person who came up with that should be the one in jail." There were alternative perspectives. "Robo-Dad" argued:

> How is it that hard-working people who have paid taxes for most of their life and who lose their jobs through no fault of their own have to jump through hoops and get hounded and humiliated to get even a pittance off the [Department of Health and Social Security], while unwashed layabouts, chancers and other assorted human garbage seem to be able to make a living out of it.

This sentiment was personalized by "Zumber," who wrote ironically: "had to resign my job recently. A single man with no kids, the £73 a week I get, I'm having an amazing time. Holidays abroad, private jets. Doesn't matter I've worked all my life." And "Zippet" sought to balance the argument, objecting: "Just one of millions of people who abuse the welfare system of this country. To the real detriment of the very needy forced to go through degrading tests … System is not fit for purpose."[86] These words are disembodied from the conversational contexts of which they were part, and in this sense are subject to multiple readings. The one preferred here is fixed by the sentiment of a car delivery driver who in January 2005 struck up an unprompted conversation with me about "lifelong dossers, skivers, you know, these people on benefits" but who also noted, "There's fraud and then there's fraud."[87] In the conversation he made a distinction between fraud occasioned by responding to *extremis* and "real" fraud. This differentiation is a constant feature of the material across all source types. By way of example, in July 1843 John Lloyd of Llandybie (Carmarthenshire) responded to claims that he had been misrepresenting his poverty by suggesting that accusations of fraud were malicious: "I offended one of the Relieving Officers and one of the Guardians by teling them that they gave relief to some that did not want and refused to those was in want." *In extremis*, Lloyd had no choice but to pursue his claims.[88] Similarly, in 1786 Edward Levies wrote home, noting that "to be poor & seen poor is the devil" such that the symbolism of poverty justified any means of rectification.[89] Coming forward again, Mr M.B. Rhys wrote to the *Daily News* in September 1891 to suggest that "our social system is hopelessly wrong," arguing that those who had worked hard all of their lives deserved "something better than the workhouse for old age" and that they had a right to welfare, given the injury inflicted upon their ability to save by "a ridiculous system of wage slavery."[90] A related sense of natural justice was invoked by Martin Ferguson, one of twenty-four people who told their life-stories for a project looking at the social, economic, and cultural development of Old Headington in Oxford. Reflecting on the early 1950s:

> We had nowhere to live and shared a wartime hut in the Slade camp off the Slade. As we shared this hut with the Johnsons, the tenants, we were evicted by the local authority six months later. My father found a disused airfield at Mount Farm in Berinsfield, and we lived in the abandoned Nissan hut near the runway and shared the site with very friendly gypsies camping with their vans next to us.[91]

The Fergusons and the Johnsons were labelled as fraudsters despite the fact that the urgent necessity of familial homelessness hurried away any intent. Closer to the present, the anger felt by disabled people as their entitlement and honesty were defined away by successive governments after 1997 morphed into a deep sense of injustice that the most vulnerable people could so easily be constructed as fraudsters.[92] These are disjointed examples from across the chronological reach of this book, but they are not random, capturing as they do a remarkably strong feature of the underlying data.

When "Zippet" argued that the welfare system "is not fit for purpose," they meant that intentional fraud was too easy but also that there was an alternative series of engagements with the welfare system which constituted an "acceptable fraud." The acknowledgement of Parliamentary Under-Secretary for Social Security Alistair Burt, in a debate about social security fraud on 16 July 1993, that some people gradually gravitate into fraud captures some of this complexity:

> [They] drift into fraud – perhaps even unwittingly at first – for example, by simply forgetting to report a change in circumstances. But later, when they reflect on the cost of rectifying what started as a small lie, they turn a blind eye and ... [t]he boundary between forgetfulness and fraud has then been crossed[93]

Chapters in part 2 thus deal with fraud by association, by definition and redefinition, and by accident. Collectively, they outline an architecture of fraud that has deep and meaningful historical roots and which complicates both public perception of welfare fraud and the scope for policy reactions to it. That this concept of architecture has meaning in the sources can be demonstrated with a closing example: On 5 May 1825 the vestry of Bishopstoke (Hampshire) received an application from "Hedges" for a pair of shoes for his son. The officers "on calculating his earnings" had "found the family had no claim," as Hedges himself must have known. Instead of seeing a fraudulent claim, the vestrymen considered that "from his character" they would in fact make an allowance of shoes.[94] It seems likely that a single mother pulling the same trick would have had a less understanding reception.

Conclusion

Judge Angela Neild is reported as suggesting that the stability of the welfare system depended on the honesty of claimants. At the conclusion of the later 2019 fraud case introduced above, she doubled down on this message:

"You fraudulently obtained tax credits, an offence made relatively easy by the fact the system of benefits in this country has largely been based on the honesty of those who claim against it."[95] Such perspectives, I have argued, are inaccurate. The British welfare system has, on the contrary, always presumed the dishonesty of welfare claimants, as have much of the general public. This contradiction is captured by a comment on the newspaper article reporting the second case (April 2019), which said: "It [the welfare system] should presuppose dishonesty And you have to prove otherwise!"[96] My point, of course, is that it already *does* presuppose dishonesty. Against this backdrop, there is consistent and widespread "public" scepticism about the accuracy of fraud data. A core message articulated in this chapter – the scale of fraud as measured has been low for centuries – stands in contradistinction to the estimates, feelings, and speculations of the broader population that it is much higher. I have been able to trace long-term (and justifiable) doubts about government statistics and methods, anchored by a generalised view based on real life experiences and "knowing stuff," that intentional fraud is and has been rife. In the comments on the newspaper article reporting the second Judge Neild case, this view is emblematized in the suggestion that: "I have a colleague who works part time, claims benefits and has just bought her neighbour's house registering it in her twenty-one-year-old son's name."[97] Such perspectives reach deep into the historical material and identify a considerable seam of welfare fraud that the state does not (and arguably does not intend to) find and stop. The various forms of life-writing used in this book all embody incredulity at this situation. Explaining four hundred years of disjuncture between measured figures and popular perceptions takes us into considerations of the role of the media and policymakers in creating and sustaining narratives of fraud, and also to the wider and historically grounded explanations developed in this chapter.

Still, a paradox remains: people believe that fraud is rife and yet there is evidence – centuries-long evidence – of popular commitment to the welfare system and to the shifting principles of welfare citizenship. Resolving this paradox begins with a comment on reporting of the 2019 fraud case of Iftikhar Sarwar already noted above: "The system is simply not set up to detect and stop those who come with the determined intention to defraud the state."[98] But what of those who had no intention of fraud, or who committed fraud *in extremis*, or were defined as fraudsters through no fault of their own? Modern and historical data point to a general public being capable of distinguishing fraud by intent and fraud committed for other reasons. Not all fraud, as we shall see, is equal.

CHAPTER 4

Cheating by Association

The previous chapter suggested that the long-term disjuncture between measured and popularly constructed welfare fraud partly reflects the sense that people simply "knew" more fraudsters than official statistics would imply. Yet, the word "knew" must be understood loosely. Branching and looping questions in interviews and focus groups were specifically designed to distinguish between fraudsters about whom respondents had first-hand knowledge and others they had heard about or (most important for this chapter) who they *assumed* were fraudsters. The results are compelling. Just 19 per cent of 1,029 named or inferred fraudsters were identified through personal knowledge as opposed to rumour, inference, and gossip. This perspective extends to modern newspaper and commentary material. The former (even sometimes where the article appears in left-leaning publications) generally tension named cases with a more general sense of "others being out there."[1] Comments on such articles usually report rumour and categorisation of certain types of people as "just" dishonest. Thus, in relation to a 2014 article on the announcement of a fraud crackdown by Iain Duncan Smith, some of the 573 comments threw doubt on the existence of large-scale fraud. The majority, however, followed the tone and sentiment of a comment which questioned recipients' authenticity:

> Come to Stockton on Tees IDS! There are DOZENS of them walking up and down the High Street without their sticks touching the ground! Visit the shopping mall and listen to them Swapping stories how to claim MORE Benefits! Tick Box Lifers !!!.[2]

Moving this perspective further back in time is problematic. The British Social Attitudes Survey, for instance, points to the same popular understanding of welfare fraud but lacks the penetrating direction to explore degrees of knowledge proximity. By contrast, a close reading of fifty-seven repurposed interview transcripts that mention or imply welfare fraud shows that only in twelve cases can we be absolutely sure that the fraudster was "known." The life-writing used here can also be quantified in functional ways as a backdrop to individual quotation. Amongst 469 instances of welfare fraud identified by fifty-six life-writers across the period from the 1730s to the 1960s, 48 per cent drew on first-hand knowledge. This figure, however, reduces significantly when excluding the writing of those who were engaged with the administration of the Old or New Poor Laws, public assistance committees, and charities. In turn, the detail on fraud by rumour and association emerging from life-writing is often rich. John Skinner recounted the story of Sarah Goold who, having been locked into the house by her errant husband, was burnt to death when her clothes caught fire. Skinner visited at length the mental illness of Mrs Goold and his attempts to get supervision for her or to have the parish pay for an asylum place. She was, however, tarred by the parochial overseer with the same moral brush as her drunken and philandering husband. The overseer refused to act, suspecting fraud. Mrs Goold was thus guilty by association and paid with her life.[3] Claims to honesty were often fragile. The seventeenth-century experience is harder to crystallize in these terms but is encapsulated in Richard Dunning's pamphlet on how to save £9,000 in poor rates for Devon parishes "without abating the Weekly Relief of any *poor* or doing a Penny damage to any *Person*." Dunning opened with an explicit acknowledgement that he knew nothing of Devon parishes and had not encountered any of the dependent poor in real life. Rather, he assumed (much as did those who ran the 1832 inquiry into the Poor Law nearly 150 years later) that rapid increases in spending on poor relief *must have* reflected the failure of officers to find and punish the idle, beggars, and vagrants.[4]

The fact that so much welfare fraud was identified on the basis of rumour or conjecture creates the framework for "fraud by association." Two initial examples help to identify the process and mechanism. First, in 1767–76, the Surrey justice of the peace Richard Wyatt recorded in his Deposition Book ten instances of welfare fraud from the 317 cases he had heard. These exclusively involved men abandoning their wives and, while the men were the focus of accusation, the women they left behind were clearly the subject of suspicion by association.[5] A second example arises in contexts where having family notionally able to provide care and resources generated suspicions about fraud such that both sets of actors (the applicant or recipient *and* the wider family) would acquire a reputation. As noted in chapter 3, through the founding statutes of the English and Welsh welfare system, first- and second-order kin acquired a legal responsibility to support relatives when able. This requirement was even more strongly articulated in the Scottish Old Poor Law prior to 1845 and in subsequent Scottish welfare arrangements.[6] Historians differ strongly on the degree to which this requirement was enforced or enforceable at any point between 1601 and its legal demise in 1948.[7] A sense of the difficulties faced by officials in trying to enforce the law can be seen in the story (19 April 1839) of the master sailmaker Samuel Bradshaw. He wrote from Great Yarmouth to complain about the New Poor Law relieving officer Thomas Thornton. The officer had visited Bradshaw's house when he was absent and presented a bill for reimbursement of relief given to his father-in-law by the union. Mrs Bradshaw claimed that the family was doing as much as it could to support the old man and then, in a small act of agency of the sort described by James Scott, "tore the Bill to pieces and threw them on the floor." Thornton took offence at this provocative act and called Mrs Bradshaw a "Trumpery Faggot." Then, "upon leaving the room but before leaving the premises he called her a Trumpery Stinking Faggot" all over again. Samuel Bradshaw thought it was unbecoming for a "person holding a Public Office ... to make use of such approbious language so insulting to any person's feeling more particularly to a female," and asked that Thornton be reprimanded. He employed a clear sense that the New Poor Law had ushered in a new era of required professionalism – though he failed to note that the actions of his wife were also out of order in terms of conduct.[8]

One reading of this material is that the Bradshaws had initiated the conflict to avoid their nominal legal responsibilities, a manoeuvre that would be consistent with a sense that all poor people were constructed as dishonest. Yet, there are also clear signals in the data that *both* officials *and* other poor people associated the presence of kin (particularly kin of working age) with dishonest intent on the part of those claiming or applying for welfare. This is emblematised in the letter of John Thompson of Rothersthorpe (Northamptonshire), who in 1786 argued that he had been denied relief even though he was genuinely kinless and friendless, "when You Noe well that others have a Familie behind them."[9] Naturally, expectations of kinship support declined in the twentieth century as welfare rights were extended, but there remains an important link in the popular imagination between the presence (broadly defined) of people with resources who ought to help those in need, and perceptions of fraud. Even so, there has been a subtle change in the rhetoric and thinking involved in this construction. In the pre-1929 period the assumption was that such people should have deployed resources to keep family members off welfare or at least to reduce the scale of their payments. In not doing so, families and individuals dishonestly shifted the costs of care to the state.[10] After this date, and more especially from the 1950s, the issue became one whereby family members provided resources over and above individual welfare payments such that some welfare recipients had more substantial "incomes" than those that could be garnered by the working population. This is clearly embodied in my modern data, with 72% of oral histories and 100% of all focus group sessions citing instances where a welfare claimant was felt to have close family helping out and was so well resourced as to be (to use a 2014 focus group phrase) "lording it up."[11]

Associational fraud, then, speaks to a sense that some groups of welfare recipients and applicants are more (to use the word of "PE") "dodgy" than others because they are associated with particular labels (single mother, vagrant, youth), behaviours, or relationships.[12] This is not a new observation. Many readers would be unsurprised that the word dodgy and its conceptual equivalents (scrounger; dosser; deadbeat; scum) appear with unerring regularity in the sample of post-1970 records from life-writing to newspapers and article comments. As this chapter shows, however, associational fraud leaves a deep and long-term imprint in the historical record, stretching right back to the foundations of the welfare system. I turn first to a broad survey of the sorts of "dodgy people" appearing in the public imagination, and then focus specifically on the group – migrants and immigrants – most clearly linked to associational fraud. While public and policy commitment to the principle of a (residual) welfare state is consistent across the period from 1601, it is equally clear that not all welfare citizens are or have been equal. We might have assumed this from modern discussions of civic stratification, but historical consistency matters here both in and of itself and for the ultimate meaning and significance of the gap between official and popular perceptions of the scale of welfare fraud.[13]

"Dodgy People"

An act of 1597 prefigured the Old Poor Law.[14] It identified two groups – those with relatives who could in theory and fact support them (clause vii) and beggars (clause x; though wandering ex-soldiers and mariners were excluded from the definition[15]) – who might be particularly likely to defraud the newly established parochial welfare system. In turn, variously constructed vagrants, rogues, vagabonds, beggars, and "the homeless" form a large and consistent seam of those who were understood as fraudsters by association, even though this group has always had a limited footprint as recipients. For much of the period under study, that linkage was embodied and materialised in law itself, as it affected vagrants both directly and tangentially via public nuisance and other legislation used to police public space.[16] Much of the modern circularity in the welfare system that makes it so hard for those with no fixed address to secure or maintain benefits flows directly from this collective legislation and speaks to the close yoking of dishonesty and rootlessness.[17] It *is* possible across my sources and chosen period to find people questioning this association. The Bedale (Yorkshire) shoemaker Robert Hird constructed his massive poetical treatment of characters and events in the area cumulatively between 1808 and 1841. Of the local squire Matthew Dodsworth, he said disparagingly: "All paupers did him fear" since:

> Out of our streets, the mendicants,
> He forc'd to go away,
> It matter'd not how great their wants,
> He would not let one stay[18]

Further into the nineteenth century the serial advocate Joseph Rowntree of Leeds (encountered in chapter 2), focussed particularly on improving welfare conditions and accessibility for vagrants. Rowntree's engagement with the Bradford poor law union (Yorkshire) came to a head on 10 March 1866 when (in a letter about Manchester but with some "first remarks on Bradford which portrays serious wrongs") he made allegations about the admission, treatment, and discharge of vagrants.[19] Across 7,606 further words and forwarded newspaper articles, Rowntree developed his "first remarks," alleging that workhouse staff refused to admit vagrants, forced them to work when they could not, withdrew or withheld food, discharged the sick, and endangered the very morals of young female travellers by forcing them out of the workhouse with no visible means of support. In relation to the latter group, he asked: "is not Board of and Guardians highly wrong in prostituting the Lass of this land towards destitute persons." Warming to the task, Rowntree asked on 27 March 1866 "whether men, when destitute and ill, are to receive the legal relief of which they are entitled to claim, or be allowed to wander the streets and perish like dogs." Later first-hand testimony also stands as a useful corrective to casual elision of vagrancy and dishonesty. In an important piece of life-writing covering the period from the 1890s to early 1900s, William Davies portrayed a life on the road in which defrauding the welfare system appeared remarkably lightly. Indeed, the only substantial elements of such fraud were the American cattlemen who supervised animals on the journey across the Atlantic but then rapidly spent all of their pay in ports like Liverpool and had to spend time in the workhouse while they waited for a boat back.[20] We also see sustained arguments in other forms of life-writing that welfare applicants deserved credit because they had an aversion to begging and wandering. This is notably true in Scotland. Hence the petition written for the illiterate Barbra MacKay in February 1847 arguing that she deserved relief because she "has not the face or boldness to beg even should not this be prohibited."[21]

Yet such perspectives are rare and the notoriety that advocates such as Rowntree persistently met – one Poor Law Board commissioner provided examples of strong-arming tactics to show how "Mr Rowntree's' complaints are got up [fabricated]"[22] – speaks to a deeply ingrained suspicion both of vagrants and beggars as citizens (or more accurately, as non-citizens) and of any interactions they had with the welfare system. This alleged dishonesty is well documented for the early modern period, but its persistence thereafter is marked. Records kept by two clergymen who were part of an initiative established by the Bishop of Salisbury in 1882 to spread the spiritual word amongst the traveller population of Wiltshire and Dorset provide a particularly detailed (but not unique) perspective. Reverend Thomas Holt kept a working diary from 1882–84, documenting visits to lodging houses and workhouse casual wards.[23] Another clergyman attached to the mission, Reverend J. Swinstead, published an account of his work, carried out mostly when he was himself a van dweller.[24] The latter account is particularly important. For Swinstead, simply being homeless or rootless did not equate to vagrancy, and he made subtle distinctions between, for instance, "the uncommercial tramp" usually to be found in lodging houses and the "out of worker," who constituted the "straightforward casual, tramping from union to union with a perseverance that lasts on average six weeks."[25] Other categories included showmen, quacks, horse-dealers, and gypsies, some of whom lived itinerant lives for only part of the year. Across all classes, sickness, bad weather, accident, economic downturn, death, and a surfeit of children could turn an independent itinerant life into an engagement with the welfare system. Notwithstanding obvious sympathies for their subjects, both Holt and Swinstead drew clear links between vagrancy and potential fraud. On a visit to the Alderbury (Wiltshire) union on 28 May 1882, Holt encountered only three vagrants: a "compositor in search of work"; a glass blower who was "an old stager, one that did not want to work and wanted not to do it while he could beg"; and the daughter of the old stager who Holt thought ought not to have been tramping.[26] Similarly, on 18 June 1882 he visited the Wilton workhouse (Wiltshire) and found only one inmate who was "not a regular tramp."[27] By contrast his trip to visit the vicar of East and West Harnham (Wiltshire) to talk about "the tramp question" implies a larger fraudulent presence. Over less than twelve hours they met ten tramps, most "old roadsters" who had "both the cant and cunning peculiar to this class," including hiding clothes prior to requesting relief, professing disabilities, and adopting various veiling techniques – disguise, fictitious stories, the persona of the "tough," sickness – when entering workhouses.[28]

Reverend Swinstead also found it useful "to occasionally penetrate[29] to the tramp wards of the union."[30] His collective account suggests that becoming a "casual" was largely a matter of choice rather than necessity; that, in other words, entering a workhouse involved a process of calculation. Fusing recount and anecdote, inmates told him of recent prior sojourns in pubs, lodging houses, doss houses, gaols, and even hotels. Swinstead also suggested that workhouses swelled with undesirable vagrants when there was a fair nearby, citing the case of a crippled man who, "appearing in the union after a fair," was found to have hidden coinage in a hollow of his crutch: "This 'Egyptian' was then despoiled of more than fifty shillings, his earnings at a single fair from the charitable but foolish."[31] This story resonates with wider nineteenth-century narratives about artful beggars and idle tramps, and pointed for Swinstead to a systemic problem with hardened wanderers for whom "mendicity is almost a synonym for mendacity, and their daring in both respects rises to a remarkable pitch in defiance of all order."[32]

A similar sense of calculative dishonesty in relation to the welfare of the homeless can be traced persistently through the twentieth and early twenty-first-century sources. The negative presence of beggars, the homeless, and variously constructed itinerants in my oral history and focus group samples is universal,[33] and is buttressed by occasional upsurges in (largely editorial and investigative) newspaper commentary, and comments on articles that mirror the moral panics over vagrants from the 1600s to the interwar period.[34] Such presence is in one sense surprising; beggars and the homeless are much more likely to be caught defrauding the general public or in criminal acts than committing welfare fraud, given the difficulty faced by such groups in getting welfare in the first place, as I have observed. Still, the vitriolic narrative is well captured by "RR," who in 2009 reasoned: "they're just druggie scum and they can get whatever they need from the state an tell all the lies they want and then just go nicking. No one cares; too much trouble for them sat in their cushdie offices."[35] These sentiments reflect closely the comments that adhere to newspaper articles and documentaries about beggars, the homeless, and other liminal groups. Thus, in relation to a 2018 story about feigned homelessness and welfare fraud, one of the eleven comments read: "Tip of the iceberg, these people know the system and take the pi55."[36] The sense that the state is not serious about combatting fraud (the tip of the iceberg) is clear.

Loosely articulated fears that "bad" parents breed and socialise "bad" children constitutes a second important strand of associational dishonesty. While historians have come to question the Malthusian view that "generous" welfare led to the poor reproducing themselves along lines of intergenerational dependency in the nineteenth century, there is no shortage of micro-claims that dishonest parents could and did pass their proclivities to dishonest children unless prevented.[37] The later nineteenth-century movements advocating social work, adoption, children's charity, resettlement, and training were underpinned by the view that cycles of poverty could and must be broken.[38] In Bolton (Lancashire), for instance, the female poor law guardian Mary Haslam routinely took children whose parents were in prison into the workhouse on the basis that they would get an education and good example, as well as boarding out the children of broadly construed defective parents to foster families. She literally sought to remake the welfare citizen from the bottom up.[39] Moving back through the data, we find thousands of references in pauper letters, vestry minutes, life-writing, and other sources to the threat of bad parents. The exchange between Thomas Bowen of Llandilofawr, the PLB, and the Llandilofawr guardians is typical of the New Poor Law material. On 9 August 1850 Bowen wrote to "inform you of The mis Conduck of our offsers be Login [belonging] to the Llandilo union." He went on to detail inadequate allowances, drunken officers, and a failure to implement due process, following up with another letter on 28 August, because "we are starving by inch." A local investigation found that Bowen "had two children of the respective ages of 16 & 14 residing with him and following no employment." Faced with demands that they find paid work, Bowen had simply failed to act, and welfare payments had been withdrawn. To avoid doubt about the link that should be made between the character of the parents and idleness of the children, the guardians in a pointed exemplum noted that six years prior to this Thomas Bowen had run away from his family leaving them dependent on the state, that he was a drunk both when he was on and off relief, and that he was well known as a "notorious bad Character."[40]

Similar reasoning is found in Old Poor Law letters, where some well-known fraudsters even tried to use the prospect of bad children to argue for support! Thus, Robert Mawman wrote to a former employer at Beverley (Yorkshire) on 9 December 1832 to say that: "Since I saw you at Calais some years ago, I have undergone various changes of fortune and things in France, having taken an unfavourable turn, in consequence of the Political events of that country." He had returned to England, having promised his home parish that he would never do so, but now argued that with five children and a sick wife he required welfare, and asked his former employer to intercede with the parish. Mawman wanted to do well for his children but warned: "I wish my case to be Put to the Authority in this way, Suppose I were to die there are four of my children who are unable to defend themselves in any way and the natural consequences would be that they must become a Fixture on the Parish, but if I had the means of Emigrating to America this possibility would be avoided altogether." Perhaps in a signal of his dubious character, Mawman suggested that the recipient might "feel disposed to enclose me with your answer, a trifle in remembrance of former days."[41]

More widely, apprenticeship was constructed from the earliest days of the Old Poor Law as one way to disrupt cycles of bad parenting and prevent the intergenerational recurrence of dependence. This was true of published pamphlets and accounts which saw apprenticeship as part of a package of measures to break the cycle, and of individual vestries and officials who made this connection explicitly. The commentator J.C. Wright, in his reconstruction of *Bygone Eastbourne*, noted that in December 1816 the town had decided as part of a long-term strategy for containing welfare bills to make the workhouse a hub for training in weaving, spinning, and clothes-making, decreeing that, "Should any parents refuse to send their children … relief was reduced or stopped."[42] Above all, the sense that bad parents made for bad children can be found in life-writing, even that of the very poor themselves. This sentiment is clearly elaborated in the memoir, essays, and poems of John Leathland of Kettering (Northamptonshire), who argued that the difference between the workhouse and independence lay "with the character of each household" and that "there is not a vice but what is more or less expensive."[43] The emotional community of parenthood had no place for the degenerate welfare-dependent mother and father, a sentiment that appears in almost all of my life-writing sample.

Modern political rhetoric – developing strongly from the 1970s and gathering pace in the 2000s – about the need to break cycles of poverty, crime, and dependence is thus not remotely novel.[44] Furious and polarised views about the state of ingrained dependency *or* the demonisation of welfare claimants in extended debate about the documentary series *Benefits Street*[45] – one commentator as late as 2021 argued that "White Dee" was "The poster chav for the thousands of benefit scroungers out there"[46] – can be replicated across the period covered by this book. While the source base does not (despite its size and reach) lend itself to measures of the exact *intensity* of commentary, it is easy to get a sense of active and latent fears about "bad" children of "bad" parents. Roger Prouse and Jeune Morris, for instance, both remembered their Oxford parents fearing the effects on morality and honesty of children mixing with gypsies.[47] More widely, post-war parliamentary debate is suffused with worry about bad parents; there are fifty-six substantial examples of this narrative in *Hansard*, 1971–2021. Some of these sentiments were a mere step away from framing real law.

In 2001, for instance, Jeff Rooker, MP, revealed that the government had until the last minute intended to target "the families of known fraudsters as a discrete group" in directing welfare fraud detection resources.[48] When one focus group participant in 2015 talked of benefit dependence and fraud (seeing them as one and the same thing) "running in the family like Syphillis, you know there are hundreds of kids here just doing nothing because they learn from their shithead parents," she was merely elaborating a sentiment that could have been held and expressed by much of the general population in the seventeenth century.[49] Stripping back the invective, there is significant statistical evidence of the transmission of intergenerational dependence.[50]

Meanwhile, single mothers are also a consistent presence in the arena of associational fraud, as we have already seen. Because they *were* single mothers, their claims *ought* to be doubted and their citizenship credentials circumscribed.[51] The endemic modern concern with this group is emblematised by a 2022 article on the sperm donor James MacDougall.[52] He had advertised his services on social media platforms despite knowingly having the genetic condition Fragile X, which can have fundamental consequences for child development. When McDougall tried to gain access to two children he had "fathered" for a lesbian couple, the judge revealed his identity as a caution to other women seeking DIY solutions to childlessness. In an investigative article ostensibly about moral responsibility and the difficulties faced by aspirant lesbian parents, its author, Frances Hardy, subtly turned the focus onto welfare. We learn that *inter alia*: MacDougall himself was living off benefits; the anonymised lesbian mother – "barely 20" – had entered into a relationship with a jobless partner and they had "decided to try for a baby together" despite having no economic security; the partner moved out a few months after the baby was born leaving her "a young single mum on benefits living alone with a small baby" in a council house; she then met a new partner and (despite being on benefits) wanted a further child so turned to MacDougall for a "full sibling." He actually moved into her home – the implication being that she had not told the welfare authorities – and the anonymous lesbian mother now lived intermittently with her new partner, though the article is unclear as to whether she remained on benefits. These sub-texts are closely woven in the article, suggesting that Hardy intended them to be part of a wider narrative. Indeed, recent newspaper and blog sources come back episodically to single women falling pregnant or pregnant again while on welfare.[53]

Moving chronologically backwards, since fatherhood prior to the 1980s had to be imputed, ascribed, or described by the mother and other interested parties rather than genetically proven, we repeatedly encounter resignation in relation to the dependence of single mothers, and deep scepticism about their honesty. I find limited support for the tolerance of single mothers identified by Andrew Blaikie in relation to northeast Scotland.[54] At the general moral level, more representative is the oral testimony of tenants on the Tollemache Estate (Suffolk) in the early twentieth century, as recorded by George Ewart Evans. He noted that parents were obliged to banish single mothers or be thrown out by the estate owner – "If they didn't they themselves and the whole family would have had to go, and would probably have finished up in the workhouse" – because the failings of their daughters raised a question mark about the moral worth, deservingness, and honesty of the parents themselves.[55] Between this date and the 1990s, there is a considerable weight of negative sentiment about welfare-dependent single mothers across all my sources. This finding is encapsulated in the writing of Grace Horsman, who notes that when the illegitimate newborn child of "Betty" died in the 1940s "we could only feel glad for her."[56] One focus group participant, reflecting on the early 1980s in the midlands, noted: "it was like rent a cock; didn't matter who or what colour, just get knocked up so they can scrounge."[57]

The denunciation of single mothers as dishonest was even more visceral in pre-1900 sources. On 6 September 1849 the PLB received a letter from Charles Spilman of Beverley (Yorkshire). He recounted the story of Elizabeth Glasby, a resident of the Beverley workhouse, who

> had three illegitimate children previous to her entering the house where she has been I think nearly from its formation After she has been in the house some time she gave birth to another child the father of the child which was never acknowledged The child is now about 12 years of age and in the House.

The moral judgement of Glasby drips from the page and constitutes the core framing mechanism. Spilman also doubted her very honesty as a welfare claimant, noting that he had visited Glasby to offer her two jobs so that she could remove herself and the children from dependence. However:

She said she would not leave the House, but live and die in it ... I then told her I should state the case to the Poor Law Commissioners, she said she did not care she should not leave the House either for me or the Commissioners. I brought the case before the Board of Guardians, but they [considered] they could do nothing in it.[58]

This is a nineteenth-century construction of an essentially timeless problem whereby the withdrawal of a total welfare package (including housing costs, clothing, and so forth) means that acceptance of paid work carries a substantial material penalty.[59] It is given added piquancy here by the extended moral discussion of the fact that Glasby was a serial begetter of illegitimate children and *must* thus have been a fraudster. Spilman assumed his readers would understand the message, they being part of the same moral and emotional community. Such attitudes translate easily for this period to the non-elite population: On 17 January 1863, seventy-nine paupers wrote a collective letter to the guardians of the Barnsley union saying that:

having been informed that the inspector was coming from London to inspect Mr Atkinson concerning the subject with Mrs Field, I with other poor paupers join unanimously to stand in his defence and we think it is our bounden duty so to do for he is worthy of it He is a friend to the poor and Needy a Father to the Fatherless & husband to the widdows and waifs upon the old and infirm and seeks out their necessities and wants and aids them in their distress ... Now just examine the woman Field she has had 9 illegitimates and on her way for the 10 and a gentleman of the description of Mr Atkinson to be branded by her we think it ridicolous and we the undersigned poor paupers hope you will think more of Mr Atkinson than be ruled by her.[60]

These more-distant historical sources ground a further theme that we can also find in both oral histories and modern newspaper commentary: the sense that whether the recipients were strictly eligible or not, the receipt of welfare allowances by single mothers of all sorts was an affront to more respectable and deserving people. Hence, when the sixty-three-year-old widow Mary Stafford wrote to the PLB in July 1861, she outlined a case in which the Basford union (Nottinghamshire) had withdrawn an outdoor relief allowance and told "me I must either do without or go into the Union House." This notwithstanding her age, widowed status, and the fact that her dead husband had served his country – all factors that should have mitigated against the workhouse. More important: "Now I should not think so much of their usage did I not see a great deal of favouritism, I see young widows with little or no incumberance having a bountiful allowance given them also single women with illegitimate children used far better than such as I."[61] The moral censure of single women oozes from the text, as it does even more firmly in Scottish sources, where in some places roughly 46 per cent of all relief cases in the years between 1845 and 1923 dealt with single mothers.[62] These threads run strongly through the earlier material and right back to William Cooke's 1636 collation of advice on parish matters from a number of legal "sages," in which the threat to parish order, morals, and finances from licentious single women was a repeated topic.[63] In short, single motherhood was seen as a clear threat to the welfare system, signalling as it did the chance of ever more progeny and intergenerational dependence, an unrootedness from the families that ought to take responsibility, and deeply ingrained moral suspicion that, to take the words of "HP," "there's always some man sniffing around; she ain't fussy."[64] Even as lifelong singleness and informal cohabitation increased from the 1920s both in numbers and as a percentage of the population, concern over the honesty and moral probity of single mothers has been maintained by policymakers, commentators, and communities.[65]

A final set of prominent "dodgy" welfare recipients were those whose honesty came into doubt because of where they lived. My father's engagement with fraud investigators was caused partly by the fact that he did not understand the forms, but also because he lived on a council housing estate with considerable benefit penetration.[66] Once I started writing to the investigators with a professorial title and from a recognisably "rich" postcode, the case evaporated. It is telling that the ensuing apology for harm caused was written to me at my address, rather than to my father at his. Even if we step aside from some of the controversial films and documentaries analysed here – which are effectively auto-correlated for place – the sense that dodgy people come from dodgy places is systemically present in the post-1945 sources. Such ideas are internalised by claimants themselves, as for instance in the case of "Sean Kelly" responding with a comment on the 2011 Panorama investigation "Britain on the Fiddle," who was "gratefully in receipt of welfare" and contrasted himself with "the scum who cheat and steal from tax payers rich or poor" on their council estate and who were "member[s] of [Gordon] Brown's client state."[67] Concentration effects clearly relate to the wider underlay of persistent inequalities in regional income and wealth in modern Britain.[68] Yet, the key point for this book is the *traction* of the association between dishonest places and dishonest people. Hence, when the House of Lords debated the report of the Select Committee on Regenerating Seaside Towns and Communities – *The Future of Seaside Towns* – on 1 July 2019, the crossbencher Lord Best noted:

> in Blackpool and similar towns, your rent will be fully covered, making these places magnets for DWP claimants and a place for other councils to send their vulnerable claimants. Every year, around 5,000 households eligible for housing benefit move into Blackpool, many of them with personal problems – of physical and mental health, drug abuse or alcoholism ... A system that concentrates the most vulnerable in one place and incentivises this trend into the future is a disaster for that place's health and well-being.[69]

Inadvertently, Best had given substance to the observation of "TM" in an interview of 2017: "I got out of Blackpool to down here and thank God, its full of druggies and benefit cheats and you sort of get tarred with the same brush."[70] The boundaries in the popular imagination between citizenship and non-citizenship become clearly defined in such stories. Indeed, an implicit bias of that sort is a familiar feature of the testimony of those sharing perspectives, who were explicitly asked about such places. Focus group participants in 2016, for instance, argued that Morecombe "is a shit hole; they dump the druggies and benefit cheats there."[71]

These cases are important for understanding how popular views of the scale of fraud can deviate so radically from official estimates. Just as important is the fact that concentration effects are a familiar feature of the historical research on welfare, especially in relation to crowded urban areas with high population turnovers.[72] They are also a constant presence in the earlier data used here, including the singling out of Nottingham in the 1940s, for instance, of Great Yarmouth in the 1850s, Manchester in the 1830s, and London in the 1790s. The location of unfavoured places flexes over time in the face of variables such as de-industrialisation and according to the system of welfare organisation, especially the legal ability or lack thereof to move recipients around. Even so, there are some remarkable continuities across multiple source types including, for instance, deeply ingrained senses that Liverpool, Birmingham, and Blackpool were "problem" places. The observation in the 2019 English Indices of Deprivation that these three communities had dominated the ranking of "most deprived" places in the country across multiple prior iterations finds its analogue in persistent suspicion of Liverpudlians in focus group meetings.[73] Locating "dodgy places" is complicated by problems of recording, autocorrelation (places with greater welfare dependence generate more welfare fraud), and definition.[74] Nonetheless, both modern and historic commentators were clear that they *could* locate such hotspots, as is well captured by *The Sun* in its benefit hotspot maps of 2018.[75] These "breeding towns for scum and cheats" (see above) are to be found in all three of the mainland countries that were moving to a common welfare system by the 1870s. There were also, however, important cross-currents of opinion about the honesty of English, Welsh, and Scottish migrants that adhered simply because of their nationality and it is to this issue, and to the wider question of immigration as the singular feature of the association between dishonesty and just "being," that the chapter now turns.

Immigrants in the Benefit System

The constructed relationship between movement and associative dishonesty operates at three levels in the sources used here: first, in suspicion of English migrants to English communities. An Act of 1662 had remedied the central problem of the Old Poor Law from its inception, which was that parishes were obliged to provide welfare for "impotent" residents wherever they actually came from. The burden thus created is reflected in petitions to Quarter Sessions where representatives of towns that attracted migrants urged action so as to prevent their bankruptcy.[76] In a little over a thousand words, the act established criteria that gave a person a legal belonging to a fixed place of settlement and provided that unless a "settlement" parish were willing to furnish a certificate promising to pay host parishes if one of their parishioners fell into poverty, migrants could be physically removed "to such Parish where he or they were last legally settled either as a native Householder Sojourner Apprentice or Servant."[77] While many early histories of the Old Poor Law focussed on the number of people who were removed under these rules, recent research has highlighted the laws' episodic and individualised application.[78] In this chapter, however, what is important is the persistent suspicion of the honesty of English migrants on the part of both officials and the settled resident population of parishes throughout the two-hundred-year period over which these settlement laws effectively operated. This ultimate expression of localism and discretion is evidenced in the pamphlet literature of the eighteenth century, including that of Roger North, who argued in 1753 that suspicion had been so much increased during the first century of the settlement laws that their utility was diminished and: "in Truth [the law was] a Snare to the Poor, and Cause of Poverty, robbing them of all Means to mend their condition."[79] Local sources lay this suspicion bare, as with George Cleaver of Kidderminster (Worcestershire), who complained in October 1825 that his wife "is become a child which we may expect she being in her 79 or 80th year" and that he could not get welfare. Cleaver asserted that "honest poverty is no disgrace" and then made a crucial distinction in trying to establish his deservingness, contrasting his position as a long-term resident – "I have been a poor Man all my life in this Town about 30 Years & never troubled you for any thing" – with those who had much more recently arrived in Kidderminster.[80] That suspicion carried on in the area under the New Poor Law is elegantly confirmed in the letter of John Whitgrove of Stourbridge (Worcestershire), who noted that his daughter was refused relief to care for him because "I was out of there union." He noted with some gusto that "my opinion of the business is planley this whas I sat in the Deepest Mine in England Ireland Scotland or Wales I should not be out of your union which is the One I have applied to."[81] We might imagine this associative link between domestic migration and honesty wasted away as urbanisation and migration increased and a rights-based national welfare system began to develop. This is incorrect. As recently as 2001 the MP Steve Webb noted that, in their consideration of a recent Social Security Fraud bill, the House of Lords had removed a government clause stating that scrutiny would fall particularly on "those in a category [undefined in the bill] more likely than others to commit fraud." He asked, perhaps not as tongue in cheek as we might assume, "whether they had in mind people ... with funny accents."[82]

A second group of movers – those crossing physical boundaries between the three home nations – merited an even closer association between welfare application or receipt and dishonesty. My oral history sample comprises almost exclusively English people, as does the sample of repurposed oral histories. They had little positive to say about perceived enclaves of welfare-dependent Scottish people in England or individual Scots. Interviewees from west- or north-west England were similarly condemnatory of the Welsh, making repeated accusations of laziness, invoking a plethora of single mothers and (to quote "KN," interviewed in Manchester in 1997) ascribing to them "backwardness."[83] Figure 4.1 is an image of writing on a road between Shrewsbury and Wales in 2001, with an arrow pointing back to Wales and derogatory comments about the Welsh living in Shrewsbury. Newspaper articles of all types for the post-1945 period, by contrast, had seemingly little to say on the honesty of UK migrants, and even exhibited some sympathy for the fate of those casually forced to move by local authorities to places such as Rhyll, Morecombe, or Paisley. The disjuncture is an important one; it reflects an alternative enduring concern for newspapers – welfare fraud and immigration – which is encountered below. Nonetheless, concerns about cross-border movement have deep historical traction. The sheer contempt for Scottish welfare claimants evidenced by an entry to the East Dereham (Norfolk) overseers' accounts for 10 October 1754 – "Funeral of a Scotchman's child 4s 6d; neither the man or his child was worthy of a name" – is replicated across all the early sources used here.[84] The fact that William Gordon of West Bromwich (Worcestershire) was obliged in 1836 to assert that Edward Shrewsbury "is no impostor – he appears a simple hearted honest Welchman," speaks volumes on the anticipated reception of applications by Welsh migrants to English parishes.[85] Thirty years later we find Alexander Sparrow making the same point to the Liverpool vestry about the Welshman John Carroll, who "was a Man with double rupture, asthma, bronchitis and disease of the heart rated like a criminal because he asked parish relief in his extremity." Sparrow characterised the conduct of the vestry to an "honest and sober" Welshman as "brutal."[86]

4.1 Picture of hostility to Welsh welfare recipients.
Source: Author's photograph.

By contrast, it is much less easy to discern matching attitudes towards English migrants in Wales and Scotland. This dichotomy reflects the direction of long-term migration flows, which favoured England, and for Scotland at least a very different welfare system, which was harsh to *all* applicants.[87] Nonetheless, particularly in rural areas of Scotland where relief applications were accompanied by investigative forms with up to sixteen columns of information recorded, parochial inspectors in the later nineteenth century seemingly viewed with suspicion those who had relatives living in England.[88]

Yet, it is and was Irish immigrants to the British mainland for whom the closest association between movement and assumed dishonesty can be traced. The Irish were a liminal group, simultaneously belonging and not. Early Irish immigration was often seasonal; they arrived, earned, and went home. Parochial officers and the settled parochial poor might grumble about the cost of welfare claims by poor harvesters but could be reasonably sure that paying a little relief would lead the Irish to move on and back to the ports. Transcripts of the Buckinghamshire Quarter Sessions record more than five hundred such cases. Even before the famine, however, migration for textile work, military service, and so forth had expanded exponentially, generating substantial problems for an Old Poor Law system in which the Irish had no legal settlement unless by accident and English women notionally lost their settlements when marrying Irishmen.[89] Thus, when Sarah O'Hara wrote from Wigton (Cumbria) on 1 June 1811 seeking welfare, she noted that although herself English, "my Husband is an Irishman and belongs to whare I belong." She justified this misinterpretation of the law by claiming that her husband had been a long-time resident, supported them through hard work "this long time Back," and that he had been recognised as belonging (that is, almost native) by parish officials: "the overseir of this Plase has forgave him the Poor Rates as he is out of work."[90] The endemic suspicion of the Irish that justified this very structured appeal is obvious. Until the 1860s and the gradual dismantling of the settlement system, such problems persisted and even intensified,[91] with the Irish or their relatives persistently suspected of fraud. This perceived injustice is exemplified in a letter of 31 August 1868 in which Michael Flannagan complained that the York guardians had mistreated him while in the workhouse infirmary to such a degree that "it is evidently known by every body who had knowledge of me that I had redu[ced] wonderfully." Having discharged himself, he was now refused outdoor relief and attributed this directly to the racism of the guardians:

> such awthority as this shuts up the sources altogether from an Irishman as the Guardians will never under any circumstances give charitable consideration to his case … it can hardly be believed in York that a person of 72 years of age as I am and my wife 70 can be deprived of out door relief on any grounds except bigotry or National hatred to the applicant.[92]

Suspicion does not dissipate in the modern welfare system. In chapter 3 we saw a 1969 example of the MP Roger Gresham Cooke being taken in by an Irishman, but he had no need in his storytelling structure to highlight nationality. Other examples abound, including for instance one in a speech by Peter Lilley, MP, in 1987 when, in a debate on Gipsy caravan sites, he elided the observation that "we must recognise the Irish dimension to the problem. In recent years, ever since the war, there has been a growing influx of Irish tinkers and didicois" with the further contention that:

We do not have obligations to provide benefits to a special category of people who are often considerably wealthy. I have visited several illegal gipsy sites in my constituency and been impressed by the quality of the cars and how new they are … We have no obligation to provide social security benefits to people who are clearly well able to look after themselves.[93]

These are important observations, but in a presentist sense the single most important group associated indelibly with welfare fraud are immigrants from further afield, especially illegal immigrants. Figure 4.2 traces the number of newspaper stories and comments *directly* about immigrants and welfare fraud found in my data for the period 1990–2023. While we see episodic peaks and troughs (especially after Tony Blair's decision to allow free movement from eastern European accession counties after 2003) the weight of this commentary is striking. Common tropes included: dishonest eastern European mothers returning home and still retaining "our" child benefits; Romanians flying in for a summer of benefits and begging; illegal immigrants "grazing" off the welfare system; and all manner of commentary on the breaking of the assumed linkage between contribution in terms of paying prior taxes, and welfare. Such associations are mostly erroneous, of course, but that is not the point in the context of this chapter.[94] Other "modern" sources confirm that such views are structural and endemic rather than linked to the political persuasion of newspapers and those who comment on their articles. Every oral history and focus group came back to the sense that immigrants have and had a privileged space in the welfare system compared to British natives. Focus group participant "PO," a self-confessed Labour voter, is typical, claiming: "They just have to click their fingers, you know, them illegals from Africa or wherever, and they gets what they want but I can't even get unemployment benefit because my husband is earning."[95] There are of course complexities; a nurse whose family hailed originally from Uganda talked to me as I waited for a procedure on 16 April 2022, telling me proudly of the record of contribution by herself and her children, before moving on to call more recent Somali immigrants "lazy," workshy, and parasites.[96] This sort of commentary from settled first- and second-generation immigrants of colour is a consistent feature of the evidence and has striking linguistic similarity to the arguments and rhetoric of the white population.

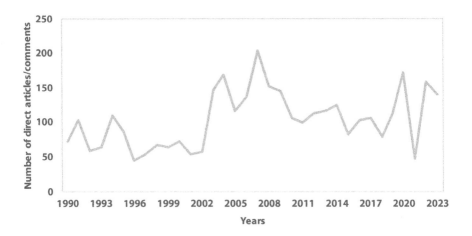

4.2 Newspaper and comment pieces on immigrants and welfare fraud, 1990–2023. *Source:* Articles and comments; see chapter 2.

The circular knowledge and attitudinal ecology in relation to immigrants is consistently demonstrated in the modern sources. High-profile cases of immigrant benefit fraud move immediately into popular conversation and memory. In November 2022, for instance, the case of criminal gangs "inventing" children to make child benefit and Universal Credit claims gained wide purchase. It was reported that "The gang members are all Somalian" and that the ringleader had already served a lengthy jail sentence for immigration and drug offences. The same articles linked the case to a further story of three Polish women inventing children for the same purposes.[97] Straight after this story broke, I had six conversations about it in my local town (equally split between those concerned about demonising immigrants and those who were condemnatory) but the reach of the case was much longer. On 15 April 2023, for instance, my local butcher started a conversation with, "You remember that story about those people inventing children …" and then proceeded to detail a local fraud case on a smaller scale. The idea from the third chapter that not all welfare fraud was equal applies very clearly to immigrants, who are routinely stripped of their citizenship potential in a rhetorical and associational sense.[98]

Even in these modern sources, however, I detect a tension between attitudes to immigrants as a group or codified "other" and individuals. While all oral history respondents had something to say about the welfare claims or honesty of "immigrants," when asked about *specific* individuals, almost everyone acknowledged that their neighbours were, to use the words of one focus group attendee in 2015, "alright."[99] This should not surprise us. Laura Tabili has argued persuasively that nineteenth-century immigrants could relatively easily integrate into local street cultures such that their naturalisation applications would be signed by their neighbours. "RK," an outspoken oral history respondent, had even signed documents for an immigrant Syrian neighbour.[100] The modern welfare system has tended to make immigrants more visible and connect them more fully, firmly, and for longer to the welfare system than pre-1945 immigrants,[101] but these stories signal an interesting complexity to the assumed dishonesty of newcomers, and one with deep historical roots. Three aspects of this historical complexity are important, even if the sources do not yield to a simple time-series analysis of the sort represented for the modern period in figure 4.2. First, before the 1960s, immigrants (other than Irish) were encountered episodically by most of those claiming, funding, or organising welfare. They rarely appear in the repurposed oral histories. Just two of the ninety-nine available for Hertford and Ware mention immigrants at all and none in relation to welfare. Similarly, immigrants are almost completely missing from the multiple volumes of Joy James's monumental autobiography recording her childhood and life in postwar Nottingham,[102] and from Reverend Oliver Wilmott's account of "doings" in his Dorset parishes.[103] Reverend John Skinner noted the presence and passage of three Black men through Camerton and recounted the dishonesty of one of them, but in relation to work and not welfare.[104] On the other hand, in places where incomers concentrated and stayed, we see a more determined linkage of immigrant status, welfare, and dishonesty. A circular printed by the Order of the White Seamen's Brotherhood in 1932 called attention to the situation in British ports where "black and yellow seamen" were being "maintained by British funds [that is, welfare payments] to supplant British labour" at a later date, and thus weaken the vital merchant marine.[105] Almost a hundred years earlier, Thomas Venes Jnr of Wimbledon had expressed a very similar sentiment. In a closely reasoned 1,218-word letter he argued that, having lost his "pension" as a result of the 1834 Poor Law Amendment Act, there was little point in challenging the decision because "in a word Gentlemen I shall be told this law was passed to make every tub stand upon its own bottom." Yet how could this be, he asked, unless "in these days of improvement a law was framed and passed that every foreigner, Scotch inclusive were to go home to their own homes." Only then, he argued, could an "empty washing tub" be given the requisite "oar a sail and compass … to propel his tub machine along."[106] Construction of immigrants as a dishonest seam of welfare recipients thus had a regional, local, and even personal flavour.

A second historical complexity is also important; that is, many immigrants came to Britain because of pre-existing settlement of prior migrants. The same is true in a modern sense, as the 2024 controversy over the raising of the income requirements for spouses of immigrants to come to Britain or remain here shows. But historic communities often developed their own welfare structures which kept recent arrivals *away* from the Old and New Poor Laws or interwar public assistance committees, and thus away from wider narratives of fraud and dishonesty. The importance of Jewish welfare organisations is well known[107] and finds its analogue in pauper letters from 1755: in over five million words of text, I find only eighty-nine references to Jews, Jewishness, or any derogatory variation – testimony to the limited place of Jews in the British welfare system. Other immigrant support structures were less systematic but still important. Joseph Ashby noted in one of his 1893 newspaper articles: "I think it would only be fair to say that Catholics as a body, throughout South-east Warwickshire have a very warm side to the poor."[108] Formal and informal support networks for Catholic immigrants and migrants wind consistently through the source base, as for instance with the Catholic Welfare Association founded in Wigan in 1784 with the explicit intention of keeping settled and migrant Catholics away from parish welfare dominated by Anglican officers and ratepayers.[109] Other religious groups keeping their immigrant brethren away from the welfare system included the Moravians in West Yorkshire and Methodists more widely.[110]

In part related to these support networks – which dripped immigrants gradually into the welfare system and thus in public and policy consciousness – a third complexity is that for much of the time immigrant welfare has been surprisingly uncontroversial. Periods of national or intense local economic stress – the 1790s, 1860s, 1880s, or 1920s – brought the probity of many claimants and especially "others" into sharp relief. Mostly, however, immigrants reached the welfare system at the extremes of need such that Old and New Poor Law obligations to prevent people from starving to death crept in. More than this, some groups of immigrants were more or less automatically given relief because they were in effect regarded as children, and thus not directly responsible for their situation.[111] The remarkable absence of references to skin colour in millions of words from vestry minutes, pauper letters, or guardian minutes is in part a reminder that ex-slaves were regarded in this way. In one of the few negative examples, "Mary the Black Girl" was admitted to the Godmanchester poorhouse (Cambridgeshire) and can be traced through clothing accounts until the point where she is herself accused of stealing items of clothing and discharged. This, however, is a remarkable incident in a landscape of historical sources in which non-white people have a fleeting or particular place.[112] These caveats and complexities notwithstanding, at certain times, in certain areas, and inexorably from the 1950s, the deep roots of presentist elisions of immigrants and fraud can still be found.

Conclusion

The strong presence of fraud by association in the data helps to explain why ordinary people constructed fraud on a much wider quantitative canvas than official measurements suggest. It is a mistake to understand these processes of association in presentist and superficially modern terms. We see modern rabble-rousing by newspapers and policymakers, to be sure, and the internet gives rapid traction to the process of othering, as scholars from many disciplines have noted.[113] Yet, the long-term continuities in associational fraud revealed by combining summative perspective on the sources, and micro-perspective and examples – the consistent presence of the homeless, single mothers, those from certain places, and the emergent narrative of welfare-dependent immigrants from the interwar period, which signals the dishonesty of these groups even apart from a wider sense that all poor people are dishonest – suggest much deeper currents of thought or influence. They speak to the traction of a complex matrix of moral, ethnic, locational, and situational othering that persists in the popular imagination beneath the changing organisation, rules, and scope of the British welfare system from its very earliest days. More than this, the ascription of a substantial seam of associational fraud *both* highlights the complexity of understanding what a welfare citizen is and was – not all voices and experiences are in this sense equal – *and* signals how difficult it will be for policymakers to reimagine the future welfare citizen without a keener understanding of the historical dimensions of that status. It is also important to understand that these models of associational fraud come to be internalized by welfare recipients. We see this clearly in films and documentaries dealing with poverty and welfare claimants or in fora where "modern" associational groups tell their stories, but the internalisation is even more visible in the distant historical sources. Rather poignantly, for instance, Reverend John Coker Egerton told the story of Mrs Isted, who in July 1874 gained a new public presence: "All this freedom I believe owing to ye taking off of ye relief. She is now not afraid of being seen about."[114]

Other examples of the internalisation of the fraudster persona wind depressingly through the corpus. Such internalisation over the very long term creates a regenerative narrative that cannot be corrected by fact or political assertion. In researching for this book, I have read thousands of online pages of *Hansard*. Most ministers, select committee members, and shadow ministers are and always have been assiduous in seeking to challenge associational structures in parliamentary debate. And none of this matters. Indeed, in some ways it is counter-productive. We cannot quantify exactly how many people are drawn into the actual or suspected fraud arena by association, but the fact that it cannot be quantified and that no one wants to try (the lesson of the *Hansard* debates) explains a fundamental characteristic of the post-1601 welfare state. That is, together with intentional deception, fraud by association goes some way towards explaining the strikingly residualist nature of the British welfare state. For the groups I have dealt with here, fraud was often constructed as simply a way of life, and this basic ecology of belief has always held back support for anything other than residuality. The alternative approach – to acknowledge the traction of associational fraud and to admit that it has had at least some basis in the lived reality of ordinary people from the very start of the British welfare system – is not one that has garnered much modern political and elite support but which might in the end be vital to understanding the deep sociocultural costs of residuality, and doing something about it.

These are matters taken up at greater length in chapters 10 and 11. For now two things are important: first, that while belief in large-scale associational fraud can and should be understood on the same canvas as intentional fraud, people do not construct all fraudulent activity in negative terms; and second, that a significant part of the gap between measured and popular estimates of the extent and cost of fraud is explained by processes and experiences that elicit sustained sympathy on the part of those looking in from the outside. These two issues inform the focus of the final two chapters of this section.

CHAPTER 5

Cheating by Definition and Redefinition

In June 2022 most UK newspapers carried editorials noting government press releases that: "People on benefits will have to work longer hours if they want to avoid regular check-ins with job coaches under plans being drawn up by ministers." Some 44 per cent of Universal Credit recipients were employed in that year, and the finding that there were "more job vacancies than unemployed people for the first time since records began" had prompted the government to "extend the amount of time claimants have to spend working each week from nine hours to 12 if they are to justify missing regular meetings."[1] This tweak to the rules would not mean that recipients would lose benefits, but ministers had calculated that the "hassle value" of attending meetings as well as working and caring would nudge people into taking on more hours in the sorts of industries that in 2022 were failing to recruit. The *Times* editorial argued that a booming jobs market post-COVID left many recipients trapped on welfare benefits:

> It is vital, for national prosperity and their own dignity, that people of working age are helped into employment and that perverse incentives to live on benefits are closed off … Though the provision of universal credit ensures that having a job always pays better than not working,[2] the marginal effect may be so small that, coupled with travel and childcare costs, an applicant may not consider it worthwhile.[3]

This editorial was followed throughout 2023 and early 2024 by announcements (or rather, largely re-announcements) of measures to force people "back to work." Such material speaks to my wider theme that the assumed dishonesty of the poor is baked into the framing and perception of the British welfare system. It also highlights the complexity of the interactions between welfare and work in fact and imagination, an issue to which I return later.

What matters here, however, is the proposed rule tweak. It is a truism that welfare changes take a long time to become part of the local ecology of knowledge amongst recipients.[4] Yet, a singular characteristic of the British welfare system from 1601 to 2023 has been the *rapidity* of changes to law, guidance, and regulation, and also to the intent and enforcement of existing laws. It has thus always been easy for those receiving, renewing, or applying to obtain payments to be accused of fraud simply because they had no functional knowledge of the rules. As focus group member "TO" said about rules on in-work benefit withdrawal rates in 2014 (and repeated in a draft autobiography shared with me), "How was I supposed to know they'd changed them?"[5] In one sense, changes to rules and some of the consequential definitions of deservingness are a variant of cheating by accident, but I have a separate chapter on that theme because of an insistent rhetorical thread in the sources which focusses on the difficulty of interpreting rather than simply *knowing* the law. In this chapter I explore a series of case studies, each dealt with (for the first time) across the whole period from 1601 to the present, to explore the dynamics of thinking about the "fraud" arising from rule changes.

We encounter three sorts of rule problem: the first is the enacting of subtle tweaks to existing rules that simultaneously affect the number of people who could be accused or suspected of fraud, the attitudinal world of claimants, *and* the perception of the general public. The second is the accumulation of case law or administrative precedent that modifies the practical scope or application of acts, or influences the consequences of breaking them, with fundamental implications for the knowability of "the" law.[6] Between the seventeenth and nineteenth centuries a complex series of courts and jurisdictions became involved in poor-law business, each creating precedent.[7] Even in a modern sense some court and tribunal decisions on fraud and entitlement create precedent, such that the rules of welfare are ultimately fluid.[8] Finally, the chapter deals with sweeping changes affecting the whole system, as for instance with the settlement acts of the 1660s (discussed at length in chapter 4), which at the stroke of a pen opened up generations of migrants to suspicions of fraud simply by dint of their arrival in a community. Overlaying these rule problems is the wider issue that right up to the 1940s the exact understanding of who could and should claim welfare was rooted in local discretion, such that it was possible to make a genuine claim in one place but for the same claim and circumstances to signal fraud in other communities. My case studies confront these complexities. A core theme of the chapter is the way claimants and the general public – and sometimes even officials themselves – have understood the episodic redefinition of entitlement and thus the re-evaluation of the honesty of welfare recipients as essentially "unfair."

Tweaking: Part-Time Work and Income

As we have seen at various points, the hope that welfare claimants would seek work and return to independence has been the single most consistent philosophical feature of the British welfare system from 1601 onwards.[9] Unsurprisingly, belief in the value of work runs deep across the period in question, and two emblematic examples capture a consistent motif. The agricultural trade unionist Joseph Ashby spoke in 1893 of the sustaining and nourishing effect of work, claiming that the ability through work to gain the "solid means of comfort" constituted the "independence [from welfare] that makes a man a man."[10] Poor applicants and recipients also consistently aspired in a rhetorical sense to build work capacity and, once able, to return to the light of the labour market. One of the earliest writers in my sample is George Bradford, settled in Oxford. His letter of 15 August 1754 is timeless in its claims, rhetoric, and intent. Setting out the prospect of being thrown into the street for arrears of rent due to illness and consequent unemployment, he promised: "If the Gentlemen will Please to Grant Me this favour," he would be able to end his dependence because "Now is the time of the Year for Fruit and other things."[11] Equally, many of those whose stories underpin some modern surveys of poverty rhetoricised a desire to get work if they could.[12] In turn, the demonisation of those who claimed to be incapable of all work, and the episodic changing of rules so as to force labour market participation by such groups, have been a constant feature of the system since 1601.[13] There are, for instance, more than 350 twentieth-century examples of such rhetoric in *Hansard*, and some 800 in letters and vestry and guardian minutes for the nineteenth century.

Yet the British welfare system has also had to persistently grapple with a more slippery problem: those people who could do *some* work or might slowly build a labour market profile over time. While the Act of 1601 contained little on this group explicitly, custom, practice, and case law coalesced over time to generate localised norms of the rate at which welfare payments might be withdrawn as individuals or families garnered more resources through work. Calculating this withdrawal rate has been a thorn in the side of policymakers ever since, especially for Gordon Brown in his tax credit regime.[14] The issue matters for this chapter at a general level: policies about the amount welfare recipients can earn without losing payments or the amount they do not earn because they want to protect payments shape broad perceptions of the honesty and moral worth of all claimants. The issue also has *particular* consequences, including ingrained beliefs across the sources that recipients are doing (and being paid for) more work than they are recording. The bricklayer George Hewins traced an intricate web of petty earning opportunities for himself and others in late Victorian and early Edwardian Stratford-upon-Avon, something that rings true for most life-writers in my sample.[15] Yet there are also more subtle issues around the intersection of work and welfare that shape the scale of measured and feared fraud. These are deeply entwined with matters of definition and redefinition, and include: What constitutes work? Whose work? What constitutes earnings? How long does "work" have to last? How should withdrawal rates be calibrated? And how do current and future applicants get to "know" about changes in rules or expectations? Some of these questions (the definition of work and earning; issues of duration) speak to the agenda of chapter 6 where we deal with fraud by accident. Others have a particular place here, given that slight tweaks to process, custom, or rules can lead to the definition or redefinition of claimants and applicants as fraudsters either in fact or in the public and policy imagination.

Let us turn first to withdrawal rates. As with the example of Universal Credit above, the modern welfare system seeks to impose a maximum limit on the acceptable amount of work to be done and withdraws benefits at a national rate if that threshold is surpassed. For a significant part of the post-1945 period, the effective marginal reductions in welfare arising from working more have been close to, at, or (for sub-groups of the poor) beyond the resources gained by working.[16] More important for this chapter is that both the withdrawal rate *and* the hours or earning limit have changed frequently in the modern period. Tracing the dynamics of such changes is a difficult endeavour. A survey of ministerial declarations on the subject in newspapers from 1981 (the year in which announcements outside parliamentary debate mushroomed after urban riots) to 2021 indicated that less than half of them could be traced through to meaningful changes in the rules connecting part-time work and welfare. The follow-through rate was lowest for announcements that appeared in Sunday newspapers, given the tendency for politicians to test public opinion in these particular editions. This in itself explains some of the disparity between official and popular understandings of the scale of welfare fraud; people simply assumed that rules *had* changed after reading announcements in the press. Reversing the analysis, it ought to have been possible to definitively trace changes to thresholds and withdrawal rates through announcements by the Department for Work and Pensions and its predecessors. This is not the case.[17]

Since the 2010s governments have become better at "advertising" rule changes, but the potential for modern recipients and applicants to be suspected of or charged with fraud because of unknown changes remains clear. The extent of misunderstanding about the rules around part-time work and welfare in my oral histories was thus profound. All interviewees were asked whether claimants could simultaneously earn and receive welfare payments: 47% thought not, 100% had no knowledge of the hours or earning limits in place at the time they were interviewed, and 63%, once alerted to the possibility of work, assumed that such earnings would top up welfare payments. These interviewees were mainly considering the post-1960 period, but there is evidence of equal ignorance from the 1920s and 1930s. Thus, Mr G.2.L of Lancaster remembered that no one saw anything wrong with "the men from the workhouse" appropriating waste wood and "wheeling barrows of it round the town to sell as firewood."[18] It is easy to see how both the suspicion of fraud and actual accusations of it can arise from the complex connections between part-time work and welfare.

There is a temptation to think of this issue as a twentieth-century problem, but to do so would be a mistake. In general, the Old and New Poor Laws – and even public assistance committees outside the means test periods – did not systematically seek to limit work or earnings. The 1601 Act framed the dependent poor as essentially dishonest, as we have seen. This presumption extended even to the impotent poor or their families, with officials entitled to expect that welfare recipients of all sorts *would* do whatever they could to limit the burden on parish taxes. Officials in their turn would tailor the withdrawal of welfare payments to exact personal (including moral) and local circumstances. Everyone knew this to be the case and so the key question for claimants, officials, and the public was: how much earning was too much? When Keleigh-Ann Groves speaks of cash-in-hand as part of the "thick" resource matrix assembled by modern welfare fraudsters, she is thus keying into a model that is hundreds of years old.[19] Withdrawal rates were not uncontentious. In one of the early sources used for this book, "poor and plain dealing farmers" wrote about their dispute with the townsmen of Buckingham and appended a pamphlet on the duties of overseers which dealt at length with the need to put the poor to work in order to minimize the rates.[20] Later sources provide a deeper understanding of local mentalities. Thus, in vestry minutes recording occasions when applicants had to present a case or might find themselves subject to information-gathering, earning and earning potential were consistent themes. This system, at its most imaginative, allowed vestry members and officials to fuse work and benefits, creating an "acceptable" income for the circumstances of individual families.[21] Thus, the vestry of Herriard (Hampshire) maintained – and in the 1820s and 1830s were guided by – multiple tables dealing with the "Scale of Wages and Parochial Relief" which effectively set knowable and scalable welfare withdrawal rates.[22] The problem for applicants, recipients, and communities, however, was that these informal rules were rarely codified, consistent, or knowable for the long term. Thresholds and withdrawal rates could fluctuate (or even disappear) as vestry members or officials changed, as economic circumstances deteriorated or improved, and as knowledge of practice elsewhere percolated, as is well illustrated by the keen interest that the Swanage Vestry (Dorset) took in the monthly price of stone, to which withdrawal rates were finely tuned.[23] It was thus possible under the Old Poor Law for an applicant to find that the rules had literally changed overnight; their application could be seen as fraudulent when it would not have been the day before. This happened to people in Devizes (Wiltshire) in 1802, when the vestry ordered a survey of poor families. The very first entry related to Henry Beans and his family, who were collectively recorded as earning 12s per week and receiving 5s of poor relief. The entry noted: "Mr Burton offers to give this man 6s [presumably for more labour] – if not accepted 2s to be taken off [the relief]."[24] The assumption was clearly that Beans would naturally prefer to rely on welfare rather than extend his labour.

A further feature of the Old Poor Law data increased background suspicions of fraud. In the early eighteenth century, officials could usually get to know the earnings or earning potential of applicants and recipients by asking around in the locality or, if the poor person was not locally resident, asking contacts in other places. From the early 1800s it became harder to obtain information, as more people moved out of their locality, earnings became more fractured, and the co-operation of employers decreased. In terms of the latter, for instance, in May 1828 Christopher Grime, writing to the parish of Kirkby Lonsdale (Cumbria) noted that his employer, Mr Clayton, "would not allow any thing of that sort [earnings per week] to be devulged to any Township."[25] He returned to the theme in December 1829 when requesting more relief, saying that: "M^r. Clayton will not give a statement of never a workmans wages about His place," but he nonetheless volunteered "a statement of my self as near truth as fasible I can The wages we earn is in a general way."[26] Crudely, the overseer was asked merely to trust the poor writer. In such circumstances, popular and official suspicion of dishonesty increased and policies became more fluid, such that changes in implicit rules (ultimately unknowable until the point of application) became more likely to generate fraud. The harshness that often accompanied such fluidity and opacity is captured in rebukes issued to the Manchester vestry in 1811 by local magistrates, who argued that welfare withdrawal rates were too "immediate."[27]

The New Poor Law theoretically solved the problem of earning thresholds and welfare withdrawal rates by requiring that relief should in most cases be given via the workhouse, where the possibility of labour other than to serve or service the institution itself was absent. Yet throughout the New Poor Law period almost all relief was given "outdoors," and at a level where the need for supplementary resources was ever-present. At no point did the *General Orders* – issued to codify practice across the whole system – deal with this matter.[28] The resulting problems were well articulated by officials who were simultaneously charged with driving down annual welfare bills *and* discouraging the melding of welfare and labour market architecture in ways which might have achieved the first objective.[29] The tension was brilliantly outlined by the Reverend John Coker Egerton of Burwash (Sussex) in his diary entry for 3 May 1875, in which he recounted the case of Widow Langridge. She received between 12 and 14 shillings of relief per week, which had been set against an income from self and family labour of 9s. However: "She has a big boy hiding at home who only pays here 9/– per week instead of 10/– as he wd. have to any where else." In addition, "now that there is no man to keep, she may be considered as well off as when her husb: was alive." Her welfare payments had thus been reduced. Egerton felt sorry for the widow but noted, "this is how a relieving officer calculates."[30] Equally, applicants themselves elaborated the problems they faced in dealing with inconsistent, unknowable, variable, or non-existent rules across the poor law system and which risked their being labelled and treated as fraudsters through no fault of their own. John Booth illustrates this issue well. He wrote from Mansfield (Nottinghamshire) in 1855 to say that he was threatened with the workhouse but: "Sir I do not wish to have my little home broke up & my children going astray like lost sheep aving no sheppard." Booth assured the Poor Law Board that with a little help he could combine work and welfare, and enquired how he should proceed:

> I read by the Review Paper as your honourable house ad ordered out doore relief to abled body men dated June 14 1855 they declining to do aney further onley under the Test Act – i do appeal to you to know what remoidey i ad better take to Beg i am ashamed to Rob & thieve i should not like to break a rightous law would hurt my feelings

Here, then, an honest man was driven to the edge of dishonesty by the Mansfield guardians' refusal to implement central guidance on how to fuse work and outdoor relief.[31] The gradual removal of particular groups from the direct ambit of the workhouse as the Cottage Homes Movement[32] took hold and then as the Liberal welfare reforms began to gain traction merely exacerbated this situation by focussing attention on a smaller group of potential wage-earners and thus on potential fraudsters.[33] Denis Warry noted that, although his father had died in 1927 "indirectly due to the gassing he had received in the war," his mother, a fit and healthy woman with only two children "received no war-widow's pension and so was expected to live and bring up two children on the paltry widows' pension of 5 shillings a week." This obligation involved her working part-time as a cook and redistributing her children in the wider family group, which was normative at this time.[34]

A second aspect of definition and tweaking – whose earnings count for the threshold measures underpinning welfare rules? – also has a strong place in the sources. The import of this question can be crystallized right at the middle of the period covered in this book. James Seely of Loddon (Norfolk) recounted his childhood from around eight years of age after his father died in 1902. His mother was left a widow with five children on an outdoor relief allowance of just 3s 6d weekly because: "They said she was young and able-bodied and could work." But:

> every Saturday morning us three children who were old enough to go to school had to take attendance cards they'd given us to the Relieving Officer to show him we'd been attending school all week. If we'd been absent it would be marked on the card, he wanted to know exactly what we'd been doing on that day. I suppose it was to see that us children didn't earn any more money working out of school.[35]

Whether relieving officers ever had the power to act in the way Seely claimed is unclear, but the memory shows how the redefinition of children as assets for education not work introduced uncertainty for relief recipients as to what children could legitimately contribute to the household, and gave officials a lever of power over them. Before this date, whether children were earning or ought to be, was a constant motif in all source-types. Indeed, the marginal earnings of co-resident children were sometimes more important in determining the pace and scale of welfare withdrawal than the earning capacities of parents themselves, though not in any predictable way even within a single locality. Thus, Hughina McKay (alias Neilson) of Tongue parish (Sutherland) found that her welfare was withdrawn in December 1845 because her illegitimate daughter was "now doing a little for herself in field work &c.," whereas other women with legitimate children in the same position were not thus treated.[36] We see even more encompassing examples in England, as for instance with the resolution of the Hursley (Hampshire) vestry on 14 July 1826 that "those who were dissatisfied with the present mode of payment should in future have the earnings of the *whole* family taken before they receive any relief."[37] As the expectations that children would generate income declined, their presence came to be tied up with positivist policies on welfare entitlement through, for instance, the family allowance system legislated in 1945[38] and the Supplementary Benefit system of 1966.[39] Even so, the residence of non-earning teenage children in the households of those on welfare was often a factor in the popular imagination of the fraud problem, as we see from life-writing. "TO"'s unpublished autobiography (see above) noted that in the 1950s his parents were suspected of fraud because he lived at home and was seen as lounging around at the state's expense. The association is even clearer in the evidence offered by the wider focus groups, where young adults of supposed working age were themselves constructed as "spongers and deadbeats."[40] On the other hand, when young people did work, often bringing in low and inconsistent income, I found considerable sympathy for the idea that such earnings ought not to be taken into account when applying benefit withdrawal rates to parents.

Other sorts of earners have also troubled policymakers, including co-resident kin other than children, and lodgers whose cash-in-hand payments might supplement welfare resources. The presence of individuals from these groups, especially undeclared lodgers, flowed easily into suspicions of fraud. Prosecutions of people, some certainly paupers, for taking in lodgers were a persistent feature of the seventeenth- and eighteenth-century Buckinghamshire Quarter Sessions reviewed in chapter 3. Even in the twenty-first century, Citizens Advice expends many hundreds of words in carefully setting out the impact of lodgers on different welfare forms in England, Wales, Scotland, and Northern Ireland.[41] But other scenarios also have a problematic place in popular and policy conceptions of fraud. How, for instance, were officials and communities at any period to conceptualise the resources offered by kin, friends, or ex-neighbours who sent regular or irregular remittances from overseas (having emigrated) or from long distances inside the UK? Whether benefit withdrawal rates were based upon fixed formulae or local discretion, such income should theoretically have counted. Indeed, across the whole period covered by this book there is evidence of ordinary people assuming exactly this and suspecting fraud as a consequence. Such was the 1823 case of Grace Fowler, whose husband "is now gone to South America." The overseer of Totnes (Devon) assured his respondent that she was "expecting an allotment of half pay" but that it had definitely not arrived and when it did she would "be able to get on without parochial aid."[42] Yet examples like this are unrepresentative, and most people most of the time conceptualised such income as gifts and thus outside the scope of welfare legislation.

Attempts to change, massage, or expand the capture rate of income were also often understood as illegitimate. In some places, for instance,

Old and New Poor Law officials seem to have expected in-laws to provide resources even though there was no legal basis for such requirement, something that attracted pushback both from welfare recipients and wider communities. An attempt by the Stamford guardians in June 1873 to compel Henry Goodwin, the brother-in-law of Rachel Scott, to pay her funeral costs using money he had got from an insurance society was met with a flat refusal and at no point thereafter did the guardians revisit the liability of in-laws.[43] Similarly, *ad hoc* support from employers, ex-employers, fellow employees, and even neighbours was often seen as uncontentious in welfare terms, given that those helping were little better off than those they supported. Mrs W.1.L. of Lancaster captures this very well for the 1920s, noting that a widowed neighbour was "very poor, and … had nothing but what she worked for and I think she got a little bit out of what they called Parish Relief in those days" and that she was consistently supported by female neighbours in small, often intangible, ways which were nonetheless incompatible with welfare rules.[44] Even in 2017 an extended discussion on the website *MoneySavingExpert* about whether welfare recipients were obliged to disclose cash gifts reveals the uncertain public understanding of income and earning thresholds.[45] Thus, while we can find a seam of public and private commentary in which writers worried about the fact that "unseen" income streams frustrated the withdrawal rules, there were and are strict limits in the popular imagination to whose income *should* "count."

This observation raises an important further issue in relation to work, earnings, and the tweaking of definition and rules: How do current claimants, future applicants, and their communities get to "know" about changes in either rules or expectations? In 1815 the Buckinghamshire autobiographer Joseph Mayett was unemployed and, "being a single man and at that time the King wanted Soldiers … the parish would not imploy me [on make work schemes]" and so he set himself up as a hawker. Yet neither of these local rules (single men were restricted from welfare and the potential for military work disqualified a man from entitlement) had any basis in law. In effect, Mayett found that his poverty and need had been defined away and his very honesty questioned.[46] The pernicious impact of silent rule changes, or at least of the leeway that opaque rules afforded local officials in discretionary welfare systems of the sort that shaped welfare pre-1945, is a core feature across the evidence-types employed here. In the 1840s, the Outdoor Labour Test Act (variously amended by circulars and orders to 1904) required able-bodied adults on outdoor relief to do specified, organised, and monitored work, thereby at a stroke defining all small supplementary earning activities as fraudulent.[47] More than this, as many officials and paupers noted, the terms of the act were not enforced consistently between poor law unions, in the same union over time, or even for all categories of the able-bodied, such that the rules were not ultimately knowable. In Nantwich (Cheshire), for instance, extensive unemployment for the town shoemakers in 1862 occasioned a decisive split amongst the ratepayers. Some argued for a make-work programme akin to a Labour Test and others were strongly opposed. Leonard Gilbert, for instance, claimed that the scheme subsidized the idle: "If this is re-garded as a labour test, let the hours be extended to those usually made by labouring men; as it is we have widows, old and poor people working to pay large and increased rates to give work to a few of the worst char-acters in our town."[48] Often officials simply classified large swaths of the able-bodied as temporarily sick, actively colluding in undermining the rules in the sense that most sick people were still expected to do things to contribute to their maintenance.[49] But not all places did this.

Further back, under the Old Poor Law long-established customs could change silently. Thus, the second action of the newly appointed Amport (Hampshire) vestry at their initial meeting on 5 April 1809 was to resolve that all paupers "residing at a great distance to have no relief" because of concerns about fraud. By July the same vestry was resolving that widows "able to work should be taken of from full pay."[50] Changes such as the dole and labour exchanges also led to complexity; for Edward Prynn in the 1920s, it was not simply that he had to sign on, but that having done so at all would limit his earning potential. After all, he reflected, "the rubbish went with the rubbish and the good went with the good."[51] Even the modern welfare system is not immune to issues of imperfect knowledge. "RK" noted in 1994 that he had been "done" for welfare fraud because rule changes in 1993 of which he claimed to have no knowledge "shifted the ground from under my feet."[52] His welfare citizenship was swept away in a "shady" act of appropriation. Exactly similar sentiments are to be found from the handful of former officials who participated in my focus groups, one of whom noted that he was dealing with "populations" that were functionally illiterate, did not read what was sent to them or "engage with any forms of authoritative publication," and who simply did not understand why they could not do "a little paid work on the side."[53] Questioned further he admitted considerable sympathy with claimants who were bamboozled by withdrawal rules, and more widely we can see a not-inconsiderable seam of public sympathy for those caught out by changes to earning thresholds or other benefit rules about which they could obtain little knowledge. We see little of this sympathy in Daniel Blake's filmic encounters with the welfare system, but the sense that endless circular rules and processes, many of which cannot be known in advance, push Blake over the edge is viscerally apparent and captures an insistent motif across all my sources and the whole period.[54]

Case Law and Precedent: Disability

The relationship between work, welfare, and fraud for the able-bodied is complex. However, the scope for redefinition and changing rules and thresholds to influence measurement and perceptions of fraud, and thus for legal and other challenges to these processes that create precedent, is most acute for those claiming disability payments.[55] In 2010 the *Guardian* carried an interview with Iain Duncan Smith, the newly appointed DWP minister. He argued that "Britain's welfare system is 'bust', with such penal disincentives to work that many people on benefits regard those who take up job offers as 'bloody morons.'"[56] This and other statements early in the term of the LibCon Government's tenure were precursors to three changes in welfare rules that have had major consequences for perceptions of fraud amongst the disabled: the introduction of Universal Credit with a cap on total income; a concerted attempt to raise the physical or mental threshold for people to be considered disabled or *more disabled* and thus to merit any or enhanced payments; and a renewed emphasis on the moral and material value of work for the disabled. These aspirations were in practice difficult to realise.[57] The number of people in work went up but it would have done so anyway, given the unwinding of the 2008 financial crisis, and the attempt to define away disability and entitlement met sustained resistance in tribunals and courts.[58] A pithy summary from the Institute for Fiscal Studies noted:

> Changes to the disability benefit system have also been rolled out much more slowly than planned. In particular the new more

stringent tests for employment and support allowance (ESA) to people already claiming support, and the replacement of disability living allowance with "personal independence payments" (PIPS), have run into problems. And fewer claimants have been found ineligible than originally expected – in part, because of successful appeals against initial decisions.[59]

Even so, by 2019 the three mechanisms of the LibCon policy had begun to bite. In a hard-hitting blog the campaigner Carole Ford emphasised that "claiming disability benefits has never been a simple process" but that post-2010 changes had made things immeasurably worse: "Continual reassessments by private companies acting on behalf of the government mean that these benefits may be reduced or lost at any time."[60] By this date some entitlements had been defined away, in effect suggesting that claimants had been fraudsters, and successive ministers had refused to undertake an impact assessment for disabled people no fewer than eight times.

But even if such an impact assessment had taken place, would the findings have changed the traction of the competing narrative of 2010 on public (particularly non-activist, non-elite) perceptions of the disabled and their entitlements? I find little evidence that it would. In a nuanced and penetrating 2017 blog, Richard Machin set out "Four reasons why welfare reform is a delusion." Of the eight people who commented, "Michele" had the most powerful voice, arguing:

> imagine having Parkinson's disease, be diagnosed with cancer and have this constant intrusion and pressure ... all this is daily occurrence in my job. This is a further shift from previous practice another twist of the screw ... I work on the front line of welfare rights and I fear I am becoming powerless to do much to support people.[61]

The author in effect constructed an emotional community of activists whose rationale was to confront the arbitrary demonisation of the disabled. But who cared about this emotional community? Such empathy was largely missing from the comments on disability fraud attached to articles in right-leaning newspapers. Even blogs and articles in left-leaning newspapers attracted a substantial seam of commentary to the effect that, "well, there are disabled people and then there are people trying it on." Focus group participants and those giving oral histories had literally no empathy. Both before and – even more – after 2010, the majority of commentators and contributors across the source base saw the changing rules in relation to disability welfare as justified and assumed that they had been implemented. Academic and activist nuance on the issue of disability deservingness is entirely missing from this material.[62] A focus group member ("UV") in 2014 claimed that "these people are still getting benefits even though they are about as disabled as I am." Either the rule changes had not gone far enough or (her clear suspicion) those like Michele "on the front line" were actively helping fraudsters to circumvent the rules. Either way, disabled claimants were, in her view, largely dishonest.[63] Others in other types of sources have been more critical of reforms. The Equality and Human Rights Commission's comprehensive 2018 evidence review, for instance, noted systemic failings of process, structure, understanding, and empathy in attempts to change disability support, and traced high success rates for both internal DWP appeals and external court cases.[64] While successful tribunal case reviews do not set universal precedent, they feed into popular perceptions of laxness in the system and, when combined with a sense that the courts themselves have an ingrained liberal bias (see chapter 9), locate very precisely the way in which changing definitions of eligibility feed into the modern chasm between popular and measured understanding of fraud. Turned on its head, however, reforms which attempt to define away entitlement, when tensioned with a system of appeal and challenge that progressively overturns such attempts, transform those receiving welfare from genuine claimants to fraudsters and back again without any change in their underlying histories and conditions. "UV" was not herself in receipt of payments, but she had seen this process in action and the taint of fraud stuck in her mind.

Whereas elsewhere in this book I have fused corpus level summary and individual example at different dates to emphasise continuity in policy and popular attitudes to and constructions of fraudsters over a very long period, the historical record in relation to those with sensory, physical, or mental impairments is more complicated. From the earliest part of my source base, concerns that such impairments could be faked or exaggerated are ubiquitous.[65] Even without these fears, new anaesthetic, surgical, and curative practices changed the threshold of ability and disability from the 1870s in particular. Such possibilities were slow to come to the dependent and marginal poor but were not absent. The effect was to change public expectations of the ability of disabled people to survive without welfare, even as formal and informal rules shaping entitlement remained remarkably static. Thus, in a community history project capturing memories of the Rochford area (Essex), people with impairments appear often but were always remembered as "doing something" rather than being welfare-dependent. The repeated appearance of dwarves navigating the formal and informal economy is particularly striking, and Anthony Armstrong Jones came specifically to the area during the making of his 1971 documentary *Born to be Small*.[66]

Yet the potential for those living with physical, mental, or sensory issues to be, or be seen as, fraudulent because of rule changes like those implemented after 2010 was fleeting. The 1601 Act established duties for parishes to provide resources for the "impotent" poor, of which those with such impairments were archetypal. Even so, it *was* possible in the discretionary welfare system of the Old Poor Law to effectively define away disability by creating local precedents both for the level of relief and for an "acceptable" level of inability to earn. This happened at the margins, especially for recipients or applicants who had not realised the potential of kinship support. In practice, however, the presence of broadly construed "disabled people" in disputes over entitlement or accusations of fraud is remarkably thin in the pre-1834 data. Where overseers doubted entitlement or continued entitlement, others were quick to intervene and make a clear association between disability and deservingness, as for instance did Robert Neil, writing from Gloucester to Cheltenham (both Gloucestershire) in the case of Nancy Williams. She "has for years received charity from Cheltenham as a Parishioner there being blind" but now found her allowance stopped or delayed. Neil thought this must be a mistake "& she from her infirmity unable to walk over to you" to clarify things.[67]

In the normal course of events, however, parochial authorities were often receptive to the claims of this group of applicants. They proved broadly unwilling to rip them out of active and passive support networks if they lived away, and recognised the place of the parish in responding to the movement of individuals back and forth across a spectrum of ability and inability.[68] Indeed, disability meant something very specific in this pre-1834 period: to be bed-ridden or housebound and thus deprived of the public sphere; to be (in the case of mental illness) incapable of being "about the place"[69] without supervision; or to be incapable of doing any work whatsoever. This state of being is well captured by Sam Murray, writing from Kirkcudbright (Dumfries) on 25 January 1895. In poor health, he had entered into disability, having been "bedfast for two months and feel that I will not trouble any one long."[70] In short, disability was defined not by welfare rules but by the intersection and interaction of individuals, communities, and officers in specific locations. Such contexts meant that precedents, appeals, and pressure on individual officers in a single place, whilst shaping who claimed and how those claims were responded to, did not become part of a general infrastructure of knowledge. Unlike the 2010s, then, "welfare law" tended merely to codify widely understood definitions of eligibility that proved remarkably hard to shift, rather than to redefine those eligibilities. For these reasons, those living with mental, physical, and sensory impairments were only episodically identified as fraudsters in the popular imagination.

The centralisation and regionalisation of welfare under the post-1834 New Poor Law did not change this situation. Indeed, the issues of mental, sensory, and physical impairment had literally no part to play in the legislation. As nineteenth-century disability historians have noted, the blind, deaf, idiots, decrepit, and "crippled" constituted a significant subset of the workhouse poor, and more widely these were the groups who found their lives medicalised and institutionalised.[71] In this sense the "inability end" of the definitional spectrum became firmer than it had been, and more people came to be labelled and categorised as disabled than had ever been the case in the eighteenth century. Nonetheless, officials and the poor still talked about a spectrum of ability and inability and sought to actively traverse it.[72] Thus the inspector of the poor for Kilmallie parish (Argyllshire) wrote to his counterpart in Aberdeen on 21 August 1851 to note that, while Angus McPhee was prevented by an ulcer from working full time, he was "not troubled with anything to prevent him from being employed at work which can be performed in a sitting position."[73] Even more clearly, John Forbes, inspector of the poor for Invergordon (Ross and Cromarty), wrote on 24 February 1863 seeking information on Catharine Fraser. In particular he wanted to know whether she was "<u>able</u>, partially <u>able</u>, or <u>wholly unfit</u> for work."[74] Moreover, in a system which never sought to define disability or to limit investment in the lives and futures of those with different sorts of impairment, it is striking how much perspectives on disability change if we switch our attention from institutions and medicalisation to questions of circulation. Families sought institutional care for relatives with impairments, but they rarely constructed them as permanently "unable." More often, they sought partnership with the poor law in ways that would be unthinkable or undoable today. They were not always successful. When Roderick McKay of Braekirkiboll (Sutherland) applied for welfare because his daughter was "deformed," he was refused since he both owned land and his other children were able-bodied and "no burden to him."[75] Yet such instances are relatively rare even in the harsh poor law of Scotland. Most requests for partnership were met. Moreover, the New Poor Law played an important role in facilitating circulation between *inter alia*: institution types and locations; families and institutions; different families; and institutions and other care or boarding arrangements. I see this played out not only in the admission and discharge registers for workhouses but also in alternative sources such as the diary and report book of the Barnet workhouse master Benjamin Woodcock, who traces an intricate pattern of "in and out" by the disabled poor and their supporters.[76] In this context, the disabled poor could not easily be defined or redefined as fraudsters, even by the most determined critics of the cost and scope of welfare in this period. Thus, the central authorities of the New Poor Law kept their own precedent books and sought to issue *General Orders* to change local practice across England and Wales, but very little of that precedent related to broadly conceived "disabled." Nor did the courts or petty sessions fill up with the disabled. The striking motif of the nineteenth- and early-twentieth centuries is actually the absence of external intervention.

This broadly supportive framework survived the Liberal welfare reforms, but the organic development of a central control process, universalising benefits and welfare forms which were specific to those who were born with or acquired physical, mental, or sensory impairments, required definitive rules to establish or confirm the nature of entitlement. An accumulation of definitions and rights, both in the sphere of welfare law and practice and more widely in terms of human rights, had fundamental consequences. These manifested slowly. Arguably Margaret Thatcher was able to legitimately create a substantial cohort of the long-term disabled in order to avoid creating an equal number of the long-term unemployed because of the accumulated memory of moral obligations to those with physical impairments.[77] Iain Duncan Smith, in his 2010 defence of the need for Universal Credit, recognised this moral footprint but inverted it, arguing that enabling work was the key moral imperative for policy-makers and a sceptical general public. He acknowledged that "both Tory and Labour governments have used incapacity benefit to keep jobless figures down" and argued: "People basically get parked on this benefit and forgotten about. If you have been on this benefit for more than two years, you are likely to die on it." The moral responsibility of the govern-ment, in his view, was thus not to pay benefits but to allow or chivvy 2.5 million people on various sorts of incapacity benefit into work: "If you are unemployed, and you come from a family that is unemployed, all you can see when you think about work is risk. It is a real risk because for all the efforts you make the rewards are very minimal and in some cases none at all."[78] In this vacuum stood the capacity for and risk of fraud, and also the operation of the courts and tribunals, and their role in subtly (and sometimes not so subtly) changing the meaning, scope, and reach of welfare law and practice.

In this sense, history matters. Whereas modern "problems" over disability welfare are almost universally constructed in presentist terms, the attempted changes to the thresholds of eligibility and ability after 2010 and the role of courts and tribunals in constraining such aspirations in fact crystallised more than a century of slow and subtle change. In this process the capture of mental and physical impairment by the medical professions on the one hand and its constraint by the universalising rules of the welfare state on the other transformed disability from an independent to a dependent variable. Post-2010, the levers of medical and state power could define away that dependent variable, thereby leaving courts and other bodies that set precedents with increased power.[79] This confused matrix of authority, information, and perception created shifting sands of definition and redefinition which were fertile ground for the popular construction of fraud. The same could not have been true in the nineteenth century and before, when a more fluid spectrum of ability and inability, dependence and independence stood at the cornerstone of an essentially localised welfare system in which the inability to define away entitlement left "the disabled" largely outside the system of precedent-setting. This much was recognised by the "almost disabled" Thomas Clarke when he was writing his autobiography in 1911. He reflected presciently that putting a doctor in charge of defining ability and disability and thus adjudicating access to welfare payments would "store up all sorts of trouble for you and so you can hope that ordinary folk will not shift their focus to thinking that it [relieving the disabled] is no longer their problem."[80] Such readings are not uncontroversial in the context of a wider literature that has focussed on legal and process advances for the disabled poor since the early twentieth century.[81]

And of course, we should be careful about emphasising discontinuity. For Duncan Smith the key task was to roll back a system that:

> at the bottom end to one of the most regressive tax and benefit withdrawal rates that it is possible to imagine. We ask people to go to work for the first time and then tell them to pay back 70%, 80% and 90% back to the state. These are levels none of the wealthiest bankers are asked to pay – they are moaning at 50%.[82]

Smith's body language in contemporaneous interviews is important. Talking of the "problem" of people remaining on benefits, he used a series of rightwards push-away hand movements; talking of the need for reform, he persistently cupped his hands; and talking of the rightness of work he used a series of open and expansive hand movements. Such body language is indivisible from the controversy of the reforms themselves.[83] The logical extension to these interventions is that there needs to be a much more subtle, responsive, and finely graded spectrum of balances between ability and inability, one that is clearly understood by a general public which has come (for all the reasons Duncan Smith noted) to elide welfare for the disabled with fraud, and to see every change to threshold and withdrawal rates as confirmation of this relationship. In other words, Duncan Smith, and before him Tony Blair and Gordon Brown, needed and wanted to generate a system not unlike that which underpinned the 1601 poor law. This has not been achieved of course. Modern policy makers focus on tweaking universal rules rather than building broad attitudinal or moral frameworks, whereas the pre-1929 welfare system operated under a loose set of rules with little consistency in application but relative uniformity in outcome because the moral framework came first. In this context, the modern disabled citizen has legal rights to welfare, but those rights can all too easily be defined away, leaving law and precedent as the only defence. The outcome of that defence, since the later twentieth century at least, has been a contested entitlement for the disabled and ingrained suspicion of fraud. Even in this context, however, we can find an understanding of the way in which changes in rule and threshold create fraudsters from what were once solid welfare citizens. A comment on a 2011 newspaper article from "Incurable" illustrates this effect. Noting "my pittance of benefits (which I paid plenty ... towards when I was well)," the comment went on to suggest that rule changes and tweaks like those imposed by the LibCon coalition from 2010 meant that "the public by and large see people like me as a 'scrounger' and a waste of money." This juxtaposition of claims to citizenship (paying taxes) and fear of public constructions of undeservingness speaks keenly to the ease with which people might find themselves suspected of fraud.[84]

Sweeping Rule Changes: Universal Credit

As we saw in chapter 4 when considering seventeenth-century settlement laws, the British welfare state has been periodically modified by sweeping rule changes that have affected the whole spectrum of welfare entitlement and both created fraud and enhanced perceptions of it. Amongst other measures, these changes include: the introduction of Gilbert Unions, which from 1782 diluted parochial control of welfare administration;[85] the 1845 Scottish Poor Law, which swept away a welfare system based largely upon the gift relationship and established a local infrastructure of deliberation even more susceptible to morally based decision-making;[86] the Liberal welfare reforms, which in defining who was *not* eligible pinpointed a considerable seam of potential welfare fraudsters; the post-1945 welfare state, which created standardised and often universal entitlement but then rapidly found itself enforcing welfare conditionality and structural suspicion of certain social groups; and the rise of "workism" in the later twentieth century, whereby to be unemployed was increasingly seen (and heavily reminiscent of the seventeenth and nineteenth centuries) as a moral and behavioural choice rather than an economic or structural reality.

All these systemic events or processes are important, changing the boundaries of actual or perceived deservingness and creating, usually at short notice, a changed underbody of "others" who might be suspected of fraud. We should, however, be wary of thinking that ordinary people constructed this underbody in solely negative terms in the sense of questioning the integrity and moral worth of claimants. On the contrary, sweeping rule changes that removed, compromised, or redefined entitlement sometimes elicited contempt for the local and national state and sympathy for those who had suddenly been constructed as dishonest welfare citizens. Thus, for years prior to the settlement laws of the 1660s, elites in wealthier (and often urban) areas had been petitioning government for some mechanism to limit their poor relief bills in relation to migrants. Such a mechanism having been obtained, its central flaws were apparent within twelve months: the numerous ways in which one could gain or lose settlement when set against imperfect prior record-keeping and equally imperfect memories pitted parishes against each other at law and generated enormous legal bills.[87] Parishes thus spent the next century unpicking the settlement laws.[88] In the meantime, vociferous voices were ranged against the concept and practice of settlement, precisely because it created so many people who were technically fraudsters and thus required the urgent attention of officials, communities, and the law.[89] Later, the wholesale changes to the Scottish poor law in 1845 were necessary to calibrate social welfare to the emergent urban industrial economy of the lowlands, but even so many shared the sentiments of Charles Manson, writing from Thurso (Caithness) on 23 April 1863, who expressed disbelief that a brother officer should try and enforce settlement on a man who had not lived in the place for over half a century.[90]

These deep historical roots to situations in which sweeping rule changes create "fraudulent others" have gone largely unnoticed by modern commentators. Yet they remain vital. As we have seen, Universal Credit is arguably the most significant change to welfare organisation, process, and actual or perceived entitlement since the 1940s. It wrapped up a variety of benefit types for working-age adults into a single envelope, the size of which varied according to whether recipients lived in London, to be actively managed by claimants. Sitting alongside a wider set of imperatives (workism, ableism, austerity, shortages in social housing, and disentanglement of work and welfare by reducing the real value of welfare payments whilst raising minimum wages), the Universal Credit initiative was dogged by claims that it undermined the health, well-being, and dignity of those subject to it.[91] This negative commentary has persisted, while the system has at the same time become so firmly embedded that it is unclear how it might be broken apart. Above all, Universal Credit has become a byword for fraud, as chapter 3 showed. Its implementation has also led to sclerotic constructions of inclusivity and otherness. Thus, a firm link between claimant family size and the number of bedrooms that the state is willing to fund through the housing benefit element of Universal Credit has led to sustained narratives of a bedroom tax on the one hand and the privilege and entitlement of claimants on the other. The rolling up of child tax credits (and associated attacks on child benefits) with other welfare forms has generated not only accusations of an assault on family life and aspirations but also outrage at the number of large families endlessly supported by the state.

Earlier in the chapter we saw that attacks on disability payments (both inside and outside the Universal Credit envelope) and a renewed emphasis on workism provoked liberal moral outrage, while at the same time other commentators saw a "crackdown" as being long overdue. As one might expect, the different positions on this spectrum were associated with political persuasion, but not always. In a 2015 focus group there was complete agreement that "genuinely" disabled people should see their payments uprated and that at the same time a radical crackdown on "lazy scroungers" was required.[92] Such complexity was also embodied in other focus group meetings, where first the prospect and then the actuality of Universal Credit and its sweeping changes to entitlement tended to elicit sympathy rather than condemnation. Members of these focus groups acknowledged the scope for welfare changes to create fraud and fraudsters of the genuinely needy, whereas what participants felt was really needed was a severe crackdown on the immigrants and others who set out intentionally to defraud the country. However, to think of these narratives and counter-narratives in presentist terms is misleading. My data shows that wherever officials, policymakers, and the general public contemplated fundamental changes to welfare packages (as opposed to individual welfare payment types) in order to combat fraud or impose stronger conditionality, there was also a likelihood that rule changes would "manufacture fraud" as well. We see this incongruity played out powerfully in a contrast between the systematic construction of the poor as fraudsters in the evidence underpinning the passage of the Poor Law Amendment Act in 1834, and the insistent assertions of honesty on the part of the poor made by advocates, some ratepayers and even officials in their thousands of letters once the system was in place.

Conclusion

In the BBC's Tuesday Documentary "The Block," a group of tenants struggles against poverty, poor housing, shambolic welfare administration, and constant suspicion on the part of social workers, council officers, and welfare officials. The programme is an essential corrective to narratives of a postwar consensus on the purpose and scale of the welfare state. It also highlights the systemic vulnerability of single mothers to changes in welfare rules or their practical interpretation by officers at street level.[93] They were literally "caught" by episodic changes to the definitions and thresholds at the heart of the modern welfare system, their experiences speaking directly to the three types of process change – tweaks, precedent, and sweeping amendment – dealt with in the current chapter. The injustice embodied in documentaries and other forms of direct testimony was not wholly shared by the broader population, some of whom seized on rule and definitional changes to highlight what they perceived as the overly generous nature of the British welfare system or to suspect fraud on a scale not measured (perhaps deliberately so) by official agencies. Contrary to the implicit assumptions of most modern commentary, these processes and views are essentially timeless; a repeated signal in the sources used here.

Yet we must be wary. Not all definitional or rule changes were negative. When nineteenth-century rules evolved to gradually eliminate the question of a legally enforceable settlement from welfare decisions, the migrant poor were given a new certainty, at least once those changed rules had percolated into common understanding. The advent of state old age pensions generated an underbelly of morally suspect and potentially fraudulent old persons through a list of exclusions, but at the same time it systematised an acceptable state of worklessness. Nor of course were those affected by changes to definitions and thresholds of whatever sort always regarded negatively. We can observe a strand of public and private sympathy for those subject to the whims of the system and the politicians or officials who controlled it, suggesting a tolerance, perhaps even support, for fraud. This idea is one to which we return later in the book as we address the question of why fraud persists when it could easily be eliminated.

In the meantime, an encounter with "RK" provides further nuance to these perspectives. He levelled the accusation that "they just lay some landmines and then you keep stepping on them."[94] That is, someone might be seen to commit several types of fraud at once or in quick succession, largely through no fault of their own. Even when rules remained unchanged for some time, their meaning and interpretation could be opaque and contested, resulting in the most resented of all forms of fraud, that which arises by accident. It is to this issue that we now move.

CHAPTER 6

Cheating by Accident

In a 2016 focus group, participant "CR" detailed three prior occasions on which she had been accused of welfare fraud.[1] In the first, she was acting as a volunteer at a charity while receiving disability benefits (allowable under the rules) but had done some paid cleaning work in the shop after hours. Like others suspected of fraud, "CR" claimed not to have known the rules on paid employment; she also deployed a more subtle argument: "it weren't really work though, because it weren't regular." On the second occasion, the fact that her boyfriend stayed over for two nights a week was the basis for an investigation. She saw this as especially unjust because the definitions and rules about a "cohabiting partner" were particularly opaque: "if they fucking mean no men in the house they should fucking say it shouldn't they?" Finally, "CR" having moved back into her parental home, both she *and* her mother were accused of fraud. In trying to adjust disability payments to reflect the new domestic arrangements, it transpired that her mother had been erroneously claiming additional support allowances for some years.[2]

In all three instances, "CR" escaped prosecution or sanction. In line with formal guidance for fraud investigation staff, the circumstances were deemed accidental.[3] In turn, accidental fraud – that which arises from confusion, short-term changes in circumstances or other factors – is a sub-category in the official statistics stretching back to 2008. Such instances are characterised by a 2013/14 welfare fraud report in these terms: "Claimants make inadvertent mistakes with no fraudulent intent."[4] The wooliness of the term "inadvertent" is of course obvious, but the question of what constitutes intent also has roots in the earliest data I have, as chapter 2 began to show. William Cooke's 1636 Q&A style book with "foure famous Sages of the common law," for instance, returned repeatedly to the question of intent and liability in cases where women bearing illegitimate children moved about in a quest to secure parochial relief.[5] Thereafter, lack of intent is both fact and claimed artefact throughout the source base. The letter series alone carries over three thousand assertions of the honesty and probity of poor writers, and such claims also wind though other ego-documents as well. Thus, seventy-five-year-old Sarah McBride of Berwick-upon-Tweed (Northumberland) committed fraud by accident in late 1860. She wrote on 10 December 1860 to explain that she had been in receipt of an allowance after her husband died but: "I went to see a son and daughter that lived in New Castle on Tyne for doing so they have withdrawn the relief from me." This reaction from the Board of Guardians arose in part because they (now) believed McBride's children could look after her and were shirking their responsibilities (cheating by association) but even more so because she was not even supposed to take such leave of absence without notice.[6] A rule of which she was unaware and which has even escaped much of the poor law historiography had turned McBride into an accidental fraudster. Moving forward to the twentieth century, Mrs H.2.B. recalled an aunt who after 1918 "fought the War Office" every time it changed the rules on widows' pensions, telling others: "I fought for my own and got it. You want to do the same."[7] These anecdotal waymarkers capture a much wider motif, which in turn suggests that accidental fraud has been a consistent backdrop to the British welfare system. The longevity of this theme arises from structural and definitional faults in the welfare system itself, the comprehension abilities of "the residuum," the complexities of navigating both discretionary and rule-based systems, and genuine confusion arising from the fact that welfare rules defy basic logic. Fraud of this sort was not random and individualised but reflected systemic failings of knowledge, understanding, rules, and process.[8]

Indeed, many of these faults are and have been acknowledged by those who administer, oversee, or look in on the welfare system. David Willetts, MP, argued in 2001 that "one of the best ways to tackle fraud is by reducing the complexity of the social security system," while Andrew Rowe, MP, in the same year ridiculed the perverse rules that stopped people from doing short-term work on a trial basis because they would then be denied renewal of welfare for several months.[9] The fact that obvious system flaws are allowed to reverberate (often for years) speaks to ingrained and long-term attitudes towards the welfare state on the part of policymakers and their agents, a matter to which we return in chapter 11.

More than this, however, accidental fraud matters because it partly informs the popular sense that dishonesty is much worse than that which is measured and caught, one of the core themes of this section. On the other hand, the presence of accidental fraud, and a wider sense in which it could happen to anyone faced with similar rules and silences, constitutes the bedrock for popular scepticism about the value and legitimacy of pursuing welfare fraudsters. The chapter takes up these broad themes, exploring the long history of three forms of accidental fraud – that associated with cohabitation, definitions of actively seeking work, and that associated with structural delays in welfare payments. We will see a considerable undetected underbelly of fraud, but one which attracted sustained sympathy in the broader population. First, however, we return to the overview of the contours of accidental fraud initially reviewed briefly in chapter 2.

Landscapes

There is no easy and intuitive way to measure accidental fraud, either now or in historical data. As we have already seen, official figures for the "accidental part" of fraud statistics (roughly half of all detected or suspected fraud) are hypothecated from tiny samples of a shifting base of payment types. In practice accidental fraud has always been higher than such figures allow. Figure 6.1 captures, categorises the explanations for, and provides a visual representation of all *mentions* of accidental fraud in the data for the whole period. While it is impossible to calculate the extent of resources that were "lost," the causative complexity of accidental fraud over the very long term is evident. In addition to the three foci of the rest of this chapter, four further categories stand out with remarkable historical consistency. The first we might construe as "fraud by form." The benefit form as we know it – the one to be filled out by applicants and recipients – is largely a product of the Liberal welfare reforms, as suggested in chapter 1. Prior to 1905 there were plenty of forms to be completed and summative returns made to central government, but these were generally for others than the applicant to fill out.[10] Some engagement with applicants and recipients required personal testimony, history, or evidence and, while these were usually mediated by others – social survey work was largely based on forms and case notes, for instance[11] – the signature or mark of the poor person was increasingly demanded. This procedure suggests that

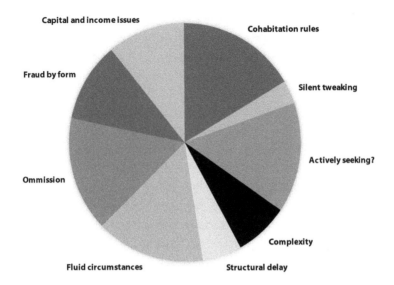

6.1 Causes of accidental fraud, 1601–2023.
Notes: 3,701 observations. Where multiple causes were implicated, only the central category was chosen. Accidental fraud is detected through self-ascription, second-hand identification (as in "I know someone who ...") and third-hand reportage (as in "I heard about this case ...").

paper forms and their requirements passed into process knowledge, as was the case, for instance, with Abigail Taylor, who learned from other applicants that a form had to be completed to support her application and asked: "I hope you will kindly send me one."[12] For most of the period up to 1929, however, applications were made in person, by advocates, or in free-form letters.

The use of more informal procedures variously reflected perceived deficiencies in the literacy of applicants,[13] the fact that those administering the system prior to the early 1900s were understood as having local knowledge trumping the need for universalising forms, and a sense that the state was less concerned with individuals than with their collective welfare cost and the broad composition of the recipient cohort.[14] Even so, the most basic form or process of exchange could involve the poor in committing (or being suspected of) fraud by accident. As an example, officials in Belgrave (Leicestershire) received a letter by hand from their counterparts in Ipswich

(Suffolk) on 1 December 1808. They were immediately suspicious – why had a letter not been sent separately in the post? – and so sought clarity as to whether the Ipswich officials had: "sent an Order by Ann Pole dated the 26 Novemb^r Wishing us to allow her three shillings a week The parish do not think the Order ann Pole brought satisfactory" because it had not been signed by both the churchwarden and overseer of the poor. They strongly suspected fraud simply because fellow officials had incorrectly completed and conveyed their request.[15] In a follow-up letter the Ipswich officials admitted their mistake,[16] but we then see another (unspoken though powerful) reason for ongoing suspicion through a letter sent by Thomas Pole from Cambridge (Cambridgeshire) on 26 December 1808. He noted: "my Wife is Now in the famley way a gane and i Must Be allways out in the Cuntrey." There was then a fear on the part of both the home and host parish of being saddled with the settlement of a child.[17] By 20 May 1809, Ann Pole had moved to Hull (Yorkshire), and the overseers of Belgrave received another letter, this time from Richard Northern, who had "been presented" with a "note purporting to be yours in which you agree to allow her two shillings per week." Once again the letter had been incorrectly or inadequately attested and so suspicion fell on Pole, presumably now a woman with a young child or heavily pregnant.[18] In a further example, from the other end of the nineteenth century, Jane Mackay wrote from Strathy (Sutherland) on 17 August 1899 to say that, although her husband had gained relief, "I his wife has'nt received anything"; having failed to understand the forms that were being completed, she added: "I may blame myself for that because I did'nt give up my name and case."[19]

In the twentieth century the "problem" of forms both in themselves and as a cause of accidental fraud becomes repetitive, and the proportions shown in figure 6.1 are overwhelmingly generated by twentieth-century examples.[20] We first detect the problem for areas other than pensions in the 1920s when, starting in Scotland and then rippling out to other nations, new forms for relief applications and recording were introduced. This new system involved the transfer of details of existing welfare claims to new paper-based record forms, updating of those forms by administrators who took new data directly from claimant interviews, and further updating from written information received. The scope for error in continuing existing claims was profound, while the new forms constituted a complex hurdle for new applicants.[21] This situation was made much worse by the sheer number of rule and process changes for unemployment relief in the interwar period and the episodic use of the means test to flatten costs in the 1920s and 1930s.[22]

An example from the post-1945 period provides a deeper perspective. When in 2003 Tom Cox, MP for Tooting, asked Malcolm Wicks (the parliamentary under-secretary of state for work and pensions) "when benefit application forms were last revised to make them easier and simpler to complete," he was told that forms were constantly under revision. Wicks reminded MPs that the form for the minimum income guarantee had been reduced from forty to ten pages and that his department had recently won a "plain English" award. From all sides of the house there followed numerous real-world examples of why neither the forms nor the language were fit for purpose.[23] More significantly, a close multi-phrase search of *Hansard* reveals more than three hundred references to the nature, complexity, and utility of welfare forms between 1945 and 2023, and a clear sense that forms do not keep up with rule changes or that the rapidity of rule changes requires repetitive form-filling. Indeed, the form problem is well illustrated by a Youtube video from CarersUK in which the presenter shows an early slide of general tips which notes, *inter alia*, that: forms may be 10–40+ pages; handwriting must be legible; applicants need to "state the obvious, even if it seems normal or easy to you"; boxes are provided at the end of most forms for contextual information, but these are only effective if cross-referenced to the questions; the process can be "completely overwhelming"; and that if applicants get stuck they should seek help, preferably from someone who is "familiar with completing the [particular] forms."[24] The forty-plus minutes of succeeding video are baffling. Fast-forwarding to my father's story, we find the essential problems with all the advice on completing paperwork: he was intimidated by a form that (with guidance notes) amounted to ninety pages; he does not use the internet and so had to fill in the forms on paper; he could not read and so guessed what should go in the boxes; he did not state the obvious or understand the need to cross-reference contextual boxes; and he did not know anyone familiar with the forms except his own son, whom he was too proud to ask. These experiences are a systemic part of the modern welfare system[25] but have very deep historical roots. It is for this reason that there was considerable sympathy for those accused of "fraud by form" in every dimension of my data.

In August 2014 a post on Mumsnet asked for advice under the head, "I think I committed benefit fraud." The person posting claimed to have understood neither the system nor the forms and had made errors which might be read as fraud. The twenty-one replies were unanimous in pointing out absence of intent, with several showing exasperation about the complexity of the forms.[26] Some 145 years earlier, Alexander Forbes had written to the Poor Law Board to express his view that the officials of Bradfield (Berkshire) were bamboozling families who needed midwifery assistance by allowing "overseers to give medical orders in Midwifery cases on loan only." What, Forbes asked, if an:

> [o]verseer fullfilled his instructions & required the applicant to sign a paper stating that he accepted the order on loan, & had the man, considering his 10s. a week, declined to do so & gone without his order, the doctor might have been justified in refusing to attend, & as he says himself the woman would most probably have died.

An ordinary labourer could not have understood in a moment of extremis a form that he was required to sign, and which would have made him a debtor to the welfare system. In a striking irony, Forbes added: "If my application to the Poor Law Board is informal I must plead ignorance for my excuse, & shall be most happy to fill up any *forms* I may receive."[27]

A second category of cheating by accident with strong signals across my period is "fraud by capital and income." We have seen that historical welfare systems relied largely on the idea that claimants *would* combine some form of work with welfare payments, shaping and tailoring welfare withdrawal rates to exogenous or personal circumstances and creating "thick" support matrices.[28] There is no need to develop these perspectives further here. Other forms of income, however, have provided fertile ground both for those wishing to see more fraud than is measured and for the scale of accidental fraud as a substratum of this picture. The nature of the "income problem" can be seen in the case of Henry Brenner, investigated in 1875 because it was alleged that he "had been in receipt of an allowance from the Marquis of Exeter at the same time as he had been receiving relief from this Board." Called to account, Brenner claimed that "Relief [from the New Poor Law] was obtained without his personal knowledge" and that he was unaware of where his welfare was coming from in to-tem.[29] In turn, discoveries that the poor were simultaneously in receipt of state welfare and payments from self-insurance schemes and friendly societies stretch across the chronological and spatial dimensions of the data. Elizabeth Roberts asked all her oral history respondents about both welfare and insurance schemes, for instance, and the difficulty of balancing and retaining the different income strands is a consistent marker in those sources. Yet, apart from groups such as vagrants, beggars, or immigrants, I find limited evidence of condemnation for people who took advantage of patchy or one-off income opportunities, a finding that fits with many modern studies of fraud.[30] Indeed, the dataset is replete with active collusion on the part of individuals, ratepayers, and communities in hiding such income streams from the prying eyes of officials, sometimes even if the individuals concerned were themselves loathed in these communities. We return to this issue in chapter 9, but it is well captured in the letter of John McLeod, who went to investigate the case of Jessie McDonald Datcharn on 8 April 1898. He was outraged at a recent petition from Datcharn signed by nine ratepayers of Kirtomy (Sutherland) claiming that she was unable to earn and thus destitute of "the necessaries of life." Upon investigation McLeod found her statement to be "a tissue of falsehoods from beginning to end." Datcharn was in regular work and had a son who was living with her and earning. The investigator reserved his strongest invective for the ratepayers who had written the original petition: "as for the parties who signed their names to her statement, I have to say they are quite ready to sign any thing provided it costs them nothing."[31] Such treatment of income by the ratepayers indicates once again that not all fraud is or has been equal in the public imagination.

The treatment of capital under welfare rules has consistently proven even more problematic. In 2021 I encountered a refugee who had fallen through the cracks of a system intended to make welfare applications for this group "seamless."[32] Faced with complex and contradictory forms – "Is a trap?" she asked (not unreasonably) as I explained what went where – her major concern was a bag of gold jewellery that a relative had given her *after* she had claimed asylum. Did this count as an asset? Should she declare it? Did it only become an asset if she sold the gold and had the money? Could gifts from family members and well-wishers affect her benefit status? The answers to these questions, drawing on official guidance, are: yes, yes, no, maybe.[33] With the clarity only afforded to someone completely new to the British welfare system, she asked, "How can [I] be sure of the rules for form?"[34] Clearly, the immigration status of this person would have made the story of a bag of gold very newsworthy, emblematising multiple levels of undeservingness for the general public. Yet this is not *just* anecdote; consistently across my data and period (with some 250 instances) applicants, claimants, officials, and policymakers struggled with how to treat capital in decisions on awarding and continuing welfare. Capital resources could shift, deliberately and fraudulently. This was the case for Joseph Pulford. On 1 October 1877 he claimed inability to pay back money expended by the Stamford poor law union in support of his mother. Yet on detailed enquiry "it appeared that on his Mothers removal from Tinwell he had obtained possession of all her Furniture and household effects" in a clear attempt to evade the capital rules in place at the time. The guardians now insisted that he return the goods in order that they might be sold. One week later Pulford grudgingly agreed to pay a weekly maintenance charge rather than deliver up the doubtless valuable possessions.[35] While such blatant cases add colour to the analysis, in most places and at most times the way to approach capital was unclear both for officials *and* for welfare applicants.

Before the introduction of universal capital threshold rules in 1980, tolerance of capital amounts varied strongly according to region and place.[36] When the Buckinghamshire magistrates decided in their midsummer 1708 sessions that Peregrine Ford had attempted to deceive the parish officers of Cuddington into giving him relief, their reasoning was that he "owned a cottage worth £40."[37] Yet in nearby Northamptonshire at exactly the same date, ownership of property did not disqualify a person.[38] Fixed and immovable thresholds introduced a misleading clarity, not least on the part of politicians. In a 2001 parliamentary debate for instance, Alistair Darling argued that half of all fraud in two key working-age welfare schemes was "due to people failing to tell the truth about their incomes, earnings or capital," as if defining any of these three variables was either easy, fixed, or agreed.[39] How, for instance should the poor who sell their own goods on eBay treat the money made if they know it will take them over a capital threshold? How should people treat capital that they cannot access? Such questions are essentially timeless. When Thomas Smith of Exeter (Devon) was accused of fraud in February 1869, for instance, "he admitted he had £24 standing in his name in a savings bank, and had two shares of £50 each in a Building Society; he had, however, no command over the amount" because the assets were held in trust and the trustees would not release the money to him. Indeed, they "had allowed a blind Brother of his to die in a Workhouse altho he was entitled to money in their possession."[40] Mary Warden of Rothersthorpe claimed in 1737 that she was entitled to keep her parish pension despite realising the value of some of her household goods at auction, because "the Officers stamped not as their own the said chattels."[41] In turn, the scale of modern public sympathy with what we might term the "capital problem" is revealed in comments on newspaper articles, blogs, and other fora, where breaching capital thresholds and hanging on to the money (or actively hiding it) was seen as legitimate in a ratio of 4:1, even as some of the same commentators raged against the scale of welfare fraud in general.

A third category of accidental fraud centres on omission rather than what was said or written. Chapter 3 has dealt with some of the intricacies of defining intent, but more discussion is required here because the question of what and when to tell is strikingly complex and intricate for welfare claimants and recipients: Should someone tell welfare authorities the location of an abusive ex-partner who ought to pay maintenance but at the risk of further abuse? If guidance associated with filling out forms leads applicants to complete them along certain lines, should they be held accountable? If an applicant had taken advice on what to include and what not, and that advice has proven incorrect, who should be held accountable? Such issues are perennial, and stories drawn from different chronological points in the data signal a complex and consistent experiential reality. Alice Geeson of Eastwood (Nottinghamshire) noted that soon after marriage in 1931 her husband lost his job. The arrival of a first child meant that they lodged with her mother who did not charge rent:

> However ... Mother had been receiving six shillings a week "parish money" in addition to her ten shillings pension. A form was filled in every six weeks stating the names of people in the household. When our names were added without a financial contribution the officials queried it. I told them my husband was unemployed and I did all the work. They replied "well, you would have to pay rent if you lived elsewhere wouldn't you?" So my mother's six shillings was taken from her.[42]

The simple exercise of a familial duty plunged the family into crisis and made them fraudsters by omission. A little earlier, Ken Marsland, reflecting on his childhood in the Welsh coalfields, noted that his father had a disability since fracturing his skull in the colliery at the age of fifteen such that he could do only "light work." He eventually retired on a pension of ten shillings a week, but "if they were caught doing other work their pension was taken away from them. There were virtually no social services."[43] But how, Marsland reflected, could a family survive on such resources without casual work? In these examples, deliberate – intentionally fraudulent – omission was either absent or opaque. For those looking in from the outside, the data attests to considerable underlying sympathy for the way in which the complexity of rules and their illogicality could lead to omission and misstatement. The issue is well captured in the deeper historical data by Mr Q.1.B. interviewed by Elizabeth Roberts in 1974, who reflected on the way in which changes to unemployment relief in the 1930s – what he referred to as "this dole trouble" – undermined parents' ability to live with their children to the benefit of both parties in what remained a residual welfare system.[44]

In chapter 7 we pick up on issues of empathy and sympathy again. For now, we take a look at a final category of accidental fraud with a persistent signature in the data – cases associated with fluidity of circumstances. In the course of the period we are examining there are some four thousand cases in which the circumstances of applicants or recipients changed so rapidly that they might move into and out of fraudulent activity and back again within weeks, days, or even hours. From the 1600s to the present, people getting sick or sicker, slightly better, and then fully better have been a constant problem for welfare officials trying to determine eligibility.[45] The shifting impact of partially disabling conditions has been equally problematic. These are obvious issues which cannot simply be designed out of welfare systems. Other situations reflect the sheer messiness of everyday life, which welfare rules and practice tend to deliberately ignore, sometimes exacerbate, and always understate.[46] Returning to Mr Q.1.B., we read that he claimed dole after a bout of paralysis in the 1920s, and that the officers "weren't bothered how they spoke to you many a time."[47] Because he had got a scribe to write for him from hospital (he was paralysed), because his discharge and case note record had been delayed in the post, and because he had once obtained benefits from a sick club – and even though he was clearly eligible for help – Q.1.B. was subjected to a tirade of abuse.[48] As with other aspects of accidental fraud, occasions when it was caused by everyday messiness sometimes belied logic for the ordinary population. Such, for instance, was the case of Richard George, writing from Perranarworthal (Cornwall) in 1849. He was incredulous that, despite being a "poor man with a sickly wife and 5 small children" and trying his best to retain his independence, he was now put in court for fraud and was therefore "saddled with 4 shillings cost which am unable to pay. Therefore I am compelled to go myself & family in the Union." Not unlike those who commented on modern newspaper articles, George concluded that, "Tis the rogue & vagabond that is encouraged in this country not the honest industrious man he is discouraged in every shape & form."[49] These complexities magnify further in our final three categories of accidental fraud.

Lovers

The question of when a lover does, or would in the eyes of officials, become a contributor to household finances has always been a bone of contention in the tri-partite world – claimants; officials and policymakers; and the wider public of national and local communities – of welfare fraud. Live-in, occasional, or visiting lovers feature prominently in modern coverage of the issue, and it presents a legible narrative of intent for the general public. In 2001 Teresa Gorman, MP, gave voice to this narrative in parliamentary debate. She claimed that in her constituency, "There were streets where perhaps three quarters of the households were headed by single women." Yet, when Tory activists were campaigning, "the door was invariably opened by a young man, who had obviously come home at the end of his day's work … he was relaxed and obviously in a family situation." Gorman noted that despite these "facts" being reported in 1997, no follow-up had been undertaken.[50] Definitive stances like this – in effect arguing that the very presence of a man or other partner ought to lead to questions about eligibility – are found in newspapers stretching back into the late nineteenth century, in pamphlets questioning the honesty of the poor, and in specific sources dealing with fornication.[51]

This simplicity is unwarranted. Current guidance on cohabitation, contributions by lovers, and related issues is remarkably loose. The charity AdviceNow argues convincingly that even DWP staff do not understand the rules, given that there is no fixed definition or threshold for cohabitation.[52] Indeed, this is a feature of the entire postwar welfare system. As Gordon Brown, MP, intervening in parliamentary debate in 1984, noted:

> Candidates for investigation are single mothers in respect of whom "no information is held regarding identity of the father and his whereabouts are not known" and against whom "the claimant refuses to take proceedings for maintenance" … Simply because they meet those criteria, individual single mothers are to be random targets for what have become early morning visits to establish whether they have sexual partners. Investigators are instructed – I quote precisely from the document – to check: "What explanation has been given to account for the presence of male items? Has this occurred frequently?" The Minister told me in a written answer that investigators have no powers of search. Is that compatible with an instruction to check for the presence of male items – clothes, shoes, and even underwear – which the police cannot do without a warrant? That is achieved by … an ability somehow to insinuate their way into the homes and even the bedrooms of ordinary citizens.[53]

In this area, the messiness of everyday life rapidly comes into juxtaposition with the rules and generates the foundation for accidental fraud, something acknowledged in the National Audit Office's 2003 pamphlet *Tackling Benefit Fraud*. Here, undeclared partners were highlighted as a major element of detected fraud: "There is considerable potential for subjectivity in what constitutes sufficient evidence to prove that a male/female couple are 'Living Together as Husband and Wife' and there is no legal definition of a 'husband and wife' relationship," such that investigators were obliged to rely "on criteria embodied in case law."[54] There is little doubt that some of the people involved in relationships and accused of fraud knew what they were doing. This claim is a compelling feature of comments on newspaper articles. But for many others the basic logic of their situation – the visitor was not contributing financially; the visits were regular but not for entire weeks; the visits were episodic; the relationship was casual; there was no sex involved – resulted in confusion over what should be told to whom, or (more frequently) led only to inaction.

These issues carried even greater weight in the pre-1948 welfare system, and particularly the period from 1601 to 1929. This partly reflected the intricacies of marriage. Women abandoned by men had little or no chance of divorce and could never know whether their husbands would return.[55] It was thus both strategic and problematic for a welfare recipient or applicant to acknowledge a new partner. Some waited until they were discovered, as did Widow Bainbridge. Overseer William Craston wrote from Manchester to his counterpart in Kirkby Lonsdale on 1 January 1827 to note that a recent pound note had been sent to her, and revealed her situation: "I have supposed by your direction to her in her former husbands name that you are not acquainted with her recent marriage to a pensioner she has been married three or four months."[56] The Bainbridge story can easily be read as deliberate rather than accidental fraud. In other cases complex courtship patterns and opaque rules shift the balance of interpretation. Martha Springer of Brockenhurst (Hampshire) got her father to seek parish support for a potential match which would remove her from relief, and then also wrote herself to the same effect.[57] Clearly, a courtship had been taking place and the couple chose to announce it to welfare officials only at the very end. This was within the implied rules of the Old Poor Law (which focussed on questions of cohabitation rather than merely courtship) but clearly risked Springer being constructed as potential fraudster. Yet, the line between secrecy and openness in terms of fraud was a fine one, as Frances Brizes of Shadwell (London) found out in July 1835 when the overseers of Sidmouth (Devon, her settlement parish) wrote suspecting her of bigamy. Wriggling repeatedly, she claimed: "I am very much surprized at your saying you Cannot send me my Money unless i do send My Marriage Certificate i Cannot send you it as it dose not lay in my Poure to Get it at present as i Am veary Badley of and my Husband out of Work." The excuses cut no ice. Her allowance was removed.[58] Men too were sometimes caught by this conundrum, given that divorce at that time was only notionally easier; such was the case of Henry Townsend of Brentford, who wrote to Lewes (Sussex) on 8 October 1822 because he:

had the misfortune to have that Wreched Wife Wich Run away from me and my deare Children Wich i searched the Country round for her and found her at hastings and Braught her Back to London With me to my dear Children We Whire together

About 15 months and she the Wrech deserted me and my deare Children again.

Townsend now found himself unable to work full time on account of caring duties but, since the officials were suspicious of the narrative of abandonment, they would not grant him "a trifle to subsist on."[59] More widely, much historiography has focussed on successful courtships, but it now becomes increasingly clear from life-writing that, for poor women and widows in particular, relationships were often fragile, fleeting, and multiple.[60] In this context, it made sense to delay declaring a new partner until near the point of marriage, and often by then in the process of asking the welfare system for financial help in bringing that marriage about.[61] Under the Old and New Poor Laws official responses to such requests depended in significant part on location and past precedent, and the existence of local discretion in the guise of organic, flexible, and even highly personalised rules certainly provided an added layer of complexity for lovers.

In turn, the issue of lovers has always figured strongly in the popular construction of welfare fraud, as I show above. This was partly connected with whether relationships were carried out (to use the words of "RK") "in your face." Brazen contempt for the known or suspected rules of welfare was more likely to sustain suspicions of fraud.[62] Duration of relationship was also an important (negatively correlated) factor; long-term lovers *just* attracted gossip, whereas a throughput of lovers was more likely to raise suspicions of fraud. The extent to which one was liked, was embedded in a community, or had a lover who was "useful" to neighbours shifted the balance of opinion from deliberative to accidental fraud, the fault of the system itself. This was true of some immigrants and regional migrants but, by the later twentieth century for most of these groups, having a lover was tantamount to an assertion of fraudulent intent. This is a clear further signal of the fact that the welfare state was increasingly constructed in the imagination rather than in light of direct knowledge, contact, and experience.

Actively Seeking?

A second prominent category of accidental fraud centres on the question of work. Between 1601 and the 1940s it was an overwhelming assumption on the part of policymakers, officials, and some communities that if you were above a certain age and able-bodied but claimed to be unemployed, then by definition you were not looking hard enough for work.[63] Even thereafter the moral failings of the unemployed have been a consistent theme for British politicians.[64] Yet from 1601 the intertwining questions of how to define "work" or "earning," what duration of work thus defined ought to be reported, and how to understand when someone was "actively seeking" work were extraordinarily complex. This complexity could lead to accidental fraud, a category of allegation well recognised by the different publics with which I deal in this book. Thus, in the film *I, Daniel Blake* the central character is obliged to confront a recurrent tension in the British welfare system. Having had a heart attack and been deemed unfit for the labour market by his doctor, Blake still had to seek work in order to retain benefits. He could be confident, if miserably so, that his lack of skills would result in no job offers, as he expressed in persistent disbelief about the system. That is, he could be seeking work but not actively and realistically so. When offered a job, Blake had to turn it down, not because he was workshy but because he was medically unfit, and he was consequently lambasted by the potential employer for being a scrounger.[65] Technically, he *was* a fraudster and yet no reasonable person would see his fraud as anything other than accidental, a result of the perverse logic of the system – which is of course the point of the film.

The fictional portrayal of Blake comes close to reality for anyone involved in helping welfare claimants in the 2000s. The historical continuities of this situation are compelling. In the late 1930s, as an example, the young teenager Mary Hewins was working in a Stratford-upon-Avon brewery but had become pregnant by a grammar school boy who abandoned her.[66] When "an opening" came for her to get the sack Mary took it because her pregnancy would have become apparent to the entire workforce had she stayed up until the point where she would have had to give notice anyway: "And I couldn't a – got no dole, then." This tactic, however, still left the "dole office … sending me away for jobs," forcing her to "be crafty … I made out I was too rough for their rotten job." Like Daniel Blake, Mary was not in truth actively seeking.[67] On the other hand, nor was she condemned for such fraud. On one occasion a female publican saw her as perfect for the job but played along: "I'm goin to tell em you's *most* unsuitable. Now where's your paper?":

How'd she guessed? You couldn't *see*. I was about six months but I'd been starving myself, practically, to keep thin. I used to get a sheet, rip up an old sheet, bind it round myself, tight … "You take care of yourself. And the babby." I could have died! She signed the paper and I thanked her and rushed out. You see if I'd refused a job I wouldn't a – got any dole. It wasn't much, but I did get some, I got a bit – o dole. I was still working at the school, o'course, but I didn't get paid for that.

Continuity in the ambiguities around the definition of seeking work (and the sympathy for those caught up in such ambiguities) is also embodied in two much earlier stories: Elizabeth Brown wrote from Gosport to Lyndhurst (both Hampshire) on 11 September 1829 to say that she was very ill and needed "to urge your Kindness in granting me some further relief, being in very great distress and misery, my little earnings with my Basket, are ~~gone~~ so trifling, that it is impossible for me to sustain the wants of nature."[68] The crossing out of "gone" emphasised the ambiguity of seeking work both in her mind and, she would have assumed, in the minds of officials. In another example more than a century earlier, Thomas Brown in 1715 told the overseers that he was willing to seek work but could not do so "if I have no shoos to my feete or close to my back."[69]

In almost all such cases we can observe additional complexities over and above the issue of active seeking. Hewins was working when she received the dole, cleaning the local schoolhouse sometimes with the help of – but usually instead of – her father (the school caretaker, who was actually paid for the work but had been wounded in the First World War) and her mother (who had an enormous hernia). She was thus a double fraudster, but no one, not least herself, seems to have regarded her in this way. In turn the corpus has a rich vein of evidence that work without earning, activities that were work-like, or work that was of actual or planned short duration did not count as labour that should compromise benefits either in the eyes of recipients or their communities, or sometimes even in the view of officials themselves. This issue is encapsulated in an 1850 letter from William Rogers Sr. He argued that the smallness of the New Poor Law "stipend" left people on the verge of starvation, "& this is the way poor people are got rid of." In his own case that stipend had been supplemented by a regular 2s 6d. allowance from a "respectable trades-man" as well as by irregular needlework, gifts of food from friends, and his own episodic work. But now the respectable tradesman was dead and "were I as perfect on my feet as some I know are, who receive a greater stipend from the parish than I do, I would not trouble you." More than this, "I have paid all kind of Taxes long enough to have entitled me" to better support. In short Rogers was technically a fraudster, having failed to declare any of this other support to the parish, but he did so now with a sense of right and even entitlement, urging the welfare authorities to set aside any preconceptions they had about him. He would not be a long-term burden, he wrote: "ere long (& I am sure the summer will do it) from the curse of nature, shake hands with the poor mans friend, His only friend Death which I shall willingly do, for I am heartily tired of the deception, hypocrisy, & villainy of the world."[70] The wonderful pathos of the letter notwithstanding, Rogers made a serious point that there was a strand of acceptable, or at least explicable fraud. In a modern sense this is one way to reconcile consistent public belief that fraud is rife with an equally consistent commitment to the principle of the residual welfare state. Nowhere is this clearer than in the question of delayed payments or decision-making, a theme to which I now turn.

Structural Delay

One of the features of Universal Credit that has captured most (critical) commentary is the inbuilt delay to the first payment. Much of that commentary treats such delay as a scandalous *new* attack on welfare claimants.[71] In fact, the opposite is true. Structural delays in paying new and even existing claims have been a normative part of the English, Welsh, and Scottish welfare system from their very inception. We return to the reasoning behind such structural delay in chapter 10, but the fact of it is vibrantly clear in my sources. One in five pauper letters from the early 1700s to the later 1830s were about reported instances of delayed payment or consideration of claims, interruptions to payment, or the difficulty of renewing claims. While the commitment to welfare structures traced in my first chapter may have been consistent, this adherence did not mean that officials behaved well. Figure 6.2 plots the duration between receipt of a *first* claim and its outcome in terms of either a dismissal or a payment

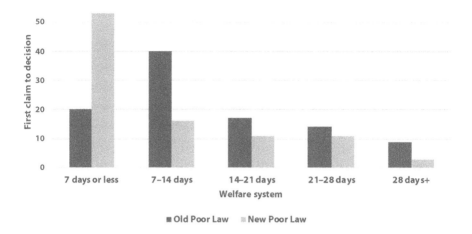

6.2 Duration between first claim and decision (days), 1601–1929.
Notes: Durations drawn from pauper letters, vestry minutes, and other supplementary poor law sources including life-writing. Where duration is broad ("I wrote last month") I have chosen mid-point dates. Requests for further information do not count as a definitive decision.

under the Old and New Poor Laws respectively, where both events can be traced in the records. While the average decreases sharply under the maturing New Poor Law because applicants could be ordered into the workhouse at will, even post-1834 systems of inspection and assessment by medical and relieving officers created inbuilt delay.[72] No matter how we look at this material, modern delays in Universal Credit payments do not jar with centuries of welfare practice.

Other types of structural delay have an equally long history. In particular, claimants' fear that withdrawing from welfare would leave them facing significant delays in receiving help should their circumstances change, is a continuous feature of the data. My focus groups came back persistently to the problems that "genuine" people faced in re-establishing their claims. Their views map onto comments attached to newspaper articles and blogs about welfare fraud. "Christopher Smith" captures this issue brilliantly in a acomment on a 2011 BBC Panorama programme on fraud, noting that those who had their benefits wrongfully removed and won tribunals faced delays of up to six months in re-acquiring entitlement.[73] Politicians of all parties have been alive to the same problem, with some two hundred post-1972 references in *Hansard* dealing either with the principle of delay, or with specific examples of individual constituents. There is little "new" in the stories told. Rachel Boothman wrote on 22 May 1825, seeking to renew her entitlement to relief now that she had moved from Manchester to Glasgow. However, as she complained: "I have wrote to you some time ago and never received any answer But I hope you will not Delay any time of writing me as I have nothing to Suport me and my tow helpless Children."[74] Deliberately or otherwise, the overseer had not replied to what should have been a mechanistic renewal, leaving Boothman in dire straits. Under the New Poor Law, payment of relief to paupers living in Scotland was outlawed, but systemic delays in dealing with English and Welsh migrants seeking to renew or extend entitlement is shown by the story of John Jones from Aberystwyth. Writing on 25 June 1847, he alleged that his pauper father had died because of "gross neglect of his Duty" by the medical officer. His account shows multiple levels of inbuilt delay for existing recipients:

> he got ill on thursday night on saturday I went myself for Mr Roberts [the medical officer] he was not at home but his Aprentice promise to let him know on sunday morning another man Isaac Edwards Bronhealog went for him again saw him and said he would not come unless he went to Llanrhystyn 3 miles further than Aberystwith to get an order from the Relieving Officer sunday night I again went and saw his father and promised to deposit £12 or 15 in his [hand] as security in case he aprehended we will deceiving him who took no notice at all of what I said he said Mr Roberts was somewhere in Town then after all this trouble and delay I went and called Dr Richard Williams who came with me and Drew his water with a silver Instrument who said that he was afraid it was to late to save him.[75]

A couple of years earlier, a pauper from the Festiniog Poor Law union (Merionethshire, now Caernarvonshire) had made an even more pointed intervention, taking an "EXTRACT FROM THE NEW POOR LAW AMENDMENT ACT, 7TH & 8TH VICTORIA, CAP. 101, SECT. 63," which listed penalties for officers delaying payment, and translated it into Welsh for the consumption of his fellow paupers:

Dyfyniad o Gyfraith newydd ddiwgiedig y Tlodion
7 fed a'r 8fed Victoria, Pen 101. Adran 63.

"Os bydd I Arolygwyr (Overseers) Tlodion unrhyw lwyf esgeuluso yn wirfoddol wneyd, neu gasglu digon drethi tu – ag – at gynorthwyo'r Tlodion, neu esgeuluso alu i Warcheidwaid unrhyw blwyf neu Undeb (Union) eyfraniadau angenrheidiol, ac os bydd trwy y cyfryw sgeulusiad i gynorthwy a orchmynir ei roddi i unrhyw lawd gan Frwdd y Gwarcheidwaid gael ei oedi neu i attal oddiwrtho am yspaid Saith niwrnod, pob cyfryw rolygwr ar euog – brofiad o hyny, a gaiff Fforfetio a nalu am bob trosedd o'r fath, unrhyw swm heb fod wehlaw Ugain Punt.[76]

At the other end of the chronological spectrum of the sources, the Buckinghamshire justices of the seventeenth and early eighteenth centuries returned repeatedly to delayed payment, and particularly the fate of paupers in disputed settlement claims who might be given a bare subsistence or nothing at all until intervention from the Quarter Sessions. Such structural delay has figured lightly in the literatures on the history of welfare, but it had an important effect in conditioning behaviour on the part of welfare recipients, claimants, and potential claimants. Patrick Butler draws this issue out in a complex 2015 *Guardian* article, but the corpus is rich with historical examples as well.[77] Focus group participant "GC" remembered her father telling her that in the 1920s once someone had established entitlement to an allowance it was best not to let anything interrupt that, even if one had to lie, because delays in re-establishing a case could result in privation.

These stories underline once more the need to acknowledge a historical grounding to problems we largely construct as "modern." For this chapter, however, they have a more important function, leading us to the question of what people "do" or are supposed to do when faced with structural delay to either processing or payment. Some modern sources yield one clear answer: claimants suffer.[78] Much the same could be said of the past, as is well illustrated by a letter to Blockley parish (Gloucestershire) from Edward Miles on behalf of Thomas Hardy and his family. Miles claimed that Hardy had been through "Trials and distresses" due to the small and episodic nature of parish relief during a winter of illness. His "sufferings have been very great."[79] A further answer is – and always has been

– an assumption that applicants and recipients can and should muddle through by using credit, cutting back, forestalling debts, and calling on family and friends. That is precisely what some of the commentators on modern newspaper articles and blogs had done, and it is a clear feature of the historical data, even if we usually only find out about such alternative support once it had run out. Such was the case with James Nelson of Horton (Lancashire), who was "in Greeat Destress all their little Credit is at an End" because the overseer of Kirkby Lonsdale had reneged on a promise "to Remitt Either every fortnit or Month but so many weeks have Elapsed and no Letter or Remittance."[80]

A final coping strategy takes us back to questions of fraud: claimants and recipients facing delays take on work or work-like activities that generate monetary or in-kind resources, ranging across the spectrum from selling petty goods – on the internet, in physical markets, or door to door[81] – through to selling themselves or taking on various paid roles. The timelessness of the dilemma for Michael Fagan as portrayed in the Netflix series *The Crown* – to take or not take cash-in-hand jobs in order to pay for repairs to his flat so that he could see his children, having been sent in endless circles of delay by the welfare system – is clear across the whole source base.[82] These activities reflected the illogicality of rules, the flawed nature of assessment regimes or simply (deliberate in the case of Fagan) administrative delay, and we might understand them as an aspect of accidental fraud. There is much evidence that those thinking about welfare fraud adopted precisely this stance, putting themselves in the shoes of others. Many hundreds of the comments I use in this book make exactly the same point, sometimes explicitly reminding other participants in the comments line that to "do" fraud by accident was so easy that even those in the thread might be caught in the future.

Conclusion

Part 2 of this book has worked through a complex architecture of welfare fraud, one in which official measurement is, and is seen to be, wanting. A well-known modern disjuncture between official measures and a popular and media sense that fraud is rife can be traced right back to the very earliest days of the British welfare system. Persistently across my sources we find significant levels of undetected fraud and even more significant levels of suspected or ascribed fraudulent activity. Life-writers and those providing oral or written testimony have identified variously constructed groups of "others." The roots of the public and private demonising of these groups run chronologically and qualitatively deep, and the remarkable inability of politicians to give definitive measurements of fraud in the postwar period does nothing to ameliorate such views.[83] In these senses we would expect – and have found across part 2 – a strongly moralistic and punitive public conversation about fraud and fraudsters in which the claims of welfare citizenship are denied, contested, delayed, or diluted. The suspicion of all of those who found themselves in a state of dependency, first outlined in chapter 1, resonates strongly in such examples.

Yet, we should not be easily led by such attitudes. As chapters 5 and 6 have shown, a significant part of the disjuncture between official measures and popular perceptions of fraud is explained by the fact that everyone seems and seemed to know someone "caught" by flaws in the design, philosophy, or execution of the welfare system itself, however it was constelled. Definitions and thresholds have often been unclear, rules unknowable or changeable, precedent has taken time to become ingrained, and each of the incarnations of our welfare system since 1601 has been underpinned by rules and processes that defy logic. The latter issue has attracted much recent public commentary, but in the deeper historical record claimants, applicants, and advocates spent hundreds of thousands of words pointing out what one called the manifest "incompetence" of every level of welfare administration from the local to the central.[84]

Once again, such observations are a useful corrective to a presentist construction of welfare problems and thus of potential welfare solutions. This chapter has, however, gone further. It begins to suggest that a seam of sympathy for some acts of fraud and for some fraudsters stretches way beyond the self-defining advocates for the poor. Not all fraud is or was equal in the popular imagination, even if most people worried about the scale of it, disbelieved official statistics, or drew in media hysteria on the subject. In turn, a complex ecology in the understanding and construction of fraud might be expected to feed into more complexity than has thus far been allowed to public and official understandings of what to "do" about it. The chapters in part 3 turn to this matter.

part three
Reacting

CHAPTER 7

To Tell or Not to Tell?

In May 1833 the overseers of Billington (Lancashire) received a brief note from Joseph Ady, of Tower Hill (London). He wrote: "The undersigned is able to inform you of something considerably to your advantage on receipt of Twenty Shillings by Post Office order or otherwise for his trouble."[1] This was the second letter received from Ady. The first, in August 1832, conveyed the same information but also established his credentials for honesty: "Forty years resident in same Parish And known to each of the 26 Aldermen of London."[2] These are two of 226 letters, some deliberately anonymous, in the pauper, union, and overseers' correspondence between 1716 and 1906 which either hint that the writer could expose fraud or refer to specific cases for which the writer wanted paying, had a grudge, or merely was acting for the public and parochial "good."

The official apparently did not reply. He had, however, acted in October 1824 after receiving an anonymous tip that Barbara Ingham was claiming welfare in Kendal (Cumbria) because her husband had run away but that he was in fact around the place. On 18 October 1824, the overseer of Kendal wrote to his counterpart in Lancashire to clarify: "Barbara Ingham of this place is informed that it is your intention to strip her pension of 4/ a week because her husband has been seen here. This I assure you is very true but he only comes to distress her and her family and goes off again in a few days nobody knows whither."[3] Mr Seed, the overseer of Billington, wrote back disbelievingly, detailing the allegations that he had "heard," prompting Ingham to ask John Taylor of Kendal to intervene:

> Barbara Ingham has placed your letter in my hands and in reply to it I have to say from her (and I know it myself as a fact) that her husband has been at home at different times for a few days but never brought a single farthing with him for his wife's

support, in her own language he came for no other purpose than to distress her … from what she has heard he is skulking around Bury or Burnley but he has declared he will not do anything to support her, he is a very bad fellow and your township ought to punish him.[4]

Taylor's view was subsequently supported by Ambrose Thwaite, his successor in office:

It was rational for you to do this [remove her welfare payments] knowing that Ingham was with his family, he certainly was with them for a short time, but instead of contributing by industry to the comforts of his family, he distressed them very much, and is now gone we cannot tell where, I would recommend him to you as a proper officer for the laws of his Country.[5]

Ultimately Ingham had her support reinstated, but the emotional impact of the anonymous accusations in this case is clear.[6]

In some of the 226 letters, the writers went out of their way to provide "proof" of fraud. Thus, and to keep our Cumbrian focus, Christopher Grime (first encountered in chapter 5) had been receiving poor relief from Kirkby Lonsdale for some time while living in Settle (Yorkshire) when the overseers of the former place received a letter in June 1823 from a "concerned citizen" called Samuel Grundy. His text is worth reproducing in full:

This morning Brother John & myself walked up to Mr. Clayton's mill, in order to enquire into the earnings of Christopher Grimes Children, the clerk was extremely civil, he gave us a written copy of their average earnings – which is as follows – The oldest Girl 8/6 pr Week, the second Girl 8/– and two Boys 3/6 each, total 23/6 pr Week, besides this, the Father is now earning under the employ of Mr. Clayton as a labourer 15/– pr Week. This fellow deserves punishing for such a rascally application to his Parish
And remain yours very respectfully
Samuel Grundy

N.B. The above statement was taken from the Books as an average for the last two months and being under their exact earnings, as the first mention'd was 8/10½ the others in proportion.[7]

Just as Grundy no doubt intended, Grime found his allowance removed. He had to spend some time and many words re-establishing his credentials in the minds of the "home" parish.[8] Turning to the wider evidence base for the period 1601–2000, we find in newspapers, life-writing, and other materials some 1,840 *detailed* cases of individuals informing on welfare recipients and 284 of being on the receiving end of such (to use a term from my oral histories) "snitching." In the twenty-first century this sense of a general population vigilant against and willing to highlight welfare fraud fits with modern state narratives and strategies. These persistently highlight the value of tip-offs, moral responsibilities to report, the possibility of anonymous engagement by phone and internet, and the value (in terms of resources, punishments, or smashing organised crime rings) of information received from the public.[9]

This chapter provides the first long-term analysis of the scale and importance of "snitching." It argues that, notwithstanding widespread doubts about the honesty of the poor across welfare state history and enduring public concern about fraud analysed here and in the work of scholars such as Keleigh-Ann Groves or Peter Golding and Sue Middleton, the public have at most times been strikingly *unwilling* to inform on neighbours or even strangers. More than this, the poor, their communities, and often those of higher social classes can sometimes be seen actively going out of their way *not* to report fraud, no matter what incarnation of the welfare state they live under. This is not to argue that snitching is unimportant – the chapter will extend backwards recent worries that certain groups of the poor are disproportionately affected by it[10] – but to illustrate that the practice has never had systemic public support. The rest of the chapter seeks to explain this long-term trend, turning away from presentist understandings to argue that moral imperatives to report have consistently proven less powerful than deeply ingrained suspicion of the state, welfare policymakers, and judges on the one hand and a complex and subtle popular toleration of fraud – acceptable fraud or fraud by necessity – on the other.

The Scale and Meaning of Snitching

The historical numbers quoted in the opening of this chapter *seem* significant. They are much surpassed by the centrally measured and publicised scale of snitching via information hotlines in the modern welfare state. In 2022 some 800 people per day used the national welfare fraud hotline.[11] While these figures represented an uptick from 2019/20, the reported scale of informing has tended to fluctuate around this broad level for most of the 2010s. Writing for *The Mirror* in 2016, Dan Bloom suggested that a million people had used the fraud hotline between 2010 and 2016.[12] Two years earlier Homa Khaleeli, authoring a critical piece on the cost effectiveness of advertising campaigns to encourage informing, noted that 600 people per day were calling the fraud hotline.[13] Between 2009 and 2010, some 253,708 cases were reported to the hotline, or 695 per day.[14] These "modern" figures can be anchored back to 1996, when encouraging snitching was a cornerstone of attempts first by Conservatives and then by New Labour to reset welfare citizenship.[15] In the first nine months of that strategy, 225,534 cases were brought to the attention of the central authorities.[16]

Yet the precision of these figures is misleading and their meaning opaque. Significant numbers of people would report the same individual or circumstance to national hotlines. It is usually unclear whether either the publicised figures or the officially mandated numbers refer to discrete cases or merely to aggregate numbers of calls.[17] This problem might in some years significantly reduce the number of "actual" fraud cases represented by the figures. On the other hand, reporting derived from national hotline data has always failed to encompass snitching in person or by letter, and every quoted national number since 1997 has ignored the fact that some individual local authorities have also used their own reporting hotlines, which are then combined haphazardly with the national reporting system. These discrepancies mean that modern official statistics on snitching may substantially overstate its scale. Other factors add layers of interpretational complexity to modern measurements: While communities with significant welfare dependency tend to generate the highest levels of snitching in absolute terms, the *rate* of snitching per welfare claimant is often much higher in areas with lower welfare penetration. More widely, even the most cursory viewing of the BBC's 1997 *Inside Story* feature "To Catch a

Cheat" shows in rich detail the extraordinarily low value of many phone calls to cheating hotlines.[18]

We can cut through these complexities and count for the period 1997–2022 all the official, media-reported, or recounted (in comments for instance) "national figures" for snitching that exist in my data.[19] To this we can add all fraud figures reported by local authorities where they could be found in their own records or via responses to questions about local fraud levels by MPs reported in *Hansard*. The net result of the different sources and the multiple over- and under-statements that they embody is that in an average year some 450,000 cases would have been reported. To this figure we can apply a deflator of 30 per cent to allow for the fact that a significant number of these reports would be about the same person or functionally useless,[20] such that perhaps 300,000–320,000 potentially "real" cases would have fallen into the initial purview of fraud investigators. These seem like "big" numbers and of course they are. Sustained over a decade, they might hypothetically add up to a majority of welfare claimants being reported. They can, however, be read in very different ways. Thus, given the scale of national advertising campaigns and concerted othering of welfare claimants by some newspapers, it is possible to ask why snitching was not *more* prevalent. Recalling chapter 3, it is apparent that the scale of informing seems modest compared to the number of welfare recipients, levels of officially measured fraud, and the scale of resources apparently lost to that fraud. Even more, these numbers seem remarkably modest in comparison to the amount of *suspected* welfare fraud in the popular imagination that I and others have traced. Certainly, they are much smaller than the people whose stories and voices constitute the data for this book *could* have reported. This much is acknowledged by persistent contributions to debates reported in *Hansard*, where hundreds of thousands of words were expended from 1997 onwards on the need to combat fraud. Yet almost every debate came back to the difficulty of really addressing the matter in the absence of widespread public take-up of fraud reporting. In a similar vein, analysis of the comments left on newspaper articles or blogs reveals just how little reporting of known or suspected welfare fraud takes place; fewer than 3 per cent of comments suggested that the writer had actually snitched. Though it is often grudgingly conceded, we can trace an underlying ecology of official knowledge that efforts to get the public to inform on people in their communities generate very partial results.

Such anomalies might be expected to echo in the farther historical data. In practice, however, it is impossible to create a quantified picture. Between 1948 and 1996 the mechanisms for reporting welfare fraud were multiple, moving slowly from the 1940s when reliance on local knowledge was an overhang of much older welfare systems, through national schemes for reporting fraud of particular benefit schemes, and to national telephone hotlines, which were trialled from 1994.[21] The records for such initiatives are patchy, and it is notable that a comprehensive review of *Hansard* for the post-1948 period usually points to the absence of evidence collection.[22] These absences magnify for the interwar period. A national record is lacking, given that "obvious" data series recording those who were turned down for or removed from the dole pattern very imperfectly onto the intent of fraud. My own sources are in turn heavily focussed on individuals rather than on system-level indicators. Even the newspapers over much of this period were more likely to carry calls for the public (and particularly "responsible" ratepayers and clergy) to inform on welfare fraudsters than to convey estimates of the scale of snitching already in place.

Figure 7.1 (which plots every incidence of snitching I can trace across my entire source base) is thus not comparable to my post-1997 rendering of informing. It is impossible to know whether rising annual totals over time reflect a growing tendency to inform or merely the multiplication and diversification of sources through which snitching can be traced the nearer we get to the present. Still, there are important features that support an attempt to contextualise snitching: The regular periodicity to spikes in reporting that we can see from 1997 is broadly consistent with earlier periods, suggesting that moments of national economic stress result in reporting upticks. This is more than simply that the level of informing was keeping pace with increased welfare expenditure or the number of welfare recipients associated with cyclical downturns. Reporting peaks generally preceded the high points of these two variables, implying that the initial economic downturn often had a deeper impact on the wider population than the troughs of depression. It is more difficult to see, as others have argued, whether moral panics and associated campaigns against welfare dependency fed through into popular perceptions of the need to inform.[23] Clear associations can be seen in the 1870s during the crusade against outdoor relief, but other well-articulated moral panics such as that in 1923 have little signature. If we delve deeper into the data,

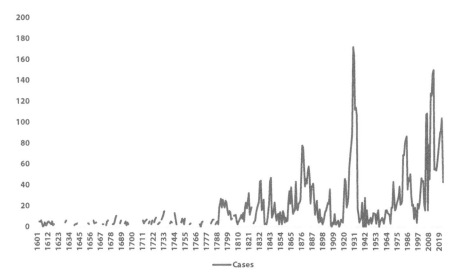

7.1 Trends in fraud reporting.

Notes: 6,943 observations. When the source deals with fraud conviction and reporting indicates someone informed on the fraudster, I have assigned the snitching to the same year as the conviction. Figures include snitching by accident, as when ratepayers or others pick up conversations in pubs or streets and are then forced to act. *Source:* All material listed in the bibliography.

further complexities can be seen across the historical record. Thus, even before the advent of state pensions in 1908, the aged appear lightly in the architecture of snitching.[24] Of the 6,943 observations underpinning figure 7.1 and which have age data, only 14 per cent of those suspected were over sixty-five. Moreover, and as we might have expected from chapter 5, those with physical, mental, or sensory impairments were rarely snitched upon in the pre-1945 period. Indeed, this only changes as of the early 2000s, when some 38 per cent of all snitching involved someone with a claimed disability – a proportion somewhat higher than the presence of the disabled in the wider population.[25]

For other sets of applicants or recipients, being snitched on was, if not systemic, nonetheless widespread and even systematic. This included immigrants and (prior to the 1930s) Welsh and Scottish migrants. Single mothers have also figured disproportionately in the history of snitching. The woman who featured in the BBC's "To Catch a Cheat" and claimed that she had been snitched on six times in a single year[26] has her analogue in a 2015 focus group participant who had been "spragged" eight times.[27] Other regularities have been submerged in the long-term data. Thus, while the seasonality of reporting to modern telephone hotlines is never routinely publicised, the lessons of the historical data are much clearer. Figure 7.2 is an index of seasonality for snitching in the pre-1929 period and we can see that the winter and early spring were a particular focus of reporting activity. This pattern to some extent reflects a long-term ingrained seasonality to relief applications and spending itself, but there are more persuasive explanations. John Knight of Axminster (Devon) locates this well. Giving background to the suicide of either his father or brother (the letter interchanges both people in the story), he said they had received notice of a reduction in relief on account of wider family earnings and thus became fearful of starvation. Knight noted: "Mr. Hugh Trenchard and Mr. Richard Perry are the guardians for this Parish I never applied to them for relief Sometimes in the Winter I cant work for 10 or 11 weeks and then I am nearly starved. I get nothing [from] the Parish," and he suggested that cutting off the resources of his father or brother in such circumstances while others continued to receive relief was wrong and had fatal consequences.[28] Crudely, past winters brought out wider discontents.

Regional and local patterns to snitching are also apparent. In constructing my historic source base, I did not seek to create any stratified sample of community types, to define a particular pattern of regional foci, or to order the data geographically according to the scale of poverty and welfare dependence in any area. The truly national elements of the different source types – pauper and advocate letters and official correspondence, for instance – would have lent themselves to this analysis but would also have made it more difficult to reliably blend in other forms of place-correlated evidence such as life-writing or oral history. In one sense, the essential randomness of the sources amplifies the observation of spatial and typological patterning. Thus, as I have already argued, at any point in the period from the 1600s to the early 2000s the correlation between levels of welfare dependency in particular towns or regions and the observable scale and regularity of snitching at the *per capita* level is a loose one. On the other hand, individuals in northern and Midland communities seem to have been more prone to snitching than their counterparts in the south and southwest. This is true both in aggregate and at source level. Thus, a close reading of vestry minutes suggests that for the period 1800–34, northern

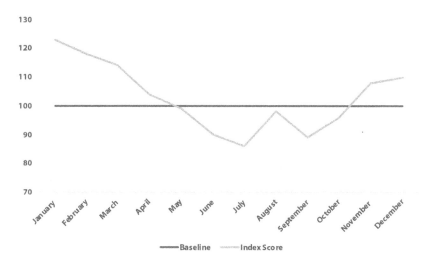

7.2 The seasonality of informing, 1601–1929.

Notes: The index line of 100 indicates the baseline of events that would be generated by an even distribution of events every month. Figures below the line indicate fewer events than we might have expected and those above the line, more events than might be expected. All dates used are those of dispatch rather than receipt; some 28% of cases cannot be reliably dated. *Source:* All material listed in the bibliography where a date of informing could be found or estimated.

officials were twice as likely to receive – to have "heard" – information on potential fraudsters than their counterparts further south. In the post-1834 New Poor Law, this pattern continued; the letter corpus for northern and north-midland poor law unions indicates snitching at almost double the rate of their southern and southwestern counterparts, with Wales generating the most significant levels of all.[29] As with so much else in this book, these long-term continuities move easily into the modern period, as an extended 2018 discussion of benefit hotspots in *The Sun* reveals.[30] Thus, while snitching might be partly related to economic cycles, the presence of immigrants, seasonal stress, or national campaigns, elements of cultural inheritance in attitudes towards welfare fraud are also evident.

Personal attitudes, grudges, and belief systems are also a factor. We see this particularly in instances where multiple people report(ed) on a single case, or where the information given was ultimately deemed malicious. Both in the modern comments attached to newspaper or blog articles and in historic data, we find with unerring regularity ex-wives, husbands, and co-habiting partners reporting on those who had abandoned them. When Colin McKay of Newtown (near Thurso, Scotland) told the parochial authorities that his wife had applied for relief and "obtained five shillings on false pretences before I knoew of it … I can prove that I am doing more fore my famely than aney working man," he was merely one of 290 paupers whom we can trace between 1800 and 1900 as having given malicious information.[31] Neighbours or workmates who had come into dispute with one another spread rumours that they knew would be picked up. One notable such case was that of the devout authoress Mrs E. Redford, the "Banbury Female Martyr." In the late 1840s the death of two children and a carting accident in which her husband was involved drove her into the hands of the New Poor Law guardians of Wantage (Oxfordshire). She had publicly blamed her husband's accident on his employer, whose wife retaliated by accusing *her* of fraud – "you have earned a great deal of money … you had flour in the house to last a month or more" – after which her relief was stopped. Redford reflected bitterly on the malicious intent directed towards her (which she trusted to God's will she would overcome), and insisted that there had been no savings and that the flour was on credit and hence constituted a liability and not a resource.[32] Comparable modern personal enmities leading to snitching include disputes over cars and children, drugs, outside space, and the presence of relatives and sexual partners.

In many cases, however, I have observed that snitching was not just wholly personal. The act of informing came, rather, at the end of a process in which those who informed (including, surprisingly often, other welfare recipients) had reached a tipping point; that is, when behaviour or (more often) stories about behaviour, had accumulated, and were magnified and re-invented, such that snitching went beyond what none other than Boris Johnson in 1995 called a "Nark's Culture."[33] This idea began to emerge when I was thinking about the impact of "brazen" behaviour for chapter 6, but three stories from very different chronological periods exemplify the reach of the observation. Thus, commenting on a 2011 newspaper story about a single UK court that considered twenty-three welfare fraud cases in one day, "Reg" claimed his daughter had told him about "a family over the road from her in North London who everyone knows are on benefits but still work." He went on to suggest that the woman was masquerading as a single mother and that both she and her partner had "cash jobs" including "ironing on an almost industrial scale" which necessitated the woman employing "some other neighbours as parttime helpers (cash)!" The clear implication was that those neighbours were also receiving welfare payments. Here, then, it was fraud at scale and the encouragement of other fraudsters that constituted the tipping point.[34] Even in this case, neither "everyone" nor the unnamed daughter had themselves snitched on the couple; rather it was left to an outraged "Reg," who suggested: "A quick call to the DSS line is in order methinks, we might see her on here next time!"[35] In the earlier years of the period I have studied, a 1710 treatise providing instructions for overseers of the poor on their day-to-day duties noted that officials could not rely either on parishioners or on ratepayers to identify the idle, charlatans, and other undeserving poor unless their behaviour was extraordinary.[36] Exactly the same perspective emerged from a 1995 interview with a retired official who had been active in investigating fraud in the 1960s. He noted (very much echoing Robin Page, whom we have encountered in earlier chapters) that the tolerance level of communities was generally high until "someone lost their head, then they got reported."[37]

The architecture of snitching is thus complex. It becomes more so when we understand that informing in other areas of economic, social, and cultural life has also been traditionally modest both in absolute terms and in comparison to the potential scale of the underlying issues. While we can trace many prosecutions for breaching "weights and measures" legislation in relation to food or other goods, the sheer turnover of buying and selling in British markets could easily have generated many more accusations.[38] The Factory and Mining Acts and the nascent Health and Safety Movement of the later nineteenth century could easily have led to millions of complaints and informing events, but they did not.[39] As interwar unemployment spiralled and the means test for unemployment payments moved in and out of legislation, it would have been easy and natural for neighbours to snitch, but they did not.[40] And while there is modern angst about popular hostility towards immigrants and asylum seekers, it is striking, both historically and in the present, how few people snitch on these groups even when they have the chance.[41] In this sense, our task is to explain both a general *and* a specific absence.

Speaking and Thinking of Absence

The disciplinary traditions on which I draw have distinct ways of conceptualising absence and silence; these run across a spectrum between absence being seen as an artefact of power (or resistance) through to a reading of absence as a function of the scale or geographical unit of analysis. In the context of this book, I understand absence of reporting as signalling a basket of imperatives – approximating to a learned and transmissible behaviour – which has remarkable consistency across the many forms of welfare state organisation from 1601 to the present. Equally, it is necessary to understand, much as an anthropologist studying body language or the intricacies of speech would, that absence is more than silence.[42] To ground these ideas we can range over the story of Percy Cross, reflecting on his early life at Eastwood (Nottinghamshire) in the years immediately after 1918. In that society, beggars looking to supplement doles and pensions would appear at the weekend: "Some of them looked cringing and beaten, others still clung to a bit of respectability and defiance. There were several shabby armless and legless soldier veterans showing off their medals (and the nation's ingratitude)." Cross felt particular sympathy for "a dirty old woman who clasped a baby tight-wrapped in her shawl" until his mother told him that she was from the nearby village of Kimberley, the "baby" was just a bundle of rags assembled to elicit sympathy, and that the woman "ought to be in prison."[43] It would have been easy for Percy or his mother to report the beggar to the local relieving officer or (given a wider moral crusade against beggars and scroungers at this time[44]) to the police. They did not. George Ewart Evans, the Suffolk ethnographer, recounting oral histories from roughly the same period, suggested that "the unconscious element in a man's speech will, to a certain extent at least, mirror the actual assumptions of the culture in which he lives."[45] The unconscious elements in the Cross testimony thus reveal much about a wider culture of tolerance for and even sympathy with welfare fraudsters. The nation had treated its veterans appallingly; inadequate welfare provision had left people "cringing and beaten"; he admired those who clung to defiance; and no mother, he thought, should be left begging for help to feed a small baby. Whether his own mother shared these views is unclear, but his quoting of her words that the supposedly fraudulent beggar "ought" to be in prison suggested that she expected someone *else* to do the informing.

The decision not to act certainly equates to absence but it also speaks to a deeper culture favouring conscious collusion rather than merely turning a blind eye or being silent.

Stories like these constitute the core of my data, and while most of them give or imply multiple reasons for silence and inaction, I can usually classify the central reasoning clearly enough to understand the longevity of opposition to snitching. Figure 7.3 summarises this classification. Some of the causes or labels are familiar from earlier chapters and require no further elaboration. Others such as fear of reprisal are simply obvious, inscribed in stories across all source genres. Sometimes references to fear are oblique or latent – as for instance in the case of an anonymous contributor to a 2012 comments thread who said: "Wish I had the balls to report em, I know quite a few people that commit benefit fraud"[46] – but they can also be visceral, as in the case of one focus group participant who was badly beaten because he was (wrongly) suspected of snitching on a single mother.[47] The historical continuities of fear are striking. Thus, David Edwards of Cardiff wrote to the Poor Law Board in 1857, observing:

> There is pauper who receives three shillings & sixpence per week from the parish known by the name of Ann Gronow She has a son Mr Edward Gronow who holds a farm of about 100 acres in the Hamlet of "Peterstone Super Montem" with a large Colliery on the same He also has an Inn of his own for which Mr John Rowe pays him £23 a year and his mother on this Parish!!!! now the mystery of the case is the following, her son is a particular friend of the Guardian whom is the Rector of the Parish We had a vestry meeting on the subject some time ago and the whole Parish voted that that her son should maintain her but the Guardian will not take the case before the Board

Edwards warned ominously that either the son or the unnamed guardian "would revenge on me and turn me out of my farm" if they knew he had complained. The PLB, alive to the threat, noted that an inspector should make inquiries but withhold the name of the informant.[48] A fundamental "unbelief"[49] that reporting would remain anonymous constitutes a sub-category of this fear across the chronological and spatial dimensions of my data. This is well crystallised in the words of Edward

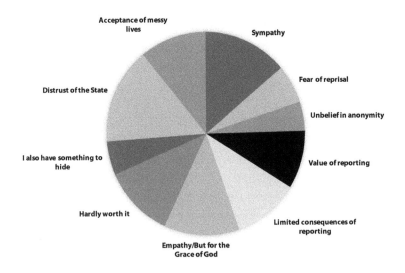

7.3 Central reasons for not informing, 1601–2023.
Notes: Original 8,243 observations, of which 18% do not give a clear enough reasoning to be included. *Source:* All material listed in the bibliography.

Thomas. Writing a snitching letter from Builth (Breconshire) in 1884 he headed it "Private and Confidential" and went on to stress that he wanted the letter to "be kept as private as possible for Several reasons," including that "I have Brothers and Sisters Tenant Farmers to Miss Thomas referred too and Father of the Officer being the Agent he will likely injure them if he can." Thomas then went on for a third time to emphasise the need for secrecy because, "in a thin populated district as this we know Each other 20 miles around."[50]

Other categories in figure 7.3 are not so obvious. One is the purchase of a view consistently elaborated across the chronological dimensions of the sample that, because the value of payments in the British welfare state has always been so low, fraud was simply not worth fighting over.[51] Commenting on a 2011 newspaper article, for instance, "kams" argued:

> I have no sympathy for greedy cheats but the reality is that you can have no quality of life on this [welfare] income. Before you judge people for making an extra £2000, think about the top 5% who steal £millions of ours every day … You could be next.[52]

In turn, on the opposite side of the coin to concerns about the value of reporting in the first place, we find the perceived muted consequences of action. While I did not ask oral history respondents about their feelings on either the investigation process for fraudsters or its consequences, all of them had something to say on the subject. In a 1995 interview, for instance, "PT" cited as a reason for not snitching that: "the watering down of the rules by these crap judges means that any bastard can pitch up and make a claim and they just don't get investigated and punishment well that's an effing joke."[53] Indeed, "PT" simultaneously cited lack of punishment as a reason for their belief that there was more fraud than was ever reported, and as a justification for not reporting the infractions they claimed to know about. A jabbing finger pressed the point that officials were not serious about punishing fraud. Lack of effective investigation and punishment mechanisms was also a core thread in comments on newspaper articles (as well as appearing in the articles themselves); some three thousand writers railed against loose or lenient punishment but had clearly not themselves reported cases they were aware of.

Such comments appeared in threads attached to articles in *both* right- and left-leaning newspapers. Commentators who did claim to have submitted reports almost universally mentioned that their actions were a waste of time, since people they had reported usually remained on or returned to welfare payments even if given suspended or custodial sentences. There is also a related sense that local anti-fraud campaigns could be counter-productive. In 2001, for instance, MPs received a report noting that a recent hotline campaign in the northwest had the effect of showing how easy it was to commit welfare fraud rather than increasing the amount of snitching.[54] We return to these matters in greater detail in chapter 9, but the strength of this argument deep into the historical data is remarkable; repeated injunctions in guidance manuals and pamphlets from the seventeenth-century onwards for overseers to inspect the poor, chase down vagrants, and enforce sanctions when someone returned to a place having been subject to removal under the settlement laws constitute *de facto* evidence that these tasks were *not* being done.[55] Printed circulars from early nineteenth-century Somerset reminding parish officers to closely inspect vagrant passes so as to prevent fraud embody this observation.[56]

Positivist variables also shape the borderline between silence and reporting. Most significantly, we find empathy as opposed to just sympathy or pity.[57] This sentiment can be illustrated for the twentieth century by three short but important stories. Nellie Wilson, recounting her teenage years before and during the First World War, noted: "With no help from the State, sickness, bereavement or loss of work for the breadwinner meant real hardship. Neighbours all rallied round to help with cooking, washing, ironing, caring for children etc., and no one went hungry."[58] The allegation of lack of state support was of course erroneous; Wilson was writing in the aftermath of the Liberal welfare reforms. Indeed, judged in terms of income replacement rates for the unemployed, welfare payments in the late 1910s and early 1920s were (for those who got them) probably more generous than they had been for more than a hundred years.[59] Yet Wilson *felt* the residuality of the state, and her testimony reveals a strong empathy with those who did a "bit on the side." Shifting the focus from England to Wales, we can turn to the testimony of George Ewart Evans. In his semi-factual collection of short stories about interwar Wales he recounted the life of Ben Griffiths: "it's pretty sticky when you've been a councillor and opened the Water Works, and now got to line up and take a pinch off the Dole every Friday at ten-thirty."[60] That someone of substance and standing could be drawn low by structural decay in the mining industry and forced into dependence speaks keenly to the idea that people could be snitching in one week and also the subject of it not long thereafter. Use of the word "pinch" here is very deliberate, simultaneously conveying the smallness of the dole (as for instance in a "pinch of snuff"), the emotional suffering occasioned by having to apply for and accept it, and the mark of poverty that might be left on the mind and body.

Similar subtleties of language and feeling are found in the case of Elizabeth Trainor, who in her unpublished autobiography reflected on being poor in the 1960s. She argued that, although work was plentiful, for those who could not keep regular employment, "doing a bit of this and that, whatever someone could get, was the only way for families to avoid getting screwed down by the benefit system."[61] The phrase "screwed down" speaks to the emotional weight of dependence and the intent of the state. And, despite the invective often aimed at welfare recipients in the online commentary analysed here, it is still possible to trace a consistent thread of support for fraudsters. This ranged from deflection rhetoric ("The focus should be on outright fraud ... not on policing whether people with disabilities and illnesses are continuously experiencing their allotted pain quotas"), through transference sentiment ("Can you blame a parent for having the best interests of their kids at heart"), to empathetic support ("for the most part [fraud] is perpetrated by desperate folk in need of an extra tenner a week, its not the chancer off the telly ad").[62] These threads also wind through records emanating from the discretionary welfare regimes of the pre-1900 period.[63] Henry Rutter of Farnham (Surrey), for instance, was well known as a serial fraudster by officials of that place in the 1830s. Indeed, he complained that people were spreading rumours to this effect about him: "The unkindness, calumny, and ingratitude of the Bennett Family; and this through their Misrepresentations of me, is more than any man can encounter." Nonetheless, he wrote to others at Farnham for "friendly interposition" and for them to use "all your interest and eloquence in my favour" to secure renewal and augmentation of relief. He was ultimately successful in this endeavour even though officials knew him to be a liar and charlatan.[64]

Figure 7.3 also flags two further important variables that have shaped inaction, silence, and active collusion between claimants and "the public" who constructed welfare fraud. One is an intense distrust of the reach, intent, and power of the state and its officers, an attitude that partly balances long-ingrained suspicions about the honesty of the poor. Such views manifest in multiple ways and stand in distinction to recent research by Marc Brodie:[65] a (well-founded) suspicion that the state manufactures crises of welfare fraud to deflect attention from other failings; a sense that the welfare system picks up the pieces of wider structural problems in society and the economy that politicians do not want to tackle; the idea that a crackdown on welfare fraud would be handled so badly that genuine applicants and recipients would suffer; latent feeling that civil servants and proxy welfare officials cannot get anything right;[66] belief that almost any form of state intervention has the capacity to make things worse; and above all a suspicion of the moral agenda of the powerful elites who dominate the policymaking arena. Support for this summative assessment – especially the quality and intent of administrators – is strong. Thus, in particularly pointed comments relating to a newspaper article on fraud prosecutions, "Roy" suggested that the Civil Service "(which includes the Benefits Agency) is filled with jobsworths who are so incompetent," while "benevolentdictator" commented that "The civil servants managing these systems are all Oxbridge educated and really do not have a clue about the real world." Much earlier, Donald Munro wrote from Skinnit (Sutherland) to contest the stories made up by Mr Sinclair, a local welfare officer. He argued that Sinclair had told "a falsehood in every word that he wrote," offered to prove this, and demanded that the parochial board "bring him to answer in the case before his superiors."[67] Concern about the partiality, competence, and prejudice of officials and guardians in England is also captured in the story of Kitty Massey from Hale (Cheshire). In 1838 the Poor Law Commission received a letter from James Thompson, who gave Massey an excellent character reference but went on to note that:

> Hannah Holme 83 years of age but strong and healthy (of this Township) having a well furnished House and keeping a dog and cat on food that the beforementioned [Kitty Massey] would be glad of has been constantly and obstinately persevering in going around the country and telling the most abominable tales and lies against Mrs. Massey for the purpose as I believe of destroying her character and income.

Thompson had sought sanctions against Holme, who was herself on poor relief, and "laid the above case through the relieving officer before the Board their reply 'they have no power to suspend relief.'" Despite Thompson's claim that he could "substantiate the charge against Hannah Holme by witnesses," the officials were unmoved because she was a favourite of the guardians; it was for that reason, Thompson said, that he now wrote to seek justice.[68] In a similar vein, a 2003 Audit Commission report on tackling fraud documented multiple occasions on which (with good reason) one part of the state apparatus doubted the will, capacity, motivations – and even the capability – of other parts of the same apparatus![69]

Finally, and returning to a theme that emerged in chapter 6, I find widespread acknowledgement that people on or on the edges of welfare have always simply had messy lives. "RK" did not report the undeclared live-in lover of a neighbour because "she's just inadequate; a crap and chaotic life what can I say."[70] In the documentary "To Catch a Cheat" one single mother detailed with penetrating clarity her complex relationship status, linked it to the scale of her benefits ("like, 78 pound, that goes nowhere"), and then moved to the question of snitching on those like her who had complex lives: "I wouldn't like it done to me, as somebody just has done, so, I wouldn't do it to anybody else."[71] For the early twentieth century, social investigators like Beatrice Webb persistently highlighted the day-to-day unpredictability of life on the margins of welfare. She found it difficult to physically and emotionally penetrate communities, given their coherence by such messiness.[72] Decisions on snitching that we see as simple – to report or not; to listen or not; to be offended or to ignore – are given complex circularity by such messiness. We see this type of situation brilliantly captured in a letter from an anguished father, Matthew Hughes, from Cambridge (Cambridgeshire). Though substantial, it is worth quoting at length:

> Gentlemen, There is a Woman named Elizabeth Haynes – residing at No. 10 Court, Holloway head in Birmingham, who has for some years past, been defrauding a Parish in Yorkshire of a Weekly allowance for either one or two children that are dead I cannot speak with precision as to dates, but the main facts of the case are these, about five or six years ago … The Parish authorities in Birmingham granted her a weekly allowance which had to come from her husbands parish in Yorkshire – Shortly after her husbands death either one or two of the children died, and she still has continued to receive the same allowance which was first Granted. Now this woman is by no means badly off – her husbands friends have had one of the children ever since his death – her eldest daughter works with herself, at Bridle Stitching, & I have known them to earn eight & twenty shillings in a week … her eldest boy is also constantly employed at Middlemores Beside, she has a well furnished house & keeps lodgers –

> All this should be no business of mine but most unhappily for me, this base woman has been the complete ruin of an Unfortunate daughter of mine, who was at Service in Birmingham … She blasted my childs Character, and I firmly believe if the Unhappy Girl did forsake the Path of Virtue – the Vile example of this woman, and her daughter were the primary cause of it –

About 15 months ago – when I first heard of my wretched childs disgrace [she had become a prostitute in London] & the author of it – I wrote to the Overserrs of Birmingham & gave the same account of Mrs Haynes as I have done now – Whether they took any notice of the Communication or not I dont know – I know she has friends in Birmingham, that will screen her if possible.[73]

For Hughes, then, the fraud perpetrated by Elizabeth Haynes would not *ordinarily* have resulted in his snitching. He came forward with his story because Haynes had encouraged his own daughter into vice. No action had been taken. Nor would it as a result of this letter. Haynes kept her allowance because this mix of rumour and gossip collided with a messy life and left officials taking no action.

Conclusion

Boris Johnson claimed in 1995 that "The state has always relied on sneaks" and that prosecuted fraudsters have "almost all been nailed by sneaks."[74] Neither of these assertions is true. While the numbers of people reporting modern welfare fraud seem significant, I am struck not by how much snitching there is but by how *little*. This observation applies forcefully to historic populations too, and such remarkable long-term continuity means we must think much more carefully about how to explain the decision whether to tell or not. The ordinary public, I have argued, are capable simultaneously of constructing high levels of actual and imagined fraud and then of not reporting the fraud that comes into their ambit. Such non-reporting is itself challenging to interpret, with individual attitudes traversing a complex spectrum between passive silence, acceptance and inaction, to active collusion or empathy. Explaining these attitudes involves taking a new approach to classifying the central sentiments that can be gleaned from written and oral testimony across this very long period. For some commentators, the dominant explanation is found in attitudes of fear or the sense that, given the inadequacy of the whole welfare system or the punishment involved, reporting was just not worthwhile. At the other end of the spectrum, inaction reflects an ambivalent relationship between the poorer elements of the population and the extending central power of the British state. In this framework, and notwithstanding often harsh comments about welfare fraudsters in many of the sources, I find a complex form of empathy rooted in the sense that, for a significant part of the variously constellated underclass, the tables might be turned on them in the end.

I do not argue that welfare fraud is or has been insignificant, that claimants and recipients have not been persistently vilified in the press, or that the public do not have a visceral loathing of shameless welfare fraudsters or groups they construct as dishonest. Nor do I step away from my argument that the poor as a group have often been seen as dishonest, or that reporting (as with Barbara Ingham) has fundamental consequences for welfare recipients. Rather, I suggest that not all fraud and not all fraudsters are or are seen to be alike. The remarkable lack of snitching traced here is both an embodiment of this observation and also the starting point for exploring a wider question that gets to the very heart of the role and function of the welfare state and its future: why does welfare fraud persist when it could so easily be confronted at the individual, community, and system level?

To continue that exploration, in the remainder of part 3 we pursue an extremely important observation, noted only in passing here: that across the period from 1601 to the present, people have not reported fraud because they do not believe either that the processes for tracking down and punishing fraud exist, or that officials and policymakers really *want* to find and eliminate such fraud in the first place.

CHAPTER 8

To Seek or Not to Seek?

In 1803 the pauper Ann Candler published a collection of poems and brief autobiographical reflections. An unnamed editor suggested: "The events of her life are, as may well be expected, few and uninteresting." In fact the stories of an errant husband, bad luck, ill-health, multiple childbirths and deaths, and her eventual decline into pauperism, encompass much of what it meant to be a poor woman in this period.[1] By 1801, when she commenced the work, Candler had been in the Tattingstone House of Industry (Suffolk) "upwards of twenty years secluded from the world." The autobiographical account was written as a familiar letter[2] to two "Ladies" who had been her benefactors and now encouraged the poetry. Indeed, Candler thanked them for "your unlimited goodness to me, in endeavouring to render the situation I am in as comfortable as possible."[3] Such "goodness" extended to cash gifts, material presents, visits, and plans to remove her from the House. Candler explicitly contrasted the effects of their behaviour ...

> My gen'rous friends, with feeling heart,
> Remove the ponderous weight,
> And those impending ills avert
> Which want and woes create

... with that of the parish:

> Within these dreary walls confin'd,
> A lone recluse, I live,
> And, with the dregs of human kind,
> A niggard alms receive.[4]

Other inmates of workhouse-like institutions constructed them in equally evocative terms, but for the purposes of this chapter the question is: why did local officials not appropriate the cash given to Candler, reduce her relief to reflect help in kind, or even eject her from the institution into the custody and provision of her "friends"? Why did they supply the candles that let her write at night and allow her to publish by subscription a book of poems and reflections which generated income, if she was in the House of Industry? Perhaps the "friends" had sufficiently high status to dissuade officials from pre-emptive action. Many did.[5] Perhaps those officials were exhibiting Christian philanthropy in the hope of restoring Candler's independence. Or maybe they were of the slovenly genre who simply neglected their duty, as many early writers suggested of Old Poor Law officials.[6] However we read the evidence, the fact is that these officials did not act even though there was a clear legal and procedural *duty* to do so.

This chapter, then, is about the question of when officials seek and do not seek out welfare fraud broadly defined. Together with chapter 9, it will argue that, while it *is* possible to fundamentally confront fraud – this is a matter of resources, people, power, and punishment – such confrontation does not happen in practice. Its absence reflects the fact that throughout the history of the British welfare state, the variously appointed enforcement officials and bodies only seek fraudulent activities selectively and (the subject of chapter 9) even more rarely find and punish such activities. I analyse the reach of "obvious" explanations for these long-term historical continuities – cost, complexity, value for money *versus* welfare resources lost – and offer new readings. Amongst them, *inter alia*, are arguments that: there has never been a mechanism in the British welfare system to sanction benefit fraudsters with permanent or meaningful exclusion and so it is best not to seek them in the first place; widespread understanding of the residual nature of the welfare system and the structural and definitional flaws that generate fraud leads to limited bottom-up pressure for concerted action; and the structural weakness of the British central state militates against co-ordinated and sustained seeking activity. We turn initially, then, and for the first time in the literature, to the question of the scale of seeking fraud between 1601 and the present.

How Much Seeking?

The episodic avalanche of newspaper stories about welfare fraud convictions and the (now) more regular summation of figures in departmental or select committee reports on investigative activity, give the impression of a highly active surveillance system in which investigative personnel have access to an ever-wider range of techniques, databases, and powers to catch fraudsters, and the funding to do so. In a parliamentary debate on 5 December 2022, Vicky Ford, MP, asked Secretary of State for Work and Pensions Mel Stride what measures were being taken to crack down on fraud. He replied: "We have recently announced two tranches of additional investment totalling £900 million to prevent more than £1 billion-worth of fraud by 2024/25. Since May 2020 it [the DWP] has suspended 170,000 claims."[7] Less than a year earlier, Will Quince, MP, had offered a written answer on fraud and error statistics. Acknowledging that normative checks were suspended during COVID, he reassured the House:

> All benefit fraud is wrong ... but it is especially disappointing to see people exploit a global pandemic in this way. We are part way through an exercise which is examining all the cases we tagged and reapplying the verification standards that would have been applied at the time, had it not been for COVID-19. We will correct each and every case where we find something is wrong, and where appropriate, we will bring to bear the full force of the law. In addition, at the Budget the Government announced £44 million of funding for a package of measures designed to prevent fraud and error entering the system.[8]

Such claims of action and new spending constitute a sustained rhetorical ecology across the post-1945 period. In a 1974 debate, for instance, the minister of state for the Department of Health and Social Security noted that "in both 1972 and 1973 the figure [for fraudulent cases] ran at about 14,500." Projecting forward, he anticipated that the "increased effectiveness" of newly appointed investigative staff would result in a further 5% of applications being deemed fraudulent. Responding to a follow-up question from Jasper More, MP, he continued: "The number of staff dealing with this kind of potential fraud and abuse has been increased quite substantially in recent years."[9] Across almost a million and a half words of debate about welfare fraud between 1968 and 2022, the repetition of claims that new technology, more staff, more public reporting, more money, and changed local and national processes would reduce the scale of individual and organized fraud is compelling.[10] Newspaper reporting, blogs, and pamphlets by campaigning and advice groups also give an overarching impression of strong, active, and comprehensive seeking. Entertainingly, in January 2023 *The Times* was "given exclusive access to [the DWP's] counterfraud regional office in Newcastle where digital forensic analysts and investigators are combatting bogus claims" and subsequently published a series of crude photoshop fails of people who had been trying to prove residence.[11]

These impressions of concerted and substantial seeking activity in the post-1945 period are remarkably far from the truth, and far from *perceptions* found in postwar life-writing, oral histories, blogs, and comments. This contrast is crystallised in Robin Page's remarkable tell-all of his time as a fraud investigator in the 1960s, in which he exposed a demoralised, understaffed civil service fighting a massive tide of fraud – "abuse of the system is so widespread that the public purse is being regularly plundered by a growing army of professional poverty pleaders" – but hamstrung by a political and management class who ensured that: "the full extent of … fraud, malingering and blatant pilfering [was] swept under official carpets." Frontline staff were "silent witnesses to maladministration, inefficiency, and sometimes even blatant misrepresentation" by ministers.[12] Rendering the conclusions of the Henry Fisher review (set up to test Page's claims) in November 1974, the minister for the Department of Health and Social Security claimed that: "Conservative Members generally have exaggerated the amount of abuse of the system. That was confirmed by the Fisher Committee."[13] Yet, the sense of an administrative apparatus neither equipped nor motivated to seek fraudsters has traction across the entire postwar period. Keyword and thematic searches of *Hansard* show that ministers and others have been persistently unable to answer questions about the number of investigative staff, numbers of fraud cases dropped before prosecution, precise amounts spent on detection, and (with breathtaking regularity) detection and prosecution figures for particular towns or areas. Just as governments failed to keep effective statistics on the scale of fraud before the 1990s, so they have signally failed to generate data on confronting such fraud.

Paradoxically, we should be surprised that so many cases *are* followed up. A close reading of the 994 pages constituting the manual for welfare fraud investigators highlights some forty trigger points for *not* starting an investigation or for *stopping* an existing one.[14] Such guidance is perhaps inevitable if we trace the number of fraud investigators employed in the modern welfare state. These figures are somewhat opaque; it is impossible to satisfactorily tension national employment levels with investigative capacity in local authority contexts. The latter is rarely declared. Politicians often consciously obfuscate the true level of engagement. Stan Orme, MP, responding in the House to a parliamentary question about the number of staff employed to fight fraud in supplementary benefit claims every year from 1973 to 1978, began:

> All staff in local offices of my Department are concerned to some extent with the prevention of fraudulent claims for social security benefits. Their general experience, coupled with their alertness and the intelligent application of the prescribed procedures for dealing with claims, forms the first stage of defence against fraud.

To make matters worse, after giving figures for specific investigation teams, he went on at length to qualify the numbers:

> The staffing figures relate to local offices only, as regional office and Headquarters staffing figures do not have their supplementary benefit element recorded separately. They also relate to complements on a given date – that is, the number of posts authorised – not the number of staff actually in post which would be rather lower. In addition, there are other staff who are fully engaged on work connected with fraud investigation, but records are not available to make such posts readily identifiable ... As a consequence it is not possible to provide full answers.[15]

Ultimately, it became clear that by 1978 *few* dedicated fraud staff were employed, both absolutely and in relation to the volume of claims received.[16]

Using DWP figures, *Hansard*, newspaper material and comments, a trawl of local authority websites, and other reporting, figure 8.1 constructs the broad range of claimed employment of *dedicated* fraud staff for each year between 2008 and 2022. The ranges are wide, but these are still small numbers. They speak to strict capacity limits in terms of seeking out welfare fraud, and thus indicate limits to what information is followed up and from whom.[17] The figures have their analogue in a widespread sense from my modern material that the DWP lacks the person-power required to carry out detailed fraud investigations. Commenting in 2011, "muggle95" suggested that:

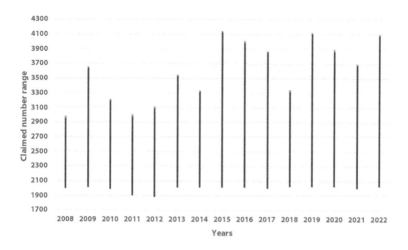

8.1 Claimed number of fraud investigators, 2008–2022.

Notes: The thirty observations represent the top and bottom estimates or claims of numbers for each year. *Source:* See text.

As a former DWP investigator, I am fascinated to note that despite the far reaching legislative powers at the disposal of DWP they continue to resort to the same archaic investigative methods they did 20 years (and more!) ago. DWP has around 3,000 investigators, many of whom will spend their day in exactly the same way as is depicted in this article. It wasn't cost effective 20 years ago and I can't imagine that it is now.[18]

Politicians shared these views. Seeking to explain a woeful lack of enforcement during a 2001 debate, speakers returned again and again to factors such as the cumulative impact of staff cuts, re-organisations, new benefit schemes that diverted experienced people, lack of specialist IT expertise, and inadequate pay structures which meant that senior staff simply tended to move on, all of which left the enforcement workforce constantly in flux.[19]

Yet, most of my respondents also felt that the state lacked the *will* to investigate egregious and deliberate fraud, the proof of which was self-evident in the everyday lives of those who told their stories. Failure to seek was about much more than *merely* the numbers of staff or even the cost of investigation. "LL," a former Jobcentre employee and later fraud investigator, noted in a 2014 focus group that they could indeed have drawn from a wider range of databases but that there was "a lack of will, you know, drive from up top," to do so.[20] Such observations have their analogue in persistent and repetitive newspaper stories drawing attention to failed fraud-reduction initiatives and the scale of fraud that could so easily be found if officials just decided to look for it. This inadequacy is well captured by "deji," commenting in 2011. Having worked in IT at HMRC, they claimed to have suggested joining up different databases but were "told that this idea would be 'totally unacceptable' as the 2 computer systems are not allowed to see each others' data." In the same set of comments, "The Gene Genie" asked why welfare payments could not be made in vouchers;[21] "West" noted from claimed personal experience the "dead wood staff" working in Jobcentres; and "mike king" was amazed that welfare applications were not linked to the passport system so that those holidaying while on welfare could be investigated.[22]

It is impossible to replicate figure 8.1 for the rest of the postwar period, but the idea that the welfare state was almost programmed *not* to seek welfare fraud is common.[23] In an unpublished autobiography covering his time as an Oxford policeman from 1948 to 1973, Alan Dent came into contact with welfare recipients only once. This was not unusual because, as he wrote: "I can only remember there being perhaps a couple of Welfare Officers" for the whole of the city.[24] Robin Page alleged that managers had a "general belief that the Department is really a public piggy bank."[25] Tim Fortescue, MP, had similar reactions when he asked in a 1968 Commons debate about the "special investigation officers" retained to investigate fraud. He was disappointed to learn that there had been no dedicated training since the investigation force was first established in 1954, mightily surprised that "there are 145 of them in the whole of Great Britain," and dumbfounded that "They have no special powers."[26] Thus, while Cathy and Reg in *Cathy Come Home* (1966) feared inspection and intervention by the welfare authorities, there was little statistical chance of their being pursued.[27]

For the interwar period and then into the New and Old Poor Laws, one might have expected a more robust approach to seeking.[28] The absence of automatic entitlement, a smaller range of welfare types, localised relief administration, and the expectation that *all* officials and ratepayers would be their own investigator on an everyday basis should have on the one hand facilitated seeking and on the other made it the norm. There are, to be sure, clear examples of robust action. James Johnson, for instance, was dismayed in August 1833 to find that an overseer from Wisbech (Norfolk) had "met him & he had Got his basket with a few cottons and tapes so on that account they stoped his pay." Johnson now wrote to clarify that he had supplies with him merely in an attempt to garner pin money since "he [writing in the third person] is not able to do anything else – and that he can do but little as he is so lame – that he can go but very little way."[29] Despite such instances of detection, I find little to support the Webbs's view that the New Poor Law resulted in claimants being "more carefully investigated, and possibly more regularly watched."[30] And while I might have expected surveillance and confrontation of fraud to break down in the dense high-turnover parishes of urban Britain from the later eighteenth century, in other sorts of places and for earlier periods than this there is also much evidence of a failure to seek. Some of this evidence is indirect. Charity Organisation Society claimed a role in monitoring outdoor relief precisely because it was felt that neither those giving out philanthropic resources nor the New Poor Law had done anywhere near enough to probe the honesty of applicants.[31] Indeed, Beatrice Webb noted that cos members and other case workers "found themselves transformed into a body of amateur detectives, in some cases initiating prosecutions of persons they thought to be imposters, and arousing more suspicion and hatred than the recognised officers of the law."[32] The 1820s diary of Robert Sharp of South Cave (Yorkshire) is replete with views (his own and from others) that the Old Poor Law recipient list was peopled by "idle Clowns" and "the worthless" who ought to have been properly investigated but were not.[33] And in 1749 James Parker and Richard Burn's *Conductor Generalis* explicitly drew attention to the fact that officers were not inspecting and seeking as part of their everyday business.[34] This is not a complete chronological survey, of course, but it does portray the remarkable consistency in the scale of not seeking.

In addition to indirect sources of this sort, there is also much *direct* evidence that officials failed to seek out fraud even in obvious cases and even after they had obtained credible proof. Some of it has been seen elsewhere in this book, as with the officials who told the 1832 enquiry into the Old Poor Law of the scale of fraudulent claims and yet had seemingly done little sustained work to find and punish it. Much else is new.

Thus, of the 226 snitching letters in my sample between 1716 and 1906, it seems that only 11 per cent were followed up. Indeed, officials sometimes noted and justified their inactivity in this area, as for instance did the overseer of Hulme (Manchester) who in 1817 told a Welsh counterpart: "the burden of this office is so great I cannot sanction my time or the cost" in following up a specific allegation of welfare fraud.[35] We might be tempted to think that questions of difficulty and cost weighed more heavily on officials dealing at a distance with the letter-writing poor, and that this separation would be a key explanation for not seeking. Yet, most of those who wrote to parishes seeking the commencement or renewal of relief did so from communities within walking (and hence knowing) distance.[36]

Moreover, vestry minutes analysed for this book also offer a clear sense that even when the poor were literally on the doorstep, officials still did not seek fraud. Evidence from these sources falls into three broad types. The first consists of injunctions on officials by vestrymen to investigate applicants and to seek vestry approval for proposed actions. Such injunctions are repeated so often in most vestry minutes that we must read them as evidence of the systemic absence of efforts to actively police applications. I find little evidence to support the claim of the Sussex farmer William Wood that Old Poor Law overseers had "complete" control over the poor in a way that "in these days [that is, by the later nineteenth century] can only be viewed as intolerable."[37] Sometimes in the data the injunctions were reversed, as in the case of Mr Mackinzie of Tongue (Sutherland), who in 1781 complained that "his Elders [vestrymen]" were neglecting their duty to help him determine cases, given that they "should know the Circumstances of the Poor better than he does."[38] Failing to seek is also revealed by a second aspect of vestry minutes: repeated renewals of individual relief payments allied with episodic "catch-up" reviews of all cases, which then resulted in some people being thrown off the relief lists. The fact that the Lancashire township of Garstang had three comprehensive reviews from 1817 to 1828, for example, is highly indicative of a substantial under-investment in the inspection regime.[39] Finally, we find some extended cases of conflict within vestries which affected their ability to seek. On 23 December 1829, for instance, the Rothwell (Northamptonshire) vestry convened a committee to consider the:

conduct of John Tomlin in his office of assistant to the overseers and reported to the vestry that they consider him to be harsh and oppressive to the labourers and that the opinion of 66 out of seventy rates payers on whom they have called consider it will tend to the peace of the parish if he were dismissed. It is resolved that this vestry … do not consider the case against him fully proved, that under the circumstances of the present times they think it would be very imprudent to give way to popular clamour and incendiary threats except in a case of manifest and substantial injustice.[40]

Here, then, Tomlin's intrusive monitoring and harsh decision-making had raised the ire of the general population. Although the vestry did not cede to its constituency, the scope of later seeking would clearly have been impaired.[41]

After 1834 vestries lost their core role in day-to-day welfare administration, but right up to 1929, similar perspectives can be gained from the letters of those who advocated for the poor or inspected their condition. These letters repeatedly pointed to the failure of officials to investigate cases properly, meaning that poor relief was denied to the truly deserving but handsomely given to the fraudster and charlatan. Such views are emblematized in a letter from Colonel McLean of Ardgour (Fort William, Scotland) in 1851. After a meeting with Angus McDonald, a local overseer, the colonel had visited Rachel McLean, who was ill and required care. At the direction of the overseer, he asked "the strongest of the Campbell Women who are Paupers" to take charge of Rachel but was met with "a refusal accompanied by words not the most polite." McLean now wrote to observe that the Campbell women ought to have their relief withheld because they were in good health and capable of working while poor Rachel McLean "requires constant attendance." He doubted, however, that this would be done.[42] In similar fashion, the Local Government Board sent a strongly worded note to the guardians of Poplar (London) on 11 June 1877 advising them that Mary Ann August "obtains relief under false pretences, because having 3/8 in her possession she was not destitute," and told the guardians that the money she now requested be returned "certainly ought not to be restored to her."[43] The LGB were to be disappointed.

This sense that officials simply lacked the will to confront fraud sits seamlessly with the evidence of modern oral histories noted above and speaks once more to remarkable long-term continuities of experience and understanding across the different chronological and organisational dimensions of the British welfare state. In practice officials were keenly aware that the life circumstances of claimants and real or imagined fraudsters were messy and fast-moving. Such circumstances – the third aspect of Jerry Mashaw's tripartite model of the role of discretion in securing administrative justice[44] – presented a substantial caution against initiating action in the first place, or (see chapter 9) following through to a prosecution end. Similar considerations affected the decision whether to inform, as we saw in chapter 7. These dilemmas are well illustrated in the BBC's 1997 documentary "To Catch a Cheat," where a detailed analysis of the observations and linguistic reference points of fraud investigators identifies considerable sympathy with those navigating a residual welfare system and with the complexity of the lives they lived. Investigator "Bess" noted that claimants were "caught in the trap of being unable to increase their income without suffering a corresponding loss in benefits," the word "trap" sending a definitive signal of sympathy. And though she had contempt for employers who knowingly employed welfare claimants, Bess was rather more sympathetic to the recipients themselves, who "find they must account for the most intimate aspects of their daily lives." Such commentary might, perhaps should, be read as a welcome sense of humanity from an employee doing a dirty job, but for many in the commentaries attached to newspaper articles, the same words and sentiments were definitive proof that officials used their considerable discretion to avoid seeking dishonesty.[45] Fraudsters *were* investigated, chased, sanctioned, and shamed. At times this process of seeking *was* broadly based in terms of spatial coverage and the types of welfare payments encompassed. But it was never substantial, either in itself or in comparison to the scale of imagined and reported fraud; nor was it sustained. It follows, then, that seeking was a selective process,[46] and it is to this issue that I now turn.

Selective Seeking

Figure 8.2 classifies the motivations for initial investigation by officers of all sorts. It is based upon the 3,863 instances, across the whole dataset and all source-types, where they *began* the process of seeking welfare fraudsters

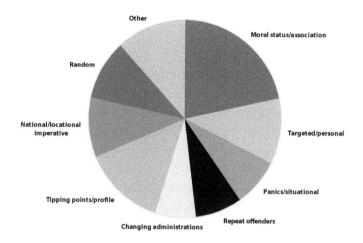

8.2 Initial motivations for seeking, 1601–2022.
Notes: 3,863 observations. Subjective decisions are made in the 30% or so of cases where multiple imperatives were noted or claimed. *Source:* See text.

and there was a given or inferred motivation.[47] Many of these motivations were clear-cut, as for instance with Sophia and Jacob Curchin of Wisbech (Norfolk), who were persistently believed to be simply morally bankrupt.[48] Others are less so. Mrs M.5.L. of Lancaster could not "remember the dole" in the 1930s but did recollect that "They used to come and weigh your circumstances up and they used to give you a food cheque." The unspecified "they" were in fact inspectors and, contrary to the latent assumption in this testimony, such people did *not* visit every family.[49] Given the intricate complexities of inferring motivations across sources like this, we should beware of reading too much into the exact distributions. The chart in figure 8.2 nonetheless points in important directions.

As I have suggested in chapters 4 and 7, being a certain type of welfare applicant or recipient shaped whether officials would ever begin fraud investigations: single mothers, immigrants, repeat offenders, and others with dubious moral credentials are all prominent. It is impossible to say whether the number of such investigations is disproportionate to the presence of these groups in the general welfare population or to the character of public reporting of fraudsters, but they constitute the largest categories transcending the data underlying figure 8.2. In the historical evidence the link between seeking and status is often transparent, as it was, for instance, in May 1817 when the Chorley vestry lost patience with a seemingly endless train of bastardy cases and ordered that "ellen hodkinson and bastard Be admitted into the workhouse she being again pregnant" and that "ellen baxendale (bastardy) to be seen after."[50] Even in the modern evidence we find links between the motivations for starting an investigation and key indicators of morality or status, as for example with assertions in March 2022 that disabled claimants were singled out by a "secret algorithm" for enhanced fraud investigation.[51] Such targeting is neither surprising (bloggers and commentators are disproportionately concerned with a narrow range of welfare recipients) nor new. The depth of the correlation between moral status and seeking can clearly be seen through the words of two officials at very different chronological points in my evidence. In 1969 and 1971 Robin Page was particularly vitriolic about the fraudulent claims of single mothers and those who worked but still claimed supplementary benefit, devoting fifty pages of his report to general commentary and case studies of these two groups.[52] Some 150 years earlier Robert Sharp of South Cave wrote in his diary that he regretted the outcome of a vestry meeting in June 1826 where "the chief consideration ... was, to make the Paupers live on the least possible allowance ... I have to communicate the results on Monday morning when the poor are paid which is not a very agreeable task." However, he also distinguished between the respectable poor and those of questionable moral status – a single mother who threw a stone at him when her allowance was reduced, the unemployed who would rather take relief than work, and "wily beggars."[53]

At the opposite end of the spectrum to this planned targeting of particular groups were essentially random instances. In 2023 Andrea Lawner was investigated for fraud after "a series of romantic selfies" suggesting that she was not in fact a single mother living alone were uncovered on Facebook.[54] Almost exactly 200 years earlier, Christopher Page wrote an apologetic letter of 694 words to the overseers of Lewes St Michael parish (Sussex), having been caught running a shop in London while leaving his wife on poor relief in Lewes when a ratepayer of the latter place happened to come in as a customer.[55] A related category of seeking was that inspired by random (or sometimes planned) changes in officials or the professionalisation of administrative structures. Almost all vestries toyed with paid officials on the basis that they would be more likely to properly investigate both new and existing claimants. The hope was not always realised but initially at least the confrontation of fraud often increased once assistant overseers and other paid officials were appointed. This is well specified in a letter from Andrew Wright to Mr Slaughter, the overseer of the parish of Caversham (Berkshire), which noted that Widow Brown had recently been refused relief for her son by the new Caversham officials. He asserted forcefully:

> If this representation is correct, then is something not right on the part of the overseer Enquire with this or give the Boy proper Relief till the next meeting of the Magistrates at Henley & then any objection you may think right to state may be heard. It's clear from what this woman says that there is a mistaken notion that the circumstance of the mother enables her & therefore that the Parish is not bound to give relief.[56]

Prior to 1834 the appointment of new magistrates hostile to the poor could also lead to increased investigation.[57] Under the New Poor Law in England and Wales and the post-1845 Scottish Poor Law, annual elections of guardians or the turnover of day-to-day staff like inspectors, relieving officers, or medical officers could equally lead to enhanced levels of seeking. Thus, James Betts wrote to the master of the Camagaul Poors House (Clackmannanshire) on 27 October 1851. He noted that a pauper named only as Mary had been jailed and that "We ought to take advantage of this & get the rooms locked up" so as to prevent her returning once free. He noted further that the recently appointed "Fiscal" (inspector) was "accusing us both of carelessness in not having at the first shown a determination in this matter."[58] This official discretion in seeking does not lessen in the twentieth century, even accepting that the scope for individual action and belief became hedged in by national welfare rules and processes. The fact that universalising guidance to fraud investigators has only recently been codified and that such guidance still does not apply to fraud investigations at local authority level highlights some of the liminal space still open for individual belief and action.

Two further categories in figure 8.2 – Panics/situational and National imperative – can be read on a single canvas. They both speak to a sense that officials chose to increase or further target their seeking activities because of broader commentary and public debate or worry, policy directions, or targeted crackdowns on particular welfare payments. Such initiatives were apparent from the earliest days of the Old Poor Law (in the form of crusades against vagrants[59]), ran through attacks on supplementary benefit claimants in the 1980s, and drove episodic campaigns against housing benefit fraud in the 2000s.[60] During such national and regional actions, significant numbers of people might find themselves subject to fraud investigation despite the absence of change in their personal circumstances (in reality or in their own mind). Thus, in 2011 there were widespread suspicions that "Jobcentre staff around the country have been involved in a drive to kick people off benefits amid pressure to meet welfare targets." While the government claimed its instructions to welfare managers had been misunderstood in a small number of cases, "A whistleblower said staff at his jobcentre were given targets of three people a week to refer for sanctions." Almost all of the 1,008 comments on the newspaper article reporting this "drive" were condemnatory, but there was also significant sentiment to reflect that of "Shocko222": "The fear and the persecution of the underclass – doesn't matter if you adhere to the political left or the political right; we're all trapped in the same eye of the storm smack bang in the centre, and we're all part of a system that simply does not work."[61]

Finally, some selective seeking can be explained by personal factors, including people reaching a tipping point (much as they might reach a tipping point for snitching) in terms of being problematic to the welfare system through repeated claims, multiple welfare forms, or particular behaviours. These experiences were not random. "MT" explained in a 2015 focus group that he "never had trouble" when "just" claiming unemployment and housing payments. An application to move onto disability-related payments, however, provoked sustained investigation. He was told by a specialist support group that officials were "particularly sensitive" about attempts to move onto "structural benefit types" and automatically assumed fraud.[62] When viewed in proper historical context, however, the circumstances encompassed by "personal factors" are rather wider: changed handwriting; aggressive behaviour towards officials;[63] inconsistent narratives; keeping a dog;[64] foreign holidays; opening or closing a social media account; a conviction for something else; and abandoning children and partners. The latter carried a particularly long reputational stigma and had consequences for all parties. Thus, Charles Allen wrote from Ealing (Surrey) on 2 July 1834 to follow up a prior unanswered letter. Noting that Mrs Charles Hall was in a "distressed situation, in consequence of her husband having entirely deserted her, although she is within a month of her confinement," he asked the overseer of Farnham to "take some steps in her behalf." Such steps did not in the end involve relief; Mrs Hall was left to deal with childbirth on her own, suspected of colluding with her husband.[65] The way personal factors fed into an enhanced risk of seeking at the process level is also exemplified in the words of the singer P.J. Proby, first encountered in chapter 3. After he had been wrongly accused of fraud in 2011, his song "We the Jury" celebrated an acquittal and drew attention to the very personalised attack on him. Proby sang that he had been "just a victim of some shabby deal" and that whatever the jury decided would not matter because "they're going to hang me anyway."[66]

Figure 8.2 also carries symbolism. While most people applying for or receiving welfare in any period were unlikely to be investigated for fraud, the complexity of the categories in figure 8.2 suggest that poor people could never be *sure* of this. When in 2012 someone on Mumsnet highlighted the case of a friend who was being investigated, the thread attracted fifty-two comments, most of them similar to that of "Tamoo":

> DWP does squillions of cross checks these days regarding a person's finances. I know someone who was interviewed by phone recently because she'd had visitors from abroad (!) and someone else who was called into the office ... When I was claiming JSA [Jobseeker's Allowance] I was randomly called in for an office interview, didn't know why.[67]

The fact of this worry would please modern welfare administrators. It would also have satisfied those who framed the 1601 Old Poor Law. Still, the key point is that historically low levels of informing map seamlessly onto historically low levels of seeking. This continuity has not figured in the current historiography (the opposite is true) and yet it is fundamental to understanding how the public construct fraud and perceive the role, purpose, and character of the wider welfare system. The question thus becomes: why do we see such continuities and what does the answer tell us about welfare citizenship? The latter issue is taken up in chapter 11. For now, we move on to the explanatory framework for *not* seeking.

Explaining Inaction

Some of the core reasons that modern investigations never start are elaborated in official guidance to officers, in some secondary literature, and in many of my post-2000 sources. Four stand out: the absolute cost (and costly administrative complexity) of seeking; the value for money of extended investigation *versus* the scale of payments lost or likely to be recouped; the quality of the initial evidence; and limitations on the actions of investigative officers. In terms of cost and value for money, detailed anatomies of individual fraud investigations reveal the remarkable disjoint between headline promises of crackdowns and costed everyday reality. A BBC Panorama investigation in 2011, for instance, suggested the ease with which a range of welfare payments could be acquired. It also referenced the "avalanche" of cases on the desks of investigators as single inquiries rapidly mushroomed into multiple accusations of fraud and criminal activity. The elephant in the room for inspectors was the degree (and cost) of prior investigation and confirmation work needed to finally charge someone with fraud.[68] The same programme (and many of the fifty-one comments to the playback edition) returned repeatedly to the question of the value of pursuing already poor people for small amounts of money that were never likely to be recouped. This pragmatism has considerable resonance in other modern sources as well. The 2002/03 National Audit Office investigation into the anti-fraud activities of the DWP, for instance, found both that regional investigation units were dropping leads in 16–31% of cases because of "overload," and that there had recently been a "major reduction" in investigation and intervention activities with a particular focus on failing to seek "small scale fraudsters" who would "yield" the lowest recovery rates.[69]

The sheer administrative and time complexity of finding, recording, and integrating enough convincing evidence, also limits seeking. On 18 August 2022, for instance, the DWP issued an urgent clarification that a letter received by some welfare recipients demanding that they attend a telephone-based compliance interview or risk losing benefits was not in fact a scam as the whole of the internet seemed (not unreasonably) to be claiming.[70] Non-attendance would in these cases have been logged as evidence of fraud. But this question of evidence has become fiendishly tricky for modern investigators, as the "proof bar" for effective prosecution or even a warning is remarkably high. Knowledge of this reality conditions decisions over whether to seek. These decisions extend from the question of the depth and quality of information required, to the means that might be used to obtain it. The NAO noted in 2003 that "the complexity of benefit regulations and inadequate computer systems will … continue to be important constraints on the Department's [DWP's] capacity" to confront fraud. But even after a massive twenty-year investment, a 2022 report branded the DWP's IT provision a "shambles."[71] Technological and process innovation and broader efforts to create golden-source information on welfare claimants ought to have increased the efficiency and effectiveness of seeking. Yet, year-on-year variability in the number of cases pursued and remarkably persistent regional differences in the scale and effectiveness of investigation suggest otherwise.[72] In any case, intrusion into the private lives of individuals has triggered significant pushback from stakeholders,[73] an important corrective to centrist and left-leaning media and interest groups that have characterised surveillance as fearsome and disproportionate to the scale of the problem. In practice, it is easy to hypothecate the additional costs arising out of each new technique or intensification of evidence-gathering and, by relating that to the overall welfare fraud budget, to see that for the most part it is more cost-effective *not* to seek in the first place. Recent legal judgements have further limited the room for fraud investigation and increased its underlying costs by putting a value on privacy and constraining the freedom of governments to use the most efficient means of surveillance and enforcement.[74] Much as the presumed attitude of magistrates in the nineteenth century shaped parochial poor law practice,[75] so the presumed complexities and costs of seeking fraud militate against action in the first place.

Yet these are not *simply* modern constraints on seeking. They have deep and compelling historical roots. When we encountered George Huish in 1832 lamenting the financial and time costs involved in seeking out fraud (chapter 3), he was picking up on a consistent theme in the historical evidence. Thus, on 14 February 1817 James Crawshaw wrote from Wakefield to Sandal Magna (West Yorkshire) to recount that James Bennett "had thrown him-self out of employ for the purpose of obtaining relief from the Town" and that "such conduct merits severe punishment." He expressed hope that prompt action in this direction would be taken, otherwise, he said, "the Township may be liable continually to be impos'd upon by such unprincipled fellows." In fact, Bennett avoided investigation because the overseer of Sandal Magna, Mr Firth, could not justify the cost of journeying to Wakefield to confirm the story.[76] Similarly, in a case dating from 16 July 1719 the overseer of Chepping Wiccombe (Buckinghamshire) prosecuted Robert Davies for having allowed his mother to remain on parish relief. The fact that she had been on such relief for "several years," that Robert had freehold property rented out to others in this small village, and that "he had £120 in money and rented a paper mill at £28 per annum and employed four workmen" speaks volumes about the time that local officials had previously devoted to seeking fraud. But he was merely required to provide ongoing support, rather than pay back the amounts defrauded.[77] The related sense that investigation was pointless given the limited likelihood of being able to recoup lost resources also has a central place in the data. Jane Vinall of Great Bookham (Sussex) was the author or subject of seven letters between 1834 and 1839. The overseer of her home parish (Worthing) made several attempts to get officials and others in Great Bookham to inspect her but, notwithstanding their being informed that she had misled the parish as to her address and living arrangements, Vinall was allowed to continue receiving parish relief because the trouble of removing her allowance was too great.[78] In January 1743, Jonathan Waters was allowed simply to apologize to the overseers of Oakham (Rutland) for defrauding them of 2s. by claiming to be sick, rather than being removed from the relief list.[79] Reflecting on her life as a teenager in the later 1920s a female oral history respondent in the Elizabeth Roberts collection noted that the introduction of the means test meant that welfare officers "wanted to know the actual wages that were coming into the house. If you gave a false statement you could be prosecuted and be jailed for it." Moreover, she supposed (but did not know), "they tried to verify it and they'd find it was right because they rung these works up, you see, they could get a statement of your wages by ringing works up." Such statements fit seamlessly with Matt Perry's figures on disallowances of claims (as opposed to prosecutions) in the 1920s, and with the oral history of "RK."[80] Recounting in 1994 his own father's experience as an inspector for the interwar "dole," he remembered being told that almost no one was actually prosecuted. It was not worth the expense.[81]

Nor are the problems of slippery evidence and the high proof threshold required for removing people from welfare lists and keeping them off remotely new – as we might perhaps have expected from prior chapters. Seventeenth-century Buckinghamshire magistrates, for instance, struggled with how to define lodgers for the purposes of prosecuting fraudsters, much as eighteenth- and nineteenth-century officials struggled to capitalise on hearsay about welfare recipients cohabiting. Even the 1973 Fisher Report devoted more than thirty pages of analysis to the difficulty of defining invalidity, sickness, dependents, "fictitious desertion," and urgent need for purposes of fraud identification.[82] It is perhaps easier to think that the imposition of limits on how far investigators could go in seeking evidence has exclusively modern connotations that are related to possibilities (new and more invasive technologies), legal constraints (notably human rights), and everyday complexities (such as modern knowledge about the episodic nature of disabling illness). Yet practical, philosophical, and moral limitations to evidence gathering – enough to dissuade seeking – are also a striking feature of the historical data. In practical terms, it took much longer to conduct surveillance in the past. Moreover evidence-gathering usually involved a network of people who were unpaid (including of course officials themselves until the 1830s) and had limited time resources. This fact is well elaborated in the case of Mary Haywood, resident in Lambeth (London) but settled in Lostwithiel (Cornwall). She had written to her Cornish parish in an undated letter to assure officials that it would be "utterly impossible to get through this winter without a little assistance."[83] A draft reply in the archive is worth quoting at length:

> In reply to your request letter the oversees have no power to grant you the assistance you have requested
> We shall do not altogether acknowledge you as belonging to this parish and before we are satisfied it is the case I will be necessary you should be examined by the officers of the parish in which you now are as we wish to know what your husband has how your husband has supported himself since he left this neighbourhood and to what acct he has rented
> There is one of the Overseer of this place now in London M^r. Treave Anderton Hotel Fleet Street I think you might call hon him also and state what would be a sufficient sum to enable you to do what you stated and what if there is a good prospect of your being in able to get sufficient to support yourself and family

<u>by</u> provided it should be granted by our Board <u>in case yo in case</u>
<u>it should be found you do belong here</u> in case this place should
appear to be your legal settlement[84]

The overseers doubted Haywood's word and insisted on seeing her, but it was only serendipity – an overseer who had travelled from Cornwall to London on other business – that allowed them to fulfil this requirement. The wider scale of the task of the overseer in carrying out constant surveillance during the period from 1601 to the 1830s is reflected in persistent attempts on the part of ratepayers to avoid serving the yearly office. And while there were no national and legal protections of privacy or rights to go about unhindered until well into the twentieth century, officials even in the past could only step so far.[85] When Mr E.1.B. was talking to Elizabeth Roberts about his experience of the dole in the 1930s, for instance, he noted appearances before a committee to tell them what work he had been seeking. After recounting his attempts – "Steel Works, Wire Works, Shipyard, Pulp Works and all these places" – the mayor as chair of the committee "turned round and said 'I don't think you've been looking for work.'" E.1.B. responded sarcastically that the mayor might try giving him a job in his own shop, at which point his dole was stopped. But the committee could not prove whether he had been looking because they did not require the keeping of a book and had no right to ask employers, so (presumably against the concerted efforts of the mayor), "I got the six weeks back pay."[86] There is much more evidence of this sort, but the key point here is that some of the core motivations for not seeking have an extended historical root.

These are important observations. Other variables suppressing seeking in the first place also take on greater significance if considered across the entire chronological canvas of the welfare state. When "KT" said in a 2015 focus group, "these people, well they just have too many rights and a right once given never gets taken away," she was expressing a view that can easily be mapped onto the modern court system, human rights, and the existence of modern commitments to mitigating the worst impacts of income inequality and relative poverty.[87] Indeed, official DWP guidance on what happens when someone is shown to have defrauded the welfare system embodies these very ideas; even where fraud is proven, some twenty-two different payment types are non-sanctionable.[88] Many comments and blogs follow the logic of this argument, suggesting (in the words of "I Wish") that: "They are all thieves and shouldn't come under the human rights umbrella either" and contending that the system itself ensures that crime does pay.[89] As readers will by now suspect, such views and sentiments are anything but modern. The founding statute of the Old Poor Law implied that parishes had a basic duty not to allow someone to starve to death. The New Poor Law took this one step further, mandating guardians and their officers to give "necessary relief," even if in the workhouse context. It was for this reason, as chapter 2 began to suggest, that paupers seeking to contest their care used a rhetoric of hunger and starvation to force action. The Jarrow March of 1936 and other demonstrations against inter-war unemployment policies can be read against the same backdrop.[90] And in 1971 Robin Page directed withering criticism against the chilling effect of concerns about human rights on the investigation of fraud process.[91] Frustrations on the part of both ordinary people and the officials responsible for administering welfare are abundantly clear across all the source types, but the issue is elegantly distilled by John Coker Egerton of Burwash (Sussex). Writing of the early 1830s he focussed on the story of "fifty or sixty persons" who were expected to work as part of receiving their relief. However, one of them: "happening one day to pick up a dead robin, was struck with the sudden humour of giving the robin a public funeral, and such was the powerlessness of authority at the time, that two days were actually wasted by all the hands on the farm in carrying out this curious freak." The parish overseers had no legal right to stop the fraudulent activity (receiving welfare without work) nor to punish the offenders for their contempt by reducing or removing their payments.[92] In other words – and to build on an earlier observation – there has *never* been a mechanism in the British welfare system to sanction welfare fraudsters with permanent or meaningful exclusion and so it is best not to seek them in the first place.

This sense of resignation is normative. Yet there is also something else that has discouraged seeking; a latent sense of sympathy is everywhere in the historical evidence if we look for it with imagination. Thus, when Carl Richards of Eastwood (Nottinghamshire) had to "sign-on" in the 1980s he noted: "The people stood in silence with bowed heads and glazed eyes, although sometimes a couple of young men would meet and their loud voices, peppered with expletives and local slang, would fill the church hall ... All-in-all the atmosphere was quite demoralising.[93] Richards constructed himself as distinct from the other people in the Dole Office, who by inference were habitual welfare dependents, but if we read carefully then we can see considerable sympathy for their position. This observation contrasts with historiographical work focussing on newspapers, which for the same period has claimed "a mounting hysteria that [in the 1980s] created a [popular] welfare backlash of cruel and massive proportions."[94] Nonetheless, a sense of sympathy that spans the evidence for this book is strong. In the 1930s everybody knew that the unemployed would be relieved only intermittently, that the "small dole allowance" only amounted to "the teens of shillings," and that respectable widows with children "only got a shilling a week, not supplementary pension."[95] It was hardly worth demanding a crackdown on welfare fraudsters for such meagre terms. Even much further back, an understanding of residuality has had considerable traction. This is captured in the letter of Jonas Crossley from Stratford (Warwickshire) to Lyndhurst (Hampshire) on 17 June 1831. Writing about Mrs Rhodes, whom the overseers had found was actually a property owner and thus a fraudster, Crossley said he was glad to hear it since selling her property might "assist her to procure some of the comforts of life for which the scanty pittance she now recives is totally inadequate although perhaps as much in the present State of things as the parish can afford."[96] Officials themselves sometimes understood that their endeavours were so scanty that investigation for fraud was unwarranted. An example is the case of Mary Chester of Basford (Nottinghamshire), who was accused of fraud because the guardians believed her four children had been (and should be) looking after her. She claimed that they were unable to help, being only poor labourers, and that to be "now parted from my children to die in a union" would "quickly bring My Grey locks with Sorrow to the grave." Officials saw little utility in pursuing the case and granted her outdoor relief.[97]

Beyond the sympathies evoked by knowledge or experience of residuality, however, we can detect a more active sympathy, even empathy, resulting in both a failure to tell and a failure to seek. Nobody sought to chase down the vagrants who Ernie Currell remembered as avoiding their allocated work by jumping over the walls of the Headington (Oxfordshire) workhouse in the 1920s.[98] Mrs D.1.P. told Elizabeth Roberts that she felt empathetic towards those struggling on the dole in the 1940s because "there is always red tape. I applied for one [a widow's pension] and I couldn't get one. I have never bothered about it since. I wasn't going to keep being insulted."[99] Writing in 2011, "kizbot" claimed that, "Even the investigators realize that the vast majority of fraud is committed by those hoping to have a little extra for Christmas or to pay off debts."[100] And somewhat further back, officials in Wighton tolerated the fact that the serial fraudster Mary Burns "Ran away for the seventh time Sep 3rd and robbed the house the 3rd time," stealing both parish property and that of other paupers. She was soon back on poor relief seemingly without any form of investigation or sanction.[101] We cannot garner a systematic perspective from such diverse and widely distributed data, but it is easy to pick up a broad sense that the pressure on officials to seek rarely reached a pitch that demanded sustained and deep, as opposed to shallow or episodic action. And while forty sets of comments referred to investigators as the lowest form of humanity, I find little evidence that they were motivated to seek "ordinary" fraudsters.

Conclusion

In chapter 3 we saw judge Angela Neild claiming that "It is not easy to detect" fraud. On the contrary, it is easily possible in a modern sense with the right resources, political will, tools, legislative framing, and intent. In this sense the disjuncture between the rhetoric of campaigns to attack fraud and the reality of detection, prosecution, and deterrence over the last three decades has been little short of woeful. This reality has strong traction in the popular imagination. In the same chapter we encountered "Zippet" arguing that the welfare system "is not fit for purpose." What they meant was that no one took seriously the need to seek, find, and punish fraud. Such views are plentiful in my recent data; commenting in 2011 "Starfinder" argued that "the powers that be have been asleep for YEARS" and had deliberately not set out to find all fraud cases as a matter of moral priority. In the same thread, "No time for deficit deniers" supposed that civil servants did not understand their own system and were not interested in pursuing all cases in order to revive the moral standing of the welfare state; and "fiflew" argued that all fraud made them "feel sick as it is them that give people like me, on benefits, a bad name;" they demanded that all cases be named and shamed.[102]

The organised agency of claimant support groups, the unwillingness of the courts to impose substantial penalties on most welfare fraudsters, and the persistent failure of government fraud units to undertake large-scale detection and evidence-gathering can be seen to coalesce in episodic "new" drives to combat welfare fraud. The modern problem is considered theoretically to be solvable by more of the same medicine. The persistence of welfare fraud and the moral and philosophical case for fraud detection, deterrence, and prevention are thus issues almost universally framed in presentist terms; a modern problem requiring modern solutions. Yet what if these same issues were consistently played out in the historical record? If the persistence of welfare fraud needs to be understood over centuries rather than decades? If episodic crackdowns on welfare fraud were a feature of centuries and not decades? If current failures are rooted in the repetitive structural weakness of the British central state?

This sort of historically grounded approach would lead us to question the motives of policymakers and officials in allowing fraud to persist and also to look at the way the public has understood benefit fraud within their wider grasp of the meaning of welfare. We might in fact find that welfare fraud persists because it is in no one's interest that it be eliminated, an idea that in turn would necessitate a radically different policy offer for the future. Focussing on the question of how much fraud officials "find" once the process of seeking has been commenced – the subject of the next chapter – throws these suggestions into sharp relief.

CHAPTER 9

To Find or Not to Find?

Reflecting on life in Stratford-upon-Avon in the early 1900s, George Hewins recounted a scene in the crowded courtyard where he lived with his wife and family. Keeping behind the curtains – "it was a daft chap poked his nose into women's quarrels" – he peered out at the scene:

> At first I thought it was the Relieving Officer come. He called at the houses with the money for the widows. He wanted to know where they worked and what they earned and what their character was – all for four shillings a week, or two if they lived with their children. Generally he was alright about her mother [Hewins's mother-in-law, with whom they lodged]; well he knowed the money wouldn't allow her to have beer much.

Hewins was actually overhearing an argument with the rent collector, but the fact that his first thoughts turned to the welfare system is important and symbolic.[1] For this chapter, the key observation is that the relieving officer *normally* entwined his giving of allowances with seeking information in a seeming attempt to find welfare fraud.[2]

Yet there are other interpretations. Working-class and poor neighbourhoods like these teemed with gossip and transient and more permanent enmities, as Hewins himself recounts admirably well.[3] Nonetheless, when it came to the presence of the relieving officer, ranks were closed. Hewins does not relate a single instance of snitching, as perhaps we might have expected from chapter 7.[4] The question for this chapter, however, is why the relieving officer asked his questions in the first place; no educated man of this town could have expected to get useful information from such enquiries. In other words, the questions were designed to be asked but not answered.[5] More than this, the relieving officer actively colluded in fraud;

the allowance to Hewins's mother-in-law ought to have been reduced or removed to allow for co-resident children.

We can see the consistent analogue of these observations in the minute books of New Poor Law guardians. Those for Belford (Northumberland) in the 1880s are typical. Each meeting opened with a statement that the clerk had examined (but not interrogated) the books of the workhouse master and relieving officer. Yet the minutes are replete with instances in which the relieving officer had failed to detect fraud: not enquiring into the finances of people applying for help in burying dead relatives (October 1883); failing to inspect outdoor relief recipients such that the guardians had to convene an extraordinary meeting to review cases themselves (June 1884) – straight afterwards a line was added to the formulaic opening: "and ascertained that the relief had been given in accordance with the instructions of the Guardians" – and neglecting the accounts (June 1886).[6] Such failings, deep into the New Poor Law period, tell us much about the (non)intent to find fraud.

This chapter, ranging across the period from 1601 to the present as others have done, takes up these themes. It argues that official reactions to suspected fraud are characterised not simply by a failure to seek, but also by a failure to *find*. The argument centres around four observations: first, that in many investigations evidence that could easily be discovered and used was not; second, that the majority of fraud cases are abandoned or reconciled before prosecution; third, that advocates and other third-party interventions often have fundamental impacts on the trajectory of cases, so that only certain types of fraudsters are pursued to the very end; and finally (to develop a theme first visited in chapter 8) that the punishments for fraud have been so weak that policymakers, judges, and civil servants could be understood as not being remotely serious about challenging fraud cultures. The chapter will also rehearse normative explanations for not-finding, including some that are implicated in the failure to seek. However, I will also argue: that officials and others collude in not prosecuting fraud because they recognise the structural and functional flaws of the British welfare system and are willing to accept some degree of fiction in the claims made; that all parties accept there is an opportunity cost to prosecution which lies in the detection of a slew of minor rule breaches requiring more direct action; and that non-prosecution manifests a desire to contain the reputational damage to the welfare system that widespread pursuit of fraudsters would involve.

Not Finding Evidence

For focus group attendees, people talking to me in chance encounters, and those responding to online material, the damning evidence of welfare fraud in individual cases would be obvious with even the slightest turning over of stones. This observation is well captured by "stalag14," commenting (in 2013) on a 2008 article calling for the government to "Make dole scroungers work for benefits." And, in a comment otherwise sympathetic to the situation of those on welfare, they added a tongue-in-cheek postscript: "We have never seen a single parent female so popular as one of our neighbours; a Housing Association Tenant with three kids by three different men, an endless parade of males coming and going, she must have a great personality! And she gets to lie in every morning because she is on benefits."[7] In practice, however, prosecutable "evidence" constitutes more than hearsay, as we see in documentaries such as "The Block" from 1972.[8] Focussing on the tenants of a condemned housing estate ("Chaucer") in Southwark, part of the programme dealt with the "spying" methods used by welfare officials. Residents "subject to inspection and suspicion" were "even suspicious of each other." Yet this attention rarely ended with sustainable action against welfare claimants. Investigators needed – and struggled to obtain – the permission of the landlord to be on the estate and faced people who had the support of a knowledgeable community.[9]

In turn, seemingly "clear" evidence can usually be subject to multiple readings or weakened by subtleties that surface under careful interrogation. We do not have national statistics on the number of cases that collapse because of problems with evidence, but websites of law firms with some specialism in welfare reveal significant instances where this happens.[10] Many of those I have encountered in writing this book had an awareness of such complexities; but there is also a deeply ingrained suspicion that officials do not *want* to find evidence, complex or otherwise. Such views are encapsulated by "Roy" who suggested:

> Now and again they'll take somebody to court, so that they can trumpet that they are on the ball, and that cheats beware. They [civil servants] are aided and abetted by our legal system who will hand down "stiff" sentences like doing 50 hours unpaid work AND a slap on the wrist, for stealing thousands.[11]

In the longer term, the complexities of effective finding are laid bare in post-1945 parliamentary debate. Of more than forty such encounters, the 24,726 words expended in 2001 over the final reading of the Social Security Fraud Bill are particularly telling. The government revealed plans for those convicted of fraud more than once to lose their access to welfare, introducing new measures against colluding employers, and adding a raft of new investigatory powers. Yet the latter powers were to be "tightly controlled" and held by only 175 authorised officers across the entire country.[12] The ensuing debate rapidly moved to discussion of how already poor people could be effectively sanctioned, the proportionality of punishment, whether welfare fraud was actually an appropriate locus for such intrusive powers, the costs of working with welfare investigators, transnational fraud, and the moral value of intruding so heavily into the lives of the poor. David Willetts, MP, thus sought to remind the House that "Political will and organisational discipline are at least as important as legal powers," a comment that feeds directly into my father's observations about fraud investigation around the same date.[13] Thus, while instruction manuals on detecting and prosecuting fraud suggest the opportunity to compose a fearsome array of evidence, we can be struck by how often these powers are *not* used to their fullest extent.[14] The same conclusion can be drawn from the statistical appendices to the 1973 report of the committee investigating welfare abuse.[15]

Many of the people who engaged in casual conversations with me once they knew I was writing this book constructed the issue of not finding evidence, or not using it to follow the full possibilities of the law, as being effectively modern. In the words of one medical consultant who happened to be interested in my subject as well as my teeth, "the system has become too complex; people can just slide down the cracks." This presentism is misleading. Suffusing the historical material is a sense that those tasked with collecting and using evidence did not do so, that the value of evidence collected was undermined by the intended ambiguity of rules, and that there were limits to the investigatory powers of officers once a decision to seek had been taken. We have already seen this with George Hewins, but several further brief case studies can ground the perspective. Should investigators, for instance, execute the full extent of their powers against people who commit fraud because of dangerous circumstances? This is an obvious modern conundrum in the context of domestic abuse. But there are also profound resonances in the historical sources, as for instance in the case of Emma Locke, who, with her children, sought out the workhouse as a refuge from such abuse in 1877 only to find herself suspected of fraudulent intent. It would have been easy for investigating officials to seek out the moral character, economic circumstances, and history of Locke, and no doubt they would have found circumstances that justified harsh action. In practice, and following the logic of the conundrum over how far to use powers, the officials instead focussed on the husband. They refused to believe his subsequent promise "not to illuse her in the future" and upon further inquiry felt that the man "would murder her if she returned to him." Locke was thus given relief and her husband charged for it, but the officials still had to justify their position in not following the evidence to its fullest extent.[16]

Mr C.1.P., speaking to Elizabeth Roberts about the immediate postwar period in Preston (Lancashire), highlights a further continuity between past and present. After his sister-in-law was abandoned and maintenance payments from her estranged husband stopped, Mr C.1.P. was amazed that the welfare authorities did nothing. So he went to London, found the chap himself and got him before the law: "the fact that I had discovered him after half a day's leave from the mill ... was a very good bit of detective work" and something that could easily have been achieved by officials truly interested in finding fraud. More tellingly, the policeman who eventually assisted him "said they get a lot of cases" where the general public were the ones tracking down fraudsters.[17] Even where evidence was clearly presented, however, ambiguity of circumstance or rules could limit its use. When the overseer of Brighton wrote to his counterpart in Lewes (both Sussex) on 22 June 1826, he noted that Mary Porter had received £1 from both Brighton and Lewes for the burial of a child, and that "if she received the money of both parties, she must of defrauded you or this parish therefore if she does not repay you the parish will endeavour to punish her for the fraud." The possibility of pursuing and punishing Porter was complicated because "it was an aunt of Mary Portor's that wrote, as she stated by the desire of her Niece," such that the fraud could have happened by miscommunication. She was eventually allowed to repay the amount in instalments.[18] Shifting our attention to Scotland, post-1845 Glasgow inspectors of the poor, knowing that the claims of many Irish paupers to have settled status were untrue, had neither the time nor the community support needed to investigate the back history of prior residence.[19]

This evidence is not systematic, and I do not of course argue that fraud prosecutions were fleetingly rare, evidence-gathering unintrusive, or that we cannot see episodic attempts to find and use evidence at scale. But stories like these emblematize a strong signal across the data; that concerns about the effectiveness of evidence-gathering and its fullest use to confront fraud characterise all organisational forms of the welfare state. The relieving officer encountered by George Hewins could not have hoped to find useful evidence. Many before and after him can be understood as setting out not to find. Such attitudes were baked into the very DNA of the British welfare system. This matters for the way welfare fraud has been and is constructed, and also for the ways in which the British public understand the role and future of that welfare state. Other dimensions to not finding fraud tend in the same direction.

Abandoned and Reconciled Cases

As previous chapters have suggested, we find "big" numbers associated with fraud investigations. Parliamentarians were reminded in 2001 that ten thousand annual prosecutions were supplemented by ten thousand further cases in which people "receive cautions and penalties as an alternative to prosecution." More widely, *Hansard* carries estimates of the savings arising from investigations in the post-1945 period, often running into the hundreds of millions or billions of pounds. Such figures are highly questionable. They are underpinned by hypothecation processes that report not the amount recovered from fraudsters, nor even the repayment orders handed down by courts, but the amount of money that *would have been* lost had the fraudsters been allowed to continue their claims.[20] Even so, extended newspaper commentary, taking hold particularly after the publication of Robin Page's *Benefits Racket* exposé in 1971, gives weight to a sense of aggressive and effective finding. The ferocity of commentary from interest groups about aggressive prosecution also gives the impression of a determined intent to find fraud in the modern period.[21] This is brilliantly captured by "angryhungry," who (replying to an earlier thread that fraudsters were stealing from "ordinary people") said: "they are [actually] stealing from the Exchequer. Pursue them with such disproportionate force as described in this article and they most likely will be stealing from those just like them soon."[22] In other words, sustained pursuit of fraud and fraudsters merely creates future burglars. What these sources collectively miss, however, is the observation that for much of the post-1945 period not only did the majority of all investigations that were initiated result in no prosecution, but very significant numbers of them were abandoned without other cautions or sanctions either.[23] In the BBC documentary "To Catch a Cheat" most cases were considered solved once someone had signed themselves off welfare, and no other sanction was invoked.[24]

Given inadequate reporting and record-keeping, and the various investigative bodies (national, regional, and local) involved, it is difficult to reliably quantify this situation.[25] Even so, the fragmentary evidence on case-closures and alternatives to prosecution is striking. In a 2003 parliamentary answer, the government suggested that it had success-fully prosecuted 62,330 people between 1997 and 2003, and that local authorities had prosecuted a further 7,660 cases. Figures for the numbers of people who were given other penalties were not available for 1997 or 1998, but hypothecating from the data available thereafter suggests that some 91,750 cases resulted in sanctions short of prosecution, with this number accelerating relative to prosecutions over time. Further evidence in different parliamentary answers reveals that over the same period there had been 1,093,627 calls to the benefit fraud hotline, alongside some 916,000 other case leads. Again, hypothecating missing figures for 1997 and 1998, it can be estimated that some 460,000 investigations were initiated between 1997 and 2003, and that at least 298,000 of those cases were abandoned with no penalty or prosecution.[26] In 1971 some 7,130 prosecutions were undertaken by the then DHSS out of a total "considered for proceedings" of 23,962. A further 11,320 cases were closed before final sanction and 29,000 went no further than initial investigation. Thus, just 11% of all cases that were opened resulted in formal prosecution.[27]

Once again, we must not think that these observations are somehow tied to the particular complexities of the modern welfare system. Even if we cannot garner "national" figures from the historical data, one of its most remarkable features is the persistent failure to prosecute or even mean-ingfully sanction when authorities had the chance. There are thousands of cases like that of Mary Shelbourne, who applied to the Stamford poor law union in September 1874 seeking an allowance for her son. Since he was in fact dead, this was a case of very deliberate fraud. On 9 September 1874 the relieving officer was authorised "to take proceedings against Mary Shelbourne for attempting to obtain money from the Guardians by false pretences." One week later, however, she "attended the Meeting [of Guardians] and having apologized for her conduct and promised not to repeat the same was reprimanded by the Chairman."[28] The offer and acceptance of an apology in this case has considerable resonance in modern commentary on blogs and newspaper articles where writers, even those who had visceral views on welfare fraud, point to the fact that politicians defrauding their expenses were often allowed merely to apologize whereas ordinary people got prosecuted.

Much *suspected* fraud also went unexplored and unpunished. To give one example, Sarah Wadsworth of Sheffield agreed in two letters, of July and September 1809, to take charge of her sister and apprentice her in return for an allowance of 3 shillings per week. By February 1811 no such apprenticeship had taken place, and a pseudonymous "nobody" sent a hastily written note in pencil to complain that "Sheffield overseers are paying 3/ a week to Hannah Wordsworth a pauper of yours: I think she is quite able to earn her own living, & that hers is a case of imposition which claims your investigation." The allowance was duly removed, and in April 1811 the overseers decided they would apprentice Hannah themselves. They did not, however, seek repayment of the three years' worth of defrauded payments.[29] A century earlier, Anne Grant wrote from Banbury to Reverend Robert Bowshaw of Wooton (Oxfordshire) to say that under the law she must be allowed a house and maintenance, and implored him, notwithstanding her shady history involving supposed abandonment, to "let the clarke acquaint your own feares of the poor and the inhabitance of the town that they may take some care of me."[30] Grant's was perhaps not so very different from the "bad cases" who stayed in or persistently returned to the workhouse in twentieth-century Barrow-in-Furness (Cumbria). There was, claimed Mr B.1.B., "something about their own make-up" which made these people idle but, as far as he knew, none were punished or prosecuted.[31]

In 2011 "Parr3" wrote about widespread welfare fraud being "entirely obvious" to anyone willing to look at Facebook. They suggested: "We should have more of these investigators and – OK if they don't want to prosecute for small amounts, they should still interview under caution … a prison sentence

… that'd deter them." At several levels – obvious evidence not collected, lack of investigators, an unwillingness to follow up "small" fraud, and the lack of proper prosecution – these views speak keenly to the idea that modern officials are not much interested in eliminating fraud.[32] Yet "Parr3" was in effect elaborating a sentiment and observation that could have been made anytime since 1601. It is also important against this backdrop to understand not just how many cases of fraud were prosecuted or otherwise sanctioned, but *who* those fraudsters were. In an important recent project David Walsh et al. conducted a two-level investigation of decisions by welfare fraud investigators on whether to proceed or not to proceed with prosecutions. In one strand they analysed field notes from actual cases. In a second, they asked fraud investigators (stratified for length of experience) to make decisions on hypothetical cases. Broadly, they found that such investigators tended to proceed to criminal prosecution – to officially "find" welfare fraud, as it were – when evidence was easy to obtain, when their experience and knowledge of prior cases suggested the evidence would be of a type to win a prosecution, and if that evidence could easily be calibrated to proving the type of fraud under consideration.[33] These observations fit seamlessly to my interviews with former officials, who universally claimed that the evidence bar needed in order to obtain "meaningful" conviction was so high that it was usually not worth pursuing cases; and they align with episodic media coverage – positive or negative – that mentions the relatively low chances of criminal prosecution.[34]

Given the thrust of chapters 3 to 6, it is unsurprising that particular sections of the dependent poor might be more subject to evidence-gathering, enforcement, and prosecution than others. But these observations are more than that; they highlight a preference for certainty, speed, and ease rather than effect and effectiveness. The historical resonance of this idea is profound; we see it played out in dramas such as *Boys from the Blackstuff*, in interviews, and also on the pages of traditional manuscript sources. In 1857, for instance, Ann Boswell could not understand why officials of the Birmingham Incorporation did not take action against the welfare fraud and criminal activities of her own sixteen-year-old daughter, who "would rob me of anything she could lay her hands upon," had defrauded tradesmen in the town, and preferred to rely on welfare rather than work. "There was not a worse girl in Birmingham," Ann concluded; "she is not to be believed in anything she says even upon her oath" and there could be no justification for not pursuing her to the full extent of the law.[35] A century earlier John Thorpe of Derby was incredulous that officials would rather "pursew old women and children then take the lawe to him [Peter Vale] that has set himself to deceive the parish year after year."[36] And, as we have seen, seventeenth- and early-eighteenth-century guidance manuals for justices of the peace and overseers assumed that neither officials nor the general public were serious about tackling determined vagrants. In short, a failure to find fraud – to comprehensively root it out – is not a matter of resource, technique, or intricate balancing by the state of individuals' rights to privacy and freedom from suspicion with their obligations as honest welfare citizens. Rather it reflects systemic flaws at the heart of the conduct of the British welfare state. In this, suspicions that third-party support allows people to escape the full extent of the law also have a place.

Third-Party Interventions

Readers will recall my account in the preface of being a third party in relation to my father. For "Jethro" I would fall into the category of "the do goders [sic] that defend them. Let's hope Covid wipes a lot of these lardy assess out."[37] In the post-1970 period I would be joined in the popular imagination of this category by MPs,[38] lawyers, Citizens Advice bureaus, local and national campaigning organisations, self-help groups,[39] doctors (especially post-2010), social workers,[40] employers, and immigrant associations. It is impossible to discern how effective such third parties have been in short-circuiting the investigation process, but they appear with notable regularity in newspaper, oral, and commentary sources that cover the period from the 1970s.[41]

Yet, the role of third-party activists runs chronologically much deeper than this. It extends to determined individuals confronting the ambiguities of different welfare types in the interwar and post-1945 periods; organized labour and clerical interventions of the eighteenth and nineteenth centuries; and employers or former employers throughout the period. In practice, three forms of intervention – passive or contextual, group, and individual – shaped the likelihood of officials "finding" fraud in the past. At the passive level we encounter people like George Savage, who in 1839 authored a pamphlet alleging that the Altrincham poor law union (Cheshire) had facilitated "The death of four children of one family, from starvation at Flixton," as a result of its persistent refusal to grant adequate relief to a family that they thought were imposing. He invited readers to "judge of the blessings the new poor law affords those who are so unfortunate as to fall under its iron grasp."[42] Other passive interventions included autonomous decisions on the part of magistrates. In 1809, for instance, Justice of the Peace Robert Houseman wrote from Lancaster (Lancashire) to tell officials that after the death of James Bagnes he had slightly reduced the amount of allowance given to his widow but would continue it whether the parish agreed or not.[43]

It was, however, usually a more active type of intervention that limited the ability of the state and its actors to successfully curtail fraud. From the 1820s forwards, groups and collectives become intricately tied into the process. We see this evidenced in a linguistic sense by the emergence in free-form letters under the Old Poor Law of phrases stating or meaning "we the undersigned." After 1834, formally constituted citizen and interest groups emerge strongly as advocates for the poor, alongside trade unions, including for instance the Watch Committee and Parochial Protection Association of the Parish of St Matthew Bethnal Green, the Social Science Association, the Liverpool Association of Unemployed, the Ripon Society for the Relief of the Poor, the Conference of St Vincent de Paul, and the Battersea Residents Association.[44] For the twentieth century I have counted seventy-six collectives that were (or were suspected of) helping fraudsters. Most modern chat and blog sites also provide further evidence for the important role of third-party groups. By way of example, tracking through the 539 comments and responses to a 2012 plea for information from someone who had committed fraud reveals the presence of staff members of well-known advice charities actively trawling the site for referrals.[45]

Above all, however, the local (and sometimes regional or national) power of individual advocates has a signature in my data. This is unsurprising. Under the Old and New Poor Law, advocates played a key role in the process through which individuals negotiated their relief and navigated the unequal power structures of the welfare system.[46] There is less appreciation of their role in preventing action even where evidence of fraud was clear. In 1854 the former vicar of Deddington (Oxfordshire) intervened with the relieving officer in the case of Mr J. Matthews, who had fraudulently claimed support for burying a dead child while not admitting his substantial weekly income.[47] The Reverend Clough of Mold (Flintshire) performed a

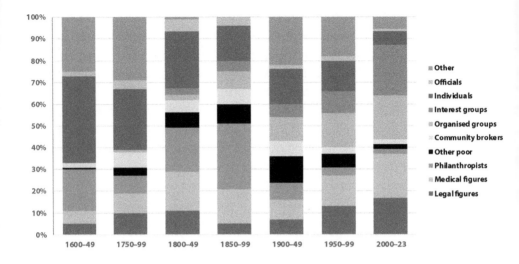

9.1 The changing composition of do-goodery.
Notes: The graph incorporates both ascribed advocacy ("doctors are complicit in …") and practical or claimed advocacy. *Source:* All material listed in the bibliography where advocacy was noted, inferred, or claimed.

similar advocacy role for the serial fraudster Eleanor Beck in 1827, arguing that "unless the clergy extend themselves on behalf of the poor they are too often neglected."[48] And between 1834 and the early 1900s there are 140 instances of Catholic clergy advocating for paupers, many deploying the argument that because the person *was* a Catholic they had been judged as inherently untrustworthy. Doctors, landlords, and even officials talking to other officials fulfilled the same advocacy functions prior to the 1900s. By the interwar period, as knowledge of new rules-based systems spread, the poor themselves became very effective advocates in their own right, as for instance in the case of Mr B.1.B., interviewed by Elizabeth Roberts, who radicalized dole queues in the late 1920s.[49] On reading his recollections, it is possible to be struck by the remarkable linguistic, rhetorical, and practical similarities between B.1.B. and Daniel Blake confronting the welfare system of the twenty-first century. Many comments on modern newspaper articles also identify individuals and "types" of people who deliberately frustrate the application of justice to scroungers.

This said, there have been significant changes in the ranks of actual or suspected "do-gooders" over the period covered here. Figure 9.1 seeks to broadly categorise the background of every advocate in my data over fifty-year periods. The results are striking; they include the consistent presence of medical and legal backgrounds on the one hand, and the long-term decline of advocacy on the part of philanthropists and officials on the other. Returning to the comment from "Roy" that officials would "Now and again … take somebody to court," we might thus understand that the people caught "now and again" were not simply the single mothers, immigrants, and disabled who were the focus of chapter 4. Rather, what really increased the risk of being pursued and prosecuted is and was being friendless or unsupported. When the 1998 green paper *New Ambitions for our Country: A New Contract for Welfare* sought to create a system "dedicated to rooting out fraud and abuse," what its authors really intended was to root out abuse on the part of the friendless. The role of advocacy is well captured by a 2014 focus group participant who noted that she had been convicted of welfare fraud in the 1990s even though others with similar records "got off," merely because "I didn't have anyone to stand up for me."[50] The net effect of advocacy, however, is and was definitely to limit both seeking *and* finding activity.[51]

Risible Punishment

A depressing sense of the persistence of welfare charlatans is engraved deeply in the public imagination and indelibly linked in the modern sources to the attitudes of courts towards such people. On 11 July 2020 the *Daily Mail* and other papers carried the story of Christina Pomfrey. Falsifying multiple identities, she had claimed to be blind, to suffer from MS, and to have other disabilities, thus establishing entitlement to welfare payments amounting to "a staggering £13,000 per month." Defrauding different parts of the welfare system to the tune of over £1m, she invented ownership of a series of newsagents to explain lavish spending and deceive her husband. The case has resonance with themes explored cumulatively in this book: Pomfrey was not "dobbed in" by her neighbours even though "we knew she was cheating the system"; illustrating the singular problem of divesting fraudsters from welfare entitlement, she launched "another bogus claim while out on bail"; and the judge in the case accused her of stealing money from her "fellow citizens. Money which could have gone to people who justly deserved it." But the case has particular traction for this chapter. Notwithstanding a DWP claim that "our detection systems make use of increasingly sophisticated techniques to identify discrepancies and thwart those seeking to rip-off taxpayers," Pomfrey had evaded detection for years. When she was prosecuted and jailed, Minister for Welfare Delivery Will Quince was quoted as saying that her sentence sent a clear message to benefit cheats. But what message? The cost of the year-long operation was not revealed but would have been substantial. Although Pomfrey had a sentence of over three years, she would have served only months, and the taxpayer recouped no money because by then Pomfrey had no assets. Indeed, upon leaving prison she would have gone straight back on benefits. The message is clear enough but not one that Quince would much have liked.[52]

In practice, and to revisit a theme from earlier in the chapter, most of the cases I have traced for the period from 1980 to the present resulted in punishments short of a custodial sentence, even for multiple sequential fraud. The failure to fully sanction serial fraudsters is striking, given 2022 rules that allow withdrawal of benefits for thirty-six months in the case of a third offence, and a plethora of Acts that allow significant custodial sentences. These failures should not surprise us. As 2014 guidance from the Sentencing Council makes clear, courts have specific reference criteria to allow them to balance culpability, harm, and aggravating factors which collectively tend away from jail or other significant punishment.[53] As one wag noted to me in a Rutland butcher's shop in 2022: "Do you know that even people who have done fraud lots of time get to keep their Christmas bonus? A present for frauding – you could not make it up."[54] In turn, the lack of custodial sentences has become part of the acquired ecology of knowledge about the welfare state. The 539 answers to the Mumsnet article cited above came back repeatedly to the theme that "my experience is that most cases are given community service and/or a suspended sentence," while many contributors considered even this sort of accountability to be harsh.[55] More widely, just over 14 per cent of the commentaries collected and analysed for this book suggested that community service and limited repayment orders (in the case of prosecution) and cautions or sanctions (in the case of investigations not ending up in court) were appropriate. Some constructed the imposition of sanctions as a plot to demonise welfare claimants. "Bulldog" wrote in 2011: "benefit claimants are being deliberately set up to fail in order to achieve sanction quotas."[56]

Most comments did not adopt this subtle view, eliding such outcomes with a soft, left-leaning, and contemptuous set of judges.[57] Perhaps this genre of sources is autocorrelated to such views, but the same broad perspective can be found in focus groups, casual conversations, and oral histories. Moreover, some MPs have also been critical of the courts; Alistair Darling, for one, expressed "frustration that sometimes the court system has not been as efficient or as enthusiastic as we might like in dealing robustly with people who have been guilty of benefit fraud."[58] He would perhaps have agreed with a 2014 focus group which, in more than twenty minutes of sustained discussion, highlighted such perceived failings: fines that would never be paid or enforced; community service work that could be avoided by claiming illness or childcare needs; repeat offenders being allowed to endlessly reapply for welfare; suspended sentences that were not then enforced; sanctioned benefits that did not end up being sanctioned; and sustained disinterest[59] in pursuing the "obvious" characters and groups likely to commit fraud.[60] One focus group participant even contacted me again in 2022 to say that they had read a BBC piece talking about fraud in which officials were quoted as being "frustrated" at the "unwillingness of senior civil servants who oversee universal credit to tackle rising fraud levels."[61] The former participant noted: "I damn well told you; I was right all along."[62]

It is natural to assume that the legal process for punishing fraud was harsher in the immediate post-1945 period, and even more so before that. But on the contrary, leniency or laxity was often the case as well. William Haynes found himself "not in a State for the Exertion attending the punishment of this Villain" Thomas Potter, who would rather lounge on poor relief than work.[63] William Story – "naturly saucey and idle too much so even to work himself or clean his own shoes" – escaped punishment from the overseers of Wimbledon despite fraudulently obtaining relief.[64] William Leeson – a "scoundrel, and a vagabond" – turned the tables on the poor law guardians of Chelsea when accused of fraudulent activity by submitting a formal complaint against them.[65] Modern comments on newspaper articles often make similar points that the best way to avoid legal sanction is to find a way to complain about process and conduct. Thomas Simcox Lea wondered what was to become of the country if officials failed to deal with scoundrels such as "James Oakes [who] had got his wife's daughter with child – I mean the daughter of his wife by a former husband." Further:

Are helpless girls – I had almost said <u>children</u> again, [this] I crossed out the word before – are helpless exposed girls to be left at the mercy of married men in whose houses they live – of overlookers in Mills who employ & discharge them at pleasure – and are men who know the force of sexual passions, to legislate as tho' these girls could protect themselves?[66]

And what were the vestrymen of Liverpool to do with the Irish servant Mary Keating, who insisted: "I do not want to be sent back to Dublin. If I am sent I will come back again"?[67] At an earlier date, seventeenth-century magistrates found themselves frustrated by the fact that officials would rather pay Irish and Scottish fraudsters than prosecute. For the interwar period we might contrast the memories of Mrs H.7.P. of her mother being summarily ejected from the sickness welfare list because she had been caught doing her own housework, with the memories of "GC," who was told by relatives about numerous people "signing on" while still wearing their painter overalls.[68] There is little sense in the historical or current record, then, that ordinary people believe either welfare officials or the legal system to be "serious" about tackling immediate welfare fraud or dissuading future fraudsters. Hence, "Hamshaw" asked without irony: "Can anybody recall ANY benefit scrounger being given a custodial sentence for fraud?"[69]

Explaining Not Finding

Some of the factors that limit initial seeking also help determine how many perpetrators officials "find," and who they are. These factors include questions of cost. The 1997 Social Security Administration (Fraud) Act gave investigators wide powers to acquire information from third parties as they thought "necessary." It devoted a full four pages to ensuring that civil servants and local authorities did as directed by the Act, but only gave three references (somewhat under one page) about meeting enforcement costs. Within five years parliamentarians were learning that the cost of each prosecution arising out of hotline reporting was roughly £20,000. Because these costs were so widely distributed within and between government departments, there was no way of putting an exact figure on the financial burden either in absolute terms or in relation to repayments obtained. The inference that prosecutions were and are rationed because of cost can clearly be seen both in law (the 1997 Act devoted three pages to recovery options instead of prosecution, ultimately acknowledging that only a small fraction of fines would be paid) and in practice. In the documentary "To Catch a Cheat," it is striking how little catching is done. The inspectors nudge – "I don't want to force you," "Everything's going to be all right," "It's not for me to make decisions for you" – and hint at the answers they want the person to give, leading them away from the prosecution (and thus formal "finding") line. As Inspector Henrietta Bess acknowledged in the programme, the intent was to get people to sign off willingly and "only the more serious cases lead to prosecution."[70]

This basic tension between law and practice percolates through all the modern sources used here. In comments on welfare fraud articles and posts across different platforms, the discrepancies between costs and the small amounts saved or retrieved are part of the basic DNA; and while some commentators push strongly for prosecution no matter what the cost, so as to properly deter fraudsters, most are more fatalistic.[71] Along these lines, "frozennorth" argued that it is not worth spending "A shed load of money for probably not much"; "Katewashere" reasoned, "Surely it costs more money to catch benefit cheats than just to let them get on with it"; and "princesschipchops" noted, "That is just crazy maths." Similar cost-benefit dilemmas have an insistent presence in the historical record. On 20 December 1821, for instance, Broughton parish (Hampshire) found it impractical to prosecute Thomas Olden for fraud and hence he was "to have a shirt if he will promise the officer to leave of thieving."[72] Thirty-six years later the guardians of Reeth (Yorkshire) were challenged by the PLB for wanting to give able-bodied miners outdoor relief *en masse* both as a matter of common sense given labour practices in the area, and because they simply had no means of weeding out fraudsters from genuine claimants without considerable cost.[73] In the same vein, "RK" remembered that welfare officials were given the run-around by the inhabitants of his boyhood Oxford council estate until they ran out of money and time to continue.[74]

A second variable that limits both seeking *and* finding is the way in which the absence of punishments, alongside a lack of court capacity, unstable budgets,[75] the role of third parties in restoring benefits rather than merely frustrating investigation,[76] and stifling red tape create a demoralised cohort of staff who accept that they can do nothing meaningful and so don't. Robin Page in 1971 spoke persuasively about the demoralisation of frontline investigative staff, but this was not new either before or after that time. Olive Malvery wrote compellingly in 1907 of the cursory checking done by dispirited staff in London vagrant wards when undertaking her social investigation work; applicants were questioned and "answers were entered into the book, often without even a look at the speaker" even though they were "answered with more or less truth by each applicant." Indeed, a whole second level of investigation had to be created because of this very demoralisation.[77] A century later, and as I outlined in the preface, one of the investigators involved in my father's case spoke just as strongly about the deflating effects of having to find examples to pursue as the political winds changed.

To these familiar variables we can add fear of reprisals or other retaliatory action on the part of those prosecuted. Comments on "investigation type" stories in recent newspapers often portray investigative staff as immoral or inadequate but some also go as far as to label them "scum" and suggest aggressive actions. The purchase of these fears is realised in the story of 'IG,' who resigned as an investigator in 2010 after an organised gang tracked down his family home and sent him an inscribed gravestone.[78] We rarely get the same degree of intimacy through historical sources, but in 1830 Mr Fry, assistant overseer, who had engaged with vigour in detection of fraud for Fawley parish (Hampshire), was run out of town by "50 or 60 persons."[79] Under the New Poor Law, Julie-Marie Strange notes, relieving officers like those whom George Hewins recounted overhearing in the opening of this chapter would often end up back in the communities where they had been responsible for investigating welfare, and fear of retrospective retribution may have limited their actions.[80] More widely, I can find numerous examples of actual or threatened violence against union officers involved in investigation and prosecution, as for instance with Cardiff guardians who in December 1855 asked Poor Law Board permission to "employ a detective Police officer from London" to identify and punish the author(s) of "a series of anonymous letters from Inmates of the Workhouse threatening to shoot the Chairman."[81]

These are significant observations, albeit based on disjointed data, but they also divert attention from the central reason for the lack of enforcement or finding, which is that officials and the public collude – both passively and actively – in the non-prosecution of fraud. Giving one example of passive collusion, Bernhard Reiger argues that, although the characters in *Boys from the Blackstuff* committed fraud the audiences reframed them as "struggling for material and moral survival" and "legitimately sidestepping and challenging rules and regulations that had been forced upon them by external circumstances."[82] There is something of the same lesson in the rhetoric of a 2001 parliamentary debate in which Alistair Darling argued that he had met both ordinary people and MPs "who say that benefit fraud does not really matter." His views were echoed by Kali Mountford, MP, who was amazed that "a large group of people believe that those who commit fraud have some excuse for doing so." They even cited the Kilroy TV programme in which people denied acting fraudulently because, given "pressure to maintain a certain standard of living," they *ought* to be able to buy the latest trainers. In the same debate Peter Lilley, MP, thought that a "two strikes and you are out" policy was too severe for the "small guy" who was "guilty of a modest element of abuse of the system." Christopher Chope, MP, similarly referred to "trivial" fraud, contrasting bob-a-jobbers with the "serious, professional fraudster."[83] This passive or latent desire not to pursue fraud seeps easily into current public consciousness – there are hundreds of comments whose writers were amazed at inspectors letting welfare recipients know when they would be coming – but it too has lineage in historical sources. The Putney vestry was clearly breaking the law when it allowed Mrs Stevens to write off the sums given to support her pauperised mother against her own poor rate bill in September 1819.[84] Alan Dent remembered the Oxford police force of the 1950s giving beggars, robbers, and fraudsters lifts out of the city rather than prosecuting such people to limited effect.[85] And in the middle of our period, the guardians of Reeth knew very well that they were turning a blind eye when they asked for permission to give outdoor relief to Phillis Brunskill and her eleven children, something codified in a sharp rebuke from the Poor Law Board in which it was suggested that her "destitution is very questionable," given that she must herself have been in some form of work and some of the children must have been capable of earning.[86]

Active collusion has an equally forceful presence. We see it in online fora where former or current investigating staff give advice on how to foil the system. More widely there are 298 comments between 2010 and 2022 in which writers alleged or cited active collusion. This process reveals itself particularly strongly through the historical sources too: in officials from the City of London poor law union, who systematically ignored paupers tapping City charities to augment welfare payments; in Ralph Blackwell, who was amazed that the overseers of Brockenhurst (Hampshire) had colluded with Martha Springer – whose "Word is Not Worth anything" – to extort money out of him for fathering an illegitimate child when he was plainly not guilty;[87] and in L.1.P. of Preston, who told Elizabeth Roberts in detail about his 1941 interactions with the Labour Exchange: he calculated that it was better for his income to remain on welfare than to work and, having "explained all my circumstances to him," the "Labour Officer … thought I was doing the right thing" and would have been "a fool to carry on in employment."[88]

Active collusion is perhaps personified by John Skinner, who was always frustrating the purpose of the welfare system even as he complained about the dependence culture of poor people. In November 1823, for instance, he bargained with the vestry over Widow Garrett: if the "Parish would continue the five shilling she received weekly for herself and two small children," then "she would contrive to pay one-half the house-rent." This notwithstanding that she was an acknowledged fraudster and he himself also referred to her as that "bad woman" and contrasted the relief she received with exclusions elsewhere, such that "parish pay is made an engine of mischief; the worthy and religious being set aside, and the bad are rewarded."[89] More directly, in November 1832 he encountered Mrs Moon (whose sister ran a bawdy house) as she was on her way to seek parish relief. Notwithstanding her suspect moral character and the implied income from managing prostitutes, Skinner "gave her five shillings" and "begged she would not mention to anyone that I had given it, but keep it to themselves, since if it were known that I did anything for them it would prevent the assistance they ought to receive from the parish."[90] These stories demonstrate consistency of experience across the different organisational forms of the welfare state and might be read as suggesting that community knowledge of active collusion reduces the stigma and moral cost of fraud.[91]

Figure 9.2 codifies every identified instance of collusion into a number of types. Defining collusion naturally rests on subjective judgement, and a single source (such as Skinner's diary) can yield multiple instances, not all of which would be classified in the same way. The categories defined here (based upon 5,068 examples) are thus broad and fluid. Even so, the lessons are instructive, pointing to a wide variety of ways in which those wielding welfare power frustrate the very rules they are notionally

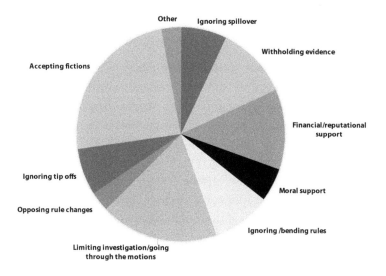

9.2 Categories of collusion, 1601–2023.

Notes: 5,068 observations. A single source may yield multiple examples.

Source: See text.

enforcing. These range from simply failing to report or act on information that welfare recipients had other resources (spillover) right through to opposing rule changes that might result in greater prosecution of fraudsters. Two large categories have a particular place in this evidence: officials actively limiting their investigations or just going through the motions; and both investigators and policymakers creating acceptable fictions that would remain acceptable as long as welfare recipients did not step outside certain boundaries. Whether collusion has been systemic is a difficult thing to test. The idea that it was widespread is an easier proposition, not least because expectations of it were written into the rules and guidance for the welfare system. An 1864 manual setting out the duties of overseers under the post-1834 regime, for instance, clearly anticipated that officials might collude in not enforcing rules about rent, casual relief, and outdoor relief.[92] An 1862 guide had more to say on the fraudulent character of the able-bodied poor in particular – arguing that giving welfare to the working poor and the able-bodied un- or underemployed was "productive of evil" – but in terms of wording and thrust the text was centrally concerned with giving specific guidance on the limits of interpretation to the "exceptions" which peppered New Poor Law rules and created a framework of local discretion.

The fear of collusion on the part of guardians is recurrent, as is its expectation. Insistent warnings that those who lived outside places of settlement presented "the difficulty of ascertaining the circumstances beyond the power of inspection of the guardians" and that "cases here indicated ... cannot without great difficulty be sufficiently investigated and watched by guardians and their officers, and are therefore such as afford frequent cases of deception," frame a sense that officials *would* simply ignore fraud. The same manuals repeatedly listed the day-to-day duties of officers and, if read in one way, such constant reminders to inspect applicants and collaborate with other officials inside and outside the union confirm the patchy nature of these practices in the first place.[93] Restated guidance to officials on their duties by vestries under the Old Poor Law, or repetitive restatement of the limitations to investigations for modern fraud investigators, can be read in exactly the same way. Certainly this is how "HenryHomer" understood it, observing that inspectors were uninterested in catching cohabiting single mothers: "I work in social housing and in my experience the incidence of 'non declared partners' for people who claim to be single parents is at least 10–20%."[94] I do not, of course, argue that everyone colludes; merely that enough people do for the public to understand the system as rigged in favour of fraudsters. Nor do I argue that the scale and intensity of collusion is constant over time or region, merely that it is constant enough to limit the desire to find as well as to seek welfare fraud.

Conclusion

On 5 September 1855 the PLB wrote to Berwick-upon-Tweed (Northumberland) enclosing a letter sent to them by Alexander Laidlaw, the master of their own workhouse. Laidlaw's letter called attention to the problem of "able-bodied females leaving the Workhouse in the morning and present[ing] themselves for re-admittance the same or the following day, spending the day in prostitution and drunkenness." Unsurprisingly the guardians were displeased that their officer should air dirty linen in public but noted an inability to do anything about these known charlatans and fraudsters. Unless they rioted, assaulted, or stole, in which case they could be jailed, such women were in the end free to leave, and the poor law union was obliged to readmit them if they could prove or confect "need." Workhouses were not prisons.[95] In short, it was best not to find fraud. For many other cases, the leeway and right of officials to confront fraud was clearer, but the evidence employed here suggests that a desire to find fraud when sought was not always present.

The motives for inaction or even active collusion, a collusion shared by a significant section of the public as chapter 7 suggests, are not always obvious. Not many people were as blatant as "HowardBeale" who suggested: "Good luck to anyone in genuine need who defrauds the benefit system … I would never vote for a conviction in such cases if I were serving on a Jury."[96] The picture is pinpointed, however, by "HC," a former inspector who quit in 2008. His teams had been well aware of the structural and functional flaws of the British welfare system and were consequently willing to accept some degree of fiction in the claims made. Even more intriguingly, he suggested that every Monday brought a balancing act because each investigation and prosecution had both a real cost and an opportunity cost. The latter had two features: the deterrence of genuine new claims or the sign-off from the system of genuinely desperate people; and the detection of a slew of minor breaches of rules, the sanctioning of which, quite apart from prosecution, was massively beyond the resources that were ever likely to be allocated to his department. In the view of "HC" widespread prosecution would have led to reputational damage for the entire welfare system, as would eventual widespread public knowledge of a "feeble" sanctions framework to substitute for prosecution.[97] For these reasons, he suggested, it was best not to seek *or* find unless driven by fleeting new targets in episodic welfare crackdowns.[98] We have seen numerous examples of broadly similar rhetorical, emotional, and strategic responses to the question of fraud in the course of preceding chapters. In the historical record at least, we also see some intriguing complexities. One is exemplified by the case of W. Lambrick, who wrote to the Local Government Board from Swansea in 1894, with a comment and a question:

> all the [guardians'] bussiness is carried on in Welsh language and Ratepayers meetings as well. As English men go to those meetings, and come away as we went, with no knowledge of what have

been transacted in that meeting, as a ratepayer is it legual for all the bussiness to be carried on all in Welsh language.

How could he fulfil his duties to the poor and to ratepayers if he could not understand the language? The LGB replied that they had no power to order the change, keenly aware no doubt that considerable prior fraud would be revealed if they acted.[99]

We thus gain a cumulative picture in which, *inter alia*: welfare fraud is and is perceived to be more extensive than official measures allow; welfare fraudsters are not all equal; there remains a degree of empathy and sympathy for some groups of fraudsters even as welfare recipients' credentials for morality and honesty have always been to some extent questionable; public knowledge of and anger about welfare fraud does not translate to extensive and sustained snitching; there are considerable doubts about whether officials and policymakers even want to seek, let alone find welfare fraud; and policymakers, officials, and the public passively and actively collude in the processes of not seeking and not finding. Against this backdrop, part 3 of the book asks (first) in whose interests is it that welfare fraud be eliminated? And (second), knowing this long cumulative history, how should we conceptualize the future of welfare citizenship?

part four
Landscapes of Cheating

CHAPTER 10

In Whose Interests?
Cheating, Residuality, and
the Meaning of Welfare

The Reverend John Coker Egerton, in his posthumous 1892 book *Sussex Folk and Sussex Ways*, shared an anecdote that tellingly captures the wry local sense of humour. He recalled an unnamed labourer who, "out of work and hungry,"

> went one morning into the surgery of a neighbouring parish doctor, sat down, and asked to have one of his teeth taken out. The doctor opened the man's mouth and looked at his teeth, but nothing seemed amiss, said –
> "Which is the tooth, friend?"
> "Oh e'er a one you like, sir," said the man. "I've got nothin' for 'em to do, so I thought I might as well get rid an 'em."
> The good doctor did not charge his patient anything for looking into his mouth, but gave him a shilling, and told him to go and get his teeth a job for one day at all events.[1]

This story enfolds some core themes from my book: when the labourer was employed, his income was low – the elision of a shilling and a day's work acknowledges crushingly low wages – and now that he was unemployed the poor law was ineffectual. The doctor should have sent him to the relieving officer but did not. Neither did he check whether the labourer was on relief when giving him the shilling – a possible act of collusion with fraud.

Mainly, however, this anecdote is about the residuality of the welfare system, something that was established by law in 1601, persists, and is arguably intensifying.[2] In a 2013 House of Commons Library Briefing Note, Tom Rutherford suggested that from 1948 until the 1970s, the uprating of individual welfare payments to reflect earnings, inflation, or some other measure was *ad hoc*. Thereafter the uplift pattern became annual, but the preferred inflation measure on which to uprate payments changed both within and between different government tenures. Rutherford's note shows that, while some welfare types (pensions, child benefit) have seen episodic or long-term real increases in the post-1948 period, most (incapacity and disability payments, unemployment allowances, and broadly defined supplementary benefit payments) have stagnated or fallen in real terms. The decline in relation to average earnings is more marked, with unemployment-related benefits falling particularly strongly to reach only 11.6 per cent of average earnings in 2012.[3] By 2019 Peter Lindert was demonstrating both that the British system was on the margins of being a functional welfare state and that, with the exception of broadly understood maternity and family benefits, it propped up international league tables of generosity and scope.[4]

Others have traced different periodicities to residuality. Bernhard Reiger suggests that Margaret Thatcher's emphasis on the moral obligation to work marked an abandonment of earlier models of social citizenship rooted in state protection of the poor. By 1982 Britain was unique in Europe in not linking unemployment welfare payments to the prior income of the claimant, and Thatcher, he concludes, viewed welfare as "a moral provocation" that undermined pride and self-reliance. Her ministers regarded themselves as engaged in a "benefits war" with endemic scrounging and dishonesty, one reaction to which was to strip back the real value of benefits.[5] Other commentators trace very similar sentiments on the part of Tony Blair and David Cameron,[6] or gloomily predict further retrenchment in the 2020s.[7]

This chapter explores the changing contours of residualism. It argues that many of the dichotomies observed in this book – rampant fraud in the popular imagination as opposed to a tendency for the public not to inform; political rhetoric about the vital task of tackling fraud *versus* an inability to even quantify the problem; leftist hysteria about the ferocity of investigation and prosecution set against very low rates of seeking and finding; the assumed dishonesty of the poor in general contrasted with clear and unambiguous public sympathy and even empathy with some groups of fraudsters; widespread popular condemnation of fraudsters *versus* an accepted architecture in which not all fraud was equal; and the eye-popping sums lost to fraud seen against a strongly elaborated sense that tackling fraud as a matter of principle is not worth the effort – can be explained by the fact of residualism. In this context, I will suggest, the history of both the welfare state and attitudes to fraud matter. Ultimately, and to pick up a theme visited briefly in chapter 9, I will argue that it is in no one's interest that welfare fraud be eliminated.

Contours of Residualism

As I have previously suggested, historians struggle with chronologies of the shifting value of welfare payments. Brodie Waddell's important survey of parochial spending concludes that, while linear patterns are absent, welfare payments broadly increased in real terms for much of the eighteenth century. Nonetheless, these approximate figures rely on multiple hypothecations and assumptions to correct for data problems and coverage.[8] Richard Smith concludes that the real value of regular payments to the aged increased in the first half of the eighteenth century, but he deals only with this older group and only with data from the midlands. Contrary perspectives pointing to low nominal and real allowances at parish level or in different regions are easy to find.[9] Such divergent views, themselves reflected in the historiography of postwar welfare as we have seen, partly reflect problems of definition, sources, and yardsticks. Thus, both historically and in the present it matters whose welfare was supposed to be encompassed by a single welfare payment. Many pauper writers of the eighteenth and nineteenth centuries made the rhetorical and factual point that an allowance of [x] shillings to a household head was a small one when it also had to meet the welfare needs of partners, dependent children, or the sick and disabled. And Universal Credit is in turn widely constructed as inadequately calibrated to individual circumstances and needs.[10] The question of what yardsticks to judge the "value" of welfare payments against is equally slippery. Across my sample, both recipients and taxpayers sought to calibrate nominal payments against inflation. Indeed, right up to 1929 it was expected that welfare payments could go down as well as up to reflect changing prices. The mantra of inflation-adjusted welfare allowances has become compelling in a modern sense, as we have seen.[11] There are and have been alternative measures, however: the level of allowances in relation to median, modal, or mean earnings in any locality or (post-1970) nationally; the income replacement rate of welfare payments for families and individuals; the relationship of welfare thresholds to indicators of relative poverty; and of course the regionally adjusted value of welfare payments relative to deeply ingrained spatial divisions in the cost of living both historically and now. Universalism ironed out very long-term differences in the nominal value of welfare payments but in so doing reduced the real value of those payments in high-cost areas and ossified their value elsewhere.

Such complexities amplify if we listen to the voices of the dependent poor across the period covered here. Many claimed that while payments might have *seemed* adequate (even at times generous), they failed to take into account the differential starting points of welfare applicants. In particular, pre-existing debt thinned out the value of allowances. Nor should we forget that the regularity and timeliness of payments had a value in and of themselves. Across the data, writers, poor people, and advocates noted that regular and timely payments, however small, allowed poor families to leverage or retain other support. For this reason, the eighteenth-century poor complained as bitterly of delayed payment and decision-making as those seeking the dole in the 1930s and critics of Universal Credit in the 2010s.[12] In short, what matters is not simply a headline rate, but its "meaning." A variant of this observation is that free-to-use money has a value over and above the amount of the cash itself. Complaints from the poor and their advocates that cash was given directly to landlords, encumbered by various restrictions on its use, or provided in the form of food and fuel which was in effect supplied at inflated prices are common. They find their analogue in the determination of ratepayers and some politicians that relief should be paid "in kind," distributed from workhouses or given in the form of vouchers that could be spent on certain forms of goods or only in certain places. Post-1997 comments on newspaper and blog articles almost always have threads that contain demands for welfare to be given in the form of vouchers; and many cite abuse of this very system, as for instance in the case of Liverpool (again) where in 1999 it was alleged that parents were exchanging milk vouchers for cigarettes and booze.[13]

Attempts to understand just *how* residual British welfare payments are and have been, are thus conceptually difficult. The historiography is mixed. There is much evidence from the very beginnings of the Old Poor Law to the present of entrenched public views that welfare payments are too high, whatever their real or nominal value.[14] In this commentary, welfare is not residual enough either to control the spiralling cost of the system or to dissuade moral hazard, idleness, and moral bankruptcy. Unsurprisingly, commentators across the period since 1601 often see welfare fraud as a signal that the system is and was simply *too* generous. We should not, however, be seduced by such narratives. Edward Hunt argues that the New Poor Law "pension" was equal to a mere 27–35% of average working-class familial income.[15] Later in the century the memoirist Samuel Kendall was scathing in his criticism, noting of the aged poor in 1870s Wiltshire and Somerset that outdoor allowances, which varied between 2/6 and 4s per week, amounted to less than 25 per cent of the average male wage.[16] Improvements over time were at best marginal; Kendall characterised small changes post-1918 with tongue in cheek. Sitting again as an elected guardian he fantasised about paupers receiving:

> relief on such a liberal scale that I have almost rubbed my eyes to assure myself we were not in the land of Arcady! Not doling but dealing out unconscionable wealth to the thousand! Even that was better than these mean and niggardly Poor Laws of the greater part of the 19th century, which I hated, indeed detested, with all the strength of my very existence.[17]

Subsequently, he wrote disparagingly about unemployment relief whereby "our truly magnanimous Poor Law system still only gives three or four shillings per week Out-of-door Relief – which was all too little for those unfortunate 'down and outs' to live on."[18] Kendall was by no means alone in opposing calls for further economy under the New Poor Law, especially as thinking on the causation of poverty changed from the 1870s. Even before this, paupers themselves regularly conducted a rhetorical engagement with officials over the adequacy of relief. Spanning the Old and New Poor Laws, the rhetoric is exemplified in a letter from William Rogers Snr (first encountered in chapter 6), written from Chelsea in 1850. He opened aggressively and sarcastically: "I would humbly beg to state that the stipend you are pleased to afford me is very inadequate to my necessities or comfort." Warming to his task, he took the whole system to charge:

> the feeble and decayed Housekeeper is stinted in order that the underlings in petty offices may be supplied with more means to fatten upon, than the distressed & destitute Housekeeper who

in fact ought to be the first considered … And here Gentlemen
I cannot omit noticing, that were I as perfect on my feet as some
I know are, who receive a greater stipend from the parish than I
do, I would not trouble you[19]

Gaining a sense of the meaning of the nominal welfare payments of the pre-
1800 period is somewhat more difficult. Notwithstanding the perspectives
of Brodie Waddell and Richard Smith, some eighteenth-century voices still
questioned the adequacy of support for individuals and families. The use
of the word "trifle" to describe allowances given or requested occurs some
500 times in pre-1834 pauper letters, pointing strongly to an expectation
of small contributions to need.

Similarly, the absence of welfare (because of threshold or contin-
gency rules) or its inadequacy are also prevalent themes across the oral
history and life-writing elements of my data from the early 1900s. Mrs
G.1.B. of Barrow (Cumbria) exemplifies the resulting dissatisfaction: "I
remember when my husband got the dole [in the 1930s], seven and six
or eleven shillings. I threw it at him. I said, 'What do you expect me to
do with that?' I was so indignant."[20] A more systematic perspective can
be reached through a comprehensive analysis of debates about welfare,
individual welfare schemes, and welfare fraud in the postwar *Hansard*
record. Such debates always involved a moral tone, usually contained some
discussion of conditionality, and sometimes led to specific commentary
that welfare payments were too high or encompassing to dissuade moral
hazard. Yet almost none failed to feature an MP stating or implying that
benefits were too low.[21] By the 1990s we can tension claims that benefits were too generous with data from the OECD and the EU, some of it
quoted in parliamentary debates, which showed convincingly that, both
absolutely and in comparison to other states, the British welfare state is
essentially residual in the support it provides.[22] In 2013 "Carol" claimed:
"The benefits system has become a magnet for the workshy and feckless.
It has also attracted vast numbers of people to our shores because we are
regarded as a 'soft touch.'"[23] As well as joining a strong theme that we can
see in public debate across my data, she was also rather missing a point,
the weight of which only truly develops through *longue-dureé* historical
analysis: the very rationale of centrally mandated English and Welsh (later
British) welfare from 1601 onwards was to be residual. Not only did this

involve "low" payments but also a high bar for deservingness and (at least in terms of practical operations) delaying payments as a way of managing and rationing demand. It follows that the welfare state plays, and is meant to play, an ambiguous role in tackling inequality through redistribution of income across life-cycles or at certain points in time. Simultaneously, a long history of extreme income inequality in Britian consistently leaves the welfare system doing more heavy lifting to support the acquisition of median or normative living standards for the poor than in other states.[24]

There is also, however, another insistent feature of residualism across the data: from the beginning of the Old Poor Law there was a determination to make obtaining, keeping, and renewing welfare payments a complex process, both as a "good" in its own right and because some or many applicants – deserving or otherwise – would thereby drop out of the system. In turn, the lengthy and often circular application process for English, Welsh, and Scottish welfare has both created fraud and reflects the fear of it. We saw a version of this observation when discussing fraud by form in chapter 6, and it constitutes rather more than the practice of conditionality that has dominated historiographical debates in public policy circles.[25] In a modern sense, "difficulty" was written into the DNA of the tax credit system, notwithstanding a commitment by Baroness Hollis in 1998 when introducing a welfare green paper that "the system of delivering modern welfare should be flexible, efficient and easy for people to use."[26] Complexity and difficulty were also features of the early Thatcher governments and indeed can easily be traced back to the mid-1950s as concerns about the spiralling cost of the National Health Service prompted wider debate over the sustainability of welfare.[27]

But once again, these issues are not unique to the modern welfare state. Under the Old Poor Law officials receiving claims by letter had to judge how and when to respond and whether to pay or to seek more clarity. Hundreds of thousands of words in the letter corpus were employed by paupers and their advocates in navigating a system that could at times be made deliberately convoluted. Claims lodged in person were less susceptible to deliberate complexification, but during the eighteenth-century vestries increasingly took on decision-making, and many applicants found themselves circling hopelessly in administrative and procedural loops. Under the New Poor Law admission to the workhouse could become a long and attenuated process, while for those (the great majority) who avoided the workhouse, gaining outdoor relief was often held up by relieving officers seeking further information, guardians refusing to make decisions, and repeated offers of amounts that would clearly be unacceptable to applicants, necessitating the re-starting of the process. This was precisely the complaint of James Miller (and many hundreds like him), writing from Reeth on 1 November 1853:

> Having in vain for nearly 12 months past entreated the Guardians of <u>Reeth</u> Union to extend me a reason – the relief, I am reluctantly compelled now to appeal to you, as my situation is such that I cannot subsist with the allowance I have namely, one shilling and sixpence halfpenny a week on the av since last Nw Year's day. I shall be 71 years of age next birthday nd am scarcely able to do any work at all.[28]

Reaching forward by more than a hundred years, focus group attendee "GC" recalled her father describing the "sheer grind" of "keeping the right side of it [the welfare state]" in the 1960s.[29] In effect he was capturing a sense not *just* that welfare was conditional and residual but that it was obtainable only through a process of attrition. We might thus think of the British welfare state not *simply* as superficially residual (for instance in ranking poorly in terms of the income replacement rate of benefits[30]) but as intensively so.

Fraud and Residualism

The links between real or imagined fraud and residualism are multiple and complex. Friedrich Heinemann makes a clear and strong association between increases in the scope of the welfare state since 1981 and the tendency for welfare recipients to see fraud as acceptable.[31] Ana Moro-Egido and Angel Solano-Garcia suggest that perceptions of substantial fraud reduce support for welfare spending and increase calls for residualism,[32] while Ruth Patrick traces a link between the "programme of welfare residualisation" instituted by the LibCon government in 2010, and the particularly striking attack on the scope and value of welfare payments for the group most closely associated with fraud in the modern public imagination, the disabled.[33] Others understand welfare fraud as a targeted construct, an attempt to create or re-create a "never-deserving poor" by chipping away at public trust in the state and an encompassing welfare system.[34]

Adding the long history of welfare to this picture introduces further complexity, suggesting in particular that harsh residualism as much as overweaning generosity might reduce benefit morale.[35] Thus, modern filmic representations often link the intense need and hopelessness generated by residualist welfare and the sense that good people are pushed unwillingly into fraud. The same idea has strong foundations in philosophical writing about the welfare state,[36] but even more so in the historical data. From at least the 1820s, parishes and then poor law unions, slum visitors, doctors, institutional visitors, court officials, and "investigators" continually rediscovered the residuum and were usually shocked to find the conditions under which the poor lived and to realise the limited role that a residualist welfare system played in alleviating need, let alone achieving redistributive effects. The very earliest advocate letters in my sample illustrate exactly this: William Smart of Northampton argued in 1714, for instance, that unless the pension of an unnamed widow was increased, she might be driven to criminal ends.[37] Accumulated knowledge of the deeply rooted residualist nature of the British welfare state also affects the way that fraud itself is understood. We see this in oral histories, comments, and life-writing where members of the public refrain from reporting fraud because anyone in that situation would struggle, or in the actions of modern fraud investigators who nudge people off benefits rather than prosecuting because the amounts involved are so small and the activities detected are not systematic.[38] The employment of private contractors or AI in fraud detection is controversial precisely because of the loss of contextual history.[39] These instances can be patterned easily onto historical examples: the overseer under the Old Poor Law who paid small amounts to people suspected of fraud because they told the right fictions; the advocate of any period who prioritized need over character in offering their support; and officials who responded to moral panics about fraud by having a drive to divest claimants, only to allow them to return to welfare lists shortly thereafter, given the grim reality that residual payments were easier to make than meeting the consequences (at law, in terms of local public reputation and order, or in terms of accusations of starvation or nakedness) of harsher policies.

In the historical data there are certainly pinch-points when rising welfare bills or particular scandals or exposés in the system generate tension, outrage, and action in terms of both "genuine" recipients and suspected or actual fraudsters.[40] But, as I suggest at the outset of this chapter, many of the attitudinal and behavioural dichotomies observed in this book can be understood as a function of the fact that the key response of the British state to the moral hazard represented and embodied in long-term belief in the inherent dishonesty of the poor has always been to keep low or to persistently reduce the value of individual benefits and welfare packages to *all* claimants, especially in relation to median living standards.[41] Perversely, the relatively small amount seemingly lost to officially measured fraud certainly reflects problems of measurement and understatement, but ultimately it embodies the fact that welfare payments are and always have been so low in the first place. This connection between fraud, honesty, and residuality has extended consequences. In the words of one ex-inspector, because governments "hack down benefits to the lowest common denominator" and most people "don't know and don't give a shit" about welfare claimants, there has always been a pressure release valve for public opinion.[42] We see this clearly through the debates recorded in *Hansard*, which return over and over to welfare fraud and mechanisms for dealing with it. Initiative after initiative is reported and debated. Then the cycle begins again. Post-1945 governments, deliberately or not, have proven themselves hopelessly incompetent at evaluating any of these measures until forced.[43] Still, this is enough to placate popular opinion at most times and in most places. The key parties in identifying and eliminating welfare fraud – politicians, policymakers, officials, and the public – thus engage in circular fictions, the outcome *and* cause of which is residuality.

The historical consistency of this story is both remarkable and, as I have suggested, absent from much modern debate. Thus, while historians, sociologists, economists, and social policy scholars have in their efforts to understand the changing character and role of the welfare state focussed on important chronological, policy, or cultural turning points – the 1790s, 1834, the 1870s, pensions in 1908, the end of the New Poor Law in 1929, Beveridge in 1942, the codification of a welfare state in the 1940s and early 1950s, supposed postwar consensus over the security and redistributive purposes of welfare, Thatcher, Blair, LibCon austerity, Universal Credit – the effect has been to lose sight of the basic DNA of British welfare. It is residual, it has almost always been residual, it is *meant* to be residual, and I contend it always will be residual without radical thinking. Yet, rhetorical, practical, conceptual, and popular attempts to think afresh about the structure, scope, quality, and longevity of entitlement between 1601 and 2024 are repetitively and remarkably fragile. It is no accident that welfare historians from their very earliest incarnations have always been writing about what Dorothy Chunn and Shelley Gavigan evocatively label "the teeter tottering of the welfare state."[44] In this framework, welfare fraud has a factual place but also a highly symbolic one, the ultimate embodiment of moral hazard and the moral uncertainty of the welfare state, and yet something that no one has ever had much interest in confronting.

In Whose Interests?

This issue of "interest" reaches deep into the very purpose of my book. It has multiple layers. The first is obvious from foregoing chapters, debates reported in *Hansard*, comments on blogs and newspaper articles, and the correspondence of officials backwards from 1945. There has always been a latent acknowledgement that systematically tackling fraud would both cost a lot and cost a lot more than would be saved. This remains true even if we accept contentions in chapter 3 that the actual scale of fraud is significantly more than official measurements show. On this level it is not in the *immediate* interests of taxpayers to undertake such an exercise even if the consequence of inaction is to continually renew doubt about the moral basis of the welfare state and welfare recipients more widely.[45] We have encountered financial and time costs in earlier chapters, but at a more systematic level concerns about cost appear or can be inferred in numerous separate source references, including 320 in *Hansard* alone.

But there are more fundamental aspects to the question, "in whose interests is it to eliminate fraud?" that require attention using a long historical canvas. Thus, in the modern arena systematically tackling welfare fraud – adopting the zero-tolerance approach periodically rolled out for other forms of crime – would involve an acknowledgement that both the residuality of welfare and systems issues (thresholds, forms, knowledge) *create* fraud at national and local levels. An army of inspectors would certainly find much undetected fraud. They would also visit considerable unmet need, a seam of people who do not apply for welfare even though eligible, and multiple interlocking process flaws that explain a significant portion of real and suspected dishonesty. In this sense, fraud is a small price to pay for avoiding the problems (including root-and-branch process reform) that would be generated by actively tackling it. Such views are not routinely or directly elaborated by officials and politicians, but I find them in thousands of comments on newspaper articles and blogs. Sometimes we also see this sense writ across the national psyche. COVID-era furlough was a direct response to the fact that a significant proportion of the population would have come into contact for the first time as adults with the residuality, complexity, inflexibility, sloth, and inadequacy of the welfare system. Yet this issue too has indelible historical imprints. The men and women conducting social surveys from the 1860s, and those alongside and before them who advocated for the poor, acknowledged fraud but drew attention to residuality, unmet need, and process failings. They often used the lens of scandal to gain traction with decision-makers, much as is true of the 2020s.[46] In turn, the Old and New Poor Laws, and even to some extent the interwar public assistance committees and other welfare bodies, were almost preprogrammed to give way in individual cases so as to prevent a wider analysis of the system itself. Just as with COVID, national or regional crises (the 1790s and early 1800s, 1840s, 1860s, 1920s, and more generally smallpox or cholera pandemics) in which large numbers of people would have been catapulted into sustained contact with a residual welfare system with which they were unfamiliar and which was ill-equipped to deal with their needs, resulted in the suspension, subversion, or amelioration of normative rules. I have demonstrated too the remarkable inability and sometimes unwillingness of welfare officials to rid the relief lists even in "standard" times of people they knew to be charlatans. These complex intersections mean that it has never been in the interest of policymakers to systemically tackle fraud, given the intimate discussion of welfare citizenship that might then be required.

I revisit this question of citizenship for chapter 11. In the meantime, a third aspect of "interest" to be noted are the considerable but subtle opportunity costs that would emerge in targeting fraud. Systematic analysis of *Hansard* for the post-1945 period identifies a cumbersome and fractured political process in relation to welfare reform in general and combatting welfare fraud in particular. Re-engineering welfare legislation and practice in the way that might be required for a zero-tolerance approach would thus carry very considerable opportunity costs in terms of other legislative agendas foregone, borne over several parliaments. In the longer historical data, significant opportunity costs included: the (unpaid) time of officials and ratepayers, the strictly limited capacities of the central welfare authorities which would have resulted in retreat from other statutory duties, and (something with considerable modern resonance) the limited capacity of the courts to deal with the extended increase in business occasioned by any serious attempt to engineer out welfare fraud. Even had court capacity existed, the requirements of multiple sequential and parallel prosecutions, alongside more encompassing and intrusive ongoing monitoring systems, would likely have led to a breakdown of local social relations and violence. The Swing Riots of the 1820s and early 1830s were notionally about wage rates and labour market architecture but in reality the rolling back of customary norms of poor relief played an unambiguous role.[47] It is too much to argue – in the modern British context, though not in France, as we have recently seen – that a systematic and extended crackdown on fraud would create riot and unrest, but an opportunity cost of such actions would certainly be even greater emotional and emotive distance between a modern underclass and the taxpayers who fund the welfare system. Perhaps the biggest opportunity cost to a zero-tolerance approach – historically or in the present – would be the revelation of accumulated political failure to control welfare and the associated risk that the general population would come to the view that getting, keeping, and sometimes defrauding benefits is a cost-free option.

We see the potential for this view in comments appended to articles and blogs covering fraud crackdowns and multiple prosecutions. The tone and focus of such commentary are generally split between support for such approaches and their condemnation, but the most consistent narrative theme is always a sense that, given the potential punishments involved, the lack of payback, and the ability of those convicted to sign straight back onto welfare, fraud is a cost-effective route for those who engage in it. Sometimes such agitational rhetoric is shared with politicians themselves,[48] but at the most basic of levels it makes more sense for policymakers to contain this narrative by concentrating on residuality for all rather than a crackdown for some. Opportunity cost also emerges in the deeper historical data. The narrative is a strong one in the 1832 report prefiguring the New Poor Law, but it is perhaps best embodied in the letters of Jospeh Rowntree of Leeds. Frustrated at his inability to get the central state to act on both fraud and unmet need, he asked in his letter of May 1866: "Am I to conclude, that 'bona fide' information is not wished for by the Board."[49] The answer, of course, was yes, they had no wish to know. The consistent presence of multi-level "costs to action" thus means that almost no one has had an interest in eliminating fraud rather than merely grumbling about it.

This impression is strengthened if we turn to a fourth line of analysis, which follows on the weakness of public and political support for a central consequence of any sustained and systematic attack on fraud: that "genuine" claimants would be either rejected or disadvantaged. Such fear is a consistent presence in modern parliamentary debate, recent and repurposed oral histories, and the material left by advocates of the poor throughout the period. Two threads of the evidence found in modern comments – the idea that fraudsters stop genuine claimants (themselves or someone they know) from gaining the (higher) benefits they deserve; and the idea that campaigns against fraud lead to the demonisation of all claimants[50] – also speak to this sense. More distantly, early-twentieth-century discussions about fingerprinting welfare claimants came to nothing because such tactics elided the poor with serious criminals.[51] Nineteenth-century officials made a distinction in their interactions with the central authorities between the able-bodied welfare scrounger on whom they were supposed to crack down, and the "good men" disadvantaged by labour market conditions and who were captured by the same harsh imperatives. Eighteenth-century people of status often appended their signatures to relief applications, in effect giving their personal weight to the idea that excluding the unworthy fraudster was not worth the effort if it came at the cost of excluding also the worthy or reformed. Similarly, all my interviewees told at least one story of their getting involved in supporting a claim or claimant for welfare, even though the circumstances they described were not so very different from those that they also assigned to people identified in the same interview as morally unworthy or actively engaged in fraud. In the very recent past, post-2010 austerity and the post-COVID explosion of sickness and disability welfare may arguably have upset the sentiment that excluding the deserving was not a price worth paying for dispensing with the fraudulent and unworthy.[52] Yet this is a short-term effect; court decisions in 2018 and politically inspired budget decisions in 2022 and 2023 have once more emphasised that the moral cost of excluding the fraudulent in liberal democracies is simply too high to sustain for any length of time.[53]

A variant of this point – and a fifth aspect of the question "in whose interests?" – might broadly be understood as "fractured intolerance" in national public opinion. Put another way, the competing influences on public perceptions of the scale and seriousness of welfare fraud generate persistent concern about the issue, but rarely the sort of sustained intolerance that precipitates lasting policy action. While think-tanks and advocates in my data have written hundreds of thousands of words in efforts to draw attention to the highly negative implications of national fraud drives or individual acts and initiatives, in practice little seems to have changed in terms of the public view of this matter. And notwithstanding many thousands of historiographical words aimed at the issue of media construction of scroungers, I see little by way of a concerted groundswell of popular opinion supporting sustained reform. This ossification is partly explained by public knowledge of the residuality of the welfare system. However, as many commentators have pointed out, such public knowledge can sometimes be imperfect and other variables thus also have an influence.[54] These include the episodic nature of media coverage and some of the perception gaps that were outlined in chapter 1. But there is something more; throughout this book I have come back to long-term understandings that there was fraud "and then there was fraud." This architecture means that not all suspected or detected dishonesty feeds into a perceived need for reform and invasive action. More than this, and as I have consistently emphasised, officials, the public, potential informants, and even some politicians have both sympathy and empathy with *some* of those caught in the residual welfare system and its arcane complexities.[55]

Robin Page's 1971 dissection of a shambolic, wasteful, and incompetent welfare system defrauded as a matter of course by the unworthy should have been a moment of systemic change. It was in no one's interest – especially the general public – that it became so. Indeed, for this reason a core theme of my book has been the issue of collusion between the different parties in the welfare bargain to create shared fictions. In the eighteenth and nineteenth centuries the poor – even and especially the fraudulent poor – used well-established rhetorical, attitudinal, and behavioural forms to establish deservingness including expressed willingness and desire to work, claiming sickness or disability, and exhausting all prior channels of help, the latter speaking to the residual nature of the British welfare system. Officials in their turn were provided through deployment of these tropes with the moral cover required by a discretionary system to grant relief even though they must have known that these signals were likely *merely* rhetorical. Official and claimant created a shared fiction because there was no desire to confront the issue of moral hazard on a regular basis.[56] The rules- and form-based welfare system of postwar Britain has also relied on such fictions. Officials (local and national) colluded with people thrown into structural unemployment in the 1970s and 1980s. More recent requirements for welfare recipients to prove they have been looking for work are also of course part of this collusion, set against the backdrop of a shared fiction that jobs and skills are there, that applications are "real," or that the jobs thus obtained are likely to be sustainable. Such collusion created a *welfare imaginary*, one in which there were real incentives not to act, reaching an apogee under Thatcher, John Major, and Blair, who among them fashioned a shared fiction of welfare as *newly* lean and mean at the same time as they created disguisable and silent corners of the welfare state. Once again this speaks to the nature and meaning of social citizenship, a matter to which we return in chapter 11.

In the meantime, and finally, fraud persists because the state has *never* really understood the inter-sectionalities and inter-operabilities of its own welfare system and arguably does not want to. In this space the claims of the unworthy – the fraudulent *and* morally suspect, which as chapter 4 showed often amount to the same thing in the public imagination – have continuing traction both because they have always had traction and because their presence is assured by the very fabric of philosophies, sentiments, structures, and safeguards of the welfare systems that we can study and through which we live. Between 1601 and 1834, rejecting a welfare claim was never a final act; a stock of community knowledge clearly existed of what sort of approaches worked. Those who were turned down because of their moral or economic position or because they had been fraudsters would come back again and again with slightly different narratives. The hierarchy of stories that I addressed in chapter 2 has real importance here. At no point in the history of English and Welsh welfare prior to the early 1900s was it possible for officials to simply reject these claims without consideration. Even thereafter, and as my interviewees often noted, welfare claimants could apply until their story was of sufficient quality to fit the rules. Disability advocates who currently advise clients on how to "properly"' fill in the extensive forms that underpin the new living allowances are replicating exactly the friendship and neighbourhood groups that Keith Snell identified as supporting welfare applications more than two hundred years ago.[57] Such activism, the failure of many benefits to have any limiting mechanism on re-application, and the complicating factor of exogenous legal decisions, has for more than four centuries constrained the capacity of the state to impose the deep conditionality required to engineer the fraudulent from the system. A modern focus on the increasing conditionality of welfare from the 1990s misses this dual point: that conditionality has been the leitmotif of most British welfare state history, and that it has effective limits.[58]

Against these backdrops, it is possible, indeed necessary, to argue that politicians, policymakers, the general public, and even officials have found it consistently difficult to take a holistic view of the welfare state. Thus, the ingrained regional nature of both need and welfare practice for much of the period between 1601 and the later 1930s generated a system that was not inherently "graspable." Indeed, when I look at Local Government Board correspondence in the later nineteenth century the frustration of civil servants at their inability to codify national practice, eliminate certain kinds of payments, and tie the rest together into welfare packages is palpable. The multiplication of benefit forms and eligibility in the twentieth century, allied with the formation of tangential benefit structures such as the NHS and the continued locus of some welfare forms (such as housing) at the local level, simply makes the system even less intelligible. Fraud thus persists not *just* because any systematic attack on it would highlight the accumulated inaction of policymakers, but also because fraudsters can cling and subsist in the cracks created by the failure of the state to conceptualize a "whole" welfare system even when (as in 1834, the early 1900s, the 1940s, and 2010s) they had the chance. We see this lack of understanding in the "shock" news that a Universal Credit cap of £26,000 per year was not actually enough to prevent hundreds of thousands of families losing significant amounts of income even outside London. Moreover, the fact that some families were getting £100,000 per year in welfare payments came as a shock to austerity Britain precisely because no previous governments had tried to think of the system as an interrelated whole. Outrage over the moral hazard embodied by such figures, an outrage replicated in historical attempts to episodically review and reduce welfare lists, is essentially a reflection of the uninformed state. In this sense, systematic confrontation of fraud carries huge risks and costs, and purging rather than consistently controlling welfare lists is and always has been a preferable option.

Moments

The argument that welfare fraud has persisted because it is in no one's interest to eliminate it reaches deep into the data deployed here. Some of it is very humorous. Several wags pointed out in comments on newspaper articles or documentaries about fraud detection that investigators themselves would be out of a job if they had got serious about fraud rather earlier. More wrote that politicians would have to find a new "other" if they had ever been determined to confront fraudsters, suggesting that footballers, the monarchy, or the House of Lords might be good targets. In the more distant historical sources, the paralysis of the authorities when welfare claimants took three days off to conduct a funeral for a robin is mirrored by eighteenth-century cases such as that in Olney (Northamptonshire) where welfare applicants who had been denied relief dismantled the overseer's house and sold off the materials while he was away.[59] The acceptance and containment of fraud was written into the basic expectational culture of the system. Unsurprisingly, the price of a low-level but consistent commitment to a residual welfare state has always been the perception of unambiguous dishonesty on the part of the poor in general and certain claimant groups in particular. Against this backdrop the fiction that twenty-first-century governments *are* tackling welfare fraud has become deeply embedded in the minds of recipients, politicians, stakeholders, and advocate groups. The same fiction has a strong spine in the historic data, running from advice books, through the job descriptions for assistant overseers, and to the records of court cases or the conclusions of parliamentary committees. But it *is* fiction; and popular perceptions of rampant fraud alongside systemic failures to report, seek, find, and punish such fraud in any meaningful way can only be reconciled with this illusion.

There have been plenty of opportunities to tear up these fictions and think more carefully about the past, present, and future of the welfare state. Instead, they have become ossifying moments. The settlement acts of the

1660s afforded poor applicants a right to apply for welfare in a defined place and assured them of a right to consideration. The ultimate effect was to make it hard and costly to exclude the charlatan, liar, and cheat. In 1834 the Central Authority of the New Poor Law was given a renewable rather than a permanent mandate and parliament specifically stated that it could not intervene in individual relief decisions. These strictures ensured that for almost a century up to 1929, officials could not be compelled either to relieve the truly deserving or to stop relieving fraudsters, the immoral, and the unworthy. The post-1945 welfare state rewrote rules of entitlement and contribution but failed to implement the wide reach of the Beveridge recommendations of 1942, in particular stepping away from an assault on residuality. When Blair and Brown came to power in 1997, they built upon the rhetorical and conceptual infrastructure of welfare reform under Thatcher and Major. They promised a radical new departure, a reset that would sweep away accepting attitudes towards scroungers and the structures that made deliberately not knowing about fraud so easy, at the same time as enhancing support for an investment in people who were "genuinely" needy.[60] In the latter endeavour they had some success, increasing the redistributive effect of the welfare state, introducing a minimum wage which (along with tax credits and tweaks to withdrawal rates) increased the number of welfare recipients in work, and of course beginning the long-term commitment to attacking pensioner poverty. On the other hand, their reforms created a cavernously complex welfare state, started the narrative that defines disability welfare as inherently fraudulent, and did little to effectively measure – let alone seek, find, and punish – structural welfare fraud.

These are important lost opportunities. Yet, the post-COVID world has been all about the imploding of comfortable illusions, and it seems likely that governments of the 2020s and 2030s will at last have to engage in rethinking the conceptual infrastructure of welfare citizenship. This endeavour will involve an intimate reconsideration of the nature and meaning of welfare entitlement, residuality, and welfare fraud, one in which the deep and long-term historical perspective will be vital. It is to this matter that I finally turn.

CHAPTER 11

The Future Welfare Citizen

In a 2022 article on British sovereign debt "spiralling out of control," Matthew Lynn argued that money-printing and low interest rates had allowed companies and governments to avoid hard choices about taxation and spending. Chief amongst the culprits were "bloated, unaffordable welfare systems that can only be kept afloat by central banks that keep the printing presses running until the financial markets call time on them."[1] Such spending, he said, is unaffordable in its own right *and* crowds out the more productive alternative investments that would allow Britain to compete with emerging economic superpowers. This sense that Western economies are hamstrung by the enormous and largely unfundable welfare states developed between the 1880s and 1950s is a contested one.[2] Nor is it new; even eighteenth-century foreign visitors wondered at the affordability of the English and Welsh welfare system, usually without balancing such views with the absence of Continental-style starvation crises.[3] But in the 2024 cost-of-living crisis, and with the British government living way beyond its current taxable means and way beyond the willingness of markets to lend further at affordable interest rates, the idea takes on more urgency.

There were converse views. Commentators (and academics) railed against austerity, workism, ableism, and the unfairness of welfare application processes – matters that could be fixed with new administrative simplification and the extension of taxation to generate new welfare resources. For many, the Tory governments of the 2020s were completing a project begun with Margaret Thatcher to rein back welfare rights, undermine the postwar welfare consensus, impose (unwarranted) harsh conditionality, and create clearly stratified degrees of citizenship status.[4] Some of that commentary helps to locate the agenda for this chapter. Thus, in a hard-hitting 2021 Citizens Advice Scotland report on Universal Credit during COVID, David Scott argued variously that: Universal Credit must be reshaped to "protect against income shocks" and "properly support those in employment"; it was wrong for applicants to have to rely on partners and family for top-up or during the waiting time for resources; payments and payment thresholds needed to rise in order to generate "the income needed for a minimum socially acceptable standard of living in 2021"; people should not have "to borrow money to pay for essentials"; and the system should be flexible enough to overlook unexpected temporary income uplifts.[5]

These dichotomous views are rooted in the conceptual infrastructure of welfare citizenship – of what that status has meant, means now, and might mean for the future. They are also rooted in a misleading and stifling presentism. Most significantly, the British welfare system, especially as it manifested in Scotland, was never meant to do *any* of the things on Scott's Universal Credit wish-list. Welfare under the Old and New Poor Laws was and was meant to be residual. Nothing that came after 1929 has changed this basic characteristic in long-term or meaningful ways. The 1942 Beveridge Report was not implemented in the form that its author intended, as we have seen.[6] It is hard to see how a "bloated unaffordable" welfare system could get much cheaper without radical thinking on the nature and scope of welfare citizenship.

A focus on recent parliamentary debate helps to pin down the competing and contested notions upon which presentist concepts of this status are predicated. Thus, in March 1998 the House of Lords debated the purpose of the welfare state.[7] Outlining eight key principles covering the relationship between the state and its welfare clients present and future, Baroness Hollis promised radical reform of a system which had to meet very different challenges "from the era when William Beveridge laid the foundation stones of today's welfare state." The limited timeframe of this observation is striking, given that Hollis is herself an historian of standing, and points to the intimate links between politics, welfare, and ironclad presentism.[8] Still, Hollis sought to rhetoricise and codify "a new welfare contract between government and citizen," the first cornerstones of which would be the opportunity and obligation to work and to plan to help oneself. Talk of supporting the disabled, the aged, and others with flexible and adequate payments was interspersed with numerous references to fraud and the need to confront and eradicate it. One leaves the Hollis speech with no clear sense of what New Labour thought a welfare citizen was or ought to be. In the same debate, however, Earl Russell, describing Hollis's rhetoric as a "sermon on duty," brilliantly crystallised the matter. He argued: "The social security system is rather like a cross word puzzle. If you change one letter, you change all the other clues across the crossword – you shift the whole pattern." But how far, he wondered, was the pattern being shifted and how far did the government understand the basic tensions inherent in any discussion of welfare citizenship? Russell referred Baroness Hollis to the work of Lord Plant, already visited in our chapter 1:

> [Plant] develops two concepts of citizenship, one resting on the concept of entitlement, where the state has to recognise the right of everybody to subsistence, and the other resting, much as the sermon [of Baroness Hollis] does, on a very stern contractual concept of duty. My own reconciliation of that, for which I shall not hold the noble Lord, Lord Plant, responsible, is that the state should act on the entitlement concept of citizenship, and the individual should act on the duty concept of citizenship, each acting on the concept more favourable to the other party.

Hollis returned to the fray at the end of the debate, arguing from the citizenship level that "the welfare state belongs to us all, [that it] is the common wealth of us all." This conceptual phrasing is important. In Britain the linkages (and breakages) between citizenship and "commonwealth" run historically deep, something that Hollis does not address in this political arena even though she does in her work as an historian.[9] On the other hand the rhetoric is a matter of choice, emerging in muffled fashion from the DNA of the historian who recognises the complex and contested place of state welfare in wider debate about balancing obligation, duty, and opportunity, in civil, social, political, and economic citizenship.[10]

Subsequent legislation and more than forty other legal changes in the New Labour tenure directly affecting the welfare state, in addition to budget announcements, actually failed to re-imagine the welfare contract or to create an acceptable welfare citizenship in the public imagination.[11] Rather, they created what Daniel Edmiston labels "conceptual indeterminacy."[12] We see this in continuous parliamentary, newspaper, think-tank, and blog interventions on the "correct" balance of rights and obligations and the wider moral standing of the poor. On 11 July 2022, for instance, the Conservative MP James Sunderland observed that his constituency

(Bracknell) had large numbers of job vacancies. He wondered "what steps" the Department for Works and Pensions was adopting "to ensure that the remaining claimants are helped into work?"[13] These words allow many readings across a spectrum from scepticism that anyone of working age really needs to be on benefits, to a genuine concern that people needed extra support to return to the workforce. However we read it, the sentiment shows the continuing problem of dealing with the crossword puzzle of the welfare state. More than this, however, the issues and rhetorics raised and applied by Hollis, Russell, and Sunderland could with almost no tweaking be patterned onto the text and intent of the 1601 Old Poor Law. More than 420 years later, Britain has still not resolved the question of what a responsible welfare citizen actually looks like, and what sort of welfare system they should confront in the guise of acceptable and accepted welfare citizens.

This circularity reflects more general confusion "out there." On 30 June 2023 I asked the AI application ChatGPT to write me an essay on definitions of "welfare citizen." I then asked for the essay to refine and extend sequentially to: British welfare citizenship, historical dimensions of such citizenship from 1601, and the relationship between welfare or benefit fraud and welfare citizenship. Distilling the more than nine thousand words of response, we can see both contested or contestable understandings and the remarkable presentism within which the debate is framed. Thus, according to ChatGPT, welfare citizenship is constructed to extend legal and political structures of citizenship and make them operational. Crudely, without "access to social rights and benefits that promote their well-being and … ensure that individuals have a reasonable standard of living and can participate fully in society," citizenship is merely rhetoric. The elision of welfare citizenship and the much wider concept of *social rights* in the ChatGPT response matches uncertainty in the historiography about whether welfare can even be disembodied from the wider contexts to which it relates.[14] Remaining with ChatGPT, however, in the particular context of postwar British society, welfare citizenship is said to impose obligations on government to underwrite "a comprehensive welfare system that supports individuals' well-being, reduces inequality, and promotes social inclusion." For an earlier period, we learn that the "Liberal reforms of the early 1900s … were intended to provide a basic level of social security and promote the well-being of citizens," while for an even earlier period we learn merely that "The term 'welfare citizenship' was not used during this specific era."[15]

As chapter 10 has suggested, the idea that a residualist British welfare state has ever been comprehensive, supported well-being, or promoted social inclusion is questionable. Its record in generating reasonable living standards and reducing inequality is woeful. Yet, what is strikingly missing from the AI trawl through web materials in relation to welfare citizenship is a single reference to obligations as opposed to opportunities, state duties, and the reasonable and just expectations of the poor. This is something we also see in the example of Universal Credit above, and it is central to Steven Jensen and Charles Walton's critique of debate about the wider basket of social rights whereby "promulgating social rights without specifying duties and duty bearers [at individual, state, and corporate levels] makes those rights … meaningless."[16] Only when we add "welfare fraud" to the ChatGPT essay requirement does the question of multi-level obligation appear:

> Welfare citizenship refers to the concept of a reciprocal relationship between the state and its citizens in terms of social welfare benefits. It implies that citizens have certain rights and entitlements to receive support from the state in times of need, and in return, citizens have responsibilities to abide by the rules and regulations governing the welfare system.

The overlap between moral and stratified welfare citizenship is evident here, and something to which I return later.[17] Playing with ChatGPT is not of course evidence or a reliable method for an historian. But the exercise reveals the disjointed nature of the conceptual underpinnings of welfare citizenship in the wider political and public spheres, and the latent bias to presentism.[18]

In the rest of this chapter I take up some of these issues, drawing on key lessons from elsewhere in the book to suggest the parameters for a new national conversation about welfare citizenship, a conversation rooted in the historical DNA of British attitudes towards welfare, welfare fraud, and welfare claimants. I focus first on more of the polarized positions that situate the "problem" of the welfare state, and then move on to the promises about welfare (to welfare citizens) that will inevitably be broken in a slow-growing and heavily indebted state such as Britain. Finally, I turn to the future of welfare citizenship and to the role that history and historians must play in shaping that future. Here I adopt questions asked by Jensen and Walton: Who owes what to whom? How are obligations conceived and enforced? Who decides?[19] To them I add: Who pays? Does moral hazard matter? Why does fraud matter? And why is history essential? In a welfare landscape of the 2020s and 2030s where the hulks of old certainties rust, residuality is always a spectre, the tax base dwindles, and the assumed dishonesty of the poor has been centuries in the making, how should we be thinking about the potential and limitations of welfare citizenship?

Polarized Positions

The problematics of welfare citizenship are centred in more of the sort of modern and historical polarities that began this chapter. I turn first to the acceptable thresholds of ability and inability in a residualist welfare state structured by clear moral rights and wrongs stemming from 1601. In a comment of 2011, "DavidG" took both the BBC and other commentators to task over lazy assumptions about disability and deservingness in a recent programme leading to the view that "all disabled people are frauds and scroungers." He himself had:

> the audacity to sail, white-water raft and fly gliders, all while disabled. None are incompatible with being severely disabled, none come without an invisible cost (costs that have lasted up to a year at times), none are incompatible with the receipt of any disability benefit. Disabled people already live in an atmosphere of suspicion, jealousy and hatred because of the failure of society to understand that disability does not mean being a wheelchair user dependent 24/7 on the charity of those around us.[20]

This expansive and fluid definition of disability drew the ire of others in the same commentary thread: white-water rafting, it was objected, absolutely *should* have been incompatible with disability welfare payments. The fact that it was not intensified latent notions of what Dorothy Chunn and Shelley Gavigan label "welfare *as* fraud."[21] By 2023 and 2024 private threads of this sort had mushroomed into a national crisis, with observations in national newspapers that 3.7 million people were too sick or disabled to be required to seek work, "meaning that taxpayers face bankrolling their benefits indefinitely." Even more strikingly, "one in eight of all working age people will be claiming some form of disability benefit by 2027." The implication that these numbers encapsulated substantial fraud was given voice by Iain Duncan Smith, who argued that most "people on these benefits should be in work."[22] In short, and to pick up a theme from chapter 10, the welfare system was not residual enough. The quoted reports are in right-leaning newspapers, but similar views about the crisis of disability percolated most arenas at this time. Similar dichotomous views of disability run through the historic data, albeit that debate in the past has centred on the relative thresholds and spectra of ability rather than on outright dependence *per se*. The macro-level decline in the moral standing of disabled welfare – a shift from inclusive to exclusive and stratified citizenship rights – has in turn made it impossible to determine what the characteristics of a disabled welfare citizen might look like. By 2024 politicians, newspapers, blogs, and comments were all asking why "the disabled" could not just work from home, given the COVID-era flexibilities then in play.

Other present and historical polarities emphasise these complexities: historians and policymakers have failed to reach a consensus over whether welfare recipients should be regarded as a disenfranchised residuum or underclass – a group that Arianna Bove evocatively conjures as "irreducible figures of otherness" who have a lesser citizenship status[23] – or as mainstream citizens.[24] Andreas Fahrmeir asks precisely this question in his work on the evolution of formal citizenship but then does not answer it.[25] Substantial historical questions thus meld seamlessly into their modern variants. Is the existence of systemic intergenerational welfare dependency – both real and extensively constructed in the public and political imagination, as we have seen – compatible with a model of welfare citizenship in which balancing obligations are never and never will be met? To what extent should the welfare system support or penalize the messy lives of those with rights to make claims on it? How far should character shape the rights and obligations associated with welfare citizenship? The New Arlseford vestry acknowledged these questions in 1820 when it gave William Smith "a voluntary donation" to recognise "the industry he has shewn in the maintenance of his wife and 8 children without having applied to the parish for relief for the same."[26] Yet the epistolary advocates of the poor in the nineteenth century wrote harrowing tales about the deserving, the inadequate, and the unworthy, often seeking to rehabilitate the latter in the eyes of officials. They did so because, when confronted with the reality of the poor on their doorsteps, the moral categories of deserving or undeserving, good or bad character, and worthy and unworthy dissolved, just as did other binary categories such as immigrant or native and White or Black.

In a modern sense these competing ideas about the importance of character in particular strike to the heart of public conceptions of welfare citizenship and fraud. For "Johny," responding to a 2008 article, "Scroungers will be the ruination of the welfare system in this country they cry about human rights but don't give a stuff once they get their money."[27] In other words, character had been outweighed by law, making citizens of those who ought not to be. A sub-strand of this issue, and one that has interwoven the entire history of the welfare system from 1601, is the question of what constitutes the balancing "contribution" to the rights associated with welfare citizenship. The ultimate fraudster – an un-citizen – was the person who had never made a contribution.[28] In 2023 Oliver Anthony's song "Rich Men North of Richmond" raced to the top of the charts. Left-leaning commentators saw it as an extreme right-wing anthem. Billy Bragg even wrote a counter-song. In fact, "Rich Men" was a powerful critique of the bloated power of elites, an issue as central to the left as to the right. Still, at its heart were questions that are relevant to this chapter: Who gets taxed? For what? Who listens to the people? Who should be eligible for welfare? What to do about scroungers? Who matters?[29]

Four further issues crystallise the enduring complexities more fully. *Should welfare citizenship be conditional on gratitude?* Margaret Downie recalled paying weekly pensions to old people in Southend (Essex) in the early 1960s. She remembered an old agricultural labourer who "always thanked me profusely despite my saying it was his pension I was giving him in his own right but I never got through."[30] Many of those writing to the Old and New Poor Laws between the early eighteenth century and 1929 also expressed gratitude, even if few of them really meant it. Some people who left comments on newspaper and blog articles and who themselves were welfare dependent expressed gratitude and made a distinction between their own attitudes and those of the shameless scrounger and fraudster. Yet throughout the period from 1601 to the present many claimants shunned any sense or rhetoric of gratitude, leading to extensive public and policy comment on the enfeebling of obligation balances to welfare citizenship.

Should welfare be retributive? Walter Rose notes that during the nineteenth-century enclosure of his village, the dependent poor found that any land due to them "was entered in the award as the property of the parish officers."[31] The ordinary household goods of the poor could also be appropriated so as to pay back welfare costs.[32] More than a century later, and reflecting on a story that Diane Halko of Arbroath had faked disability to claim £40,000 in benefits but had only been ordered to pay back £1, "Bulldogsrul" said: "a total slap in the face to every tax payer in Scotland! She should be made to repay the money even if it takes the rest of her life. Going into court wheezing and hobbling, aye right."[33] As Wim van Oorschot notes, the need for signs of superficial gratitude has strong modern traction.[34] On the other hand, and as we have seen in several earlier chapters, ordinary people seem to have had a strong tolerance for the fallout of messy lives and shunned opportunities to make the welfare system retributive (by reporting fraud) when they had the chance.

Should welfare citizenship be dependent upon taking any old work? The economist Patrick Minford argued that Margaret Thatcher had broken the "huge support of anyone who wanted to be unemployed for as long as they liked" and that post-COVID the key imperative had to be: "You've got to get a job if you possibly can, and you can't be too fussy about what it is … we can't have people retiring early on the basis of benefits."[35] Minford overstated ingrained benefit-dependency in the late 1970s but Mrs D.1.P., reflecting on Preston in the 1920s and 1930s, made an exactly similar point about work. She claimed that the interwar generations would do any job so as *not* to be on welfare but (talking about the contemporary situation in 1979), "Today, they don't want it, they are being kept too easily."[36] Mr M.8.B. of Barrow recollected an interwar character called "mothballs." In one conversation, as he stood in the doorway of M.8.B.'s family shop watching workers knocking off for lunch, he commented, "and in about quarter of an hour they'll come dashing back" repeating the same pattern forever: "I haven't done a day's work in my life and they call me silly old mothballs" but "what would you call that lot?"[37] "Mothballs," then, encapsulates a central problem for the welfare state: what to do when someone refuses just to do any old work, or indeed anything at all? There are modern resonances. In responding to a blog on dole scroungers in

2008, "ahforfoulkessake" asked why on earth he should take "a job that pays hardly any more than I would be getting on benefits," but he nonetheless made a distinction between himself and the "lazy bums" who had *never* worked.[38] This distinction between a welfare conditionality based upon any work, and a different sort of conditionality that relates continuing welfare support to the opportunity for remuneration carrying a person above a meaningful gain threshold, is one that deeply colours the whole of the welfare debate from 1601.

Finally, should welfare citizenship be (to use the words of several focus group participants) about living or existing? On 18 December 1846 the Parochial Board of Tongue challenged a claim that they had neglected Isabella Kay of Oag (Sutherland), arguing that: "the allowance now given to this pauper is in the opinion of the meeting, exceedingly liberal, and perfectly adequate to meet all her needs and wants."[39] Recalling early nineteenth-century Burwash, Mr Noakes told the story of his grandfather who "got into some trouble" as parish overseer "because he would not allow a labouring man pumps for his daughter to go to a dance in."[40] The modern equivalent might be an expectation that welfare payments should be given to support white-water rafting. If in turn we fast-forward through the subsequent history of the British welfare state, a group of related questions – Should someone be able to achieve a better standard of living by exploring and exploiting the rights of welfare citizenship than someone who was working? Should the welfare system meet the costs of wants rather than merely needs? Should there be time limits to support? Is adequacy enough? – hove episodically into view. Modern studies that trace a progressive retreat of public support for living as opposed to merely existing are usually disengaged from this long and episodic history, in which such retreat may just represent a return to the welfare norm.[41] Compelling psychological experiments (albeit in non-British contexts) in which empathy-inducing case studies of hardship and suffering on the part of welfare claimants and applicants barely shift the dial in terms of attitudes towards redistribution, tend strongly in this direction.[42]

In my brief flirtation with ChatGPT I learned that:

> fraud disrupts this social contract [the rights associated with welfare citizenship] by creating an imbalance. It diverts resources from those who genuinely need assistance, undermining

the fairness and effectiveness of the welfare system. Benefit fraud erodes public trust in the system and can lead to negative perceptions of welfare recipients, which can further stigmatize those in need.

More than 1,600 of the comments that I have harvested made exactly this point, and we can trace the same sentiment stretching back to guidance manuals in the seventeenth century. The presence, perception, detection, and punishment of fraud is perhaps the single most important variable shaping the meaning of and support for welfare citizenship. As my father said endlessly when (falsely) accused, if he could be "had up" after a lifetime of tax and "stamp" contributions while others had just "dossed all their lives," why not just close the welfare state and "it's every person for themselves?" The fact that the obvious system flaws which made my father a fraudster are still allowed to reverberate suggests policymakers might quite like this idea.[43] Yet if these have been and still are important questions, it seems entirely possible that welfare citizenship (and with it the presence and continuance of fraud) will become very much more fraught in the later 2020s.

Promises to Be Broken

The question of what the state is "for" has arisen several times so far. In terms of welfare, the issue has in the 2020s reverberated across Europe as the unfunded and (currently) un-fundable promises accumulated across the post-1945 European welfare systems are finally confronted.[44] Modest growth, spiralling national debts, very significant off-balance sheet liabilities, and tensions over the rights of immigrants have fuelled rising pension ages, cutbacks to working-age welfare, increasing conditionality, and even doubts about the universalism of flagship allowances.[45] These debates and changes have much further to go, given the blistering cost of servicing national debts and Europe-wide angst about the practical limits of individual and corporate tax burdens. According to Peter Taylor-Gooby, modern and shared pressures on the European welfare states have generated either "adaptation, evolution or recalibration of the welfare settlement" rather than serious attempts at systemic change, or calls for managed decline and dismantling. In this context the British welfare settlement "appears robust" because, he argues, both governing parties adopt a commitment to residualist liberal market welfare.[46] I am somewhat less sanguine either that the settlement has ever been really settled, or that it has a future.

In Britain, promises broken or soon to be broken stand out clearly. The brief (in terms of the time-scales of this book) flirtation with universal child benefits from 1979[47] was ended by LibCon and Conservative administrations between 2010 and 2017, the changes in effect creating an army of tax and benefit fraudsters at the same time as hitting the very poorest households hardest.[48] In 2023 Chancellor Jeremy Hunt pulled back from further increases in the qualifying age for state pensions. Others before him had used that ruse to preserve universalism, justifying later retirement primarily in terms of growing life expectancy. Yet pre-COVID, increasingly unhealthy middle-class and middle-age lifestyles had begun to both limit rises in life expectancy and narrow the difference between men and women. By 2021/22 life expectancy was falling, brutally exposing some of the baked-in faults of the universal system (not least the fact that working-class people contribute the longest and yet enjoy the shortest retirements), encouraging widespread reflection on the costs of universal pensions and at last drawing attention to eye-watering unfunded public-sector pension liabilities that do not sit on the state balance sheet. Britain is not Italy (where an impossibly high 17 per cent of 2020 national income was already spent on pensions[49]) but by 2023 political and popular rumblings about the sustainability of universalism were heard.[50] The SNP's disastrous handling in February 2022 of the question of accumulated pension rights and the future of universalism in a potentially independent Scotland was a caution to other parties, but the pressure is clear even as the evidence builds strongly that restricting welfare access for average and middle income taxpayers fundamentally undermines public support for welfare and progressive taxation.[51] There is historical precedent: In a House of Lords debate on 26 March 1998, the Earl of Onslow noted of the welfare state that "the only thing that has become absolutely clear is that every single cash forecast has been quite horrendously wrong. It is stated old age pensions in 1905 were expected to cost 2.5 million, but in four years they cost £5 million. I know the cost of the disability allowance was way in excess of what we thought it was going to be." While he was not questioning the principles, he warned that we cannot do "what President Kennedy did as regards going to the moon" and simply keep adding noughts on the end.[52] Even without big debate about cold hard cash, Jeremy Hunt's freezing of tax allowances at the same time as uprating pensions will inevitably lead to the effective means-testing of pension income – a return to the basic ideas of 1908. Pensions are one of the least defrauded payments in the welfare system, but changes in the profile of the "average pensioner" (more indebted, living longer but with poorer health, and with higher expectations of relative living standards) will inevitably generate more pressure in this area. While John Macnicol argues that "retired people are never members of the underclass," the 2020s have seen definitive signs of a change in this arena.[53]

Long-term care of the aged has likewise been the subject of seemingly unending broken promises and has generated increasingly blatant fraud. Regulations that family must look after the dependent poor are still on the statute book in Germany and Switzerland. Such requirements were, as we have seen in several chapters of this book, also part of the conceptual infrastructure of welfare up to the 1940s.[54] The principle was well enunciated by the Somerset rector John Skinner, who in 1822 argued that the poor laws had "a bad influence" in undermining the "natural affection which ought to bind a human creature in a more especial manner to his kindred" because the dishonest and morally bankrupt argued that alleviating destitution was the responsibility of the parish rather than the family.[55] The modern welfare state (through payment limits and welfare withdrawal thresholds) focuses familial and affective responsibilities on the co-resident household, leading to arcane rules on who "counts" and, subsequently, to both fraud and perceptions of fraud. But for aged adults in need of domiciliary or institutional care the situation is even further complicated, ruled by a tax on inheritance for those who have been fortunate or cautious or both, and caps on the quality and availability of support for others. The assertion that old people are acting to reduce their assets in anticipation of the need for care and the hope of securing state funding has become increasingly common, and the surveillance methods and rules have correspondingly multiplied. Comprehensive schemes to deal with these circularities have floundered for proximate reasons including cost, intergenerational fairness, and an unwillingness to impose compulsory insurance schemes on a younger generation already pinned to the ground with housing costs and student loans. But the actual reason for delay and dissembling is that no one has yet been able to deal with the moral hazards of state-financed elder care.

The slippery citizenship positions of other groups in the British welfare system have been an ongoing feature of this book. The unemployed of the seventeenth, eighteenth, and nineteenth centuries moved slowly and imperfectly from being constructed as unworthy and dishonest – eligible for the most residual elements of a residual welfare state – to becoming upright citizens with benefits as of right.[56] Even here, however, gains were fragile and unemployment welfare carried a stigma.[57] The latter is well located in the 1950s by the actress Joy James. Reflecting across several autobiographical texts on her time growing up poor in Nottingham, she tells of being sixteen and getting dressed up for Friday night out. In one poem about her encounters with sharply dressed teenage Teddy Boys, she writes:

A matter of pride, never been on the dole,
As they Creep and Jive and Rock and Roll.
This is the cream of fifties youth
Fresh and pure and short in tooth.[58]

By the 1980s and certainly after 1997, as we have seen, governments were once again constructing benefit dependence of working-age adults as reflecting lack of pride, energy, and moral worth.[59] Datafication of the welfare state threatens to make this situation immeasurably worse.[60] British government promises to this group in terms of access to welfare and its value were at best vague and fleeting. Even so, the question of how to balance the rights and responsibilities of the unemployed will be one of the key areas in which the nature and limits of welfare citizenship are tested in the 2020s as new and revived powers to inspect bank accounts roll out across the welfare recipient cohort.

The other major area of reckoning will be in the sphere of support for the disabled. Between 1601 and the interwar period, as I argued in chapter 5, the disabled were amongst the most conceptually secure groups of welfare recipients. This status has not only gone into reverse from the later twentieth century, but (and as we began to see above) decisively so.[61] The "problem" of the disabled welfare recipient has magnified as they have become casually elided with spiralling numbers of the long-term sick (who may or may not be disabled), massive job vacancies, and a rising minimum wage which increases the moral as well as economic value of work.[62] Given the enlarged cohort of disabled and long-term sick in the 2020s, restoring the real value of (and access to) disability benefits and undoing the work of the LibCon coalition would cost more than £5bn per year. Restoring the moral rights of the disabled poor, so systematically stripped by all governments from the early 1980s, would cost much more than this in the sense of establishing new expectations of the purpose of disabled welfare. A return to an even longer-term historical norm would truly test the limits of a residual welfare state.

Ultimately, then, we come back to the question of what welfare citizenship has and can look like in a residualist welfare state where recipients are *expected* to be dishonest. There have been times when the nature, scope, and limits of that citizenship were well defined in either a negative or positive sense: 1601, the 1660s, the 1790s, and early 1800s (when widespread child benefits were first tested), 1906–12, and 1942–49, 1997, or the 2010s. Such periods have been fleeting and most individuals at most times can have had only the most intangible grasp of what it meant to be a welfare citizen. The speech that Daniel Blake intended to make to the court about his treatment at the hands of the welfare system ends: "I, Daniel Blake, am a citizen, nothing more, and nothing less."[63] But none of those who participated in my oral history project and focus groups even understood themselves as citizens, full stop. We see this too in the huge spectrum of philosophical, economic, cultural, and political views underpinning the modern comment data that I have collected. As the crisis of the 2020s and 2030s unfolds, governments will have to properly confront longer-term issues about how generous the welfare system broadly defined should be, who should have eligibility, what their obligations and those of their families should be, and who should pay for it. The post-COVID "workshy," people with mental and physical impairments, immigrants, and pensioners will become even more firmly part of this debate, and the linguistic registers of deservingness, fraud, and moral eligibility so redolent of the nineteenth century will re-emerge or be reinforced.[64] In this there is an irony. Broadly defined, historians and historical sociologists played an important part in shaping the welfare settlement – a "new" welfare citizenship; even a new language and rhetoric of welfare – that crystallised with the Liberal welfare reforms in the post-1905 period. Now, more than a century later, these same groups have been largely absent from the debate about the future of welfare. Even more strikingly, while the Webbs felt that their interventions in policy demanded a foundation in the deep history of welfare structures and philosophies, for most modern commentators "history" begins with Beveridge in 1942 or later.[65] In turn, and as John Macnicol eloquently declares in the context of the recycling of conceptual models of the underclass, "politicians have learned nothing and forgotten nothing."[66]

Future Welfare Citizens

To revisit my introductory agenda, who is the future welfare citizen and what matrices of obligation and duty, tax and spend, residuality or comprehensiveness, and morality and empathy should they be expected to traverse? Very different attitudes to concepts of a Universal Basic Income (UBI) in different European states speak to these questions.[67] So do long-term comparisons between the (now dissolving) Nordic welfare model and that in Britain, riots in France over the raising of pension ages, and a deepening right-wing political consensus on the need to contest welfare eligibility for immigrants. The dividend for welfare resources promised by politicians, unions, and think-tanks in their agitation for wealth (for which read "property") taxes, and more generally persistent, often hysterical calls for the same energy to be devoted to curtailing corporate and individual tax avoidance as to confronting welfare fraud, point to a widespread desire to simply kick the can down the road a little more. But for the future welfare citizen, history matters as never before. So, what *should* politicians have learned, given that (returning to Patricia Hollis) the welfare state "is the common wealth of us all"?[68] By inference, how can history help in what Lydia Morris identifies as the need for "civil repair"?[69]

First, by reminding us that the British welfare system has a basic DNA laid down in 1601, one that cannot be wished, rhetoricized, or even legislated away. Welfare was supposed to be residual, both as a matter of practical necessity and because the Old Poor Law was framed in anticipation of the dishonesty of all poor people throughout their lives and inter-generationally. The postwar consensus over the purpose and scope of the welfare state, if in fact there was such a consensus,[70] was a mere blip; it was only a work of twenty-five or so years before it began to revert to this basic DNA.[71] The welfare system was never supposed to iron out the regional economic inequalities on which it was superimposed.[72] Nor was it ever meant to be strongly or persistently redistributive.[73] Even at the height of the moral belonging of the disabled, no one could have conceived of the disabled welfare citizen having rights to the equivalents of gliding and white-water rafting. And, of course, the poor were never expected to be honest for very long, if at all, so that residualism was justified.

I have in this book outlined much excellent work from the perspectives of social policy, sociology, economics, law, media, and anthropology which evidences creeping conditionality in modern welfare policy, stigmatisation, demonisation of welfare claimants (especially immigrants), and the chilling effects of cuts to welfare programmes. Equally I have dealt with much evidence from the poor and their advocates of the emotional, physical, and mental toll of grinding need both within and outside the welfare state. But presentism does not serve us well, allowing as it does academics as well as policymakers to see newly minted gold instead of tired old copper.[74] When Mrs Redford, the nineteenth-century "Banbury Female Martyr," wrote that society was full of "the cruel enemies of the poor" who would "treat them as something inferior to human beings," she could just as well have been writing of attempts in the 2010 to define away welfare eligibility for the disabled.[75] The moral considerations shaping welfare citizenship under the Liberal welfare reforms[76] are being debated afresh in the 2020s. Attempts to purge the seventeenth-century welfare accounts of the wandering poor have their analogue in the most difficult of all welfare cases: how to get payments for those without a long-term address? The welfare state is residual. It was always supposed to be residual. Without fundamental rethinking and refinancing, it will *remain* residual. And whatever the poor, interest groups, and left-leaning politicians think, we must understand that residuality and expected dishonesty are and always have been intimately linked.

The second history lesson for future welfare citizenship flows from these observations: the public suspects much more fraudulent activity in the welfare system than is ever officially measured or publicised. This is not, or not merely, a function of rabble-rousing politicians and the press. The consistency of the observation all through the period from 1601 is literally breathtaking. People (including very often those receiving welfare[77]) see, suspect, infer, hear, and gossip about fraud on a substantial canvas. They always have, and this has reinforcement and agenda-setting effects for wider attitudes towards welfare and welfare recipients.[78] Yet, the tone and consequences of these beliefs is not inevitably negative; I have traced an architecture in which not all fraud is equal and not all of it is constructed negatively. Modern legal and philosophical conceptions of basic human and social rights have their analogue in historical narratives of fraud by necessity. People have always understood that fraud can be accidental or, worse, a pitfall for the unwary, given the complexity of welfare systems and the messy lives many welfare recipients lead.[79] And while single mothers have a consistently negative place in public constructions, the fact that groups like the disabled can move from being morally cast-iron to systemic fraudsters in the popular imagination also suggests that movement in the opposite direction is possible. But there *is* much more fraud than is officially measured, let alone sought and found, even if elite commentators contest this idea in historically uninformed ways.[80] Persistent political fictions reported in *Hansard* that welfare fraud eats up a small proportion of welfare resources thus become part of the public "problem" of welfare and increase latent support for residuality and the demonisation of welfare recipients.[81]

A third lesson of history is thus that any attempt to refashion welfare citizenship for the 2020s and beyond requires a fundamental engagement with the complexities of welfare fraud.[82] It is not a bug in the modern welfare system but a systemic feature that spans all the organisational forms of the British welfare state. Its existence over the long-term justifies an intensively residualist welfare state and stratified citizenship. As Keleigh-Ann Groves suggests, such views are unlikely to be popular.[83] Yet, across chapters 7 to 10, I have developed an argument that, whatever the screaming headlines, it has been and is in no one's interest (even historians') to report, seek, and find fraud. Unpicking this long history of collusion and illusion would be costly at multiple levels: political (acknowledging a long history of undetected fraud; headlines about investigatory methods); financial (seeking and finding is hugely costly even if predictive analytics become a comprehensive technological reality;[84] addressing the causes of non-intentional fraud in my architectural model costs even more); social (the impact of fraud sanctions on individuals and families; the divisive aspects of encouraging a zero-tolerance approach to free-riding); and cultural (generating new intergenerational understandings of citizenship, entitlement, and obligation is inevitably painful and involves giving up entrenched rhetorical and philosophical positions; the welfare status of immigrants would have to be settled for the long term[85]). Done creatively and cumulatively – traversing staged vistas of the sort envisaged by Ben Baumberg in his ideas for saving the welfare state[86] – the project would take a long time, inevitably so, given more than 420 years of calculated under-action. Continuing the illusion that anyone actually wants to seek and find fraud would also of course have its immense costs which will accelerate as the economic, social, and labour market changes of the 2020s rip through the social fabric. There are, too, deep socio-cultural and economic costs to residuality, something that the (in their own eyes) deserving poor of any period elaborate when they suggest that benefits could be much higher for them if the fraudsters were not using up the money. Sustained exposure of the effects of such fraud appears to be a necessary prerequisite for addressing such costs.

Research by GfK NOP provides some sense that, if executed over an appropriate time-scale, the confrontation of fraud does not have to be framed as a war or involve vast numbers of new prosecutions. In evaluating the 2006 *Targeting Benefit Fraud* campaign, the researchers found that multi-channel advertising on a tri-partite basis – the dangers of getting caught for fraud, the consequences, and the damage to the moral fabric of fraudulent actions – left 60 per cent of *existing* claimants unmoved. However, they found that the same messages were particularly effective in generating lasting recall on the part of those on the "cusp of fraud" – new applicants or claimants, and those in areas of high welfare penetration who were not currently fraudsters – such that "sustained PR activity at a low level over a longer time period may be more effective than shorter more expensive activity." In short, and with associated attempts to improve communication for younger claimants who are the least likely to "get" the welfare rules, it might be possible to reduce the flow of fraud and thus over time reduce the stock of fraudsters.[87]

The derivation of policy constitutes a fourth history lesson. Across Europe, the crisis of the Western European welfare state has involved many politicians stepping back in haphazard and uninformed ways to the welfare past. Examples include the extension of working lives, withdrawal or capping of universal allowances, emphasis on the primacy of work and the honest payment of associated taxes, shifting boundaries of measured ability and disability, and all manner of rules to slow down applications, reduce the scale of payments, or make keeping payments more difficult. Read in one way, these measures are a statement that the duties on welfare recipients to go with the obligations of states have become unbalanced. Or, provocatively, since lots of people who got welfare a few years ago would not now qualify, they are an acknowledgement of fraudulent practice and intent. In postwar Britain, nothing has drawn more ire than Universal Credit.[88] But it is not new. Instead, it patterns seamlessly if accidentally onto the basic conception of how to run a welfare system under the Old Poor Law, 1601 to 1834. Similarly, the prospect of the British state pension age rising to seventy for modern twenty-somethings is not new; it merely takes us back to where the state pension started. The workism that so many modern commentators have located as developing from the 1980s onwards is not new;[89] it reflects the basic intent of the founding welfare statutes of 1601. And modern emphasis on welfare dependency as a moral and behavioural choice rather than a medical, structural, or cyclical necessity is not new;[90] it too can be traced in an unbroken line right back to 1601. Such historical perspective is lacking from parliamentary debate. This has consequences.

Most significantly, as policymakers selectively track back to a welfare past, they singularly fail to notice or reinvigorate the associated practical measures and organisational or philosophical structures that made residualist welfare a workable proposition. Several are important. *First* are the mechanisms which meant that the poor retained agency – that "fraught apportionment of personal capability and incapability"[91] – to challenge narrative and practice, whatever the law might have said.[92] We should not overstate the degree of agency open to the historical poor. But it *was* there. The Reverend Skinner recognized it in 1821, lamenting that "it is not merely in the microcosm of this Parish that the lower orders are striving to supplant their superiors."[93] In researching this book I have met few poor people who would even know the taste of such agency. Its progressive demise has meaning for the process of establishing a new and acceptable welfare citizenship for the 2020s. Systems which are incapable of receiving or acting upon signals from clients, rather than merely funders and policy masters, never become truly settled. If residuality is to remain the core economic and ideological underpinning of the British welfare state, a key task must be to re-establish the diverse mechanisms through which the state can listen to its welfare citizens and re-impose the legal and process obligations on administrations to actively hear them. The need for the modern historian in this endeavour is compelling.

The *second* necessary measures are meaningful localism and official discretion, the two factors that effectively made the Old Poor Law precursor to Universal Credit workable by tying local economic and political elites into sophisticated signalling systems of need, and required the balancing of individual obligation with parochial duty. I do not argue here that the Old and New Poor Law or the interwar public assistance committees avoided harsh moral judgement, scandal, or episodic attempts to crush the poor (though of course these are also features of the modern welfare system) but I do suggest that these practices could not be enacted easily or without contention. Peter Taylor-Gooby notes that in the modern system those most in need of welfare are also those least able to have or to exercise political influence.[94] In pre-1930s Britain the poor were formally disenfranchised, and yet the politics of localism and local discretion gave them a real practical influence. As Miles Ogborn observes, in a situation where the "centre" of the British state constitutes a "kaleidoscopic array" that has consistently necessitated and fostered regional and local autonomy, localism is the only way to develop the "best practicable form" of the welfare state.[95]

Third, policymakers (and much of modern historiography) have lost sight of the importance of local taxation. Martin Halla and Friedrich Schneider argue that growing national tax burdens enhance the acceptability of fraud, both because people come to believe that having paid heavily into a system it is acceptable to get something out and because in a high-tax environment people "view both tax evasion and benefit fraud as tools to restore purchasing power."[96] Crudely put, the higher tax rates and reduced eligibilities for welfare that are the favourite sticking plaster for many of those grappling with the modern crisis of welfare both undermine the moral standing of the welfare state and increase fraud.[97] Prior to the 1930s, all, most, or some welfare was variously financed by local tax structures in which officials could both define need and choose the rate at which to fund it and thus how much to tax themselves. The consequences for claimants could have been catastrophic, especially when set against ingrained doubts about the honesty of the poor and sustained belief that welfare fraud was rife. They were not. Although poor areas could find themselves overwhelmed by too much need and too few tax resources, they generally did not.[98] There was plenty of grumbling, but in the end when officials were faced with need and the messiness of everyday life, they raised taxes at a rate that would have been inconceivable for the national state to have invoked. As local taxation has receded, so the moral standing of groups like the disabled has also collapsed.

Fourth, accidental policymaking trips into the past have lost sight of the meaning of residuality. The pre-1930s welfare system assumed that state welfare payments would be topped up, that there would be what Groves calls "thick" resource matrices.[99] The only question was how to calibrate the local and individual rates of payment withdrawal to other resources. This was a flexible and localised system in which, rather surprisingly, many of the poor made absolutely no effort to hide top-up resources once they had obtained welfare payments in the first place. Decisions and withdrawal formulae were not always opaque, consistent, or free from estimations of moral worth, but they were ultimately contestable. A new standard of welfare citizenship, if set alongside a residual welfare state, will require a fundamental rethinking of the meaning and acceptable scale of top-up resources.[100] In other words, Britain will need UBI in reverse.

Finally, I have spent most of my adult life advocating for the poor. I am, to borrow a phrase from a comment used in an earlier chapter, one of those "lardy assess." Organized groups, interest groups, and individuals such as myself are a vital part of the mechanism by which the very poor manage to navigate a deliberately complex welfare system.[101] Advocates have always been important in this role, as I have argued, and modern governments make implicit assumptions that such advocates *are* at work. But something *has* changed. In the modern era I – we – can change the experience of individuals; in the welfare past, advocates could realistically expect to change the experiential infrastructure of the whole system. Debates about the future of welfare citizenship thus need to include the renewal of the channels of influence that once existed, and without which the residual welfare state will continue to be a *Hansard* parody.

I do not, of course, argue that knowledge of history is the only required component in a new conversation about welfare citizenship of the sort that will, like it or not, be a feature of the 2020s. Nor do I argue that the mechanisms, philosophies, structures, and sentiments of historical welfare regimes pattern inevitably onto modern problems, though many do. But we *have* reached a crisis point with multiple layers: crises of taxation, debt, entitlement, and trust in the state and welfare state, the deepening of moral judgements about welfare claimants, and an uninformed policymaking class who fail to acknowledge that the model *is* actually broken. In this the poor suffer. And they really do suffer. Stephen Reynolds argued in his 1908 memoir of life in the poor community of Sidmouth, that: "the air is full of social remedies [that is the LWR], mostly quack." Real reform he argued did not have roots in politics, laws, societies, social surveys, and investigations or publications, but in "sympathetic understanding." And "Reform without understanding *is* quackery – in every sense of the word." He went on: "for the supposed welfare of the people will continue to be the handiest political weapon; for the property-owning articulate classes are better able to prevent themselves being played with … to learn to care for the poor, for their own sake, is to fear for them nothing so much as slap-dash, short-sighted social legislation."[102]

Reynolds was not a rabid opposer of welfare. Nor am I. While a fundamental zero-tolerance of welfare fraud is necessary whatever the cost, this would go hand-in-hand with a reconsideration of the residual welfare state, the nature of entitlement, and the confrontation of centuries-old concerns about the very honesty of the poor. Illusion, collusion, and fiction would be put to good use in reimagining the welfare citizen of the 2020s and onwards, moving from contempt or conditional reciprocity to understanding or empathy and ultimately altruism.[103] The exercise would be costly in a financial sense. Indeed localism, discretion, the renewal of the moral mandate of the disabled and other things for which I have advocated above – the expansion and recapturing of what Morris understands as the "boundary of our social and moral community"[104] – would be, to use the words of a local butcher on whom I tried out these ideas in 2023, "arse-squeakingly expensive." A new welfare contract, as opposed to the rhetorical hope of it in the Blair and Cameron years, will require new income streams and new moral acceptances. This will not be achieved easily, as Peter Taylor-Gooby recognizes in his own assessment of how to address current welfare crises. He and his collaborators remind us that solutions require that those with "relevant interests are included within the consensus"[105] (including of course activist claimants[106]) if the relatively uninformed querulous citizen is to be satisfied.[107] Historians have just such a place in the Royal Commission on the Future Welfare Citizen that is now required. They are a resource much as the historical sources interrogated here have been a resource to deconstruct presentist dilemmas.

Can such aspirations be realized? The Conservative Party in 2024 stands hopelessly split between those who wish to protect the real value of welfare payments and others who want to cut the welfare bill through enhanced conditionality in order to fund tax cuts. The Labour Party is largely silent on welfare, acutely aware of the tax-and-spend traps being laid by the government ahead of a 2024 election. Both the Scottish- and Welsh-devolved administrations have done more to protect and even extend welfare schemes, but the costs of doing so in terms of required budgetary savings have now become acute. This is not the rich fertiliser for sweeping change, and it is thus unsurprising that activists, lawyers, and claimant groups have gained increasing traction in challenging aspects of conditionality and stratification through courts and tribunals. But in the end a reckoning has arrived. The wider meltdown of the western-European welfare model is happening now. Patch and repair options have been exhausted. Britain will not perhaps take the lead in a conversation about what we might call "new welfare citizenship" but our political and elite classes are not able to avoid the wash of this particular boat. A 2024 election will result in one group of that elite frantically grasping for levers of change against the backdrop of unsustainable structural deficit. A new welfare citizenship is the *only* answer.

NOTES

Preface

1   From 6 July 2021: https://www.pinsentmasons.com/out–law/news/
    covid-19-support-cost-uk-taxpayers-billions-fraud-error.
2   From 13 July 2021: https://www.ftadviser.com/companies/2021/07/13/
    how-hmrc-is-stepping-up-its-furlough-fraud-investigations/.
3   S-M. Bates, "NHS Swindler," *Daily Mail*, 12 January 2019, 51.
4   L. Crossley, "The Stripping Ninja," *Daily Mail*, 17 December 2015, 23.
5   Clery, "Welfare," 24–44; Mau, *The Moral Economy*.
6   From 18 December 2014: https://www.dailymail.co.uk/femail/article-2877774/
    The-single-mother-eight-children-planning-lavish-Christmas-funded-benefits-
    worth-2-200-MONTH.html. On the singular importance of Christmas for
    welfare recipients: Seabrook, *Cut Out*, 134.
7   Golding and Middleton, *Images*.
8   Dorey, "A Poverty," 333–43.
9   See https://forums.digitalspy.com/discussion/2090969/mother-of-eight-marie-
    buchan-the-benefits-cap-will-make-me-homeless/p9; accessed 31 December 2016.
10 Hills, *Good Times*, 13.
11 OECD Policy Tables (2018).
12 Taylor-Gooby, "Re-doubling," 815–35; McKay and Rowlingson, "Social Security,"
    179–200.
13 *The Guardian*, 13 May 2013.
14 BBC Online, 5 June 2017.
15 *The Independent*, 16 November 2017; C. Moran, "Benefit Fraud versus Tax
    Fraud?" *The Times Magazine*, 2 December 2023. Comparison to tax avoidance
    is a motif in the wider academic literature: Dorey, "A Farewell to Alms," 93.
    Yet this too has deeper roots as a public narrative. Frederick Purdy's "The
    Statistics," 291–9, carried extended discussion on the matter.
16 Hayton and McEnhill, "Rhetoric," 101–15; Taylor-Gooby et al., "Moral
    Economies," 9.
17 Taylor-Gooby, "The Divisive," 721; Heron and Dwyer, "Doing," 91–104;
    Seabrook, *Cut Out*, 115.
18 Rieger, "Making Britain," 634–66; Drake, "Disabled People," 421–39; Andrews
    and Jacobs, *Punishing the Poor*; and Hill and Walker, "What Were," 77–99.
19 Innes, King, and Winter, "Settlement," 1–28.
20 Pugh, "Working-Class Experience," 775–96; and Cooper. *The British*.
21 Harris, "Nationality," 73–91.

22 Evans et al., "Whom," 361–80; Deacon, "The Scrounging," 120–35.

23 Finlayson, *Citizen, State*, 43–52; Hennock, "Poverty," 67–91.

24 King, "The British," 37–41.

25 AHRC grants: AH/R002770/1; AH/V010565/1.

26 "RAGE" funded by the EU Justice and Home Affairs programme. CO-PI Dr Gabriella Lazarides.

27 King, *Writing the Lives*, 16–23.

28 Mitchison, *The Old Poor Law*, and Cage, *The Scottish*. Ireland likewise had a very different welfare system throughout our period.

29 Jones and King, "Voices," 76–98. I do not in this analysis consider the Channel Islands, which throughout the period under study had a different welfare and taxation system and where the legal system carried very different penalties for fraud. See Crossan, *Poverty and Welfare*.

30 Harris, "Political Thought," 43–68. King, *Writing the Lives*, 1–28. Progressive means-testing from the 1980s also nullifies a sense of right.

31 I deliberately do not have chapters on individual payment types because beneficiaries tend to traverse multiple forms at any point in time or over a life-cycle.

32 For the same reason I do not consider "education" or arm's-length charities. The boundaries between state and charity have been a topic of considerable debate: Boyer, "The Evolution," 408 and 424–9.

33 Harris, *The Origins*; Digby, *British Welfare*; Levitt, *Poverty and Welfare*; Allen, "Class structure," 88–125; and León and De Jong, "Inequality," 1073–98.

34 On HMRC's 'Connect' database see https://www.ft.com/content/0640f6ac-5ce9-11e7-9bc8-8055f264aa8b.

35 Focus group, 17 August 2016.

Chapter One

1 The 1601 law applied to England and Wales. The differentiation of social policy in the devolved administrations traced by Curtice and Ormston, "Devolution," 21–36, is merely a return to historic norms.

2 Carter and King, "'I think,'" 117–44; Evans and Jones, "'A stubborn,'" 101–21.

3 Harris, "Parsimony," 44–5, 60–2.

4 Deacon, *In Search*, 9. For localism in the 1905 Unemployed Workmen Act: Boyer, "The Evolution," 424–9. Also Digby, "Changing Welfare," 297–322.

5 Kjaer, *The Medieval*, 4–11 and 160–83, and van Bavel and Rijpma, "How Important," 159–87.

6 Feldman, "Migrants," 88, describes the line between deservingness and

its opposite as being thin and fragile. The same point is made by Shepard, "Honesty, Worth," 95–6.

7 Pugh, "Working Class," 786, notes that the clause excluding those already in receipt of poor relief instantaneously created 160,000 "undeserving" people.

8 Harris, *The Origins*, 1.

9 Paz-Fuchs, *Welfare to Work*, 75–91.

10 King, *Poverty and Welfare*, 181–226.

11 King, "The rights," 235–62; Morris, "Reconfiguring," 271–91.

12 King, *Writing the Lives*, passim; Carter and King, "'I think,'" 117–44.

13 The character of modern local discretion is complex: contrast the positivism in House of Commons Work and Pension Committee, *The Local*, with negative behavioural conditionality highlighted in Park, *The Implementation*, and localism as buck-passing in Meers, "Discretion," 41–60, or Meers, "Panacean Payments," 115–29.

14 Grover, "Localism," 349–65; Molander, *Discretion*, 128–41.

15 Paterson, "The Poor Law," 171–93; Mitchison, "Who Were," 140–8.

16 Saraceno, "Retrenching," 35–41.

17 Chinn, *Poverty*, 81–8; King, *Poverty and Welfare*, 111–40; Hunt, "Paupers," 408–22; Perry, *Bread*, 40, 44, 45.

18 Scott, *"I Am Constantly"*; Brewer et al., *Social Insecurity*.

19 Though see Paz-Fuchs, *Welfare to Work*, 75–91.

20 Groves, "Understanding," 47–51.

21 King, "'In These,'" 51–66.

22 Innes, "The Experience," 221–47.

23 Williams, *From Pauperism*.

24 On "datafication" of the modern welfare state, see Dencik, "The Datafied Welfare State," 145–66. A "golden" source for government-held data was only launched in late 2022.

25 Fraser, "The Urban," 128–48.

26 Ferguson, "The Political Economy," 27–50, and Hitchcock, *Down and Out*.

27 Golding and Middleton, *Images*, 59–111.

28 Curchin, "From the Moral," 101–18.

29 Park, Clery, Curtice, Phillips, and Utting, *British Social Attitudes*, 28.

30 Jones and King, *Pauper Voices*, passim.

31 Hobbs, *A Fleet Street*.

32 Jones and King, *Pauper Voices*, 17–56.

33 Donovan and Rubery, "Doing the Amateur," 401–30; Seaber, *Incognito*; and Beier, "'Takin' it to the streets,'" 88–116.

34 King et al., *In Their Own Write*, chapter 6.

35 Kendall, *Farming Memoirs*, 181.
36 My father recalls his whole street being profoundly shocked by the residual nature of the welfare state and its rigid rules as portrayed in *Cathy Come Home*.
37 Dixon et al., *The Disability*.
38 Golding and Middleton, *Images*, passim.
39 Groves, "Understanding," 2, 7, 167–94. The same absence was reported in 2011 by Tunley, "Need, Greed," 303.
40 Lindbeck et al., "Social Norms," 534.
41 Tunley, "Need, Greed."
42 Dean and Melrose, "Manageable Discord," 103–18.
43 Dyson and King, "'The streets," 71–102, and Hitchcock, "Vagrant Lives," 125–44.
44 King, *Writing the Lives*, 145–70; Kidd, *State, Society*, 8–64; Hollen-Lees, *The Solidarities*, 126–34 and 210–19; Lowe, *The Welfare State*, 31–44.
45 Golding and Middleton, *Images*, passim.
46 Thane and Evans, *Sinners?* chapters 3 and 5; Evans, *'Unfortunate Objects'*; Williams, *Unmarried Motherhood*; Fink, "Private Lives," 135–48; and Cook, *Rich Law*.
47 Turner, "'Fraudulent' Disability"; Hirschmann and Linker, *Civil Disabilities*.
48 Donoghue and Kuisma, "Taking Back Control," 177–99. Cook, *Rich Law*, 25.
49 J. Reed and E. Bailey, "The Puzzle of UK's Half a Million Missing Workers," *BBC News*, 23 November 2022; T. Wallace and S. Ping Chang, "How Worklessness and School Truancy Drove Britain into Recession," *Daily Telegraph*, 15 February 2024; and Anon., "One Million More People Cite Mental Health Battle: Nearly Half of Working-Age Disability Claims," *The Times*, 22 March 2024.
50 de Vries, Reeves, and Geiger, "Social Class," 843–58; Harris, "Between Civic Virtue," 67–87.
51 Fraser, "The English Poor Law," 24; Collard, "Malthus," 700 and 708; and Crossick, "From Gentlemen," 150–78. Also, Morris, *Dangerous Classes*.
52 Macnicol, "Reconstructing," 99–108.
53 Welshman, *Underclass*; Hitchcock, *Vagrancy*, chapter 4; and Hayward and Yar, "The 'Chav' Phenomenon," 9–28.
54 McArthur and Reeves, "The Rhetoric," 1005–25.
55 Lassalle, "Policing the Margins," 192–202.
56 Issues of composition are also affected by supplementary narratives from literature and science: Alexander, "The Residuum," 99–120.
57 Golding and Middleton, *Images*, 186–201.
58 A point also made by Webb: *My Apprenticeship*.
59 Sen, "Poor," 153–69; Vizard, *Poverty*; Shildrick and MacDonald, "Poverty Talk," 285–303; and Dean, *Social Rights*.
60 In Scotland church and philanthropic welfare remained: Smyth, "'Seems Decent,'" 251–72.

61 Fideler, *Social Welfare*.

62 Hollen-Lees, *The Solidarities*, 88–92; Thiel, "'It isn't,'" 291–318.

63 King and Stewart, *Welfare Peripheries*. On empathy and welfare in periods of austerity see Koch and James, "The State," 1–21.

64 See widespread concern in early 2024 that the DWP was to start direct monitoring of the bank accounts of some welfare recipients.

65 Anon, *Shedding Light*.

66 Hurren, *Protesting*, passim.

67 Lindert, "Poor Relief," 101–40.

68 Lindert, *Growing Public*, and Boyer, *The Winding*, 30–4.

69 Greve, "The Hidden," 203–11.

70 Rarely fully. The "spare room" in Universal Credit has deeper roots than the debate thus far allows.

71 Waddell, "The Rise," 154, 178, and 180. For competing estimates, and figures post-1800, see Taylor, *The Problem*, 12 and 86.

72 Kidd, *State*, 32–44.

73 Hurren, *Protesting*, 128–55, provides a particularly acute account of disguised welfarism.

74 Boyer, *The Winding*, 18.

75 Harris, *The Origins*, 10–13.

76 Boyer, *The Winding*, 18.

77 Keen, *Welfare Savings*, and https://www.statista.com/statistics/283954/benefit-expenditure-in-the-uk/, accessed 9 September 2022; Dilnot, "The future," 492–3.

78 Taylor-Gooby and Taylor, "Benefits and Welfare," 1–28; Gough, "The Crisis," 459–77; Dwyer, "Creeping Conditionality," 265–87; Morris, "New Labour's," 39–57.

79 Hindle, "Civility, Honesty," 40 and 47, and Hindle, "Dependency," 6–35.

80 For an important rebuttal of this view: Williams, "Malthus," 56–82.

81 For modern arguments: K. McKenna, "Unlike the Royals, the Poor Mustn't Be Allowed to Breed like Rabbits," *The Observer*, 28 October 2018, and C. Cooper, "Five Ways the State Could Discourage People on Benefits from Having Large Numbers of Children," *The Independent*, 6 April 2013.

82 Butler and Drakeford, *Social Policy*, 5, suggest that such fracture points are often tied up with national scandals.

83 King et al., *In Their Own Write*, 316–31.

84 Gibson-Bryden, *The Moral Mapping*; Gillie, "Identifying the Poor," 302–25; and Gillie, "The Origin," 715–30. Poverty lines changed concepts of entitlement amongst groups such as the aged. See Boyer and Schmidle, "Poverty," 249–78.

85 The rhetorical similarity in the construction of deservingness by Thiel's Essex interviewees is remarkable. Thiel, "It Isn't."

86 Levine-Clark, *Unemployment*, 6 and 9.

87 Wessel Hansen, "Grief," 35–50.

88 Hennock, "The Measurement," 208–27; Hennock, *The Origin*; and Hennock, "Poverty," 67–91.

89 King, *"We Might be Trusted"*; Lewis, "Gender," 37–55.

90 Whiteside, "Who Were the Unemployed?" 150–69.

91 Jensen and Tyler, "'Benefit broods,'" 5; Edmiston, "Welfare, Austerity," 267.

92 Noble, *Inside*; Jones, "The Illusion," 109–20.

93 I am grateful to an anonymous referee for this point. On Beveridge's own frustrations, see Harris, *William Beveridge*.

94 Whiteside, "Creating," 83–103; Ellis, "No Hammock," 441–70; Neill, "Conservative Thinkers," 162–77; and Jones, "A Bloodless," 1–16.

95 See contributions to Oppenheimer et al., *The State*.

96 Page, *Clear Blue Water?* 77–116; Raison, *Tories*, 146–67; and Römer, "Poverty," 513–51.

97 Hayton and McEnhill, "Rhetoric and Morality," 102.

98 Jensen and Tyler, "'Benefit Broods,'" 480; Chunn and Gavigan, "Welfare Law," 223 and 231.

99 Deeming, "Foundations," 862–86; C. Green, "British People Stopped Believing in the Benefits System Due to Tony Blair, Researchers Claim," *The Independent*, 25 September 2014.

100 Lupton et al., *Social Policy*; Patrick, "All in it Together?," 307–10.

101 Edmiston, *Welfare, Inequality*.

102 The existence of this transfer is disputed by Bradshaw and Holmes, "An Analysis," 39–56.

103 Questions of stigma have a deeper historical grounding: Baumberg, "The Stigma," 181–99.

104 E. Munbodh, "UK Benefit Claims: What DWP Check for When They Investigate Universal Credit Fraud," *Daily Mirror*, 26 August (2021). Comment by "IAmISaid" on the same date.

105 Field notes, 27 August 2021.

106 Coombs and Coombs, *The Journal*, 314, 318, 322, 329, and (quote at this point) 353. My italics.

Chapter Two

1 D. Gadher, "Benefit Cheat Hangs on to Chelsea Flat," *Sunday Times*, 6 May 2012.

2 Likely someone literate and white: Headworth and Rios, "Listening to Snitches," 319–47. Also Taylor-Gooby, "The Divisive," 723 and 728.

3 Morris, "Reconfiguring," 273, 280–2.

4 Morissens and Sainsbury, "Migrants,'" 637–60.

5 Chishimba was also technically defrauding the NHS. No article or comment made this point.

6 https://www.zambiawatchdog.com/zambian-woman-who-obtained-london-flat-by-fraud-loses-it/; accessed 8 April 2022. The word "relieved" is important, signalling doubt over whether the case would be successful.

7 https://www.gov.uk/benefit-fraud/; accessed 2 April 2022.

8 Plant, *Citizenship,* 12. In the theoretical model offered by Groves, "Understanding," chapter 6, Chishimba was navigating a "thin" patchwork of welfare resources.

9 Meers, "Discretion," 46–7, argues that devolving resources to localities is a strategy for avoiding human rights law.

10 "RK" interview, 12 January 1994.

11 Reynolds, *A Poor,* 169.

12 CRO WPR/19/7/6/16/14, Letter.

13 For moral imperatives generated by hunger/starvation: Gurney, *Wanting,* and Griffin, *The Politics.*

14 For comparison see Golding and Middleton, *Images,* 68, and Groves, "Understanding," 116.

15 C. Hayhurst and B. Wright, "Golfer Who Pocketed £26,000 in Disability Benefits while Winning Tournaments Caught Playing 18 Holes," *Daily Mirror,* 12 March 2015; N. Sears, "Afghan Asylum Seeker Who Lived in £1.2 Million House Faces Jail over £30,000 Benefit Fraud," *Daily Mail,* 15 March 2011.

16 M. Chorley, "Ministers Name and Shame Five Biggest Cheats Who between Them Stole £750,000," *Daily Mail,* 16 May 2014.

17 C. Ellicott. "Sixties Pop Star P J Proby Charged with £47,000 Benefit Fraud," *Daily Mail,* 3 February 2011.

18 The headline is from the *Daily Mail* on 19 February 2014, but the case was widely reported.

19 A. Singh, "Humphrey Lyttleton's Son Claimed Thousands in Illegal Benefits, *Daily Telegraph,* 5 August 2011.

20 Golding and Middleton, *Images,* 3, 65, argue that a single 1976 case came to crystallize and drive a wider public narrative on the need to attack scrounging. On concepts of welfare porn see Gavin, "Below the Radar," 707–24.

21 Loveland, "Policing Welfare," 187–209.

22 Connor, "'We're onto You,'" 231–52.

23 K. Ahmed and G. Hinsliff, "Blair Launches Attack on Britain's 'Sick Note' Culture," *Guardian,* 9 June 2002. See also the deeply critical Owen and Harris, "'No Rights," 1–21, and Patrick, "Work," 5–15.

24 F. Ryan, "Is This Truly Britain – A Land That Spies on Sick and Poor People?" *Guardian,* 1 February 2018.

25 Hence the limited usefulness of fraud hotlines: A. Cowburn, "Benefit Fraud

'Witch-Hunt': 280,000 Public Tip-Offs Led to No Action Taken Due to Lack of Evidence," *The Independent*, 15 January 2018.

26 P. Butler, "DWP Hope for £1.3bn Fraud-and-Error Savings Fade with £6bn Loss from Universal Credit Overpayments," *Guardian*, 13 May 2021.

27 The 2021 report is: https://www.gov.uk/government/collections/fraud-and-error-in-the-benefit-system. Accessed 14 September 2022.

28 Levine-Clark, *Unemployment*; Paterson, Coffey-Glover and Peplow, "Negotiating," 195–214.

29 Second World War bombing destroyed the central letter set that would have continued to 1929. These letters are different in style and intent to the petitions considered in Miller, *A Nation*.

30 I have analysed 72 sets of vestry minutes from Berkshire (13), Hampshire (26), Lancashire (8) Northamptonshire (7), Surrey (3), Dorset (2), Norfolk (5), Wiltshire (4), Somerset (1), and Yorkshire (3). I am grateful to Bruce Balmer, Richard Dyson, Margaret Hanly, Peter Jones, Alison Stringer, and Colin Wright for transcribed material in addition to my own.

31 King, *Writing the Lives*, chap. 2, and King et al., *In Their Own Write*, 27–70. The letters have *not* previously been used to analyse welfare fraud or welfare citizenship.

32 Griffin, *Liberty's Dawn*; Humphries, *Childhood*; Tomkins, "Poor-law institutions," 434–72; Mack, *Heart Religion*. My focus on memorials means that overlap with the samples employed by these authors is limited.

33 Torr, *Small Talk*; Kendall, *Farming Memoirs*.

34 Knight et al., "Re-using Community," 63–72.

35 Groves, "Understanding," 97, 102.

36 Berridge and Taylor, "The Problems," 86–94.

37 For the use of such *ad hoc* conversations in pubs, taxis, and the street as evidence, see Samuel, "'Quarry Rough,'" 139–263.

38 I am grateful to Peter Jones for assistance in these multiple sweeps.

39 Waddell, "Writing History," 239–64.

40 Healey, "Kin Support," 318–39, and King, "The Rights," 235–62.

41 Kendall, *Farming Memoirs*, 101–2.

42 "VC" interview, 17 January 1989.

43 Martin and Rose, *Genre Relations*.

44 Rutherford, *Indoor Paupers*.

45 The Rowntree correspondence is the subject of ongoing work by the author. Full transcripts will be available at: policyfactory.org.

46 On concepts of "they" see Hupe et al., "Defining," 3–24.

47 Scott, *Domination*.

48 Bennett, *A Century*, 80. On graffiti see Forman Cody, "'Every lane,'" 82–100,

and Giles and Giles, "The Writing," 336–57. Southwell workhouse graffiti can be found in a blog by Karen Logan, or by visiting the property and the "men's yard" there: https://www.karenlogan.com/2019/11/workhouse-graffiti.html.

49 Rosenwein, *Emotional Communities*. For a clearer location in mass observation: Jones, "Emotional Communities," 102–20.

50 Reynolds, *A Poor*, 168.

51 BBC News, accessed 23 March 2022: https://www.bbc.co.uk/news/uk-59067101

52 In series 4 of the Netflix drama *The Crown*, for instance, Michael Fagan is shown being progressively driven to welfare fraud by the absurdity of the welfare rules in the 1980s, before he eventually breaks in to confront Queen Elizabeth in her bedroom.

Chapter Three

1 *The Times*, 19 January 2019, 15.

2 43 Eliz. 1 c.2, *Act for the Relief of the Poor*, 1601.

3 On the philosophical underpinning of the Old Poor Law: Fideler, *Social Welfare*, and Patriquin, *Agrarian Capitalism*.

4 Charlesworth, *Welfare's Forgotten Past*.

5 Coombs and Coombs, *The Journal*, 27–8.

6 NRO 249p/216/95, Letter. On wider narratives of moral hazard: Hitchcock, "The London," 59–72, and (in the modern context) McKeever, "Social Citizenship," 465–82.

7 ORO, Oxford St Michael, PAR 211/5/C1/1/25, Letter.

8 Wrigley and Smith, "Malthus," 33–62; Himmelfarb, *The Idea*, 100–44 and 156.

9 J. Groves, "Benefit fraud jumps by £500 million in just a year despite ministers' pledges of a crackdown," *Daily Mail*, 9 July 2016, Comment 10 of 281. The word "easy" is a key motif in the underlying data.

10 Less eligibility embodied the principle that welfare should not be at a level which stymied work and self-reliance: MacNicol, "Family Allowances," 137–202.

11 King et al., *In Their Own Write*, 19–23.

12 Harris, "Parsimony," 67–72.

13 Beveridge, *Social Insurance*. The clauses are: 9, 19(v), 19 (vii), 21, 22, 44(g), 98, 110, 112, 122, 125, 128, 130, 131(i–v), 136, 163, 210, 238, 239, 244, 248, 260, 174(ii), 317, 325(ii), 326, 327, 347, 348, 349, 371(b),372, 398, 412, and 417–19. For some consequences of these passages see Nijhuis, "Rethinking," 370–95.

14 See Hills, *Good Times*, 4–5, and Sloman, "Beveridge's Rival," 203–23.

15 Lacey, *Cathy Come Home*; Paget, "'Cathy Come Home,'" 75–90; Gibbs and Lehtonen, "I, Daniel Blake," 49–63; and Sticchi, *Mapping*, 49–62. The latent sub-text that much fraud was "of necessity" can be seen in all these broadcasts.

16 House of Commons Committee of Public Accounts, *The Department*, 3–4.

17 Ibid., 6.

18 DWP, *Fraud and Error*, 1–8. The figures elide in opaque ways the activities of new claimants, existing recipients, and those renewing or extending payments.

19 Ibid., Appendix 1, 10.

20 Ibid., Appendix 5.

21 Anon., *Fraud and Error*. These figures broadly accord with Scampion, *Organised Benefit Fraud*.

22 Anon., *Beating Fraud*, Appendix 1; *Hansard*, vol. 273, "Benefit Fraud," 5 March 1996, in which Peter Lilley noted for 1995 that new fraud detection processes had located "previous undetected fraud of about 10%, which amounts to £1.5 billion a year on income support and unemployment benefit alone" with 2.7% of the budget lost. See also the datasets used by Geiger, *Benefit 'Myths,'* 1, 5–6.

23 *Hansard*, Vol. 146: Debated Tuesday 31 January 1989. This even though Cook, *Rich Law* and Groves, "Understanding," 125, identify the late 1970s as marking a visceral interest in fraud.

24 Fisher, *Report of the Committee*.

25 *Hansard*, Vol. 788: Debated 20 October 1969.

26 The 1958 figures were obtained by cross-referencing figures on the disallowance of claims for maternity and sickness benefits (for all reasons including lateness of application, which was the primary focus of this debate) contained in *Hansard*, "National Insurance Benefits (Claims)," Vol. 587, 8 May 1958, and TNA PIN 60/118, Part-time employment report. The figures for 1952 were obtained by cross-referencing TNA PIN 60/67, National Insurance Advisory Committee: Time limit Report (also referenced in the 1958 debate) and personal estimates contained in *Hansard*, "National Assistance (Increased Scales)," Vol. 499, 29 April 1952.

27 TNA, CAB 23/84 C 44 (36), 25 June 1936.

28 Boyer, *The Winding*, 235–38. Deacon, *In Search*, 97–107.

29 *Fifth Annual Report of the Local Government Board, 1875–76* (London: Eyre and Spottiswoode, 1876), xxxiii, 30–43, 130–1.

30 Hurren, *Protesting*.

31 For the full run of reports: https://www.amdigital.co.uk/primary-sources/poverty-philanthropy-and-social-conditions-in-victorian-britain.

32 Huish is briefly mentioned by Golding and Middleton, *Images*, 16.

33 The surprising absence of this word from letters and ego-documents suggests the particular scope for inquiries to generate invective.

34 For the report: https://ia801203.us.archive.org/0/items/b28746119/b28746119.pdf.

35 Tunley, "Need, greed," 308–10.

36 Brundage, *The Making*.

37 Shave, *Pauper Policies*, 48–51.

38 Sweeping reviews were also a feature of the post-1834 period: Wells, *Victorian Village*, 111–12.

39 Magistrates had some place in overturning these decisions: See Morgan and Rushton, "The Magistrate," 54–77.

40 These are LRO DDX 386/3, Garstang Vestry Minutes Garstang; Chorley Public Library, Chorley Vestry Minutes 1781–1823; NRO 249p/164–66, Oundle Vestry Minutes; Putney and Wandsworth History Centre, PP/1/2/1, Putney Vestry Rough Minutes 1819–1831.

41 For Lancaster (Lancashire) see: LRO PR 866 and 867, Lancaster Letter Books, 1809–19.

42 King, *Crime and Law*, 1–70.

43 Healey, *The First Century*. See also his excellent "Kin support," 318–39.

44 Le Hardy, *Buckinghamshire*. Figures exclude prosecutions for abandonment or bastardy.

45 Haines, *England's Weal*, 4–5.

46 A. Chakelain, "New: You're 23 times more likely to be prosecuted for benefit fraud than tax fraud in the UK," *New Statesman*, 19 February 2021.

47 For comparable European data: Moro-Egido and Solano-Garcia, "Does the perception," 1101.

48 "TY" interview, 15 August 1994. Robin Page – then a welfare official – kicked off 1970s soul-searching about the nature and purpose of the welfare system with his book *The Benefits Racket*. On belief in widespread fraud in the 1970s and 1980s: Reiger, "Making Britain," 653–4.

49 These figures are higher than those found from survey data by Geiger, *Benefit 'Myths,'* 6–9, but Geiger also tries to categorise "reasonable" and "unreasonable" definitions of fraud whereas for my study the precise point is not to conduct such an exercise.

50 Golding and Middleton, *Images*, passim. Also, Duffy and Wolff, "No more," 103–18; Jensen and Tyler, "'Benefit broods,'" 479. Livingstone and Lunt, *Talk*.

51 "KR" interview, 23 August 2008. Contrast Brodie, *Neighbours*, who argues that people trusted the state much more than other people in their communities.

52 On unbelief as a mode of resistance to elite power: Scott, *Domination*, 205.

53 Vincent, *Literacy*; Vincent, *Bread*; and Lyons, *The Writing Culture*.

54 Wells, *Victorian Village*, 148.

55 Webb, *My Apprenticeship*, 376.

56 C. Riches, "Judge slams misuse of welfare state after woman lied to fiddle handouts," *Daily Express*, 19 January 2019.

57 ESRO, PAR 496/37/3/4, Letter. The word "lend" is deliberately used here, implying that her case would not take much time to consider and resolve.

58 Wood, *Some Accounts*, 6.

59 Valentine and Harris, "Strivers," 84–92.

60 NRO, ZB 68/1/306, Newspaper Clipping.

61 See for instance Brome, *A Jovial Crew*, published at the height of a moral panic over begging. For context: Steggle, *Richard Brome*.

62 Golding and Middleton, *Images*.

63 HAC, Tongue Letter Book 1845–68.

64 "KP" interview, 26 September 2016. I thus became a community information-broker.

65 Focus Group, 17 August 2016. Some noted specifically the guidance provided by rightsnet.org.uk. I am grateful to participant "GC," who also allowed me to read an unpublished life-story making these points.

66 Anon., *Truth and Lies*.

67 John Humphreys, "Is Britain Witnessing a Shift in Public Mood over Benefit Dependency and the Beginning of the End for the 'Age of Entitlement'?" *Daily Mail*, 1 August 2013.

68 *Hansard*, Vol. 365, "Social Security Fraud Bill," 27 March 2001.

69 Humphreys, "Is Britain."

70 "RK" interview, 12 January 1994.

71 "B.1.P." interview, Elizabeth Roberts Collection.

72 Foster, "The Poor Laws," xxviii, 624, and 625.

73 Though contrast this with Brodie, *Neighbours*.

74 Razzell, *Life*.

75 HRO, 4M69/PV1, Vestry Minutes of Romsey and Eling, 1816–33.

76 On public reception see: Robert Odams (aka Robin Page): "Harold Wilson Is My Daddy," *The Spectator*, 27 September 1969, 3.

77 For the full debate: https://hansard.parliament.uk/Commons/1969-10-20/debates/8b54e374-eb65-441c-af40-efcf72aff853/SupplementaryBenefits(Payment).

78 Coombs and Coombs, *The Journal*, 12.

79 With good reason. See Okoroji et al., "Elite Stigmatisation," 207–29.

80 Focus group, 1 December 2016.

81 James, *Yo'd Mek*.

82 HRO, 40M75A/PV1 and PV2, Botley Vestry Minutes 1818–1826.

83 Sutton Local Studies Library, LG 15/37/1, Sutton Vestry Book 1810–1829, quoted entry for 6 December 1826.

84 HRO, 95M95, PV2, Ringwood Vestry Minute Book 1811–1850, entry quoted 9 August 1832.

85 J. Wood, "Judge condemns open benefits system after drug dealer scammed £21,000 in handouts and used the money to buy a house," *Daily Mail*, 18 April 2019.

86 For the resonance of these views in the 1970s see Golding and Middleton, *Images*, 112–56.

87 Field notes, 18 January 2005.
88 TNA, MH12,15922, Letter from John Lloyd to the PLC, 22 July 1843.
89 LERO, Constable-Maxwell Collection DG 39/1189, Letter, 1786.
90 *Daily News*, 4 September 1891.
91 M. Ferguson, "Memories of the Slade Camp and Wood Farm (1950s)": Reminiscences of Headington.
92 Well captured by "Debs," commenting on M. Duell, "The Staggering Scale of Britain's Underclass," *Daily Mail*, 17 August 2014, who argued that "So being disabled and living in a council house is two of the three pointers to being part of the 'underclass'?"
93 *Hansard*, debated 16 July 1993.
94 HRO, 145M82/PV1, Bishopstoke Vestry Minutes 1826–1839.
95 Wood, "Judge Condemns."
96 A. Walker, "Judge Blasts How 'Easy' It Is to Steal Benefits as Drug Dealer Jailed for Pocketing £21,000 and Using It to Buy a House," *Manchester Evening News*, 18 April 2019.
97 Wood, "Judge Condemns."
98 Ibid.

Chapter Four

1 A response also noted for the 1970s by Golding and Middleton, *Images*, 63–4, 77–81.
2 M. Chorley, "Benefit Cheats Using the Welfare State as a Money Making Scam," *Daily Mail*, 29 December 2014.
3 Coombs and Coombs, *Journal*, 186–218.
4 Dunning, *A Plain*, 1.
5 Silverthorne, *Deposition Book*.
6 Crowther, "Family," 132.
7 Thomson, "The Decline," 451–82; Thomson, "'I Am Not,'" 265–86; and Hunt, "Paupers," 408–22. Crowther, "Family," 133–4 notes that there were only 7,000 prosecutions nationally in 1880, and 6,000 by 1936.
8 TNA, MH12/8630,3098/A/1839, Samuel Bradshaw, Great Yarmouth, to the PLC, 19 April 1839.
9 Rothersthorpe Parish Church, Letter, 1 November 1786.
10 Ottaway, "Introduction," 5; Prochaska, "Philanthropy," 363; and Goose, "Poverty," passim. We still see this residual narrative in debates over who should pay for care home places.
11 Focus group, 4 April 2014.

12 "PE" interview, 12 December 2008.

13 Morris, "New Labour's," 46; Morris, "The Topology," 247.

14 *An Act for the Relief of the Poor* (39 Eliz. c.3).

15 In 1597 alone there were three further acts – 39 Eliz. c.4; 39 Eliz. c.17; and 39 Eliz. c.21 – clarifying the rights of ex-military as against the casual wandering poor: Gruber von Arni, *Justice*, 73–94. Also Hitchcock, "Begging," 479, and Schen, "Constructing," 453.

16 Beier, *Masterless Men*; Vorspan, 'Vagrancy," 59–81; Slack, *Poverty*; and Lawrence, "The Vagrancy Act," 513–31.

17 Charlesworth, "How Poor Law," 274.

18 Lewis, *Hird's Annales*, 426.

19 TNA, MH12/14736: Six letters and two enclosures, from which all quotes are drawn.

20 Davies, *The Autobiography*. An inspector visiting the Holywell workhouse (Flintshire) noted a poem scratched into the wall of the vagrant ward. Authored by "Yankee Sailor," it lamented the plight of tramps and asked God to "Send the Guardians to hell as soon as they die." TNA, MH12/1333,15567/1871, Andrew Doyle's inspection report, 4 September 1871.

21 HAC, Tongue Letter Book 1845–68.

22 TNA, MH12/14736,15345/1866, Letter annotation, 25 April 1866.

23 The text covers the first two years of a four-year ministry: Church, *Travelling Folk*.

24 Church, *Parish on Wheels*.

25 Ibid., 11.

26 Church, *Travelling Folk*, 15–16.

27 Ibid., 16.

28 Ibid., 18; 29–30 June 1882.

29 On the identity implications of constructing the workhouse as a body to be penetrated see Wahrman, *The Making*.

30 Church, *Parish on Wheels*, 38.

31 Ibid., 39. The term "Egyptian" to indicate fraudster has seventeenth-century origins. See Anon., *The Complete*, 4, column 4. The Welsh poor routinely discharged themselves from workhouses at fair time. TNA, MH12/15924, Letter annotation, 29 May 1845.

32 Ibid., 40. Also contributions to Althammer et al., *Rescuing*; and Althammer et al., *The Welfare*.

33 I find little of the positive attitude identified in Dromi, "Penny," 847–71.

34 Critcher, "Moral Panic," 1127–44.

35 "RR" interview, 14 March 2009.

36 L. O'Callaghan, "Mum-of-Three Who Lied about Being Homeless and Claimed £75k in Benefits Escapes Jail Time," *Guardian Series*, 7 September 2018.

37 In addition to chapter 1 references, see Forrest, "Familial Poverty," 508–28.

38 Mair, *Religion*; Skinner, *Behind*; and Koven, "Borderlands," 94–135.

39 Bolton Local Studies Library, ZHA 17/17, Diary of a Female Poor Law Guardian.

40 TNA, MH12/15924/50, Four letters and associated annotations.

41 EYRO, PE1-702-91, Letter, 9 December 1832.

42 Wright, *Bygone*, 131–2.

43 Leathland, *Essays*, 45–6.

44 Todd, "Family Welfare," 362–87.

45 *Benefits Street* (eOne Films, 2014). Gibbs and Lehtonen, "I, Daniel Blake," 50.

46 K. O'Sullivan, "Where White Dee Is Now," *Daily Mirror*, 14 July 2021, and Paterson et al., "Negotiating," 199–209. For wider context: Macdonald et al., "'Benefits Street,'" and L. Hanley, "Channel 4 Has Betrayed the Residents of Benefits Street," *Guardian*, 8 January 2014.

47 Roger Prouse and Jeune Morris: "Reminiscences of Headington."

48 *Hansard*, vol. 365, "Social Security Fraud Bill, Second Reading," 27 March 2001.

49 Focus group, 11 June 2015.

50 Heinemann, "Is the Welfare State," 241; Macnicol, "Reconstructing," 106.

51 Seccombe et al., "'They think,'" 849–65.

52 F. Hardy, "How Could They All Be So Reckless?" *Daily Mail*, 11 June 2022, 34–5.

53 Fusing newspaper commentary, *Hansard*, life-writing, and oral histories, I find panics in 1963, 1967, 1974, 1983–86, 1998, 2004, 2010, and more consistent concern from 2016.

54 Blaikie, *Illegitimacy*, passim.

55 Ewart Evans, *Where Beards*, 122.

56 Horsman, *Growing up*, 125.

57 Focus group, 4 April 2014. On the wider traction of such narratives: Jensen and Tyler, "'Benefit broods,'" 474.

58 TNA, MH12/14235,26327/1849, Charles Spilman, South Cave, 6 September 1849. For earlier commentary on the unworthy poor of South Cave see Crowther and Crowther, *The Diary*, passim.

59 Royston, *Mending*, 4–7, 9, 16–37.

60 TNA, MH12/14680, 2225/1863, Letter.

61 TNA, MH12/9247/439, 26770/1861, Letter from Mary Stafford, 26 July 1861. Also Griffin, "The Value," 167–85.

62 HAC, CS/6/32–44, Farr Parochial Board. Record of Applications for Relief, and CS/6/13/23–29 & 31, General Register of Poor; HAC, Tongue Parochial Board Correspondence, Letter 162.

63 Cooke, *A Brief*, 30–6.

64 "HP" interview, 23 March 2004.

65 On single mothers as part of the "never deserving poor" see Chunn and Gavigan, "Welfare Law," 220, 230–2.

66 The DWP press release "Campaign says no compromise in crackdown on benefit fraud," 21 October 2014, noted that its advertising campaign to increase the level of snitching on fraudsters had been targeted at only "50 towns and cities across the country."

67 BBC Panorama, "Britain on the Fiddle," 3 November 2011. On internalisation see Baumberg, "The Stigma," 192–3.

68 See Geary and Stark, "What Happened," 215–28.

69 *Hansard*, 1 July 2019.

70 "TM" interview, 3 July 2016. See also N. Gutteridge, "Quarter of Working Age People in Blackpool Are on Benefits," *Daily Telegraph*, 4 September 2023.

71 Focus group, 17 August 2016. For context see Lupton and Power, "Disadvantaged," 119, 126, 134, 136.

72 For a particularly important study of London see Boulton, "Double Deterrence," 54–80.

73 Bowie, *English Indices*, 1, 5–7, 11, 14–15, and 18. Golding and Middleton, *Images*, 60, also centre their work around a case from Liverpool.

74 Contrast poverty line/human need definitions 1870–1980s with the newer indices of deprivation or multiple deprivation that now direct both resources and analysis. See Gazeley, *Poverty*; Andrews, "Multiple Deprivation," 605–24; and Understanding towns in England and Wales-Office for National Statistics (ons.gov.uk).

75 H. Gye, "Benefits Streets," *The Sun*, 12 September 2018.

76 See for instance SORO, Q/SPET/1/148, Petition of the Churchwardens and Overseers of Wellington, which noted that migrants, "although warned to depart, they will not do so." On the "politics of settlement": Hindle, "Destitution," 56–63.

77 *An Act for the better Releife of the Poore of this Kingdom* (1662, Chas II, c.1–3). Such certificates required precise naming of those covered so as to avoid fraud.

78 King, "Poor Relief," 81–101.

79 North, *A Discourse*, 13.

80 GRO, P328 OV 7–8, Letter 11 October 1825.

81 TNA, MH12,14018/290,8574/B/1846, Letter 17 June 1846.

82 *Hansard*, Vol. 365, "Social Security Fraud Bill; Second Reading," 27 March 2001.

83 "KN" interview, 4 September 1997.

84 NORO, PD86, East Dereham Overseer's Accounts, 1726 – 1819.

85 GRO, PD-38-1-180, Letter, 30 March 1836.

86 TNA, MH12/5979,12455/1866, Letter, 13 February 1866.

87 Kevin Schürer and Eilidh Garrett have used the 1861, 1881, and 1901 censuses to calculate that Welsh and Scottish people were between eight and twenty times

more likely to move to England than their English counterparts were to move in the opposite directions. Personal communication.

88 DGAC, K7/15/14, Kirkcudbright Parochial Board Record of Applications, 1883–92.

89 Ashforth, "Settlement," 62, and Darwen et al., "'Unhappy,'" 589–619.

90 CRO WPR/19/7/6/4/15, Letter.

91 Bauke, *The Poor*, 84–101. The Irish remained the one group of migrants who could be imprisoned for refusing settlement examinations.

92 TNA, MH12/14408,43551/1868, Letter 31 August 1868.

93 *Hansard*, Vol. 112, "Gipsy Caravan Sites," 13 April 1987.

94 For refutation see Lindert, *Welfare States*, 21, 23.

95 Focus group, 10 December 2014.

96 Field notes, 1 March 2022.

97 B. Ellery, "Gang Invented 188 Children and Used Them in £1.7m Benefit Scam," *The Times*, 12 November 2022, 16.

98 Morris, "Reconfiguring Rights," 274, 283–7.

99 Focus group, 11 June 2015.

100 Tabili, "'Having Lived,'" 369–87; Tabili, *Global Migrants*, 1–4; "RK" interview, 20 December 2016.

101 McCarthy, "Pearl Jephcott," 779–93.

102 James, *Yo'd Mek*; James, *Yo'd Mek a Parson Swear … Again*; James, *Bog All*.

103 Willmott, *Yours Reverently*.

104 Coombs and Coombs, *Journal*, 78, 146.

105 Warwick University Archives, Circulars: The Order of the White Seamen's Brotherhood, 1932.

106 SURO, P5–5–393, Letter to Wimbledon St Mary Parish, 7 March 1836.

107 Marks, "'The Luckless,'" 113–37; Levene, *Jews*, passim.

108 Langley, *Joseph Ashby's*, 26.

109 I am grateful to Margaret Hanly for sight of the founding articles.

110 Cudworth, *Round About*, 287–93; Chapman, *The Autobiography*.

111 By contrast, Land, "Bread," 96–8, contends that bloodline mattered for welfare decisions.

112 Huntingdonshire Record Office, KHP34/18/1/4. I am grateful to Prisca Greenhow for this information and reference. It seems likely that Reverend Philip Castel Sherard brought Mary to Britain through his West Indian merchanting business but that his wife Sarah placed her in the poorhouse near or at his death. See https://www.ucl.ac.uk/lbs/person/view/2146658879.

113 Morrison, "'Scrounger-bashing,'" 383–401.

114 Wells, *Victorian Village*, 149.

Chapter Five

1 "Changes to Benefit Rules Aim to Tackle Gaps in Job Market," *The Times*, 4 June 2022, 14–15.
2 This is untrue, especially for disabled children. See Anon., *Universal Credit*, 2.
3 Anon., "Welfare into Work," *The Times*, 4 June 2022, 33.
4 See Parliamentary Health Ombudsman, *Women's*.
5 Focus group, 10 December 2014.
6 King, "The Summary," 125–72.
7 Costello, "'More Equitable," 3–26.
8 See for instance a blog from MIND on 18 July 2019 announcing: "Landmark Supreme Court judgment means thousands could get disability benefit for struggling in social situations."
9 Other studies focus core discussion of work and welfare on the Blair reforms: Deeming and Johnston, "From 'Welfare,'" 157–70.
10 Langley, *Joseph Ashby's*, 26.
11 ORO, Oxford St Martin, PAR 207/5/A7/6, Letter.
12 Seabrook, *Cut Out*.
13 Okoroji et al., "Elite Stigmatization," 207–29; Lain et al., "Older Workers," 90–114; Reiss, "The Image," 389–415.
14 F. Field, "Budget 2015: Gordon Brown's Tax Credits Monster Must Be Slain," *Daily Telegraph*, 7 July 2015.
15 Hewins, *The Dillen*.
16 Geiger, "Benefit 'Myths'?" 998–1018.
17 David Willetts claimed – *Hansard*, Vol. 365, "Social Security Fraud Bill; Second Reading," 27 March 2001 – to have identified forty-five instances but provided no detail. I have been unable to corroborate such figures.
18 Elizabeth Roberts collection, Mr G.2.L.
19 Groves, "Understanding," 141–65.
20 S.T., R.W., &c., *A Mild*, 107–37. Also Hindle, "Civility," 41–4.
21 Sokoll, "Families," 78–106.
22 HRO 44M69/J9/23, 77A–E, 77F, 77i and HRO 86M82/PV1, Herriard Vestry Minutes.
23 Dorset History Centre, PE/SW, VE 1/1, Vestry Minute Book 1788–1818.
24 Hurley, *Devizes*, 4.
25 CRO WPR/19/7/6/21/11, Letter, 2 May 1828.
26 CRO WPR/19/7/6/22/51, Letter, 15 December 1829.
27 Redford, *The History*, 98.
28 On *General Orders*, see King et al., *In Their Own Write*, 166 and 255.
29 Boyer, "The Evolution," 408–9.
30 Wells, *Victorian Village*, 158.

31 TNA, MH12/9362/292,32124/1855, Letter 11 August 1855.

32 Cottam, "Small," 175–92.

33 Cooper, *The British*, chapters 4 and 5.

34 Denis Warry: Reminiscences of Headington. Boyer and Schmidle, "Poverty," 258–9.

35 Ewart Evans, *Where Beards*, 99, and Crowther, "Family," 143.

36 HAC, Tongue Parochial Board Minutes, 1845–1868, 26 December 1845.

37 HRO, 39M69/PV1, Hursley Vestry Minutes 1824–1944.

38 Land, "The Introduction," 9–29.

39 Spicker, "The Case," 28–44.

40 Hills, *Good Times*, 6, notes that the 1989 documentary of the same name crystallised this word.

41 *Taking in a lodger – what you need to think about first – Citizens Advice*. For wider context: Davidoff, "The Separation," 64–97.

42 DRO, 1579A-24-117-21, Letter, 1 May 1823.

43 LIRO, PL15/102/13, Guardian Minute Book, entry for 11 June 1873.

44 Elizabeth Roberts collection, Mrs W.1.L. The fact that she still referred to the welfare structure of the Old Poor Law – Parish Relief – strikingly confirms the lack of background knowledge about the operation of the nascent welfare state in this period.

45 The consensus was "not." See: *Cash gifts whilst on benefits? — MoneySavingExpert Forum*.

46 Kussmaul, *The Autobiography*, 61.

47 King et al., *In Their Own Write*, 235–61.

48 TNA, MH12/1023, 19826/1862, Letter, 13 May 1862.

49 Hurren, *Protesting*, 84–116.

50 HRO, 43M67/PV1, Amport Vestry Minute Book.

51 Park, *Edward Prynn*, 60.

52 "RK" interview, 12 January 1994.

53 "TP," Focus group participant, 4 April 2014.

54 *I, Daniel Blake* (2016).

55 Though see Morris, "Asylum," 5, who argues that courts and tribunals are vital for securing the welfare rights of asylum seekers for whom public and political opinion cannot be mobilized.

56 P. Wintour, "Coalition Government Sets Out Radical Welfare Reforms," *Guardian*, 26 May 2010.

57 Beatty and Fothergill, "Welfare Reform," 145–56.

58 Note the far-reaching 2012 court decision to strike down new government restrictions on the amount of space that young disabled adults could claim for: Housing Benefit: Disability News Service, 17 May 2012.

59 Hood and Phillips, "Benefit Spending."

60 C. Ford, Alumni Blog, King's College, 15 January 2019: https://www.kcl.ac.uk/carole-ford-urgent-policy-reform-is-needed-for-disabled-welfare-claimants

61 R. Machin, "Four Reasons Why Welfare Reform Is a Delusion," 28 June 2017: https://blogs.lse.ac.uk/politicsandpolicy/four-reasons-why-welfare-reform-is-a-delusion/. The formatting is faithful to the original rather than indicating missed text.

62 Geiger, "Disabled," 337–51.

63 "UV," Focus group participant, 4 January 2014.

64 Hudson-Sharp et al., *The Impact*, 72–9.

65 For instance, the ballad *The Stout Cripple of Cornwall* (1693). Dalton's *The Countrey Justice*, conveys eight warnings against imposition.

66 Disability is mentioned thirteen times in the life stories and comments: A dozen – never to be forgotten | Exceptional Rayleigh Characters | Rayleigh | ... by Places | Rochford District Community Archive (rochforddistricthistory.org.uk). Also: *Born To Be Small* YouTube, accessed 13 April 2023.

67 GRO, P78-1 OV 7-1, Letter, 6 June 1797.

68 Turner and Blackie, *Disability*, 78–83, and Turner, "Impaired Children," 788–806.

69 King, "'still about,'" 98–120.

70 DGAC, K7/15/14, Kirkcudbright Parochial Board Record of Application, 1883–1892.

71 Borsay, *Disability*.

72 Hayward, "'Those who,'" 53–71.

73 SLAC, Kilmallie Parochial Board Letter Book, 1851–1853.

74 HAC, Tongue Parochial Board Minutes, 1845–1868.

75 Ibid.

76 Gear, *The Diary*, 222–51.

77 Pierson, *Dismantling*.

78 Wintour, "Coalition Government." On the political roots of this view: Deeming, "Foundations," 862–86, and Deeming and Johnston, "Coming Together," 395–413.

79 Morris, "Activating," 283.

80 I am grateful to focus group member "GC" for allowing me access to the unpublished manuscript of her father.

81 Gulland, *Gender*; Hampton, *Disability*.

82 Wintour, "Coalition Government."

83 "Iain Duncan Smith announces plans to reform benefits" – YouTube.

84 A. Gentleman, "Benefit Fraud: Spies in the Welfare War," *Guardian*, 1 February 2011. Comment posted 1 February 2011.

85 Rawson, "Poor Relief," 78–96.
86 Harris, "Parsimony," 40–74.
87 Snell, *Parish and Belonging*.
88 Muldrew and King, "Cash, Wages," 267–306.
89 See the biting critique of settlement in Hale, *A Method*, 6–20.
90 HAC, Tongue Letter Book, Letter 132.
91 Millar and Bennett, "Universal Credit," 169–82.
92 Focus group, 11 June 2015.
93 BBC, "The Block," 1972: https://www.bbc.co.uk/iplayer/episode/p055vzj1/ tuesday – documentary-the-block.
94 "RK" interview, 12 January 1994.

Chapter Six

 1 "CR," focus group participant, 17 August 2016.
 2 Trigger events are a persistent problem for modern welfare recipients as they tend to lead to an evaluation of all benefits. See https://www.netmums. com/coffeehouse/legal-social-services-1109/court-cases-43/1091874-possible-accidental-benefit-fraud.html; https://www.netmums.com/coffeehouse/legal – social – services – 1109/court – cases – 43/1091874 – possible – accidental – benefit – fraud.html. Accessed 14 September 2022.
 3 DWP, *Fraud Investigations*, 443–7. This two-part guide extends to 995 pages.
 4 DWP, *Fraud and Error in the Benefits System, 2013–14*: https:// publications.parliament.uk/pa/cm201415/cmselect/cmworpen/627/62704. htm#:~:text=The%202013-14%20initial%20estimates%20show%20that%20 fraud%20and,their%20lowest%20rate%20of%200.4%25%20of%20benefit%20 expenditure.
 5 Cooke, *A Brief*, 30–4.
 6 TNA, MH12/8985,43103/1860, Letter.
 7 Elizabeth Roberts collection, Mrs H.2.B.
 8 Golding and Middleton, *Images*, 84–9.
 9 *Hansard*, Vol. 365, "Social Security Fraud Bill," 27 March 2001.
10 Tadmor, "The Settlement," 43–97.
11 Peretz, "The forgotten," 103–13; Freeman, "The Provincial," 73–89.
12 HAC, Tongue and Farr Correspondence, letter 86, 31 August 1887.
13 For a corrective see King, *Writing the Lives*, and Crone, "Educating," 161–85.
14 Williams, *From Pauperism*.
15 LERO 17D 64/F/222, Letter.
16 LERO 17D 64/F/223, Letter.

17 LERO 17D 64/F/224, Letter. On settlement liabilities for illegitimate children: Harvey, "The Putative," 373–98.

18 LERO 17D 64/P/226, Letter. By 5 September 1809 Pole had returned to Ipswich, with the overseer there requesting reimbursement of relief given. See LERO 17D 64/F/226, Letter. On dealing with mobile populations in London see: Schürer and Day, "Migration," 26–56.

19 HAC, Tongue Parochial Board Correspondence.

20 Perry, *Bread*, 15.

21 See surviving forms and correspondence in HAC, Miscellaneous Record CS/D/1, County of Sutherland Public Assistance Office/Social Work Department Records c.1925–1974, Registers, c.1925–1948.

22 Golding and Middleton, *Images*, 42–7.

23 *Hansard*, vol. 403, "Benefit Application Forms," 14 April 2003.

24 See: https://www.youtube.com/watch?v=a9Vig-cvLV4. Accessed 17 October 2022.

25 Groves, "Understanding," passim.

26 https://www.mumsnet.com/talk/am_i_being_unreasonable/2165362-I-think-I-committed-benefit-fraud. Accessed 27 March 2024.

27 TNA, MH12/169,3860/1859, Letter to the PLB, 26 January 1859. My italics.

28 Groves, "Understanding," 164.

29 LIRO, PL15/102/14, Guardian Minute Book, 1873–76, 24 & 31 March 1875.

30 For summation see Groves, "Understanding," 58–64.

31 HAC, Tongue Parochial Board Correspondence, letters 66 and 67.

32 Claiming Universal Credit and other benefits if you are a refugee – GOV.UK (WWW.GOV.UK). Accessed 22 November 2022; Morris, "Reconfiguring," 283–6.

33 On withholding or artificially disposing of capital see: The Deprivation of Capital Rule in Welfare Benefits | Social Welfare Updates | News | Garden Court Chambers | Leading Barristers located in London, UK. Accessed 16 November 2022.

34 Field notes, 29 August 2021.

35 LIRO, PL15/102/12 – 20, Guardian Minute Books.

36 Perry, *Bread*, 3. The modern welfare system also, unlike its locally focussed predecessors, treats all capital as unencumbered.

37 Le Hardy, *Buckinghamshire*, 276.

38 NRO, 356p/28, Welton Vestry Minutes.

39 *Hansard*, Vol. 365, "Social Security Fraud Bill," 27 March 2001.

40 TNA, MH12/2243,10591/1869, Letter, 22 February 1869.

41 Rothersthorpe Parish Church, Letter, 16 May 1737.

42 Bennett, *A Century*, 77.

43 Ewart Evans, *Where Beards*, 79.

44 Elizabeth Roberts collection, Mr Q.1.B.

45 Kilburne's precedent book, *Choice Presidents*, 274–5, gives a model warrant forcing overseers to pay arrears of and continue relief in complex cases.

46 On this issue in the modern system see Rowlingson et al., *Social Security*, 40–53.

47 A common enough accusation in the modern welfare state: Cook, *Rich Law*, 91–4.

48 Elizabeth Roberts collection, Mr Q.1.B.

49 TNA, MH12/1530/514,19543/1849, Letter 25 June 1849.

50 *Hansard*, Vol. 365, "Social Security Fraud Bill, second Reading," 27 March 2001.

51 See for instance the colourful invective in the pseudonymous Poussin, *Pretty doings*. The Buckingham Quarter Sessions calendars contain hundreds of examples of fraud by cohabitation.

52 Advicenow, *A Survival Guide*, 3–6.

53 *Hansard*, Vol. 55, "Specialist Claims Control," 28 February 1984.

54 NAO, *Tackling*, 16 and 17.

55 Savage, "They Would," 173–90; Leneman, *Alienated Affections*; Savage, "'The Magistrates,'" 231–49; Menefee, *Wives for Sale*.

56 CRO, WPR/19/7/6/20/29, Letter.

57 HRO, 4M81, PO40, Overseers' correspondence of Brockenhurst.

58 DRO, 1855A-PO40 to 44–45, Letter, 15 July 1835.

59 SURO, PAR 412-35-54, Letter.

60 King, "Fractured courtships," 38–56.

61 Hindle, "The problem," 71–89. In practice, officials and communities actively sought such unions as a way of reducing long-term bills.

62 "RK" interview, 20 December 2016.

63 Shepard, "Honesty, Worth," 94; Whiteside, "Who Were," 150–69; Sohn, "Did Unemployed Workers," 377–92; and Reiss, "From Poor Relief," 75–107.

64 Wiede, "The Poor," 307–34; Golding and Middleton, *Images*, 38–47, 91–5, 174–8.

65 *I, Daniel Blake*, 2016.

66 All the quotations below are drawn from Hewins, *Mary*, 61–2.

67 On the complex definitions of genuinely seeking, see Deacon, *In Search*, appendix 1.

68 HRO, 25M84, PO71-21-15, Letter.

69 Rothersthorpe Parish Church, Letter, 11 April 1715.

70 TNA, MH12/6989,35326/1850, Letter, 24 April 1850.

71 S. O'Sullivan, "Credit crunch: Universal Credit five-week wait 'makes debts worse' as 4 in 5 have first payment docked," *The Sun*, 10 July 2020; Klair, *Universal Credit*, 6.

72 King, "Remembering," 292–312.

73 BBC Panorama, "Britain on the Fiddle," 3 November 2011, comment 6.

74 CRO, WPR/19/7/6/18/15, Letter.

75 TNA, MH12/15797, 13770/B/1847, Letter.

76 TNA, MH12/16522,6216/A/1845, Letter, May 1845. "If the Overseers of the Poor of any parish voluntarily neglect to make, or collect enough taxes to help the Poor, or neglect to send to the Guardians of any parish or Union (Union) the necessary contributions, and if by such neglect that assistance ordered to be given to any person by the Board of Guardians be delayed or withheld from him for a space of Seven days, every such person guilty - experience of that, shall be Forfeited and fined for every crime of the kind, any amount not exceeding Twenty Pounds." Extract from the new revised Poor Law, 7th and 8th Victoria, Chap. 101. Section 63.

77 P. Butler, "Welfare system failing thousands of its most vulnerable claimants, MPs told," *Guardian*, 19 October 2015.

78 S. Walker, "PAY WAIT Urgent warning as benefit payments could be DELAYED including Universal Credit and state pension," *The Sun*, 21 October 2022, and P. Butler, "Five-month disability benefits delay causing hardship, says Citizens Advice," *Guardian*, 6 July 2022.

79 GRO, OV 7-1-1, Letter, 17 February 1831.

80 CRO, WPR/19/7/6/14/34, Letter, 1821.

81 King, "Women," 119–40.

82 Netflix, *The Crown*, Series 4.

83 Alistair Darling suggested that the Conservative administration ending in 1997 "did not even attempt to measure fraud for the first 15 years, and they did precious little to stop it for their entire 18 years in office." *Hansard*, Vol. 365, 27 March 2001. His own party was later (rightly) accused of the same thing.

84 TNA, MH12/7979,60193/1882, Letter, 14 June 1882.

Chapter Seven

1 LRO, PR2391/43, Letter, 18 May 1833.

2 LRO, PR2391/39, Letter, 16 August 1832.

3 LRO, PR2391/11, Letter, 18 October 1824.

4 LRO, PR2391/12, Letter, 23 October 1824.

5 LRO, PR2391/13, Letter, 2 November 1824.

6 Many modern commentators also focus on impact: https://www.disability north.org.uk/horrific-stats-show-how-most-disability-benefit-fraud-allegations-are-false/.

7 CRO, WPR/19/7/6/16/40, Letter 5 June 1823.

8 Jones and King, *Navigating*, 141–64.

9 Anon., *Fighting Fraud*; F. Ryan, "The Phantom Benefit Cheat Is the Perfect Patsy for Austerity," *Guardian*, 8 March 2016.

10 See debates about informing on disabled claimants that accompanied Liz Carr's contribution – "The Real Deal" – to BBC 4's *CripTales* series in 2020.

11 https://www.gov.uk/government/news/new-benefit-counter-fraud-plan-set-to-save-taxpayer-2-billion.

12 D. Bloom, "85% of Calls to DWP's "Benefit Cheat Hotline" Are Closed Due to Lack of Evidence," *The Mirror*, 28 February 2016.

13 H. Khaleeli, "Benefit Fraud – the Facts and Figures," *Guardian*, 21 October 2014.

14 *Full Fact*, "Benefit Fraud: Has DWP Hotline Increased Prosecutions?" 5 December 2011.

15 *Hansard*, Vol. 310, "Benefit Fraud," 20 April 1998, response of John Denham to a question by David Rendel.

16 *Hansard*, Vol. 296, "Benefit Fraud," 25 June 1997.

17 In 2008, some twelve years after hotlines proper had been introduced, James Plaskitt was obliged to correct a previous parliamentary answer to acknowledge that hotline figures were not the same as discrete cases. *Hansard*, Vol. 479, "Social Security Benefits," 15 July 2008.

18 I. Stuttard, *Inside Story*, "To Catch a Cheat."

19 Where only "daily" figures were noted, I have applied the same daily rate to a whole calendar year; where aggregate figures for a period were reported I have assumed equal division between the years covered.

20 This figure emerged from a focus group session involving former administrators. Also Morris, "The Topology," 250.

21 The roots of the policy were established in an ill-tempered 1993 debate. See *Hansard*, vol. 228, "Social Security Fraud," 16 July 1993.

22 Data collection was driven by keyword and phrase searching at three levels: "benefit fraud" and its multiple linguistic equivalencies; the names of particular welfare payments; and generic terms such as "hotlines."

23 Golding and Middleton, *Images*, 159–78.

24 The state pension flattens accusations because only at the very lowest end of the income distribution was it associated with easily fraudable welfare payments.

25 Between 15% and 26% of the adult population. See: Diversity, equity and inclusion strategy | Wellcome.

26 Stuttard, *Inside Story*, "To Catch a Cheat."

27 Focus group, 11 June 2015.

28 TNA, MH12/2095,4734/B/1837, Letter 19 June 1837.

29 Given that I have suggested that northern and western communities prioritised self-reliance, this is unsurprising: King, *Poverty and Welfare*, 63–86.

30 H. Gye, "Half of Britain's Top 10 Benefits Hotspots Are in Birmingham," *The Sun*, 12 September 2018.

31 HAC, Tongue Parochial Minutes and Correspondence, Item 144, dated 7 July 1862.

32 Redford, *"Die Veult,"* 20–2.

33 B. Johnson, "Is the State Encouraging Britain to Become a Nation of Curtain-Twitchers and Whisperers?" *The Spectator*, 28 October 1995.

34 Scale and aggravating factors shape popular attitudes towards fraud more widely: Kerr and Button, *Research*, 56.

35 C. Ellicott, "Benefit Cheats UK," *Daily Mail*, 5 March 2011.

36 S.C., *Legal Provisions*, chapters 1, 3, 5.

37 "PT" Interview, 16 March 1995.

38 See Hoppit, "Reforming," 82–104, and Zupko, "The Weights," 119–45.

39 Mills, *Regulating*; McIvor, "Guardians," 1–30.

40 Deacon, *In Search*, 42 and 54–66, notes that contemporary committees of enquiry found little evidence on malingering because they relied on outside inspectors rather than local community intelligence.

41 Tabili, *Global*. Morris, "Reconfiguring."

42 Scott, *Weapons*, 78.

43 Bennett, *A Century*, 72. Also Crowson, "'Tramps' Tales," 1488–526.

44 Deacon, *In Search*.

45 Ewart Evans, *Where Beards*, 174.

46 See: https://www.netmums.com/coffeehouse/money-advice-1127/benefits-entitlements-267/788840-caught-doing-benefit-fraud-what-will-happen.html. Comment nine of ninety.

47 Focus group, 11 June 2015.

48 TNA, MH12/16252,20371/1857, Letter, 3 June 1857. For modern fears of reprisal: Evans et al., "Whom can you trust?" 361–80.

49 "VD," focus group participant in 2014 and 2015. When pressed, she made a distinction between distrust or suspicion and unbelief, the latter signifying something knowable from experience.

50 TNA, MH12/15742,116126/1884, Letter, 6 December 1884.

51 This also partly explains the cyclical or seasonal nature of informing; people see more value in reporting when they themselves are suffering.

52 Ellicott, "Benefit Cheats UK." Comment 104 of 265.

53 "PT" interview, 16 March 1995.

54 *Hansard*, Vol. 365, "Social Security Fraud Bill, 27 March 2001.

55 Layer, *The Office*.

56 SORO, PE/OV/8/5, Overseers' Papers for St George's Parish Fordington.

57 On the importance of empathy versus pity and sympathy: Gordon, *Pitied*, and Hunt, *Governing Morals*.

58 Bennett, *A Century*, 71.

59 Deacon, *In Search*, 9.

60 Ewart Evans, *Let Dogs*, 76.

61 I am grateful to Helen Trainor for sharing her mother's text.

62 A. Gentleman, "Benefit Fraud: Spies in the Welfare War," *Guardian*, 1 February 2011.

63 DBAC, GD 226, Sanquhar Letter Book.

64 SURO, 1505–BOX37–F1–42, Letter 19 November 1832; SURO, 1505–BOX37–F1–41, Undated letter but clearly after November.

65 Brodie, *Neighbours*.

66 Ellicott, "Benefit Cheats UK." Groves, "Understanding," chapter 3.

67 HAC, Tongue Parochial Minutes and Correspondence, Item 144, dated 17 July 1850.

68 TNA, MH12/770,7932/C/1838, Letter 14 August 1838.

69 NAO, *Tackling*.

70 "RK" interview, 12 January 1994.

71 Stuttard, *Inside Story*, "To Catch a Cheat."

72 Webb, *Our Partnership*, chapters 7 and 8.

73 TNA, MH12/13287,8758/A/1843, Letter, 23 July 1843.

74 Johnson, "Is the State."

Chapter Eight

1 Candler, *Poetical Attempts*, 1.

2 Fitzmaurice, *The Familiar*.

3 Candler, *Poetical Attempts*, 15.

4 Ibid., 54 and 53. Rhetorical threads of niggardliness and respectable people being lumped in with the dregs of humanity have remarkable longevity.

5 King and Jones, "Fragments," 235–66; King and Jones, "Testifying," 784–807.

6 Marshall, *The English*, 78, and Webb and Webb, *English Poor Law*, 168.

7 *Hansard*, vol. 724, "Questions for the DWP," 5 December 2022.

8 *Hansard*, vol. 695, "Benefit Fraud and Error Statistics," 13 May 2021.

9 *Hansard*, vol. 881, "Supplementary Benefit (Fraudulent Claims)," 12 November 1974. This figure of 14,500 was constructed as a conscious fabrication by Page, *Benefits Racket*, 29.

10 Heron and Dwyer, "Doing," 91–104.

11 B. Ellery, "Photoshop Fraudsters Stand Out in £8.5bn of Fake Benefit Claims," *The Times*, 21 January 2023.

12 Page, *Benefits Racket*, 7, 22, 46.

13 *Hansard*, vol. 881, "Supplementary Benefit (Fraudulent Claims)," 12 November 1974.

14 Anon., *Fraud Investigations*.

15 *Hansard*, vol. 955, "Supplementary Benefit Staff," 24 October 1978.

16 This continued a long-term pattern of underinvestment: *Report of the Committee*, 274–82.

17 Headworth and Rios, "Listening to Snitches," passim.

18 A. Gentleman, "Benefit Fraud: Spies in the Welfare War," *Guardian*, 1 February 2011.

19 *Hansard*, "Social Security Fraud Bill," 27 March 2001.

20 "LL," focus group, 10 December 2014.

21 Alec Shelbrooke, MP, subsequently tried to make this a reality: *Hansard*, "Welfare Cash Card," vol. 555, 18 December 2012.

22 C. Ellicott, "Benefit Cheats UK," *Daily Mail*, 5 March 2011.

23 For the 1970s see Golding and Middleton, *Images*, 112–41.

24 A. Dent, *My Story: An Oxford Policeman's Lot 1948–1973*, 17: https://www.headington.org.uk/history/reminiscences/dent.pdf. There is no reference to welfare fraud in Cherrill, *Cherrill*.

25 Page, *Benefits Racket*, 40.

26 *Hansard*, vol. 773, "Special Investigators," 18 November 1968.

27 BBC, *Cathy Come Home*, 1966.

28 Hindle, "'Goodly, godly,'" 181, 187–8.

29 NRO, 261p, Peterborough St John Overseers Correspondence, Letter, 17 August 1833.

30 Webb and Webb, *English Poor Law*, 145.

31 Humphreys, *Poor Relief*; Vincent, "The Poor Law," 64–85.

32 Webb, *My Apprenticeship*, 183.

33 Crowther and Crowther, *The Diary*, 66 and 72.

34 Parker and Burn, *Conductor Generalis*.

35 MCL, M10/809, Hulme Letters Book, 5 January 1817. Even though by 1808 Manchester was employing eleven people to support elected overseers in processing claims. Rose, *The English*, 64.

36 Jones and King, *Navigating*, 25–53.

37 Wood, *A Sussex*, 54.

38 HAC, CH2/509/3, Tongue Kirk Session Minutes 1777–1826.

39 LRO, DDX 386/3, Garstang Vestry Minutes.

40 NRO, 284P/190, Rothwell Vestry Minutes, 1828–1833.

41 White, *Memoirs*, 42, remembered that his father and a neighbour "had a serious fall-out [over welfare] at a vestry meeting and did not speak to each other for many years."

42 SLAC, Kilmallie Parochial Board Letter Book, 1851–53, 4 August 1851.

43 TNA MH12/7695,42769/77, Letter, 11 June 1877.

44 Mashaw, *Bureaucratic*.

45 I. Stuttard, *Inside Story*, "To Catch a Cheat," BBC 1997; Molander, *Discretion*. The latter deals with Norway but the principle is portable.

46 As Tunley, "Need, greed," 304, and Morris, "Reconfiguring," also argue.

47 Outcomes, or lack of them, are dealt with in chapter 9.

48 NRO, 194p, Thrapston Overseers' Letter Book.

49 Elizabeth Roberts Collection, Mrs M.5.L.

50 Chorley Public Library, Chorley Vestry Minutes 1781–1823.

51 https://www.huckmag.com/article/disabled-benefits-claimant-are-being-unfairly-investigated.

52 Page, *Benefits Racket*, 50–90.

53 Crowther and Crowther, eds, *The Diary*, 38, 51, 60; Bartholomew, *The Welfare*, 163–88.

54 K. Parker, "Single Mum Benefits Cheat Caught Out after Posting Loved Up Pics on Her Facebook," *The Mirror*, 15 February 2023. See also Groves, "Understanding," 67–8.

55 ESRO, PAR 414–35–1–356, Undated Letter. Likely 1823 given sequencing.

56 BRO, D/P 162/18/1, Caversham Overseers Papers 1749–1821. Undated letter.

57 Ryland-Epton, "'The Source,'" 326–40; Rushton, "Local laws," 185–206.

58 SLAC, Kilmallie Parochial Board Letter Book, 1851–53, 27 October 1851.

59 Slack, "Vagrants," 360–79.

60 DWP, *Tackling*, 43–56.

61 J. Domokos, "Government Admits Jobcentres Set Targets to Take Away Benefits," *Guardian*, 8 April 2011.

62 "MT," focus group, 11 June 2015.

63 Stevenson, *Mid-Victorian*. There were six instances between 1849 and 1856 alone.

64 Keeping dogs is also a persistent theme in modern comments, with such pets signalling that someone is not "really" disabled.

65 SURO, 1505–BOX37–F3–16, Letter.

66 P.J. Proby, "We the Jury," 2012.

67 https://www.mumsnet.com/talk/am_i_being_unreasonable/1380481-to-think-that-DWP-would-ONLY-investigate-someone-for-suspected-benefit-fraud-if-someone-had-reported-them.

68 BBC *Panorama*, "Britain on the Fiddle," 4 November 2011.

69 NAO, *Tackling*, 33–4.

70 https://www.dailymail.co.uk/news/article-11122903/Department-Work-Pensions-insists-letters-real-social-media-scam-warning.html.

71 NAO, *Tackling*, 3.

72 Ibid., *passim*.

73 See for instance the EDRi analysis of the extent and limits of powers: https://edri.org/our-work/shedding-light-dwp-uk-investigation-surveillance/. Also pushback on use of AI: Dencik, "The Datafied," 146 –7, 150, 160.

74 For a 2020 Hague decision: https://privacyinternational.org/news-analysis/3363/syri-case-landmark-ruling-benefits-claimants-around-world; more widely see Morris, "Welfare," 120.

75 See for instance the significant interventions on behalf of the poor by the magistrate Robert Lee of Berkshire: Leonard, *Diaries*.

76 WYRO, WDP20/9/3/8/7, Letter.

77 Le Hardy, *Buckinghamshire*, 70.

78 WSRO PAR, 29/37/10/10, 23, 26, 28, 34, 41.

79 Rothersthorpe Parish Church, accessed December 1997.

80 Perry, *Bread*, 43.

81 Elizabeth Roberts collection, Mrs A.1.P; "RK" interview, 12 January 1994.

82 Anon., *Report of the Committee*, 44–55, and chapters 9, 11–13, 14, and 16.

83 CORO, P128–19–24, Letter.

84 CORO, P128–19–25, Draft Letter. The tightening implied by the crossing out is intriguing.

85 Higgs, "Fingerprints," 52–67; Ellis, "No Hammock," 441–70.

86 Elizabeth Roberts collection, Mr E.1.B.

87 "KT," focus group, 11 June 2015.

88 https://www.gov.uk/benefit-fraud.

89 Ellicott, "Benefits Cheat UK."

90 See Perry, *The Jarrow*, 23–52.

91 Page, *Benefits Racket*, 107.

92 Coker Egerton, *Sussex Folk*, 45.

93 Bennett, *A Century*, 80. On the poor physical state of benefit offices in the 1960s see Page, *Benefits Racket*, 50–8.

94 Golding and Middleton, *Images*, 3.

95 Elizabeth Roberts collection, C.1.B. and C.2.B.

96 HRO, 25M84–PO71–24–7–1, Letter.

97 TNA, MH12/9248,23894, Letter, 23 June 1862.

98 Bloxham and Shatford, *The Changing Faces*, 76.

99 Elizabeth Roberts collection, Mrs D.1.P.

100 Gentleman, "Benefit Fraud," comment 9.

101 NORO, PDD 553/102, Workhouse Account Book 1789–1796.

102 Ellicott, "Benefits Cheat UK."

Chapter Nine

1 Hewins, *The Dillen*, 76.

2 For the powers of relieving officers: Horn, *Oxfordshire*.

3 Walton, "Taking Control," 23–41; Tebbutt, *Women's Talk?*

4 For similar observations see Samuel, "Quarry Roughs," 227.

5 Derek Wileman (personal communication) calculated that the average relieving officer in Southwell (Nottinghamshire) could have spent only one minute per person per week dealing with relief recipients, so the visit would have been fleeting and the questions literally cursory.

6 NDRO, GBF 10, Belford Guardian Minutes 1882–1888.

7 "Make dole scroungers work for benefits," *The Daily Gripe*, 2008. The blog still attracted comments in 2022.

8 BBC *Tuesday Documentary*, "The Block," 19 September 1972.

9 More widely: Davis, "Reshaping," 197–212.

10 See: https://mosslaw.co.uk/welfare-benefits/benefits-fraud/.

11 C. Ellicott, "Benefits Cheat UK," *Daily Mail*, 5 March 2011.

12 Somewhat fewer than for the single Canadian province of Ontario: Chunn and Gavigan, "Welfare Law," 234.

13 *Hansard*, Vol. 365, "Social Security Fraud bill," 27 March 2001.

14 Privacy International, "Shedding Light on the DWP Staff Guide on Conducting Fraud Investigations," 24 February 2021.

15 Anon, *Report*, appendices 7, 10, 12.

16 LIRO, PL15/102/14, Guardian Minute Book 1873–76, 12 November–21 January 1878.

17 Elizabeth Roberts Collection, Mr C.1.P.

18 ESRO, PAR 411–35–1–22, Letter.

19 I am grateful to Lewis Darwen for this observation.

20 Cabinet Office, *National Fraud*. Compare page 10 (on recovery rates) with page 11 (estimated value of fraud detected and future losses prevented) and pages 37–8 (methodologies for estimating).

21 Morris, "Reconfiguring," 275; Morris, "The Topology," 256.

22 A. Gentleman, "Benefit Fraud: Spies in the Welfare War," *Guardian*, 1 February 2011.

23 M. Ledwith, "More than Three Quarters of Benefit Cheats Go Unpunished," *Daily Mail*, 13 December 2013.

24 I. Stuttard, *Inside Story*, "To Catch a Cheat," BBC 1997.

25 For a rendering, see the ministerial response to a question on this matter from Neil Kinnock in *Hansard*, vol. 932, "Fraud and Abuse," 18 May 1977.

26 *Hansard*, vol. 409, "Benefit Fraud," 16 July 2003, and vol. 417, 5 February 2004.

27 Anon., *Report*, tables 2–5 and 8–9.

28 LIRO PL15/102/14, Guardian Minute Book 1873–76.

29 WYRO, WDP20-9-3-6-9-12 AND 15, Letters.

30 ORO, WOOTON P.C. IX/IV/3, Letter, 27 March 1711.

31 Elizabeth Roberts Collection, Mr B.1.B.

32 Gentleman, "Benefit Fraud."

33 Walsh et al., "Triage," 82–91.

34 E. Munboth, "What DWP Checks for When They Investigate Universal Credit Fraud," *Daily Mirror*, 26 August 2021, explained the practical thresholds for readers.

35 TNA, MH12/13306,6355/1857, Letter, 17 February 1857.

36 Rothersthorpe Parish Church, Letter, 3 March 1757.

37 "Make Dole Scroungers," comment 212.

38 Page, *Benefits Racket*, 42.

39 The "Claimants Union" in BBC 2's *Tuesday Documentary* "The Block" can be seen taking claimants through the circularity of rules, forms, and strategies.

40 Golding and Middleton, *Images*, 89–91.

41 Morrison, "'Scrounger-Bashing,'" 383–401; Roberts, "The Language," 189–204.

42 TNA, MH12/770,2920/C/1839, Letter with pamphlet enclosure: AN ACCOUNT OF THE DEATHS BY DESTITUTION & STARVATION OF THE FOUR CHILDREN OF THOMAS HARDY, WEAVER OF BAGULEY, IN THE ALTRINCHAM UNION, AT FLIXTON, NEAR MANCHESTER, *With the Depositions of his Neighbours and Others*, 27 March 1839.

43 CRO, WPR19/7/6/2/19, Letter, 14 July 1809.

44 TNA, MH12/6854,31943/1867, Letter, 7 August 1867; MH12/13317,6616/1869, Letter, 30 January 1869; MH12/6010,124293/1894, Letter, 14 December 1893; MH12/15352, 8201/1851, Letter, February 1851; MH12/15487, 77136/1881, Letter, 25 July 1881; MH12/12702, 59930/1869, Letter, December 1869.

45 https://www.netmums.com/coffeehouse/legal-social-services-1109/court-cases-43/846301-stupidly-committed-benefit-fraud-now-so-scared-i-have-go-court.html.

46 King and Jones, "Testifying"; King et al., *In Their Own Write*, 73–105.

47 Stevenson, *Mid-Victorian Squarson*, 339.

48 CRO, WPR19/7/6/20/46, Letter, 19 October 1827.

49 Elizabeth Roberts collection, Mr B.1.B.

50 "ON," focus group, 4 January 2014.

51 Morris, "Asylum," 367, 369, 374, 376.

52 Tom Rawstorne, "£1million Benefits Fraudster Who's Taken Us ALL for a Ride," *Daily Mail*, 11 July 2020, 48–9.

53 https://www.sentencingcouncil.org.uk/offences/magistrates-court/item/benefit-fraud/.

54 I noted above that many benefits are not sanctionable but was surprised at this comment, and even more surprised to find that it is true. See L. Trevelyan, "Committing Benefit Fraud," *In Brief*, 2022, 3.

55 https://www.netmums.com/coffeehouse/legal-social-services-1109/court-cases-43/846301-stupidly-committed-benefit-fraud-now-so-scared-i-have-go-court.html.

56 Gentleman, "Benefit Fraud."

57 Even some of the comments on S. Marsh, "DWP Uses Excessive Surveillance on Suspected Fraudsters," *Guardian*, 14 February 2021.

58 *Hansard*, vol. 365, "Social Security Fraud Bill," 27 March 2001.

59 In 2011 the government was "outed" for failing to acknowledge that during 2009/10 "just 12 per cent" of closed cases led to sanction of any sort. See *Full Fact*, "Benefit fraud: Has DWP Hotline Increased Prosecutions?" 5 December 2022.

60 Focus group, 4 January 2014. In 2004 the government could not say how many serial fraudsters had been prosecuted; *Hansard*, vol. 418, "Benefit Fraud," 24 February 2004.

61 My subsequent research focusses these comments to: BBC, "Benefit Fraud: Government to Spend £500m to Tackle Overpayment," 13 December 2021.

62 "ON," focus group, 4 January 2014.

63 HRO, 25M60-PO35-851, Letter to Fawley parish, 1 March 1830.

64 COWAC, P5-5-416, Letter, 12 September 1835.

65 TNA, MH12/6994,34141/1866, Letter, 16 August 1866.

66 TNA, MH12/14016/193,2268/C/1838, Letter, 24 July 1838.

67 TNA, MH12/5983,59409/1871, Letter, 19 October 1871.

68 Elizabeth Roberts collection, Mrs H.7.P. and "GC" interview, 28 August 2009. This claim about painters can also be found in a modern sense: BBC *Panorama*, "Britain on the Fiddle," 3 November 2011, comment 17.

69 Gentleman, "Benefit Fraud."

70 Stuttard, *Inside Story*, "To Catch a Cheat."

71 Gentleman, "Benefit Fraud."

72 HRO, 137M71/PV1, Broughton Vestry Minute Book, volume 1.

73 TNA, MH12/14588, Letter 10 December 1847.

74 "RK" interview, 20 December 2016.

75 In 1981 investigative resources were cut by 42%: Reiger, "Making Britain," 654.

76 Todd notes that welfare workers intervened "with the National Assistance Board where necessary to help restore or increase benefit payments": Todd, "Family Welfare," 383.

77 Malvery, *The Soul*, 55, 58–9. I am grateful to Alannah Tomkins for this reference.
78 "IG," focus group, 10 December 2014.
79 HRO, 25M60, Fawley Parish Papers.
80 Julie-Marie Strange, personal communication.
81 TNA, MH12/16250,47409/1855, Letter.
82 Reiger, "Making Britain," 647.
83 *Hansard*, vol. 365, "Social Security Fraud bill," 27 March 2001.
84 Wandsworth and Putney History Centre, PP/1/2/2, Putney Vestry Rough Minutes, 1819–1831.
85 Dent, *An Oxford*, 14.
86 TNA, MH12/14588,26348/1848, Letter, 18 September 1848.
87 HRO, 4M81/PO40, Letter series, 2 July to 23 August 1815.
88 Elizabeth Roberts collection, Mr and Mrs L.1.P.
89 Coombs and Coombs, *The Journal*, 253, 293.
90 Ibid., 464.
91 Heinemann, "Is the Welfare State," 240.
92 Davies and Owston, *Overseers' Manual*, especially 101–4.
93 Bauke, *The Poor Law*, 37, 44, 52, 70.
94 Gentleman, "Benefit Fraud."
95 NDRO, GBR 77/659–662, and 680–81, Letters and correspondence, 5 September 1855 and 19 October 1855.
96 Gentleman, "Benefit Fraud."
97 Contrast this view with Beatty and Fothergill, "Welfare Reform," 147, who argue that the financial impact of sanctions since 2010 has been substantial.
98 "HC" interview, 28 August 2009.
99 TNA, MH12/16471,30230/1894, Letter, 20 March 1894.

Chapter Ten

1 Coker Egerton, *Sussex Folk*, 36.
2 Though see Taylor-Gooby et al., "Market Means," 586–9 for a more upbeat assessment of New Labour welfare investment.
3 Rutherford, *Historical Rates*, 1 and 10.
4 Lindert, *Welfare*, 2, 4, 18, 29, 31.
5 Reiger, "Making Britain," 634–5, 649, 653; Golding and Middelton, *Images*, 66–7.
6 Morris, "The Topology," 246, 248, 256, 258.
7 Daguerre and Etherington, *Workfare*; Power and Willmot, "Bringing Up," 277–96.
8 Waddell, "The Rise."

9 Smith, "Ageing," 64–95. For contrasting views: Ottaway, "Introduction," 7.

10 Millar and Bennett, "Universal Credit," 169–82, and Andersen, "Universal Credit," 430–49.

11 H. Barnard, "Inflation Is Hitting the Most Vulnerable Families Hardest," *Financial Times*, 27 May 2023.

12 Daly and Kelly, *Families*; Hartfree, "Universal Credit," 15–26.

13 P. Kelso, "Parents 'Exchanging Milk Tokens for Alcohol,'" *Guardian*, 20 October 1999. For a compelling analysis of this issue using American data see Kim and Maroulis, "Rethinking," 78–100.

14 Connor, "We're onto You." 231–52; Baumberg, "Three Ways," 149.

15 Hunt, "Paupers," 422.

16 Kendall, *Farming Memoirs*, 99–102.

17 Ibid., 176.

18 Ibid., 203. Pugh, "Working Class," 791, notes that the pension set a new standard for outdoor relief of not less than 5s per week.

19 TNA, MH12/6989,35326/1850, Letter, 24 April 1850.

20 Elizabeth Roberts collection, Mrs G.1.B. Also Roberts, "The recipients' view," 205–27.

21 See also "councillor alan sanders" commenting on a 2011 BBC Panorama programme and where they claimed to have seen "my MP George Eustice ... and his words were it is a disgrace the £55.00 that carers get it should [not] be at less £150.00 a week," BBC Panorama, "Britain on the Fiddle," 3 November 2011, comment 15.

22 Hills, "Policy Dilemmas," 135, considers the relative UK position as "dismal," having fallen back since the 1970s.

23 J. Humphreys, "How Our Welfare System Has Created an Age of Entitlement," *Daily Mail*, 8 August 2013. Also Hancock and Mooney, "'Welfare Ghettos,'" 46–64.

24 Hills, *Good Times*, 10–32.

25 Lundström, "Framing Fraud," 630–45.

26 *Hansard*, "Welfare Green Paper," vol. 587, 26 March 1998.

27 Hickson, "Conservatism," 341–62; Lowe, *The Welfare*, 190–6.

28 TNA, MH12/12884, Letter.

29 Focus group, 17 August 2016.

30 OECD comparison tables: Net pension replacement rates | Pensions at a Glance 2019 : OECD and G20 Indicators. Accessed 4 December 2022.

31 Heinemman, "Is the Welfare State," 249–52.

32 Moro-Egido and Solano-Garcia, "Does the Perception," 1095.

33 Patrick, "All in it Together?" 309.

34 Chunn and Gavigan, "Welfare Law," 220, 230.

35 Contrast Lindbeck, Nyberg, and Weibull, "Social Norms," 533, who argue that social norms rather than residuality are the more effective solution to fraud.

36 D'Arcy, "Is There," 377–87.

37 Rothersthorpe Parish Church, Letter, 5 June 1714.

38 McKeever, "Detecting, Prosecuting," 266.

39 Ranchordás and Schuurmans, "Outsourcing," 5–42.

40 As Golding and Middleton, *Images*, 3, claim of 1976.

41 Though Taylor-Gooby, "The Divisive," 713, is also clearly correct that governments use welfare to reward their own clients.

42 Focus group, 17 August 2016.

43 Butler and Drakeford, *Social Policy*, passim.

44 Chunn and Gavigan, "Welfare Law," 227.

45 Taylor-Gooby et al., "Moral Economies," 1–16.

46 Brown et al., "Understanding Policy," 125–43.

47 Griffin, *The Rural War*, passim.

48 Bove, "For Whose Benefit?" 108–26.

49 TNA, MH12/6058,17943/1866, Letter May 1866.

50 Murphy, *The Politics*, 95–120; Hughes, "Disabled People," 991–1004; and Mooney, *Stigmatising*.

51 Higgs, "Fingerprints," 59–62.

52 Tunley, "COUNTERBLAST," 314–17.

53 Curchin, "From the Moral," 114.

54 Taylor-Gooby, *A Left Trilemma*.

55 Contrast this with the harsh attitudes assigned to American investigators: Headworth, "Broke People," 24–46.

56 King, *Writing the Lives*, chapter 4.

57 Snell, "Belonging," 1–25.

58 Dwyer and Wright, "Universal Credit," 27–35; Lister, "The Age," 63–84.

59 I am grateful to Margaret Hanly for this story.

60 Morris, "New Labour's," passim.

Chapter Eleven

1 M. Lynn, "The 'British Disease' Is Already Spreading across the World," *Daily Telegraph*, 22 October 2022, 34.

2 Di Matteo, *Measuring*, 9, 36, 58, and 71–7; Lindert, *Welfare*, 1–12.

3 King, *Poverty and Welfare*, 62.

4 For a review: Edmiston, "Welfare," 261–3; Dwyer, "Conditional Citizens," 519–43.

5 Scott, "I Am Constantly," 5, 8, 10, 27, 34.

6 Notwithstanding brief periods of relative generosity when measured internationally: Fahrmeir, Citizenship, 109–12.

7 *Hansard*, vol. 587, "Welfare Green Paper," 26 March 1998. All quoted material is from this debate. See also Morris, "New Labour's," 41, 45.

8 Also in academic debate: Lowe, *The Welfare State*, 12, argues that talk of a welfare state before 1945 cannot be taken "seriously."

9 Hollis, *Ladies Elect*. For slightly different models of a "welfare commons" see Jensen and Tyler, "Benefit Broods," 471.

10 For a succinct discussion of these themes, going beyond the classic constructions of T.H. Marshall, see Fahrmeir, *Citizenship*, 2–4.

11 Bove, "For Whose Benefit?" 110, 114, 116.

12 Edmiston, "Welfare," 263; Morris, "Moral Economy," passim.

13 *Hansard*, vol. 418, "Fraud and Error in the Welfare System," 11 July 2022.

14 Jensen and Walton, "Not," 4–5, 18–19.

15 The failure to pick up equivalencies is telling.

16 Jensen and Walton, "Not," 18.

17 Morris, "The Topology," 247.

18 For these reasons Farhmeir, *Citizenship*, suggests that the term citizen has "come to mean anything and nothing."

19 Jensen and Walton, "Not," 18.

20 BBC Panorama, "Britain on the Fiddle," 3 November 2011.

21 Chunn and Gavigan, "Welfare," 220; Hughes, "Disabled People," 991–1004.

22 S. Chan and D. Martin, "Millions Paid Benefits without Ever Having to Find a Job," *Daily Telegraph*, 24 May 2023; I. Duncan Smith, "Stop Sick People from Languishing on Benefits," *Daily Telegraph*, 23 May 2023. Also M. Parris, "Flood of Mental Health Diagnoses Isn't Working," *The Times*, 25 November 2023; T. Saunders and T. Witherow, "Rising Number of Young Given Incapacity Benefits," *The Times*, 25 November 2023; and T. Wallace, E. Nolsoe, and S. Ping Chan, "Sickness Benefit Bills to Rise by a Third," *Daily Telegraph*, 22 March 2024.

23 Bove, "For Whose Benefit?" 116.

24 Morris, "Activating," 276; Field, *Losing Out*; Harris, "Between," 67–87.

25 Fahrmeir, *Citizenship*, 51–3.

26 HRO, 45M83/PV1, New Alresford Vestry Minutes 1819–1842, entry for 5 March 1820.

27 "Make Dole Scroungers Work for Benefits," *The Daily Gripe*, 2008.

28 On the moral rights yielded, in the eyes of welfare recipients, by prior tax contribution: Thiel, "'It Isn't Charity,'" passim.

29 O. Anthony, "Rich Men North of Richmond," August 2023.

30 Rochford District Community Archive (rochforddistricthistory.org.uk).

31 Rose, *Good Neighbours*, 7.

32 Harley, "Pauper Inventories," 375–98.

33 "Disabled Scots Benefit Cheat Who Conned £40K from Taxpayers Ordered to Repay Just £1," *The Daily Record*, 10 February 2022, comment 7.

34 van Oorschot, "Who," 33–48.

35 P. Minford, "We Can't Have People Retiring Early on the Basis of Benefits," *Daily Telegraph*, 27 August 2022, 27.

36 Elizabeth Roberts collection, Mrs D.1.P.

37 Elizabeth Roberts collection, Mr M.8.B.

38 "Make Dole Scroungers," my italics.

39 HAC, Tongue Letter Book 1845 – 68.

40 Coker Egerton, *Sussex Folk*, 157.

41 See Deeming and Johnston, "From 'Welfare,'" 164–6, and Heron and Dwyer, "Doing the Right Thing," 101.

42 Bor and Simonovits, "Empathy," 1247–64, passim; Hansen, "Who Cares," 413–30.

43 As Bove, "For Whose Benefit?" points out, this sort of questioning could reflect government "agitation" on welfare citizenship from the 1990s.

44 Contrast this with pre-millenium optimism: Dilnot, "The Future," 493, 495, 497–8.

45 Timonen, "Earning," 29–51. See also S. Ping Chan, "Public Sector Pensions Bill Hits Record £2.6 Trillion," *Daily Telegraph*, 30 March 2024; and R. Vaughan, A. Forrest, and H. Gye, "Waspi Women Demand Help from Labour," *The I*, 22 March 2024.

46 Taylor-Gooby, "Polity," 171 and 180; Taylor-Gooby et al., "Market Means," 586–9; Lindert, *Welfare*, 1–3, 9–10. Contrast Edmiston, "Welfare," 263.

47 Davidson, "Family Politics," 101–24.

48 M. Reader and J. Portes, "Who Paid the Price Of George Osborne's Two-Child Benefit Cap? Britain's Poorest Children," *Guardian*, 6 April 2022.

49 G. Fonte and G. Jones, "Italy Makes Fresh Attempt at Pension Reform as Debt Worries Mount," *Reuters*, 17 February 2022.

50 "Should the State Pension Be Means-Tested," *The Times*, 7 January 2023, 58.

51 Moro-Egido and Solano-Garcia, "Does," 1087, 1097–9.

52 *Hansard*, Vol. 587, "Welfare Green Paper," 26 March 1998. On the massive understatement of eligibility for pensions see Boyer and Schmidle, "Poverty," 272.

53 Macnicol, "Reconstructing," 105.

54 Gazeley, *Poverty*, 40.

55 Coombs and Coombs, *The Journal*, 216.

56 Burnett, *Idle Hands*.

57 Boyer, "The Evolution," 394–5, 408, 412.

58 James, *Poverty*, 251–3.

59 Baumberg, *Benefit Myths*, 13–16 and Baumberg Geiger, "False Belief," 73–92.

60 Dencik, "The Datafied," 153, 156–7, 161.

61 Briant et al., "Reporting," 874–89.

62 Garthwaite, "The Language," 369–72. See also "One Million More People Cite Mental Health Battle," *The Times*, 22 March 2024.

63 *I, Daniel Blake* (2016).

64 Morris, "Reconfiguring," 274, 283; Bagguley and Mann, "Idle Thieving," 113–26; Etzioni, *The New*.

65 Webb, *My Apprenticeship*, 404.

66 Macnicol, "Reconstructing," 107.

67 See Shin et al., "Precarious Work," table 1. Observe the indifference to UBI in Britain compared to other states, even though labour market and welfare conditions should have encouraged support.

68 For some authors the answer is "nothing." See Seabrook, *Cut Out*, 9.

69 Morris, "Asylum," 365.

70 Chunn and Gavigan, "Welfare," 233, label postwar welfare rights "slight and grudging" and they are not alone: Hickson, "The Postwar," 142–54.

71 Contrast Lowe, *The Welfare*, 4, 15, 17, 21–2, who suggests that reform of the 1940s welfare state has not made it an aberration. Also Clasen, "Towards," 573–86.

72 Paterson and Gregory, "Characterising," 159–92.

73 Though the sense that there has been a new and modern neoliberal agenda to denude this aspect of the welfare state persists strongly in the historiography. See for reviews Gavin, "Below the Radar," 708.

74 For reviews that constructs a post-2010 "hollowing out" of welfare citizenship, rather than simply a return to the norm, see Edmiston, "Welfare," 264–6, and Tyler and Jensen, "Benefit Broods," 480–3.

75 Redford, *"Die Veult,"* 5.

76 Sutton, "Liberalism," 74.

77 Patrick, "Living with," 245–59. Seabrook, *Cut Out*, 126.

78 Gavin, Below the radar," 719–21; Hudson et al., "Exploring Public," 691–711.

79 Gibbs and Lehtonen, "I, Daniel Blake," 56.

80 C. Moran, "Benefit Fraud versus Tax Fraud?" *The Times Magazine*, 2 December 2023.

81 Heinemann, "Is the Welfare State," 239–41.

82 For economic modelling of the positive association between tackling fraud and support for progressive taxation and welfare policies, see Moro-Egido and Solano- Garcia, "Does," 1095–102. But contrast Tunley, "Need, Greed," 315, who argues that prosecution should be reserved only for the "greedy systematic fraudster."

83 Groves, "Understanding," 55–6.

84 Dencik, "The Datafied," 146, 151.

85 Including acknowledgement of the long-term net-positive contribution of immigrants to spendable resources. See Lindert, *Welfare*, 21–3.

86 Baumberg, "Three Ways," 157. To be clear, Baumberg sees the key public issue for the future of welfare as redistribution rather than fraud.

87 Anon., *Targeting*, 12–20.

88 For the assertion that Universal Credit and associated benefit caps represent a "dissolving of a rights-based understanding of state support" see Jensen and Tyler, "Benefit Broods," 484, and Dwyer and Wright, "Universal Credit," 27–35.

89 Deeming and Johnston, "Coming Together," 413.

90 Pemberton et al., 21–37.

91 Dierks, *In my Power*, 5.

92 King, *Writing the Lives*; King et al., *In Their Own Write*.

93 Coombs and Coombs, *The Journal*, 173.

94 Taylor-Gooby, "Welfare Reform," 147, 149.

95 Ogborn, "Local Power," 223.

96 Halla and Schneider, "Taxes and Benefits," 413–14, 416, 424, 428.

97 Heinemann, "Is the Welfare State," 252, also shows how a consolidated history of increased spending on welfare increases the risk of fraud.

98 Harris, "Parsimony," table ten.

99 Groves, "Understanding," 64.

100 Gibbs and Lehtonen, "I, Daniel Blake," 58–9, also make this point about resources from prostitution and off-market selling in *I, Daniel Blake*, reminding us that moral as well as economic and expectational thresholds need work.

101 Though see Edmiston et al., "Mediating the Claim," for the sense that the activities of advocates are not always positive.

102 Reynolds, *A Poor*, xiii–xiv, 170–5.

103 Murphy, *The Politics*, 95–120.

104 Morris, "Welfare, Asylum," 119.

105 Taylor-Gooby, "Polity, Policy," 186.

106 Edmiston and Humpage, "Resistance," 481–2.

107 Taylor-Gooby et al., "Querulous Citizens," 1–20. Also Morris, "New Labour's," 44.

BIBLIOGRAPHY

County Record Offices

Pre-1834 letters quoted in this book will be available (with equivalent German material) in an open access coded database hosted by the University of Trier in 2025. In the meantime, transcripts can be downloaded at: policyfactory.org.

Berkshire Record Office (BRO).
    D/P 162, Caversham Overseers Papers 1749–1821.
Cornwall Record Office (CORO).
    P128, Overseers' Paper of Lostwithiel.
City of Westminster Archive Centre (COWAC).
    P5, Overseer's Correspondence, Wimbledon St Mary.
Cumbria Record Office (CRO).
    WPR19, Kirkby Lonsdale Overseers' Correspondence.
Dumfries and Galloway Archive Centre (DAGA).
    K7/15/14, Kirkcudbright Parochial Board Record of Applications, 1883–92.
    GD 226, Sanquhar Letter Book.
Denbighshire Record Office.
    PD–38, Henllan Parish Correspondence.
Dorset History Centre.
    PE/SW, VE 1/1, Swanage Vestry Minute Book 1788–1818.
Devon Record Office (DRO).
    1579A, Totnes Overseers' Accounts.
    1855A, Sidmouth Overseers' Correspondence.
East Sussex Record Office (ESRO).
    PAR 411, Lewes St Anne Overseers' Correspondence.
    PAR 414, Lewes St Michael Overseers' Correspondence.
    PAR 496, Uckfield Parish Records.
East Yorkshire Record Office (EYRO).
    PE1, Beverley Overseers' Papers.
Gloucestershire Record Office (GRO).
    P78–1, Cheltenham St Mary Overseers' correspondence.
    P328 OV 7, Tetbury Overseers' Papers.
Hampshire Record Office (HRO).
    4M69/PV1, Vestry Minutes of Romsey and Eling, 1816–1833.
    4M81, Overseers' correspondence of Brockenhurst.
    25M60, Fawley Parish Papers.
    25M84, Lyndhurst Overseers' Correspondence.
    39M69/PV1, Hursley Vestry Minutes, 1824–1944.
    40M75A/PV1 and PV2, Botley Vestry Minutes, 1818–1826.

43M67/PVI, Amport Vestry Minute Book.

44M69/J9/23, 77a-e, 77f, 77i and HRO 86M82/PV1, Herriard Vestry Minutes.

95M95/PV2, Ringwood Vestry Minute Book 1811–1850.

137M71/PV1, Broughton Vestry Minute Book, volume 1.

145M82/PV1, Bishopstoke Vestry Minutes 1826–1839.

Highlands Archive Centre (HAC).

Tongue Parochial Board Correspondence and Minutes, 1845–68.

CH2/509/3, Tongue Kirk Session Minutes 1777–1826.

CS/6/32-44, Farr Parochial Board. Record of Applications for Relief

CS/6/13/23-29 & 31, General Register of Poor

CS/D/1, Miscellaneous Record, County of Sutherland Public Assistance Office/Social Work Department Records c.1925–1974 and Registers, c.1925–1948.

Huntingdonshire Record Office.

KHP34, Godmanchester Parish Papers.

Lancashire Record Office (LRO).

DDX 386/3, Garstang Vestry Minutes.

PR 866 and 867, Lancaster Letter Books, 1809–1819.

PR 2391, Billington Overseers' Correspondence.

Leicestershire Record Office (LERO).

DG 39, Constable-Maxwell Collection.

17D, Belgrave St Peter Parish Records.

Lincolnshire Record Office (LIRO).

PL15/ Guardian Minute Books for Stamford Union.

Norfolk Record Office (NORO).

PD 86, East Dereham Overseer's Accounts, 1726–1819.

PD 553/102, Wighton Workhouse Account Book 1789–1796.

Northamptonshire Record Office (NRO).

194p/ Thrapston Overseers' Letter Book.

249p/216, Oundle Overseer's Letter Book.

249p/164-66, Oundle Vestry Minutes.

261p/ Peterborough St John Overseers Correspondence.

284p/190, Rothwell Vestry Minutes 1828–1833.

356p/28, Welton Vestry Minutes.

ZB 68/1/306, Newspaper Clipping.

Northumberland Record Office (NDRO).

GBF 10, Belford Guardian Minutes, 1882–1888.

GBR 77/659–662, and 680–81, Belford Letters and Correspondence.

Oxfordshire Record Office (ORO).

Oxford St Michael, PAR 211, Overseers' Correspondence.

Oxford St Martin, PAR 207, Overseers' Papers.

Wooton P.C. IX, Overseers' Correspondence.

Sutherland Local Archive Centre (SLAC).

Kilmallie Parochial Board Letter Book, 1851–1853.

Somerset Record Office (SORO).
   Q/SPET, Quarter Sessions Petitions.
   PE/OV/8/5, Overseers' Papers for St George's Parish Fordington.
Surrey Record Office (SURO).
   1505-Box37, Farnham Overseers' Papers.
West Sussex Record Office (WSRO).
   Par.29, Broadwater Parish Records.
West Yorkshire Record Office (WYRO).
   WDP20, Sandal Magna Parish Papers.

Films/Series/Documentaries/Songs

BBC, "The Real Deal" in CripTales (2020).
BBC, Panorama, "Britain on the Fiddle" (2011).
BBC, Inside Story, "To Catch a Cheat?" (1997).
BBC, Boys from the Blackstuff (1982).
BBC, "The Block" (1972).
BBC, Cathy Come Home (1966).
Entertainment One, I, Daniel Blake (2016).
Entertainment One, Benefits Street (2014).
Netflix, The Crown.
O. Anthony, "Rich Men North of Richmond" (2023).
P.J. Proby, "We the Jury" (2012).

Legislation

An Act for the Relief of the Poor (1598, 39 Eliz. c.3).
An Act for punishment of Rogues, Vagabonds, and Sturdie Beggers (1598, 39 Eliz. c.4).
An Act against lewd and wandering Persons pretending themselves to be Soldiers or Mariners (1598, 39 Eliz. c.17).
Disabled Soldiers Act (1598, 39 Eliz. c.21)
Act for the Relief of the Poor (1601, 43 Eliz. 1, c.2).
An Act for the better Releife of the Poore of this Kingdom (1662, Chas. II, c.1–3).

Local Studies and Other Libraries

Bolton Local Studies Library, ZHA 17/17, Diary of a Female Poor Law Guardian.
Chorley Public Library, Chorley Vestry Minutes 1781–1823.
Manchester Central Library, M10/ Hulme Parochial Correspondence.
Putney and Wandsworth History Centre, PP/1/2, Putney Vestry Rough Minutes 1819–1831.

Rothersthorpe Parish Church.
Sutton Local Studies Library, LG 15/37/1, Sutton Vestry Book 1810–1829.
Warwick University Archive Centre.

Newspapers/Magazines

Daily Mail
Daily Mirror
Financial Times
New Statesman
Reuters
The Daily Record
The Daily Telegraph
The I
The Financial Times
The Guardian
The Independent
The Spectator
The Sun
The Times

Oral Histories/Focus Groups

Transcripts of all oral histories used here, along with pdf scans of the Focus Group notes taken at the meetings, can be accessed on policyfactory.org.

"VC," interviewed by Steven King, 17 January 1989, and 4 May 1996.
"LN," interviewed by Steven King, 26 June 1991.
"RK," interviewed by Steven King, 12 January 1994, and 20 December 2016.
"TY," interviewed by Steven King, 15 August 1994.
"PT," interviewed by Steven King and Margaret Hanly, 16 March 1995.
"KN," interviewed by Margaret Hanly, 4 September 1997, and 15 March 1999.
"LU," interviewed by Steven King and Margaret Hanly, 19 February 2000.
"MK," interviewed by Steven King, 29 June 2001.
"GC," interviewed by Steven King and Margaret Hanly, 6 July 2002, and by Steven King, 26 August 2009.
"NN," interviewed by Margaret Hanly, 23 September 2002.
"HP," interviewed by Steven King and Margaret Hanly, 23 March 2004.
"AN," interviewed by Margaret Hanly, 16 November 2005.
"AW," interviewed by Margaret Hanly, 6 May 2006.

"KR," interviewed by Steven King, 23 August 2008.
"PE," interviewed by Steven King, 12 December 2008.
"RR," interviewed by Steven King, 14 March 2009.
"HC," interviewed by Steven King, 28 August 2009.
"OM," interviewed by Steven King, 9 September 2009.
"TM," interviewed by Steven King, 3 July 2016
"KP," interviewed by Steven King, 26 September 2016.

Focus Group One: 4 January 2014; 4 April 2014.
Focus Group Two: 10 December 2014; 17 August 2016.
Focus Group Three: 11 June 2015; 1 December 2016.

Other Websites

Amdigital.co.uk
Blogs.lse.ac.uk
Carers UK
Citizens Advice
DailyGripe
Digitalspy.com
Disability News Service
Disability North
East Midlands Oral History Archive
EDRi.org
Elizabeth Roberts Working Class Oral History Archive, Lancaster University
Full Fact
Garden Court Chambers
Hansard
Headington.org.uk
Hertford Oral History Group
History and Policy
HMRC
Huckmag.com
InBrief
Intheirownwriteblog.wordpress.com
Karenlogan.com
King's College, Alumni Blog
Mind
Moneysavingexpert.com
Mosslaw.co.uk

Mumsnet.com
Office for National Statistics
Pinsentmasons.com
Privacyinternational.org
Rochforddistricthistory.org.uk
Sentencingcouncil.org.uk
Statista.com
The OECD
UCL Legacies of British Slavery Database
Youtube
Zambiawatchdog.com
Wellcome Trust

Private Papers

Trainor Family Papers
Clarke Family Papers

The National Archives

TNA, CAB, Cabinet Minutes and Papers.
TNA: MH12 Local Government Board and predecessors: Correspondence with Poor Law Unions and Other Local Authorities. The pauper letter collection for the New Poor Law used here has been coded and is available in perpetuity on TNA's educational resource website: https://www.nationalarchives.gov.uk/education/resources/voices-of-the-victorian-poor/.
TNA PIN: Ministry of Pensions and Successors.

Printed Sources

Advicenow. *A Survival Guide to Living with a Partner and Benefits*. London: Law for Life, 2022.
Annual Reports of the Local Government Board.
Annual Reports of the Poor Law Board.
Annual Reports of the Poor Law Commission.
Anon. *Beating Fraud is Everyone's Business*. London: HMSO for the Department of Social Security, 1998.
Anon. *The Complete Justice*. London: NP, 1637.
Anon. *Fighting Fraud in the Welfare System*. London: DWP, 2022.
Anon. *Fraud and Error in Benefit Expenditure*. London: HMSO for the House of Commons Public Accounts Committee, 2005.

Anon. *Fraud Investigations: Staff Guide*, Volumes 1 and 2. London: DWP, 2019.

Anon. *Report from His Majesty's Commissioners for Inquiring into the Administration and Practical Operation of the Poor Laws*. London. B. Fellowes, 1834.

Anon. *Report of the Committee on Abuse of Social Security Benefits*. London: HMSO, 1973.

Anon. *Shedding Light on the DWP Staff Guide on Conducting Fraud Investigations*. Online: Privacy International, 2021.

Anon. *State of the Nation 2015: Social Mobility and Child Poverty in Great Britain*. London: The Social Mobility and Child Poverty Commission, 2015.

Anon. *The Stout Cripple of Cornwall* (1693).

Anon. *Targeting Benefit Fraud Campaign Tracking Research*. London: GFK NOP, 2008.

Anon. *Truth and Lies about Poverty: Ending Comfortable Myths about Poverty*. Cardiff: The Church in Wales/Oxfam Cymru, 2021.

Anon. *Universal Credit & Disabled Children*. London: Contact, 2019.

Bauke, Algernon. *The Poor Law Guardian; His Powers and Duties in the Right Execution of His Office*. London: Shaw and Sons, 1862.

Bennett, Michael, ed. *A Century Remembered: Reminiscences of Everyday Life in the Eastwood Area*. Lenton: Eastwood Historical Society, 2000.

Beveridge, William. *Social Insurance and Allied Services*. London: HMSO, 1942.

Bloxham, Christine, and Suzanne Shatford. *The Changing Faces of Headington Book One*.Witney: Robert Boyd, 1996.

Bowie, Peter. *English Indices of Deprivation 2019 (IoD2019)*. London: Ministry of Housing, Communities and Local Government, 2019.

Brome, Richard. *A Jovial Crew, Or The Merry Beggars, a Comedy as it is Acted at the Theatre Royal*. London: Joseph Hindmarsh, 1684.

Cabinet Office. *National Fraud Initiative Report*. London: Cabinet Office, 2020.

Candler, Anne. *Poetical Attempts by Ann Candler, a Suffolk Cottager, With a Short Narrative of Her Life*. Ipswich: John Raw, 1803.

Chapman, Stanley, ed. *The Autobiography of David Whitehead of Rawtenstall (1790–1865) Cotton Spinner and Merchant*. Leeds: Helmshore Local History Society, 2001.

Cherrill, Fred. *Cherrill of the Yard*. London: Popular Book Club, 1955.

Church, Rosemary, ed. *Parish on Wheels*. Devizes: Wiltshire Family History Society, 1999.

– ed. *Travelling Folk: Itinerant Mission in the Diocese of Salisbury 1882, 1883*. Devizes: Wiltshire Family History Society, 1999.

Coker Egerton, John. *Sussex Folk and Sussex Ways*. London: Methuen, 1924.

Cooke, William. *A Brief Declaration*. London: William Cooke, 1636.

Coombs, John, and Howard Coombs, eds. *The Journal of a Somerset Rector 1803–1834*. Oxford: Oxford University Press, 1971.

Crowther, Janice, and Peter Crowther, eds. *The Diary of Robert Sharp of South Cave: Life in a Yorkshire Village 1812–1837*. Oxford: Oxford University Press, 1997.

Cudworth, William. *Round About Bradford: A Series of Sketches (descriptive and Semi-historical) of Forty- two Places Within Six Miles of Bradford*. Bradford: T. Brear, 1876.

Dalton, Michael. *The Countrey Justice: Containing the Practice of the Justices of the Peace out of their Sessions*. London: G. Sawbridge, T. Roycroft, and W. Rawlins, 1677.

Davies, William. *The Autobiography of a Supertramp*. London: A.C. Fifield, 1908.

Davies, Harry, and Henry Owston. *Overseers' Manual Showing Their Duties, Liabilities and Responsibilities*. London: Shaw and Sons, 1864.

Dixon, Simon, Ceri Smith, and Annel Touchet. *The Disability Perception Gap Policy Report*. London: SCOPE, 2018.

Dunning, Richard. *A Plain and Easie Method*. London: NP, 1685.

DWP. *Fraud and Error in the Benefit System 2019–20*. London: DWP, 2020.

Ewart Evans, George. *Let Dogs Delight*. London: Faber and Faber, 1975.

– *Where Beards Wag All: The Relevance of the Oral Tradition*. London: Faber and Faber, 1973.

Fisher, Henry. Cmnd 5228, *Report of the Committee on Abuse of Social Security Benefits*. London: HMSO, 1973.

Foster, John. "The poor laws, settlement and removal, irremovable poor." In G. Hastings, ed., *Transactions of the National Association for the Promotion of Social Science. York Meeting, 1864*, 623–7. London: Longman, Green and Co, 1865.

Gear, Gillian, ed., *The Diary of Benjamin Woodcock, Master of the Barnet Union Workhouse 1836–1838*. Hertford: Hertfordshire Record Society, 2008.

Haines, Richard. *England's Weal of Prosperity Proposed*. London: Langley Curtis, 1681.

Hale, Matthew. *A Method Concerning the Relief and Employment of the Poor*. London: Parsons and Son, 1690.

Hewins, Angela. *The Dillen: Memories of a Man of Stratford-upon-Avon*. Banbury: Elm Tree Books, 1981.

– *Mary, After the Queen: Memories of a Working Girl*. Oxford: Oxford University Press, 1985.

Horn, Pamela. *Oxfordshire Village Life: The Diaries of George James Dew (1846–1928), Relieving Officer*. Abingdon: Beacon, 1983.

Horsman, Grace. *Growing up in the Forties*. Newton Abbott: Forest Publishing, 1997.

Hood, Andrew, and David Phillips. "Benefit Spending and Reforms: The Coalition Government's Record," Briefing Note, IFS, 28 January 2015.

House of Commons Committee of Public Accounts. *The Department for Work and Pensions' Accounts 2020-21-Fraud and Error in the Benefits System* 25th Report of Session 2021–22; 4 November 2021.

House of Commons Work and Pension Committee. *The Local Welfare Safety Net*. London: HMSO, 2016.

Hudson-Sharp, Nathan, Naomi Munro-Lott, Heather Rolfe, and Johnny Runge. *The Impact of Welfare Reform and Welfare-to-Work Programmes: An Evidence Review*. London: National Institute of Economic and Social Research, 2018.

Hurley, Janet, ed. *Devizes St. Mary Survey of the Poor 1802–1808*. Devizes: Wiltshire Family History Society, 2003.

James, Joy. *Bog All To Swear About*. Nottingham: SP, 2009.

– *Poverty and Rhyme!* Nottingham: Nottingham City Council, 2008.

– *Yo'd Mek a Parson Swear*. Nottingham: SP, 2008.

– *Yo'd Mek a Parson Swear…. Again*. Nottingham: SP, 2008.

Jones, Peter, and Steven King. *Navigating the Old English Poor Law: The Kirkby Lonsdale Letters, 1809-1836*. Oxford: Oxford University Press, 2020.

Keen, Richard. *Welfare Savings 2010–11 to 2020–21*. London: House of Commons Briefing Paper 7667, 2016.

Kendall, Samuel. *Farming Memoirs of a West Country Yeoman*. London: Faber and Faber, 1924.

Kerr, Jane, and Mark Button. *Research on Sentencing Online Fraud Offences*. London: Sentencing Council, 2013.

Kilburne, Richard. *Choice Presidents upon all Acts of Parliament Relating to the Office and Duty of a Justice of the Peace*. London: Richard and Edward Atkins, 1681.

Kussmaul, Ann. *The Autobiography of Joseph Mayett of Quainton 1783–1839*. Cambridge: Buckinghamshire Record Society, 1986.

Langley, Anne, ed. *Joseph Ashby's Victorian Warwickshire*. Studley: Brewin Books, 2007.

Layer, John. *The Office and Dutie of Constables, Churchwardens, and Other the Overseers of the Poore*. Cambridge: Roger Daniel, 1641.

Le Hardy, William, ed. *Buckinghamshire Sessions Records*. Buckingham: Buckinghamshire County Council, 8 volumes 1933 to 1980.

Leathland, John. *Essays and Poems, With a Brief Autobiographical Memoir*. London: W. Tweedie, 1862.

Leonard, Harry. *Diaries and Correspondence of Robert Lee of Binfield, 1736–44*. Reading: Berkshire Record Society, 2012.

Lewis, Lesley, ed. *Hird's Annales of Bedale: From the Papers of Robert Hird, 1768–1841, shoemaker, of Bedale, North Riding, Yorkshire*. Ripon: North Yorkshire County Record Office, 1975.

Malvery, Olive. *The Soul Market*. London: Hutchinson and Co., 1907.

NAO. *Tackling Benefit Fraud*. London: HMSO, 2003.

North, Roger. *A Discourse of the Poor*. London: M. Cooper, 1753.

Page, Robin. *The Benefits Racket*. London: Temple Smith, 1971.

Park, Jo, ed. *Edward Prynn, A Boy in Hob-Nailed Boots*. Padstow: Tabb House, 1981.

Park, Megan. *The Implementation of Discretionary Housing Payments by Local Authorities in England: Exploring Accountability, Equity and the Meeting of Need*. London: i-sphere, 2019.

Parker, James, and Richard Burn. *Conductor Generalis: Or the Office, Duty and Authority of Justices of the Peace, High-Sheriffs, Under-Sheriffs, Coroners, Constables, Goalers, Jury-Men, and Overseers of the Poor*. New York: J. Parker, 1749.

Parliamentary and Health Ombudsman. *Women's State Pension Age: Our Findings on the Department for Work and Pensions' Communication of Changes*. London: HMSO, 2021.

Poussin, Fr. *Pretty doings in a Protestant nation. Being a view of the present state of fornication, whorecraft, and adultery, in Great-Britain, and the territories and dependencies thereunto belonging. Written originally in French by Father Poussin, priest regular of the Order of St. Dominick*. London: J. Roberts, 1734.

Purdy, Frederick. "The Statistics of the English Poor Rate before and since the Passing of the Poor Law Amendment Act." *Journal of the Statistical Society of London* 23 (1860): 286–39.

Razzell, Peter, ed. *Life in the Victorian Village: The Daily News Survey of 1891. Volume II*. Chichester: Caliban Books, 1999.

Redford, Elizabeth. *"Die Veult:" God Wills It: The Banbury Female Martyr (Composed by Herself) Who Never Had Any Opportunity of Learning How to Write and Written by Her Daughter Only Nine Years Old*. Banbury: Hard Press Publishing, 2019.

Reynolds, Stephen. *A Poor Man's House*. Oxford: Oxford University Press, 1982.

Rose, Walter. *Good Neighbours: Some Recollections of an English Village and its People*. Oxford: ISIS Press, 1999 Reprint.

Rutherford, James (alias Thor Fredur). *Indoor Paupers, by 'One of Them'*. London: Chatto, 1886.

Rutherford, Tom. *Historical Rates of Social Security Benefits*. London: House of Commons Library, 2013.

S.C. *Legal Provisions for the Poor, or a Treatise of the Common and Statute Laws Concerning the Poor Either as to Relief, Settlement or Punishment*. London: John Nutt, 1710.

Scampion, John. *Organised Benefit Fraud: A Report*. London: DSS, 2000.

Scott, David. *"I am constantly penny pinching." Research into Living on Universal Credit during the Pandemic*. Edinburgh: Citizens Advice Scotland, 2021.

Silverthorne, Elizabeth, ed., *Deposition Book of Richard Wyatt, J.P, 1767–1776*. Guildford: Surrey Record Society, 1978.

S.T., R.W., &c. *A Mild but Expostulatory Letter*. Buckingham: NP, 1680.

Stevenson, Geoffrey, ed. *Mid Victorian Squarson. The Diaries of William Cotton Risley, Former Vicar of Deddington 1849-1869*. Banbury: Banbury Historical Society, 2012.

Torr, Cecil. *Small Talk at Wreyland*, 3 vols. Cambridge: Cambridge University Press, 1918, 1921, and 1923.

Webb, Beatrice. *My Apprenticeship vols. I and II*. London: Benediction Classics, 2007.

– *Our Partnership*. London: Longmans, Green and Co., 1948.

Wells, Roger, ed. *Victorian Village: The Diaries of the Reverend John Coker Egerton of Burwash 1857–1888*. Stroud: Alan Sutton, 1992.

White, Richard. *Memoirs of a Victorian Farmer: Richard White of Mells, Norridge and Zeals (1828–1905)*. Frome: Downland Press, 1990.

Willmott, Oliver. *Yours Reverently... from the Pulpit, the Pub and the "Parish Notes," 1948–53*. Bridport: Bishop Street Press, 1998.

Wood, Iain. *Some Accounts of the Shrewsbury House of Industry, Its Establishment and Regulations, with hints to those who may have similar institutions in view, 4th Edition*. Shrewsbury: J and W Eddowes, 1795.

Wood, William. *A Sussex Farmer*. London: Jonathan Cape, 1938.

Wright, John. *Bygone Eastbourne*. London: Spottiswoode and Co., 1902.

Secondary Sources

Alexander, Sarah. "The Residuum, Victorian Naturalism, and the Entropic Narrative." *Nineteenth-Century Contexts* 35 (2013): 99–120.

Allen, Robert. "Class Structure and Inequality during the Industrial Revolution: Lessons From England's Social Tables, 1688–1867." *Economic History Review* 72 (2019): 88–125.

Althammer, Beate, Lutz Raphael, and Tamara Stazic-Wendt, eds. *Rescuing the Vulnerable: Poverty, Welfare and Social Ties in Modern Europe*. Oxford: Berghahn, 2016.

Althammer, Beate, Andreas Gestrich, and Jens Gründler, eds. *The Welfare State and the 'Deviant Poor' in Europe, 1870–1933*. Basingstoke: Palgrave, 2014.

Andersen, Kate. "Universal Credit, Gender and Unpaid Childcare: Mothers' Accounts of the New Welfare Conditionality Regime." *Critical Social Policy* 40 (2019): 430–49.

Andrews, Aaron. "Multiple Deprivation, the Inner City, and the Fracturing of the Welfare State: Glasgow, c.1968–78." *Twentieth Century British History* 29 (2018): 605–24.

Andrews, Kay, and John Jacobs. *Punishing the Poor: Poverty under Thatcher*. London: Macmillan, 1990.

Ashforth, David. "Settlement and Removal in Urban Areas: Bradford 1834–71." In M. Rose, ed., *The Poor and the City: The English Poor Law in its Urban Context 1834–1914*, 58–91. Leicester: Leicester University Press, 1985.

Bagguley, Paul, and Kirk Mann. "Idle Thieving Bastards? Scholarly Representations of the Underclass." *Work, Employment and Society* 6 (1992): 113–26.

Bartholomew, James. *The Welfare of Nations*. London: Biteback Publishing, 2017.

Baumberg, Ben. "The Stigma of Claiming Benefits: A Quantitative Study." *Journal of Social Policy* 45 (2016): 181–99.

– "Three Ways to Defend Social Security in Britain." *Journal of Poverty and Social Justice* 20 (2012): 149–61.

van Bavel, Bas, and Auke Rijpma. "How Important Were Formalised Charity and Social Spending before the Rise of the Welfare State? A Long-Run Analysis of Selected Western European Cases, 1400–1850." *Economic History Review* 69 (2016): 159–87.

Beatty, Christina, and Steve Fothergill. "Welfare Reform: National Policies with Local Impacts." In J. Evans, S. Ruane, and H. Southall, eds, *Data in Society: Challenging Statistics in an Age of Globalisation*, 145–56. Basingstoke: Palgrave, 2019.

Beier, Lee. *Masterless Men: The Vagrancy Problem in England, 1560-1640*. London: Methuen, 1985.

– "'Takin' it to the streets': Henry Mayhew and the language of the underclass in mid-nineteenth-century London." In A. Beier and P. Ocobock, eds, *Cast Out: Vagrancy and Homelessness in Global and Historical Perspective*, 88–116. Athens: Ohio University Press, 2008.

Berridge, Virginia, and Suzanne Taylor. "The Problems of Commissioned Oral History: The Swine Flu 'Crisis' of 2009." *Oral History* 47 (2019): 86–94.

Blaikie, Andrew. *Illegitimacy, Sex and Society: Northeast Scotland, 1750–1900*. Oxford: Clarendon Press, 1994.

Bor, Alexander, and Gabor Simonovits. "Empathy, Deservingness, and Preferences for Welfare Assistance: A Large-Scale Online Perspective-Taking Experiment." *Political Behavior* 43 (2021): 1247–64.

Borsay, Anne. *Disability and Social Policy in Britain since 1750: A History of Exclusion*. Basingstoke: Palgrave, 2005.

Boulton, Jeremy. "Double Deterrence: Settlement and Practice in London's West End, 1725–1824." In S. King and A. Winter, eds, *Migration, Settlement and Belonging in Europe, 1500s-1930s*, 54–80. Oxford: Berghahn, 2013.

Bove, Arianna. "For Whose Benefit? Fear and Loathing in the Welfare State." *Journal of Political Marketing* 13 (2014): 108–26.

Boyer, George. "The Evolution of Unemployment Relief in Great Britain." *Journal of Interdisciplinary History* 34 (2004): 393–433.

– *The Winding Road to the Welfare State: Economic Insecurity & Social Welfare Policy in Britain*. Princeton: Princeton University Press, 2019.

Boyer, George, and Timothy Schmidle. "Poverty among the Elderly in Late-Victorian England." *Economic History Review* 62 (2009): 249–78.

Bradshaw, Jonathan, and John Holmes. "An analysis of equity in redistribution to the retired and children over recent decades in the OECD and UK." *Journal of Social Policy* 42 (2013): 39–56.

Brewer, Mike, Karl Handscomb, Gavin Kelly, James Smith, and Lalitha Try. *Social Insecurity: Assessing Trends in Social Security to Prepare for the Decade of Change Ahead.* London: Resolution Foundation, 2022.

Briant, Emma, Nick Watson, and Gregory Philo. "Reporting Disability in the Age of Austerity: The Changing Face of Media Representation of Disability and Disabled People in the United Kingdom and the Creation of New 'Folk Devils.'" *Disability and Society* 28 (2013): 874–9.

Brodie, Marc. *Neighbours, Distrust & the State: What the Poorer Working Class in Britain Felt about Government and Each Other, 1860s–1930s.* Oxford: Oxford University Press, 2022.

Brown, Patrick, Rubén Flores, and Andy Alaszewski. "Understanding Policy Scandals in Historical Context: A Longer-Term Lens for Policy Analysis." *Journal of Social Policy* 49 (2020): 125–43.

Brundage, Anthony. *The Making of the New Poor Law: The Politics of Inquiry, Enactment and Implementation, 1832–39.* London: Hutchinson, 1978.

Burnett, John. *Idle Hands: The Experience of Unemployment 1790–1990.* Abingdon: Routledge, 1994.

Butler, Ian, and Mark Drakeford. *Social Policy, Social Welfare and Scandal.* Basingstoke: Palgrave, 2003.

Cage, Robert. *The Scottish Poor Law 1745–1845.* Edinburgh: Edinburgh University Press, 1981.

Carter, Natalie, and Steven King. "'I think we ought not to acknowledge them [paupers] as that encourages them to write': The Administrative State, Power and the Victorian Pauper." *Social History* 46 (2021): 117–44.

Charlesworth, Lori. "How Poor Law Rights Were Lost but Victorian Values Survived: A Reconsideration of Some of the Hidden Values of Welfare Provision." In A. Hudson, ed., *New Perspectives on Property Law, Human Rights and the Home*, 271–93. London: Cavendish Publishing, 2004.

– *Welfare's Forgotten Past: A Socio-Legal History of the Poor Law.* Abingdon: Routledge, 2011.

Chinn, Carl. *Poverty amidst Prosperity: The Urban Poor in England, 1834–1914.* Preston: Carnegie: 2006 reprint.

Chunn, Dorothy, and Shelley Gavigan. "Welfare Law, Welfare Fraud, and the Moral Regulation of the 'Never Deserving' Poor." *Social and Legal Studies* 13 (2004): 219–43.

Clasen, Jochen. "Towards a New Welfare State or Reverting to Type? Some Major Trends in British Social Policy since the Early 1980s." *The European Legacy* 8 (2005): 573–86.

Clery, Elizabeth. "Welfare." In J. Curtice, M. Phillips, and E. Clery, eds, BSA 33, 24–44. London: National Centre for Social Research, 2016.

Collard, David. "Malthus, Population and the Generational Bargain." *History of Political Economy* 33 (2001), 697–716.

Connor, Stuart. "'We're onto you': A Critical Examination of the Department for Work and Pensions 'Targeting Benefit Fraud' Campaign." *Critical Social Policy* 27 (2007): 231–52.

Cook, Dee. *Rich Law, Poor Law: Differential Responses to Tax and Supplementary Benefit Fraud*. Milton Keynes: Open University Press, 1989.

Cooper, John. *The British Welfare Revolution, 1906–15*. London: Bloomsbury, 2017.

Costello, Kevin. "'More equitable than the Judgement of the Justices of the Peace': The King's Bench and the Poor Law 1630–1800." *Journal of Legal History* 35 (2014): 3–26.

Cottam, Susan. "Small and Scattered: Poor Law Children's Homes in Leeds, 1900–1950." *Family and Community History* 20 (2017): 175–92.

Critcher, Chas. "Moral Panic Analysis: Past, Present and Future." *Sociology Compass* 2 (2008): 1127–44.

Crone, Ros. "Educating the Labouring Poor in Nineteenth-Century Suffolk." *Social History* 43 (2018): 161–85.

Crossan, Rose-Marie. *Poverty and Welfare in Guernsey 1560–2015*. Woodbridge: Boydell, 2015.

Crossick, Geoffrey. "From Gentlemen to the Residuum: Languages of Social Description in Victorian Britain." In P. Corfield, ed., *Language, History and Class*, 150–78. Oxford: Oxford University Press, 1991.

Crowson, Nicholas. "'Tramps' Tales: Discovering the Life-Stories of Late Victorian and Edwardian Vagrants." *English Historical Review* 135 (2020): 1488–526.

Crowther, Anne. "Family Responsibility and State Responsibility in Britian before the Welfare State." *Historical Journal* 25 (1982): 131–45.

Curchin, Katherine. "From the Moral Limits of Markets to the Moral Limits of Welfare." *Journal of Social Policy* 45 (2016): 101–18.

Curtice, John, and Rachel Ormston. "Devolution: On the Road to Divergence? Trends in Public Opinion in Scotland and England." In A. Park, E. Clery, J, Curtice, M. Phillips, and D. Utting, eds, *BSA 28*, 21–36. London: National Centre for Social Research, 2012.

Daly, Mary, and Grace Kelly. *Families and Poverty: Everyday Life on a Low Income*. Bristol: Policy Press, 2015.

Daguerre, Anne, and David Etherington. *Workfare in 21st Century Britain: The Erosion of Rights to Social Assistance*. Middlesex: Middlesex University Press, 2014.

D'Arcy, Stephen. "Is There Ever an Obligation to Commit Welfare Fraud?" *The Journal of Value Inquiry* 42 (2008): 377–87.

Darwen, Lewis, Donald MacRaild, Brian Gurrin, and Liam Kennedy. "'Unhappy and Wretched Creatures': Charity, Poor Relief and Pauper Removal in Britain and

Ireland during the Great Famine." *English Historical Review* 134 (2019): 589–619.

Davidoff, Leonore. "The Separation of Home and Work? Landladies and Lodgers in Nineteenth and Twentieth Century England." In S. Burman, ed., *Fit Work for Women*, 64–97. Oxford: Oxford University Press, 1979.

Davidson, Ruth. "Family Politics: Campaigning for Child Benefits in the 1980s." *Twentieth Century British History* 31 (2019): 101–24.

Davis, John. "Reshaping the Welfare State? Voluntary Action and Community in London. 1960–75." In L. Goldman, ed., *Welfare and Social Policy in Britain since 1870*, 197–212. Oxford: Oxford University Press, 2019.

Deacon, Alan. "The Scrounging Controversy: Public Attitudes towards the Unemployed in Contemporary Britain." *Social and Economic Administration* 12 (1978): 120–35.

– *In Search of the Scrounger: The Administration of Unemployment Insurance in Britain 1920–1931*. London: Bell, 1976.

Dean, Hartley. *Social Rights and Human Welfare*. Abingdon: Routledge, 2015.

Dean, Hartley, and Margaret Melrose. "Manageable Discord: Fraud & Resistance in the Social Security System." *Social Policy & Administration* 31 (1997): 103–18.

Deeming, Christopher. "Foundations of the Workfare State-Reflections on the Political Transformation of the Welfare State in Britain." *Social Policy and Administration* 49 (2015): 862–86.

Deeming, Christopher, and Ron Johnston. "Coming Together in a Rightward Direction: Post-1980s Changing Attitudes to the British Welfare State." *Quality & Quantity* 52 (2018): 395–413.

– "From 'Welfare' to 'Workfare', and Back Again? Social Insecurity and the Changing Role of the State." In J. Evans, S. Ruane, and H. Southall, eds, *Data in Society: Challenging Statistics in an Age of Globalisation*, 157–70. Bristol: Policy Press, 2019.

Dencik, Lina. "The Datafied Welfare State: A Perspective from the UK." In A. Hepp, J. Jarke and L. Kramp, eds, *New Perspectives in Critical Data Studies: The Ambivalences of Data Power*, 145–66. Basingstoke: Palgrave, 2022.

Dierks, Konstantin. *In My Power: Letter Writing and Communications in Early America*. Philadelphia: University of Pennsylvania Press, 2011.

Digby, Anne. *British Welfare Policy: Workhouse to Workfare*. London: Faber & Faber, 1989.

– "Changing Welfare Cultures in Region and State." *Twentieth Century British History* 17 (2006): 297–322.

Dilnot, Andrew. "The Future Welfare Burden." *Scottish Journal of Political Economy* 46 (1999): 489–504.

Di Matteo, Livio. *Measuring Government in the 21st Century*. Vancouver: The Fraser Institute, 2013.

Donoghue, Matthew, and Mikko Kuisma. "Taking Back Control of the Welfare State: Brexit, Rational-Imaginaries and Welfare Chauvinism." *West European Politics* 45 (2022): 177–99.

Donovan, Stephen, and Matthew Rubery. "Doing the Amateur Casual: Victorian Investigative Journalism and the Legacy of James Greenwood's 'A Night in the Workhouse.'" *Victorian Studies* 63 (2021): 401–30.

Dorey, Peter. "A Farewell to Alms: Thatcherism's Legacy of Inequality." *British Politics* 10 (2015): 79–98.

– "A Poverty of Imagination: Blaming the Poor for Inequality." *The Political Quarterly* 81 (2010): 333–43.

Drake, Robert. "Disabled People, New Labour, Benefits and Work." *Critical Social Policy* 20 (2000): 421–39.

Drakeford, Mark. "Devolution and the Welfare State: The Case of Wales." In G. Calder, J. Grass, and K. Merrill-Glover, eds, *Changing Directions of the British Welfare State*, 177–94. Cardiff: University of Wales Press, 2012.

Dromi, Shai. "Penny for Your Thoughts: Beggars and the Exercise of Morality in Daily Life." *Sociological Forum* 27 (2012): 847–71.

Duffy, Simon, and Jonathan Wolff. "No More Benefit Cheats." in J. Baggini, ed., *A Philosopher's Manifesto: Ideas and Arguments to Change the World*, 103–18. Cambridge: Cambridge University Press, 2022.

Dwyer, Peter. "Creeping Conditionality in the UK: From Welfare Rights to Conditional Entitlements?" *The Canadian Journal of Sociology* 29 (2004): 265–87.

Dwyer, Peter, and Sharon Wright. "Universal Credit, Ubiquitous Conditionality and Its Implications for Social Citizenship." *Journal of Poverty and Social Justice* 22 (2014): 27–35.

Dyson, Richard, and Steven King. "'The streets are paved with idle beggars': Experiences and Perceptions of Beggars in Nineteenth Century Oxford." In B. Althammer, ed., *Bettler in der Europäischen Stadt der Moderne: Zwischen Barmherzigkeit, Repression und Sozialreform*, 71–102. Oxford: Peter Lang, 2007.

Edmiston, Daniel. "Welfare, Austerity and Social Citizenship in the UK." *Social Policy and Society* 16 (2017): 261–70.

– *Welfare, Inequality and Social Citizenship: Deprivation and Affluence in Austerity Britain*. Bristol: Policy Press, 2020.

Edmiston, Daniel, and Louise Humpage. "Resistance or resignation to welfare reform? The activist politics for and against social citizenship." *Policy and Politics* 46 (2018): 467–84.

Ellis, Catherine. "No Hammock for the Idle: The Conservative Party, 'Youth' and the Welfare State in the 1960s." *Twentieth Century British History* 16 (2005): 441–70.

Etzioni, Amitai. *The New Golden Rule*. London: Profile, 1997.

Evans, Karen, Penny Fraser, and Sandra Walklate. "Whom can you trust? The Politics of 'grassing' on an inner-city housing estate." *Sociological Review* 44 (1996): 361–80.

Evans, Megan, and Peter Jones. "'A Stubborn and Intractable Body': Resistance to the Workhouse in Wales, 1834-1877." *Family and Community History* 17 (2014): 101–21.

Evans, Tanya. *'Unfortunate objects': Lone Mothers in Eighteenth-Century London.* Basingstoke: Palgrave Macmillan, 2005.

Fahrmeir, Andreas. *Citizenship: The Rise and Fall of a Modern Concept.* New Haven: Yale University Press, 2007.

Feldman, David. "Migrants, immigrants and welfare from the Old Poor Law to the welfare state." *Transactions of the Royal Historical Society* 13 (2003): 79–104.

Ferguson, Christopher. "The Political Economy of the Street and its Discontents: Beggars and Pedestrians in Mid-Nineteenth-Century London." *Cultural and Social History* 12 (2015): 27–50.

Fideler, Paul. *Social Welfare in Pre-Industrial England: The Old Poor Law Tradition.* Basingstoke: Palgrave, 2006.

Field, Frank. *Losing Out: The Emergence of Britain's Underclass.* Oxford: Blackwell, 1989.

Fink, Janet. "Private Lives, Public Issues: Moral Panics and 'the Family' in 20th-Century Britain" *Journal for the Study of British Cultures* 9 (2002): 135–48.

Finlayson, Geoffrey. *Citizen, State and Social Welfare in Britain, 1830-1990.* Oxford: Clarendon Press, 1994.

Fitzmaurice, Susan. *The Familiar Letter in Early Modern English: A Pragmatic Approach* Amsterdam: John Benjamin's Publishing, 2002.

Forman Cody, Lisa. "'Every lane teems with instruction, and every alley is big with erudition': Graffiti in eighteenth-century London." In T. Hitchcock and H. Shore, eds, *The Streets of London: From the Great Fire to the Great Stink*, 82–100. London: Rovers Oram, 2003.

Forrest, Colleen. "Familial poverty, family allowances, and the normative family structure in Britain, 1917-1945." *Journal of Family History* 26 (2001): 508–28.

Fraser, Derek. "The English Poor Law and the Origins of the British Welfare State." In W. Mommsen, ed., *The Emergence of the Welfare State in Britain and Germany 1850-1950*, 9–31. London: Croom Helm, 1981.

– "The urban poor law." In D. Fraser, ed., *The New Poor Law in the Nineteenth Century*, 128–48. Basingstoke: Macmillan, 1976.

Freeman, Mark. "The provincial social survey in Edwardian Britain." *Historical Research* 75 (2002): 73–89.

Garthwaite, Kayleigh. "The language of shirkers and scroungers? Talking about illness, disability and coalition welfare reforms." *Disability and Society* 26 (2011): 369–72.

Gazeley, Ian. *Poverty in Britain, 1900-1965*. Basingstoke: Palgrave, 2003.

Gavin, Neil. "Below the radar: A UK benefit fraud media coverage tsunami-impact, ideology, and society." *British Journal of Sociology* 72 (2021): 707–24.

Geary, Frank, and Tim Stark. "What happened to regional inequality in Britain in the twentieth-century?" *Economic History Review* 69 (2016): 215–28.

Geiger, Baumberg. "Benefit 'myths'? The accuracy and inaccuracy of public beliefs about the benefits system." *Social Policy and Administration* 52 (2017): 998–1018.

– *Benefit 'Myths'? The Accuracy and Inaccuracy of Public Beliefs about the Benefits System*. London: CASE, 2016.

–"Disabled but not deserving? The perceived deservingness of disability welfare benefit claimants." *Journal of European Social Policy* 31 (2021): 337–51.

– "False belief and the perceived deservingness of social security benefit claimants." In W. van Oorschot, F. Roosma, B. Meuleman, and T. Reeskens, eds, *The Social Legitimacy of Targeted Welfare: Attitudes to Welfare Deservingness*, 73–92. Cheltenham: Edward Elgar, 2017.

Gibbs, Jacqueline, and Aura Lehtonen. "I, Daniel Blake (2016): Vulnerability, Care and Citizenship in Austerity Politics." *Feminist Review* 122 (2019): 49–63.

Gibson-Bryden, Thomas. *The Moral Mapping of Victorian and Edwardian London: Charles Booth, Christian Charity, and the Poor-But-Respectable*. London: McGill–Queen's University Press, 2016.

Giles, Kate, and Melanie Giles. "The Writing on the Wall: The Concealed Communities of the East Yorkshire Horselads." *International Journal of Historical Archaeology* 11 (2007): 336–57.

Gillie, Alan. "Identifying the Poor in the 1870s and 1880s." *Economic History Review* 61 (2008): 302–25.

– "The Origin of the Poverty Line." *Economic History Review* 49 (1996): 715–30.

Golding, Peter, and Sue Middleton. *Images of Welfare: Press and Public Attitudes to Poverty*. Oxford: Martin Robertson, 1982.

Goose, Nigel. "Poverty, Old Age and Gender in Nineteenth-Century England: The case of Hertfordshire." *Continuity and Change* 20 (2005): 351–84.

Gordon, Linda. *Pitied but not Entitled: Single Mothers and the History of Welfare*. Cambridge, MA: Harvard University Press, 1994.

Gough, Ian. "The Crisis of the British Welfare State." *International Journal of Health Services* 13 (1983): 459–77.

Greve, Bent. "The Hidden Welfare State, Tax Expenditure and Social Policy: A Comparative Overview." *International Journal of Social Welfare* 3 (1994): 203–11.

Griffin, Carl. *The Politics of Hunger: Protest, Poverty and Policy in England, 1750–1840*. Manchester: Manchester University Press, 2020.

– *The Rural War: Captain Swing and the Politics of Protest*. Manchester: Manchester University Press, 2012.

Griffin, Emma. *Liberty's Dawn: A People's History of the Industrial Revolution*. New Haven: Yale University Press, 2013.

– "The Value of Motherhood: Understanding Motherhood from Maternal Absence in Victorian Britain." *Past and Present* 246 (2020): 167–85.

Grover, Chris. "Localism and Poverty in the United Kingdom: The Case of Local Welfare Assistance." *Policy Studies* 33 (2012): 349–65.

Groves, Keleigh-Ann. "Understanding Benefit Fraud: A Qualitative Analysis." Unpublished PhD diss., University of Leeds, 2002.

Gruber von Arni, Eric. *Justice to the Maimed Soldier: Nursing, Medical Care and Welfare for Sick and Wounded Soldiers and Their Families during the English Civil Wars and Interregnum, 1642–1660*. Aldershot: Ashgate, 2001.

Gulland, Jackie. *Gender, Work and Social Control: A Century of Disability Benefits*. Basingstoke: Palgrave, 2019.

Gurney, Peter. *Wanting and Having: Popular Politics and Liberal Consumerism in England 1830-1870*. Manchester: Manchester University Press, 2015.

Halla, Martin, and Friedrich Schneider. "Taxes and Benefits: Two Options to Cheat on the State." *Oxford Bulletin of Economics and Statistics* 76 (2014): 411–31.

Hancock, Lynn, and Gerry Mooney. "'Welfare Ghettos' and the 'Broken Society': Territorial Stigmatisation in the Contemporary UK." *Housing, Theory and Society* 30 (2013): 46–64.

Hansen, Kristina. "Who Cares if They Need Help? The Deservingness Heuristic, Humanitarianism, and Welfare Opinions." *Political Psychology* 40 (2019): 413–30.

Harley, Joseph. "Pauper Inventories, Social Relations, and the Nature of Poor Relief under the Old Poor Law, England, c. 1601–1834." *Historical Journal* 62 (2019): 375–98.

Harris, Bernard. *The Origins of the British Welfare State: Social Welfare in England and Wales, 1800–1945*. Basingstoke: Macmillan, 2004.

– "Parsimony and Pauperism: Poor Relief in England, Scotland And Wales in the Nineteenth and Early-Twentieth Centuries." *Journal of Scottish Historical Studies* 39 (2019): 40–74.

Harris, Jose. "Between Civic Virtue and Social Darwinism: The Concept of the Residuum." In D. Englander and R. O'Day, eds, *Retrieved Riches: Social Investigation in Britain, 1840–1914*, 67–87. Aldershot: Scolar, 1995.

– "Nationality, Rights and Virtue: Some Approaches to Citizenship in Great Britain." In R. Bellamy, D. Castiglione, and E. Santoro, eds, *Lineages of European Citizenship: Rights, Belonging and Participation in Eleven Nation-States*, 73–91. Basingstoke: Palgrave, 2004.

– "Political Thought and Welfare State 1870–1940: An Intellectual Framework for British Social Policy." In D. Gladstone, ed., *Before Beveridge: Welfare Before the Welfare State*, 43–68. London: Civitas, 1999.

– *William Beveridge: A Biography*. Oxford: Oxford University Press, 1998.

Hartfree, Yvette. "Universal Credit: The Impact of Monthly Payments on Low Income Households." *Journal of Poverty and Social Justice* 22 (2014): 15–26.

Harvey, Ben. "The Putative Fathers of Swinton, England: Illegitimate Behavior under the Old Poor Laws, 1797–1835." *Journal of Family History* 40 (2015): 373–98.

Hayton, Richard, and Libby McEnhill. "Rhetoric and Morality: How the Coalition Justifies Welfare Policy." In J. Atkins, A. Finlayson, J. Martin and N. Turnbull, eds, *Rhetoric in British Society and Politics*, 101–15. Basingstoke: Palgrave, 2014.

Hayward, Keith, and Majid Yar. "The 'Chav' Phenomenon: Consumption, Media and the Construction of a New Underclass." *Crime, Media, Culture* 2 (2006), 9–28.

Hayward, Sally. "'Those who cannot work': An Exploration of Disabled Men and Masculinity in Henry Mayhew's London Labour and the London Poor." *Prose Studies* 21 (2005): 53–71.

Headworth, Spencer. "Broke People, Broken Rules: Explaining Welfare Fraud Investigators' Attributions." *Punishment and Society* 23 (2021): 24–46.

Headworth, Spencer, and Viridiana Rios. "Listening to Snitches: Race/Ethnicity, English Proficiency, and Access to Welfare Fraud Enforcement Systems." *Law and Policy* 43 (2021): 319–47.

Healey, Jonathan. *The First Century of Welfare: Poverty and Poor Relief in Lancashire, 1620–1730*. Woodbridge: Boydell, 2014.

– "Kin Support and the English Poor: Evidence from Lancashire, c.1620–1710." *Historical Research* 92 (2019): 318–39.

Heinemann, Friedrich. "Is the Welfare State Self-Destructive? A Study of Government Benefit Morale." *Kyklos* 61 (2008): 237–57.

Hennock, Peter. "The Measurement of Urban Poverty: From the Metropolis to the Nation, 1880–1920." *Economic History Review* 40 (1987): 208–27.

– *The Origin of the Welfare State in England and Germany, 1850–1914: Social Policies Compared*. Cambridge: Cambridge University Press, 2007.

– "Poverty and Social Theory in England: The Experience of the 1880s." *Social History* 1 (1976): 67–91.

Heron, Emma, and Peter Dwyer. "Doing the Right Thing: Labour's Attempt to Forge a New Welfare Deal between the Individual and the State." *Social Policy and Administration* 33 (1999): 91–104.

Hickson, Kevin. "Conservatism and the Poor: Conservative Party Attitudes to Poverty and Inequality since the 1970s." *British Politics* 4 (2009): 341–62.

– "The Postwar Consensus Revisited." *Political Quarterly* 75 (2004): 142–54.

Higgs, Edward. "Fingerprints and Citizenship: the British State and the Identification of Pensioners in the Interwar Period." *History Workshop Journal* 69 (2010): 52–67.

– *The Information State in England: The Central Collection of Information on Citizens since 1500*. Basingstoke: Palgrave, 2003.

Hills, John. *Good Times, Bad Times: The Welfare Myth of Them and Us*. Bristol: Policy Press, 2014.

– "Policy Dilemmas and Challenges for the Next 20 Years." In H. Glennerster, J. Hills, D. Piachaud, and J. Webb, eds, *One Hundred Years of Poverty and Policy*, 135–60. York: JRF, 2004.

Hill, Michael, and Alan Walker. "What Were the Lasting Effects of Thatcher's Legacy for Social Security? The Burial of Beveridge?" In S. Farrall and C. Hay, eds, *The Legacy of Thatcherism: Assessing and Exploring Thatcherite Social and Economic Policies*, 77–99. Oxford: Oxford University Press, 2014.

Himmelfarb, Gertrude. *The Idea of Poverty: England in the Early Industrial Age*. London: Faber and Faber, 1984.

Hindle, Steve. "Civility, Honesty and the Identification of the Deserving Poor in Seventeenth-Century England." In H. French and J. Barry, eds, *Identity and Agency in England, 1500–1800*, 38–59. Basingstoke: Palgrave, 2004.

– "Dependency, Shame and Belonging: Badging the Deserving Poor c.1550–1750." *Social and Cultural History* 1 (2004): 6–35.

– "Destitution, Liminality and Belonging: The Church Porch and the Politics of Settlement in English Rural Communities c.1590–1660." In C. Dyer, ed., *The Self-Contained Village? The Social History of Rural Communities 1250–1900*, 46–71. Hatfield: Hertfordshire University Press, 2007.

– "'Goodly, Godly and Charitable Uses': Endowed Charity and the Relief of Poverty in Rural England c.1555–1750." In A. Goldgar and R. Frost, eds, *Institutional Culture in Early Modern Society*, 164–89. Leiden: Brill, 2004.

– "The Problem of Pauper Marriage in Seventeenth-Century England." *Transactions of the Royal Historical Society* 8 (1998): 71–89.

Hirschmann, Nancy, and Beth Linker, eds. *Civil Disabilities: Citizenship, Membership and Belonging*. Philadelphia: Pennsylvania University Press, 2015.

Hitchcock, David. "A Typology of Travellers: Migration, Justice, and Vagrancy in Warwickshire, 1670–1830." *Rural History* 23 (2012): 21–39.

– *Vagrancy in English Culture and Society, 1650–1750*. London: Bloomsbury, 2016.

Hitchcock, Tim. "Begging on the Streets of Eighteenth Century London." *Journal of British Studies* 44 (2005): 478–98.

– *Down and Out in Eighteenth-Century London*. London: Hambledon, 2004.

– "The London Vagrancy Crisis of the 1780s." *Rural History* 24 (2013): 59–72.

– "Vagrant lives." In J. McEwan and P. Sharpe, eds, *Accommodating Poverty: The Housing and Living Arrangements of the English Poor, c.1600–1850*, 125–144. Basingstoke: Palgrave Macmillan, 2011.

Hobbs, Andrew. *A Fleet Street in Every Town: The Provincial Press in England, 1855–1900.* Cambridge: Open Book, 2018.

Hollen Lees, Lynn. *The Solidarities of Strangers: The English Poor Laws and the People, 1700–1948.* Cambridge: Cambridge University Press, 1998.

Hollis, Patricia. *Ladies Elect: Women in English Local Government, 1865–1914.* Oxford: Oxford University Press, 1987.

Hoppit, Julian. "Reforming Britain's Weights and Measures, 1600–1824." *English Historical Review* 108 (1993): 82–104.

Hudson, John, Neil Lunt, Charlotte Hamilton, Sophie Mackinder, Jed Meers, and Chelsea Swift. "Exploring Public Attitudes to Welfare over the Longue Durée: Re-Examination of Survey Evidence from Beveridge, Beatlemania, Blair and Beyond." *Social Policy and Administration* 50 (2015): 691–711.

Hughes, Bill. "Disabled People as Counterfeit Citizens: The Politics of Resentment Past and Present." *Disability and Society* 30 (2015): 991–1004.

Humphries, Jane. *Childhood and Child Labour in the British Industrial Revolution.* Cambridge: Cambridge University Press, 2010.

Humphreys, Robert. *Poor Relief and Charity 1869–1945: The London Charity Organization Society.* Basingstoke: Palgrave, 2001.

Hunt, Alan. *Governing Morals: A Social History of Moral Regulation.* Cambridge: Cambridge University Press, 1999.

Hunt, Edward. "Paupers and Pensioners, Past and Present." *Ageing and Society,* 9 (1989): 408–22.

Hupe, Peter, Michael Hill, and Aurélien Buffat. "Defining and Understanding Street-Level Bureaucracy." In P. Hupe, M. Hill, and A. Buffat, eds, *Understanding Street-Level Bureaucracy,* 3–24. Bristol: Policy Press, 2015.

Hurren, Elizabeth. *Protesting About Pauperism: Poverty, Politics and Poor Relief in Late-Victorian England, 1870–1900.* Woodbridge: Boydell and Brewer, 2007.

Innes, Joanna. "The Experience of 'Reform' in English Local Governance in the Era of the 'Reform Ministry' (1830–1841)." In J. Pollmann and H. te Velde, eds, *Civic Continuities in an Age of Revolutionary Change, c.1750–1850,* 221–47. Basingstoke: Palgrave, 2023.

Innes, Joanna, Steven King, and Anne Winter. "Settlement and Belonging in Europe, 1500–1930s: Structures, Negotiations and Experiences." In S. King and A. Winter, eds, *Migration, Settlement and Belonging in Europe, 1500s–1930s,* 1–28. Oxford: Berghahn, 2013.

Jensen, Steven, and Charles Walton. "Not 'Second-Generation Rights': Rethinking the History of Social Rights." In S. Jensen and C. Walton, eds, *Social Rights and the Politics of Obligation in History,* 1–25. Cambridge: Cambridge University Press, 2022.

Jensen, Tracey, and Imogen Tyler. "'Benefit Broods': The Cultural and Political

Crafting of Anti-Welfare Commonsense." *Critical Social Policy* 35 (2015): 470–91.

Jones, Harriett. "A Bloodless Counter-Revolution: The Conservative Party and the Defence of Inequality, 1945–51." In H. Jones and M. Kandiah, eds, *The Myth of Consensus: New Views on British History 1945–64*, 1–16. Basingstoke: Macmillan, 1996.

– "The Illusion of Conservative Support for the Welfare State, 1942–1959." In A. Capet, ed., *Pauvreté et Inegalités en Grande-Bretagne, 1942–1990*, 109–20. Lyon: University of Lyon Press, 2011.

Jones, James. "Emotional Communities in the Cinema: Tracing Emotion in Mass Observation Cinema Records, 1937–1950." In K. Egan, M. Smith and K. Terrill, eds, *Researching Historical Screen Audiences*, 102–20. Edinburgh: Edinburgh University Press, 2022.

Jones, Peter, and Steven King. *Pauper Voices, Public Opinion and Workhouse Reform in Mid-Victorian England-Bearing Witness*. Cham: Palgrave, 2020.

– "Voices from the Far North: Pauper Letters and the Provision of Welfare in Sutherland, 1845–1900." *Journal of British Studies* 55 (2016): 76–98.

Kidd, Alan. State, *Society and the Poor in Nineteenth Century England*. Basingstoke: Macmillan, 1999.

Kim, Yushim, and Spiro Maroulis. "Rethinking Social Welfare Fraud from a Complex Adaptive Systems Perspective." *Administration & Society* 50 (2018): 78–100.

King, Peter. *Crime and Law in England, 1750–1840: Remaking Justice from the Margins*. Cambridge: Cambridge University Press, 2006.

– "The Rights of the Poor and the Role of the Law: The Impact of Pauper Appeals to the Summary Courts 1750–1834." In P. Jones and S. King, eds, *Obligation, Entitlement and Dispute under the English Poor Laws*, 235–62. Newcastle: Cambridge Scholars Press, 2015.

– "The Summary Courts and Social Relations in Eighteenth-Century England." *Past and Present* 183 (2004): 125–72.

King, Steven. "The British Welfare Citizen: Past, Present, Future." In G. Gregorini, M. Taccolini, and R. Semeraro, eds, *I Volti della Povertá. Temi, parole,fonti per la stria dei sistemi di support sociale tra modernitá e globalizzazione*, 37–41. Milan: Trebateur, 2022.

– "Fractured Courtships in Britain in the Long Nineteenth-Century." *Family and Community History* 21 (2023): 38–56.

– "'In These You May Trust': Numerical Information, Accounting Practices and the Poor Law, c.1790 to 1840." In T. Crook and G. O'Hara, eds, *Statistics and the Public Sphere: Numbers and the People in Modern Britain, c.1750–2000*, 51–66. London: Routledge, 2011.

– "Poor Relief, Settlement and Belonging in England 1780s to 1840s." In S. King and A. Winter, eds, *Migration, Settlement and Belonging in Europe, 1500s–1930s*, 81–101. Oxford: Berghahn, 2013.

– *Poverty and Welfare in England 1700–1850: A Regional Perspective*. Manchester: Manchester University Press, 2000.

– "Remembering the Dead Poor in the Midlands, 1750s to 1880s." *Midland History* 47 (2022): 292–312.

– "'still about the town': Constructing Disability in Small Town Nineteenth Century England." *Family and Community History* 25 (2022): 98–120.

– "*We Might be Trusted*": Women, Welfare and Local Politics 1880–1920. Brighton: Sussex Academic Press, 2005.

– "Women, Work and the Economy of Makeshifts in Midland and Northern England, 1700 –1840." In P. Lane, N. Raven, and K. Snell, eds, *Women, Work and Wages in England, 1600–1850*, 119–40. Woodbridge: Boydell, 2004.

– *Writing the Lives of the English Poor, 1750s–1830s*. London: McGill-Queen's University Press, 2019.

King, Steven, Paul Carter, Natalie Carter, Peter Jones, and Carol Beardmore. *In Their Own Write: Contesting the New Poor Law, 1834–1900*. London: McGill-Queen's University Press, 2023.

King, Steven, and Peter Jones. "Fragments of Fury? Lunacy, Agency and Contestation in the Great Yarmouth Workhouse, 1890s–1900s." *Journal of Interdisciplinary History* 51 (2020): 235–66.

– "Testifying for the Poor: Epistolary Advocates for the Poor in Nineteenth Century England and Wales." *Journal of Social History*, 49 (2016), 784–807.

King, Steven, and John Stewart, eds. *Welfare Peripheries*. Oxford: Peter Lang, 2007.

Kjaer, Lars. *The Medieval Gift and the Classical Tradition: Ideals and the Performance of Generosity in Medieval England, 1100-1300*. Cambridge: Cambridge University Press, 2019.

Klair, Andrew. *Universal Credit and the Impact of the Five Week Wait for Payment*. London: TUC, 2020.

Knight, Abigail, Julia Brannen, and Rebecca O' Connell. "Re-using Community Oral History Sources on Food and Family Life in the First World War." *Oral History* 43 (2015): 63–72.

Koch, Insa, and Deborah James. "The State of the Welfare State: Advice, Governance and Care in Settings of Austerity." *Journal of Anthropology* 87 (2022): 1–21.

Koven, Seth. "Borderlands: Women, Voluntary Action, and Child Welfare in Britain, 1840-1914." In S. Koven and S.Michel, eds, *Mothers of a New World: Maternalist Politics and the Origins of Welfare States*, 94–135. London: Routledge, 1993.

Lacey, Stephen. *Cathy Come Home*. Basingstoke: Palgrave, 2011.

Lain, David, Laua Airey, Wendy Loretto, and Sarah Vickersatff. "Older Workers and

Ontological Precarity: Between Precarious Employment, Precarious Welfare and Precarious Households." In A. Grenier, C. Phillipson, and R. Settersten Jr, eds, *Precarity and Ageing*, 90–114. Bristol: Policy Press, 2021.

Land, Hilary. "The Introduction of Family Allowances: an Act of Historic Justice?" In C. Ungerson, ed., *Women and Social Policy: A Reader*, 9–29. Basingstoke: Macmillan, 1985.

Land, Isaac. "Bread and Arsenic: Citizenship from the Bottom up in Georgian London." *Journal of Social History* 45 (2005): 89–110.

Lassalle, Didier. "Policing the Margins: Anti-Social Behaviour and the 'Underclass Discourse.'" In S. Pickard, ed., *Anti-Social Behaviour in Britain: Victorian and Contemporary Perspectives*, 192–202. Basingstoke: Palgrave Macmillan, 2014.

Lawrence, Paul. "The Vagrancy Act (1824) and the Persistence of Pre-emptive Policing in England since 1750." *British Journal of Criminology* 57 (2017): 513–31.

Leneman, Leah. *Alienated Affections: The Scottish Experience of Divorce and Separation, 1684–1830*. Edinburgh: Edinburgh University Press, 1998.

León, María Gómez, and Herman De Jong. "Inequality in Turbulent Times: Income Distribution in Germany and Britain, 1900–50." *Economic History Review* 72 (2019): 1073–98.

Levene, Alysa. *Jews in Nineteenth-Century Britain: Charity, Community and Religion, 1830–1880*. London: Bloomsbury, 2020.

Levine-Clark, Marjorie. *Unemployment, Welfare and Masculine Citizenship: So Much Honest Poverty in Britain 1870–1930*. Basingstoke: Palgrave, 2015.

Levitt, Ian. *Poverty and Welfare in Scotland 1890–1948*. Edinburgh: Edinburgh University Press, 1988.

Lewis, Jane. "Gender, the Family and Women's Agency in the Building of 'Welfare States': The British Case." *Social History* 19 (1996): 37–55.

Lindbeck, Assar, Nyberg Sten, and Weibull Jörgen. "Social Norms and Welfare State Dynamics." *Journal of the European Economic Association* 1 (2003): 533–42.

Lindert, Peter. *Growing Public: Social Spending and Economic Growth since the Eighteenth Century, Volume 2, Further Evidence*. Cambridge: Cambridge University Press, 2004.

– "Poor Relief before the Welfare State: Britain versus the Continent, 1780–1880." *European Review of Economic History* 2 (1998): 101–40.

– *Welfare States: Achievements and Threats*. Cambridge: Cambridge University Press, 2019.

Lister, Ruth. "The Age of Responsibility: Social Policy and Citizenship in the Early 21st Century." *Social Policy Review* 23 (2011): 63–84.

Livingstone, Sonya, and Peter Lunt. *Talk on Television: TV Talk Shows and Public Debate*. London: Routledge, 1994.

Loveland, Ian. "Policing Welfare: Local Authority Responses to Claimant Fraud in the Housing Benefit Scheme." *Journal of Law and Society* 16 (1989): 187–209.

Lowe, Rodney. *The Welfare State in Britain since 1945*, 3rd ed. Basingstoke: Palgrave Macmillan, 2005.

Lundström, Ragnar. "Framing Fraud: Discourse on Benefit Cheating in Sweden and the UK." *European Journal of Communication* 28 (2013): 630–45.

Lupton, Ruth, Tania Burchardt, John Hills, Kitty Stewart, and Polly Vizard, eds. *Social Policy in a Cold Climate Policies and their Consequences since the Crisis.* Bristol: Policy Press, 2016.

Lupton, Ruth, and Anne Power. "Disadvantaged by Where You Live? New Labour and Neighbourhood Renewal." In J. Hills and K. Stewart, eds, *A More Equal Society? New Labour, Poverty, Inequality and Exclusion*, 119–42. Bristol: Policy Press, 2005.

Lyons, Martyn. *The Writing Culture of Ordinary People in Europe c.1860–1920.* Cambridge: Cambridge University Press, 2013.

Macdonald, Robert, Tracy Shildrick, and Andy Furlong. "'Benefits Street' and the Myth of Workless Communities." *Sociological Research Online* 19 (2014). Unpaginated.

Mack, Phyllis. *Heart Religion in the British Enlightenment: Gender and Emotion in Early Methodism.* Cambridge: Cambridge University Press, 2008.

MacNicol, John. "Family Allowances and Less Eligibility." In P. Thane, ed., *The Origins of British Social Policy*, 137–202. London: Routledge, 1978.

–"Reconstructing the Underclass." *Social Policy and Society* 16 (2017): 99–108.

Mair, Laura. *Religion and Relationships in Ragged Schools: An Intimate History of Educating the Poor, 1844-1870.* London: Routledge, 2019.

Marks, Lara. "'The Luckless Waifs and Strays of Humanity': Irish and Jewish Immigrant Unwed Mothers in London, 1870–1939." *Twentieth Century British History* 3 (1992): 113–37.

Marshall, Dorothy. *The English Poor in the Eighteenth Century.* New York: Augustus Kelley, 1969.

Martin, Jim, and David Rose. *Genre Relations: Mapping Culture.* London: Equinox Books, 2008.

Mashaw, Jerry. *Bureaucratic Justice: Managing Social Security Disability Claims.* New Haven: Yale University Press, 1983.

Mau, Steffen. *The Moral Economy of the Welfare State.* London: Routledge, 2003.

McArthur, Daniel, and Aaron Reeves. "The Rhetoric of Recessions: How British Newspapers Talk about the Poor When Unemployment Rises, 1896–2000." *Sociology* 53 (2019): 1005–25.

McCarthy, Helen. "Pearl Jephcott and the Politics of Gender, Class and Race in Postwar Britain." *Women's History Review* 28 (2019): 779–93.

McKay, Stephen, and Karen Rowlingson. "Social Security under the Coalition and

Conservatives. Shredding the System for People of Working Age: Privileging Pensioners." In H. Bochel and M. Powell, eds, *The Coalition Government and Social Policy: Restructuring the Welfare State*, 179–200. Bristol: Policy Press, 2016.

McKeever, Gráinne. "Detecting, Prosecuting and Punishing Benefit Fraud: The Social Security Administration (Fraud) Act 1997." *The Modern Law Review* 62 (1999): 261–70.

– "Social Citizenship and Social Security Fraud in the UK and Australia." *Social Policy and Administration* 46 (2012): 465–82.

McIvor, Arthus. "Guardians of Workers' Bodies? Trade Unions and the History of Occupational Health and Safety." *Labour History* 119 (2020): 1–30.

Meers, Jed. "Discretion as Blame Avoidance: Passing the Buck to Local Authorities in 'Welfare Reform.'" *Journal of Poverty and Social Justice* 27 (2019): 41–60.

– "Panacean Payments: The Role of Discretionary Housing Payments in the Welfare Reform Agenda." *Journal of Social Security Law* 22 (2015): 115–29.

Menefee, Samuel. *Wives for Sale: An Ethnographic Study of British Popular Divorce*. Oxford: Blackwell, 1981.

Millar, Jane, and Fran Bennett. "Universal Credit: Assumptions, Contradictions and Virtual Reality." *Social Policy and Society* 16 (2017): 169–82.

Miller, Henry. *A Nation of Petitioners: Petitions and Petitioners in the United Kingdom, 1780–1918*. Cambridge: Cambridge University Press, 2023.

Mills, Catherine. *Regulating Health and Safety in the British Mining Industries, 1800–1914*. Farnham: Ashgate, 2010.

Mitchison, Rosalind. *The Old Poor Law in Scotland: The Experience of Poverty, 1574–1845*. Edinburgh: Edinburgh University Press, 2000.

– "Who were the poor in Scotland 1690-1830." In R. Mitchison and P. Roebuck, eds, *Economy and Society in Scotland and Ireland*, 140–8. Edinburgh: John Donald, 1988.

Molander, Anders. *Discretion in the Welfare State: Social Rights and Professional Judgement*. Abingdon: Routledge, 2016.

Mooney, Gerry. *Stigmatising Poverty? The Broken Society and Reflections on Anti -Welfarism in the UK Today*. London: Oxfam, 2011.

Morgan, Gwenda, and Peter Rushton. "The Magistrate, the Community and the Maintenance of an Orderly Society in Eighteenth Century England." *Historical Research* 76 (2003): 54–77.

Moro-Egido, Ana, and Ángel Solano-Garcia. "Does the Perception of Benefit Fraud Shape Tax Attitudes in Europe?" *Journal of Policy Modelling* 42 (2020): 1085–105.

Morris, Charlotte, and Sally Munt. "Classed Formations of Shame in White, British Single Mothers." *Feminism & Psychology* 29 (2019): 231–49.

Morris, Lydia. "Activating, the Welfare Subject: The Problem of Agency." *Sociology* 54 (2020): 275–91.

–"Asylum, Welfare and Civil Society: A Case Study in Civil Repair." *Citizenship Studies* 13 (2009): 365–79.

– *Dangerous Classes: The Underclass and Social Citizenship.* London: Routledge, 1994.

–"Moral Economy from above and below: Contesting Contraction of Migrant Rights in Austerity Britain." *Journal of Ethnic and Migration Studies* 47 (2021): 1686–1703.

– "New Labour's Community of Rights: Welfare, Immigration and Asylum." *Journal of Social Policy* 36 (2007): 39–57.

– "Reconfiguring Rights in Austerity Britain: Boundaries, Behaviours and Contestable Margins." *Journal of Social Policy* 48 (2019): 271–91.

– "The Topology of Welfare-Migration-Asylum: Britain's Outsiders Inside." *Journal of Poverty and Social Justice* 28 (2020): 245–64.

– "Welfare, Asylum and the Politics of Judgement." *Journal of Social Policy* 39 (2009): 119–38.

Morissens, Ann, and Diane Sainsbury. "Migrants' Social Rights, Ethnicity and Welfare Regimes." *Journal of Social Policy* 34 (2005): 637–60.

Morrison, James. "'Scrounger-Bashing' as National Pastime: The Prevalence and Ferocity of Anti-welfare Ideology on Niche-Interest Online Forums." *Social Semiotics* 31 (2021): 383–401.

Muldrew, Craig, and Steven King. "Cash, Wages and the Economy of Makeshifts, 1650–1800." In J. Hatcher and J. Stephenson, eds, *Seven Centuries of Unreal Wages*, 267–306. Basingstoke: Palgrave, 2018.

Murphy, Edward. *The Politics of Compassion: The Challenge to Care for the Stranger.* New York: Rowman and Littlefield, 2018.

Neill, Edmund. "Conservative Thinkers and the Post-War State, 1945–79." In L. Goldman, ed., *Welfare and Social Policy in Britain since 1870: Essays in Honour of Jose Harris*, 162–77. Oxford: Oxford University Press, 2019.

Nijhuis, Dennie. "Rethinking the Beveridge Strait-jacket: The Labour Party, the TUC and the Introduction of Superannuation." *Twentieth Century British History* 20 (2009), 70–95.

Noble, Virginia. *Inside the Welfare State: Foundations of Policy and Practice in Post-War Britain.* London: Routledge, 2009.

Ogborn, Miles. "Local Power and State Regulation in Nineteenth Century Britain." *Transactions of the Institute of British Geographers* 17 (1992): 215–26.

Okoroji, Celestin, Ilka Gleibsand, and Sandra Jovchelovitch. "Elite Stigmatisation of the Unemployed: The Association between Framing and Public Attitudes." *British Journal of Psychology* 112 (2021): 207–29.

Oppenheimer, Melanie, Erik Eklund, and Joanne Scott, eds. *The State of Welfare: Comparative Studies of the Welfare State at the End of the Long Boom, 1965–1980.* Oxford: Peter Lang, 2018.

Ottaway, Suzanna. "Introduction: authority, autonomy, and responsibility among the aged in the pre-industrial past." In S. Ottaway, L. Botelho and K. Kitteridge, eds, *Power and Poverty: Old Age in the Pre-Industrial Past*, 1–12. Westport, CT: Greenwood, 2002.

Owen, Randall, and Sarah Harris. "'No Rights without Responsibilities': Disability Rights and Neoliberal Reform under New Labour." *Disability Studies Quarterly* 32 (2012): 1–21.

Page, Robert. *Clear Blue Water? The Conservative Party and the Welfare State since 1940*. Bristol: Policy Press, 2015.

Paget, David. "'Cathy Come Home' and 'Accuracy' in British Television Drama." *New Theatre Quarterly*, 15 (1999): 75–90.

Paterson, Audrey. "The Poor Law in Nineteenth-Century Scotland." In D. Fraser, ed., *The New Poor Law in the Nineteenth Century*, 171–93. Basingstoke: Macmillan, 1976.

Paterson, Laura, and Ian Gregory. "Characterising Poverty in Place: Benefit Receipts in Britain." In L. Paterson and I. Gregory, eds, *Representations of Poverty and Place*, 159–92. Basingstoke: Palgrave, 2019.

Paterson, Laura, Laura Coffey-Glover, and David Peplow. "Negotiating Stance within Discourses of Class: Reactions to Benefits Street." *Discourse and Society* 27 (2016): 195–214.

Patrick, Ruth. "All in It Together? Disabled People, the Coalition and Welfare to Work." *Journal of Poverty and Social Justice* 20 (2012): 307–10.

– "Living with and Responding to the 'Scrounger' Narrative in the UK: Exploring Everyday Strategies of Acceptance, Resistance and Deflection." *Journal of Poverty and Social Justice* 24 (2016): 245–59.

– "Work as the Primary 'Duty' of the Responsible Citizen: A Critique of this Work-Centric Approach." *People, Place & Policy Online* 6 (2012): 5–15.

Patriquin, Larry. *Agrarian Capitalism and Poor Relief in England, 1500–1860: Rethinking the Origins of the Welfare State*. Basingstoke: Palgrave, 2007.

Paz-Fuchs, Amir. *Welfare to Work: Conditional Rights in Social Policy*. Oxford: Oxford University Press, 2008.

Pemberton, Simon, Eldin Fahmy, Eileen Sitton, and Karen Bell. "Navigating the Stigmatised Identities of Poverty in Austere Times: Resisting and Responding to Narratives of Personal Failure." *Critical Social Policy* 36 (2016): 21–37.

Peretz, Elizabeth. "The Forgotten Survey: Social Services in the Oxford District: 1935-40." *Twentieth Century British History* 22 (2011): 103–13.

Perry, Matt. *Bread and Work: The Experience of Unemployment, 1918–39*. London: Pluto, 2000.

– *The Jarrow Crusade: Protest and Legend*. Sunderland: University of Sunderland Press, 2005.

Pierson, Paul. *Dismantling the Welfare State: Reagan, Thatcher and the Politics of*

Retrenchment. Cambridge: Cambridge University Press, 1994.

Plant, Raymond. *Citizenship, Rights and Socialism*. London: Fabian Society, 1988.

Power, Anne, and Helen Willmot. "Bringing up Families in Poor Neighbourhoods under New Labour." In J. Hills and K. Stewart, eds, *A more Equal Society: New Labour, Poverty, Inequality and Exclusion*, 277–96. Bristol: Policy Press, 2005.

Prochaska, Frank. "Philanthropy." In F. Thompson, ed, *The Cambridge Social History of Britain 1750-1950*, 357–93. Cambridge: Cambridge University Press, 1990.

Pugh, Martyn. "Working-Class Experience and State Social Welfare, 1908–1914: Old Age Pensions Reconsidered." *Historical Journal* 45 (2002): 775–96.

Raison, Timothy. *Tories and the Welfare State: A History of Conservative Social Policy since the Second World War*. Basingstoke: Macmillan, 1990.

Ranchordás, Sofia, and Ymre Schuurmans. "Outsourcing the Welfare State: The Role of Private Actors in Welfare Fraud Investigations." *European Journal of Comparative Law and Governance* 7 (2020): 5–42.

Rawson, Graham. "Poor Relief Administration in the 1840s, and Its Effect on the Poor: The Carlton Gilbert Incorporation, and Holbeck, Leeds." *Northern History* 56 (2019): 78–96.

Redford, Arthur. *The History of Local Government in Manchester. Volume II: Borough and City*. London: Longman, 1940.

Reiss, Matthias. "From Poor Relief to Politics: The Protest of the British Unemployed in the 1870s and 1880s." In M. Reiss and M. Perry, eds, *Unemployment and Protest: New Perspectives on Two Centuries of Contention*, 75–107. Oxford: Oxford University Press, 2011.

Reiss, Matthias. "The Image of the Poor and the Unemployed: The Example of Punch, 1841–1939." In A. Gestrich, S. King, and L. Raphael, eds, *Being Poor in Modern Europe: Historical Perspectives 1800-1940*, 389–415. Oxford: Peter Lang, 2006.

Rieger, Bernhard. "Making Britain Work Again: Unemployment and the Remaking of British Social Policy in the Eighties." *English Historical Review* 133 (2018): 634–66.

Roberts, Christopher. "The Language of 'Welfare Dependency' and 'Benefit Cheats': Internalising and Reproducing the Hegemonic and Discursive Rhetoric of 'Benefit Scroungers.'" In A. Mooney and E. Sifaki, eds, *The Language of Money and Debt*, 189–204. Cham: Palgrave, 2017.

Roberts, Elizabeth. "The Recipients' View of Welfare." In J. Bornat, R. Perks, P. Thompson, and J. Walmsley, eds, *Oral History, Health and Welfare*, 205–27. London: Routledge, 1999.

Römer, Felix. "Poverty, Inequality Statistics and Knowledge Politics under Thatcher." *English Historical Review* 137 (2022): 513–51.

Rose, Michael. *The English Poor Law 1780–1930*. Newton Abbot: David and Charles, 1971.

Rosenwein, Barbara. *Emotional Communities in the Early Middle Ages*. Ithaca, NY: Cornell University Press, 2006.

Rowlingson, Karen, Claire Whyley, Tony Newburn, and Ryan Berthoud. *Social Security Fraud: The Role of Penalties*. London: HMSO, 1997.

Royston, Sue. *Mending the Holes: Restoring Lost Disability Elements to Universal Credit*. London: DBC, 2019.

Rushton, Peter. "Local Laws, Local Principles: The Paradoxes of Local Legal Processes in Early Modern England." In M. Lobban, J. Begiato, and A. Green, eds, *Law, Lawyers, and Litigants in Early Modern England*, 185–206. Cambridge: Cambridge University Press, 2019.

Ryland-Epton, Louise. "'The Source of All Local Authority': The Role of Gloucestershire Magistrates in Local Government 1800–1834." *Midland History* 45 (2020): 326–40.

Samuel, Raphael. "'Quarry Roughs': Life and Labour in Headington Quarry 1860–1920." In R. Samuel, ed., *Village Life and Labour*, 139–263. London: Routledge and Kegan Paul, 1975.

Saraceno, Chiara. "Retrenching, Recalibrating, Pre-distributing. The Welfare State Facing Old and New Inequalities." *Structural Change and Economic Dynamics* 51 (2019): 35–41.

Savage, Gail. "'The magistrates are men': Working-Class Marital Conflict and Appeals from the Magistrates Court to the Divorce Court after 1895." In G. Robb and N. Erber, eds, *Disorder in the Court: Trials and Sexual Conflict at the Turn of the Century*, 231–49. Basingstoke: Macmillan, 1999.

– "They Would if They Could: Class, Gender, and Popular Representation of English Divorce Litigation, 1858–1908." *Journal of Family History* 36 (2011): 173–90.

Schürer, Kevin, and Joseph Day. "Migration to London and the Development of the North-South Divide, 1851–1911." *Social History* 44 (2019): 26–56.

Scott, James. *Domination and the Arts of Resistance: Hidden Transcripts*. New Haven: Yale University Press, 1990.

– *Weapons of the Weak: Everyday Forms of Peasant Resistance*. New Haven: Yale University Press, 1987.

Seaber, Luke. *Incognito Social Investigation in British Literature: Certainties in Degradation*. Cham: Springer, 2017.

Seabrook, Jeremy. *Cut Out: Living Without Welfare*. London. Left Book Club/Pluto, 2016.

Seccombe, Karen, Delores James, and Kimberley Walters. "'They think you ain't much of nothing': The Social Construction of the Welfare Mother." *Journal of*

Marriage and Family 60 (1998): 849–65.

Sen, Amartya. "Poor Relatively Speaking." *Oxford Economic Papers* 35 (1983): 153–69.

Shave, Samantha. *Pauper Policies: Poor Law Practice in England, 1780–1850.* Manchester: Manchester University Press, 2017.

Shepard, Alexandra. "Honesty, Worth and Gender in Early Modern England." In H. French and J. Barry, eds, *Identity and Agency in England 1500–1800*, 87–105. Basingstoke: Palgrave, 2004.

Shildrick, Tracy, and Robert MacDonald. "Poverty Talk: How People Experiencing Poverty Deny Their Poverty and Why They Blame 'The Poor.'" *The Sociological Review* 61 (2013), 285–303.

Y-K Shin, Young-Kyu, Teemu Kemppainen, and Kati Kuitto. "Precarious Work, Unemployment Benefit Generosity and Universal Basic Income Preferences: A Multilevel Study on 21 European Countries." *Journal of Social Policy* 50 (2021): 323–45.

Skinner, Annie. *Behind Closed Doors: Hidden Histories of Children Committed to Care in the Late Nineteenth Century (1882–1899).* Oxford: Peter Lang, 2021.

Slack, Paul. *Poverty and Policy in Tudor and Stuart England.* New York: Longman, 1988.

– "Vagrants and Vagrancy in England, 1598–1664." *Economic History Review* 27 (1974): 360–79.

Sloman, Peter. "Beveridge's Rival: Juliet Rhys-Williams and the Campaign for Basic Income, 1942–55." *Contemporary British History* 30 (2016): 203–23.

Smith, Richard. "Ageing and Well-Being in Early Modern England: Pension Trends and Gender Preference under the English Old Poor Law 1650–1800." In P. Johnson and P. Thane, eds, *Old Age from Antiquity to Postmodernity*, 64–95 . London: Routledge, 1998.

Smyth, James. "'Seems decent': Respectability and poor relief in Glasgow." In A. Gestrich, S. King and L. Raphael, eds, *Being Poor in Modern Europe*, 251–72. Oxford: Peter Lang, 2006.

Snell, Keith. "Belonging and Community: Understandings of 'Home' and 'Friends' among the English Poor, 1750–1850." *Economic History Review* 65 (2011): 1–25.

–*Parish and Belonging: Community, Identity, and Welfare in England and Wales, 1700–1950.* Cambridge: Cambridge University Press, 2006.

Sohn, Kitae. "Did Unemployed Workers Choose Not to Work in Interwar Britain? Evidence from the Voices of Unemployed Workers." *Labor History* 54 (2013): 377–92.

Sokoll, Thomas. "Families, Wheat Prices and the Allowance Cycle: Poverty and Poor Relief in the Agricultural Community of Ardleigh 1794–1801." In P. Jones and S. King, eds, *Obligation, Entitlement and Dispute under the English Poor*

Laws, 78–106. Newcastle: Cambridge Scholars Press, 2015.

Spicker, Paul. "The Case for Supplementary Benefit." *Fiscal Studies* 7 (1986): 28–44.

Steggle, Matthew. *Richard Brome: Place and Politics on the Caroline Stage*. Manchester: Manchester University Press, 2004.

Sticchi, Francesco. *Mapping Precarity in Contemporary Cinema and Television: Chronotopes of Anxiety, Depression, Expulsion/Extinction*. Cham: Palgrave, 2021.

Sutton, David. "Liberalism, State Collectivism and the Social Relations of Citizenship." In M. Langan and B. Schwarz, eds, *Crises in the British State, 1880–1930*, 63–79. London: Hutchinson, 1985.

Tabili, Laura. *Global Migrants, Local Culture: Natives and Newcomers in Provincial England, 1841–1939*. Basingstoke: Palgrave, 2011.

– "'Having Lived Close Beside Them All the Time': Negotiating National Identities Through Personal Networks." *Journal of Social History* 40 (2005): 369–87.

Tadmor, Naomi. "The Settlement of the Poor and the Rise of the Form in England, c.1662–1780." *Past and Present* 236 (2017): 43–97.

Taylor, Geoffrey. *The Problem of Poverty 1660–1834*. London: Longman, 1969.

Taylor–Gooby, Peter. "The Divisive Welfare State." *Social Policy and Administration* 50 (2016): 712–33.

– *A Left Trilemma: Progressive Public Policy in an Age of Austerity*. London, Policy Network, 2012.

– "Polity, Policy-Making and Welfare Futures." In P. Taylor-Gooby. ed., *Welfare States under Pressure*, 171–88. London: Sage, 2002.

– "Re-doubling the Crises of the Welfare State: The Impact of Brexit on UK Welfare Politics." *Journal of Social Policy* 46 (2017): 815–35.

– "Welfare Reform in the UK: The Construction of a Liberal Consensus." In P. Taylor-Gooby, ed., *Welfare States under Pressure*, 147–70. London: Sage, 2002.

Taylor-Gooby, Peter, Charlotte Hastie, and Catherine Bromley. "Querulous Citizens: Welfare Knowledge and the Limits to Welfare Reform." *Social Policy and Administration* 37 (2003): 1–20.

Taylor-Gooby, Peter, Bjørn Hvinden, Steffen Mau, Benjamin Leruth, Miah Schoyen, and Adrienn Gyory. "Moral Economies of the Welfare State: A Qualitative Comparative Study." *Acta Sociologica* 20 (2018): 1–16.

Taylor-Gooby, Peter, Trine Larsen, and Johannes Kananen. "Market Means and Welfare Ends: The UK Welfare Experiment." *Journal of Social Policy* 33 (2004): 573–92.

Taylor-Gooby, Peter, and Eleanor Taylor. "Benefits and Welfare: Long-Term Trends or Short-Term Reactions." In J. Curtice and R. Ormston, eds, *BSA 32*, 1–28. London: National Centre for Social Research, 2015.

Tebbutt, Melanie. *Women's Talk?: A Social History of 'Gossip' in Working-Class Neighbourhoods, 1880–1960*. Aldershot: Scolar, 1995.

Thane, Pat, and Tanya Evans. *Sinners? Scroungers? Saints?: Unmarried Motherhood in Twentieth-Century England*. Oxford: Oxford University Press, 2012.

Thiel, Darren. "'It isn't charity because we've paid into it': Social Citizenship and the Moral Economy of Welfare Recipients in the Wake of 2012 UK Welfare Reform Act." *Qualitative Sociology*, 45 (2022): 291–318.

Thomson, David. "The Decline of Social Welfare: Falling State Support for the Elderly since Early Victorian Times." *Ageing and Society* 4 (1984): 451–82.

– "'I Am Not My Father's Keeper': Families and the Elderly in Nineteenth Century England." *Law and History Review* 2 (1984): 265–86.

Timonen, Virpi. "Earning Welfare Citizenship: Welfare State Reform in Finland and Sweden." In P. Taylor-Gooby, ed., *Welfare States under Pressure*, 29–51. London: Sage, 2002.

Todd, Selina. "Family Welfare and Social Work in Post-War England, c.1948–1970." *English Historical Review* 129 (2014): 362–87.

Tomkins, Alannah. "Poor-Law Institutions through Working-Class Eyes: Autobiography, Emotion, and Family Context 1834–1914." *Journal of British Studies* 60 (2021): 434–72.

Tunley, Martin. "Need, Greed or Opportunity? An Examination of Who Commits Benefit Fraud and Why They Do It." *Security Journal* 24 (2011): 302–19.

– "COUNTERBLAST: Another Case of Old Wine in New Bottles? The Coalition's Misguided Strategy to Reduce Benefit Fraud." *The Howard Journal of Criminal Justice* 50 (2011): 314–17.

Turner, David. "Impaired Children in Eighteenth-century England." *Social History of Medicine* 30 (2017): 788–806.

Turner, David, and Daniel Blackie. *Disability in the Industrial Revolution: Physical Impairment in British Coalmining 1780–1880*. Manchester: Manchester University Press, 2018.

Valentine, Gill, and Catherine Harris. "Strivers vs Skivers: Class Prejudice and the Demonisation of Dependency in Everyday Life." *Geoforum* 53 (2014): 84–92.

van Oorschot, Wim. "Who Should Get What and Why? On Deservingness Criteria and the Conditionality of Solidarity among the Public." *Policy & Politics* 28 (2000): 33–48.

Vincent, Andrew. "The Poor Law Reports of 1909 and the Social Theory of the Charity Organisation Society." In D. Gladstone, ed., *Before Beveridge: Welfare Before the Welfare State*, 64–85. London: IEA, 1999.

Vincent, David. *Bread, Knowledge and Freedom: A Study of Nineteenth-Century Working Class Autobiography*. London: Europa, 1981.

– *Literacy and Popular Culture: England 1750–1914*. Cambridge: Cambridge University Press, 1989.

Vizard, Polly. *Poverty and Human Rights: Sen's 'Capability Perspective' Explored.* Oxford: Oxford University Press, 2006.

Vorspan, Rachel. "Vagrancy and the New Poor Law in Late Victorian and Edwardian England.", *English Historical Review* 92 (1977): 59–81.

de Vries, Robert, Aaron Reeves, and Geiger Baumberg, "Social Class Bias in Welfare Sanctioning Judgements: Experimental Evidence from a Nationally Representative Sample." *Social Policy and Administration* 56 (2022): 843–58.

Waddell, Brodie. "The Rise of the Parish Welfare State in England, c. 1600–1800." *Past and Present* 253 (2021): 151–94.

– "Writing History from Below: Chronicling and Record-Keeping in Early Modern England." *History Workshop Journal* 85 (2018): 239–64.

Wahrman, Dror. *The Making of the Modern Self: Identity and Culture in Eighteenth Century England.* New Haven: Yale University Press, 2004.

Walsh, David, Coral Dando, and Thomas Ormerod. "Triage Decision-Making by Welfare Fraud Investigators." *Journal of Applied Research in Memory and Cognition* 7 (2018): 82–91.

Walton, Caroline. "Taking Control: Gossip, Community and Conflict in Basford Union Workhouse 1836 to 1871." *Family and Community History* 23 (2020): 23–41.

Welshman, John. *Underclass: A History of the Excluded 1880-2000.* London: Hambledon Continuum, 2006.

Webb, Sydney, and Beatrice Webb. *English Poor Law History Part I: The Old Poor Law* and *Part II: The Last Hundred Years.* London: Cass, 1963 reprint.

Wessel Hansen, Peter. "Grief, Sickness and Emotions in the Narratives of the Shamefaced Poor in Late Eighteenth–Century Copenhagen." In A. Gestrich, E. Hurren, and S. King, eds, *Poverty and Sickness in Modern Europe: Narratives of the Sick Poor 1780–1938*, 35–50. London: Bloomsbury, 2012.

Whiteside, Noel. "Who Were the Unemployed? Conventions, Classifications and Social Security Law in Britain (1911–1934)." *Historical Social Research* 40 (2015): 150–69.

– "Creating the Welfare State in Britain, 1945–1960." *Journal of Social Policy* 26 (1996): 83–103.

Wiede, Wiebke. "The Poor Unemployed: Diagnoses of Unemployment in Britain and West Germany in the 1970s and 1980s." In B. Althammer, L. Raphael and T. Stazic-Wendt, eds, *Rescuing the Vulnerable: Poverty, Welfare and Social Ties in Modern Europe*, 307–34. Oxford: Berghahn, 2016.

Williams, Karel. *From Pauperism to Poverty.* Oxford: Routledge and Kegan Paul, 1981.

Williams, Samantha. "Malthus, Marriage and Poor Law Allowances Revisited: A Bedfordshire Case Study, 1770–1834." *Agricultural History Review* 52 (2004): 56–82.

– *Unmarried Motherhood in the Metropolis, 1700–1850: Pregnancy, the Poor Law and Provision*. Basingstoke, Palgrave, 2018.

Wrigley, Anthony, and Richard Smith. "Malthus and the Poor Law." *Historical Journal* 63 (2020): 33–62.

Zupko, Ronald. "The Weights and Measures of Scotland before the Union." *Scottish Historical Review* 56 (1977): 119–45.

INDEX

Please note that the term *pauper* in the index is understood as an umbrella term, including those receiving welfare (both before and after the reforms of 1929) and those mentioned in the book in their capacity as experiencing poverty. Some of the people mentioned acted in more than one capacity, such as advocating for one pauper and then snitching on another. For example, James Thompson (and several others like him) therefore appears under both "paupers and the poor: advocates for" and "paupers and the poor: informants on." Long strings of undifferentiated page references can be found in three places: "government: departments and functions: *Hansard*"; "oral history, focus groups and interviews: participants, comments made by"; and "oral history, focus groups and interviews: Roberts, Elizabeth, work of." Each of these strings reflects both the huge amount of discourse that the poor and how they should be treated generates, and the repetitive nature of that discourse. An index lacks the power necessary to break that cycle. It is hoped that the page references listed under "oral history" will assist readers who wish to consult the original transcripts when they become available online. Finally, page numbers in italics refer the reader to tables or other images.

(*see* writers and commentators: Egerton, Rev. John Coker); Rev. J.L. Foster, 60; Rev. Thomas Holt, 74–5; Rev. Skinner (*see* writers and commentators: Skinner, Rev. John); Rev. J. Swinstead, 74–6; Rev. Oliver Wilmott, 91

Cottage Homes Movement, 103

crime: fraud (*see* fraud); organised, 45; prison, 75–6, 90, 181, 205–8; prostitution, 74, 142, 166, 212–14; theft, 76, 93, 191, 201, 209; vagrancy (*see* travellers: vagrants and beggars)

disability: blindness, 56, 111, 130, 205; definitions of, 108–15; Disability Living Allowance (*see* welfare: Disability Living Allowance); disabled adults, children of, 25; dogs, ability to keep, 291n64; dwarfism, 110, 212; fraud and/or dishonesty, elision with, xi, 10, 25, 109–10, 227, 243–4; Incapacity Benefit (*see* welfare: Incapacity Benefit); lameness, 56, 111, 158; mental (*see* illness and injury, mental). *See also* illness and injury, physical

Dodsworth, Matthew, 73

economic matters: cost-of-living crisis, 18, 238; downturns, 4–5, 8, 15–16, 63, 75, 92, 152; inflation, 220–1, 248; MoneySaving Expert, 106; national debt, ix, 156, 248; pensions (*see* pensions); unemployment (*see* unemployment); tax (*see* tax); Universal Basic Income (UBI), 253, 259

ego-documents: blogs, 30–4, 52, 53, 109–10, 170–1, 246–7, 271n48; diaries, autobiographies, and memoirs (*see* letters; writers and commentators: Egerton, Rev. John Coker; writers and commentators: Skinner, Rev. John)

emigration, 77, 141. *See also* immigrants and immigration, 77, 141

employment: agricultural labour and farming, 56, 74–5, 101, 159–60, 176, 245; apprenticeship, 41–2, 78, 85, 200; brewing and publicans, 136–7; building and bricklaying, 99; children in, 104–5; compositors, 75; domestic service and cleaning, 56, 85, 121, 137, 165, 208; glass-blowing, 75; hawking and selling, 106, 175; leatherwork (bridle-stitching), 165; medics (doctors, midwives), 127, 140, 219; merchant navy, 91; military service, 62–3, 73, 82, 88, 106, 158; mining, 42, 62, 85, 131, 159, 209; needlework, 138; painting, 165, 208; sailmaking, 71; shoemaking, 73, 107; spinning, 78; weaving, 78; wood-selling, 56, 100. *See also* unemployment

England

– Belgrave (Leicestershire), 124
– Berkshire: Bracknell, 240–1; Bradfield, 127; Caversham, 181
– Birmingham: 84, 165–6, 201
– Buckinghamshire, 50, 105–6, 129, 141, 187; Buckingham, 101; Chepping Wiccombe, 186; Cuddington, 129
– Cambridgeshire: Cambridge, 124, 165; Godmanchester, 93; Peterborough, 42–3
– Cheshire: Altrincham, 202–3; Hale, 164; Nantwich, 107

West Bromwich, 86
- Yorkshire, 165; Barnsley, 81; Bedale, 73; Beverley, 77, 80–1; Bradford, 73; Hull, 125; Reeth, 211, 226; Sandal Magna, 185 Settle, 148–9; Sheffield, 200; South Cave, 175, 180; Wakefield, 185; York, 60, 88
Exeter, Marquis of, 127–8

film and TV: *Benefits Street*, x, 78; *The Block*, 119, 195; *Born to Be Small*, 111; *Boys from the Blackstuff*, 201, 210–11; *Cathy Come Home*, 8, 33, 44, 174; *The Crown*, 142; *I, Daniel Blake*, 33, 44, 108, 136, 204, 252; *Kilroy*, 211; *Panorama*, 83, 139, 184, 295n68, 297n21; *Skint*, 33; *To Catch a Cheat*, 150–1, 164–5, 178, 199, 209
Ford, Carole, 109–10
France, 77, 253
fraud
- accidental: capital, status of, 129–30; cash-in-hand, status of, 142, 157; change in circumstance, failing to report, 66; cohabitation and lovers, 121–2, 132–5, 156 (*see also* marriage); forms, complexity of, xvi, 24, 82, 123–8, 226, 235: gifts, 128–9, 168; income, overseas, 105; law, complexity of ("knowability"), 96–7, 225; work, actively seeking, 123, *124*, 135–8. *See also* paupers and the poor: "deserving," features of
- associational, 25, 69–95
- attitudes to: benefit dependence, elision with, 79; cultural representations of (*see* film and TV); disability, elision with, xi, 10, 25, 109–10, 227, 243–4; "familiarity gap," 6–7; immigration, elision with, xi, 10, 25, 90–3, *90*, 97, 129;

Scottishness, elision with (*see* Scotland); single motherhood, elision with, ix–xi, 54–5, 79–81, 86, 153–4, 179–80, 194 (*see also* parents and parenting: mothers and motherhood; parents and parenting: single); tolerance of (empathy, sympathy), xvii, 158–63, *160*, 167–8, 189–90, 216; Welshness, elision with, 86, *87*
- definition and redefinition of (changes, rules, tests), xi–xiii, xvi, 7, 20–5, 63–4, 96–122, 126, 161
- exposure of (detection, reporting, "snitching"), 147–68, 153, 155, 160, 179; hotline, 151, 157, 161, 199, 208. *See also* paupers and the poor: informants on ("snitches")
- intentional, 22–5; Chishimba, Joy, 20–1, 24; David, Elise, ix, 206; Hetherington, Mark ("The Stripping Ninja"), ix; Lyttleton, David, 23; Matthews, Mr J., 203; Mole, Joanne, 41, 44; Sarwar, Iftikhar, 67; Shelbourne, Mary, 199–200; Stevens, Mrs, 211; Story, William, 207; Waters, Jonathan, 186
- professional, skilled. *See* crime: organised
- prosecution of (conviction), 28, 41, 50, 178, 186, 194, 201; alternatives to, 198–200
- scale of, assumed, 51–3, *51*, 53, 59–61, 67, 72, 151–2, 229, 254–5, 258; scale of, assumed (inflated), 33–5, 62–5, 69–70, 100–1, 129–30, 164, 180, 197
- staff employed to prevent, 172–4, *173*, 178, 181–5, 193; collusion with fraudsters, 193, 210–13, *213*, 219; *Targeting Benefit Fraud* (2006), 256. *See also* welfare

heart disease, 136; injuries and accidents, 21–2, 156 (*see also* Health and Safety Movement); lameness (inability to walk), 56, 111, 158; long-term (*see* disability); medical neglect, 140; multiple sclerosis, 205; paralysis, 131; Parkinson's disease, 109; sensory, 111–13, 153; smallpox, 230; temporary (chronic, fluctuating, episodic), 23–4, 107, 131, 137; ulcers, 112. *See also* disability

immigrants and immigration: Afghan, 23; Catholic, 92; English, 84, 87; entitlement to welfare (prior contribution, lack of), 4, 117; fraud, elision with, 10; illegal, 20; Irish, 87–8, 197, 208; Jewish, 92; Methodist, 92; Moravian, 92; Polish, 90; Romanian, 89; Scottish, 84, 91–2, 153, 208; Somali, 89; Syrian, 91; Welsh, 84–6, 140, 153

information brokers, 59, 71

information state, 60

Ireland: Dublin, 208; Irish Potato Famine, 87–8; migration (*see* immigrants)

journalists. *See* writers and commentators

legal matters. *See* crime; officials: legal knowledge of

letters, 26–7, 50; advocates', addressed to officials (*see* paupers and the poor: advocates for); anonymous, 147–8, 210; confidential, 160; hand-delivered, 124; paupers', addressed to newspapers, 30, 60, 65; paupers' and advocates', addressed to officials, 91–2, 98, 112, 127, 137;

officials', addressed to other officials, 134, 147–8, 214; postal orders, 147; snitches', addressed to officials (*see* paupers and the poor: informants on ["snitches"]); social investigators', addressed to officials, 73–4

life-writing. *See* ego-documents

literacy and illiteracy, xvi–xvii, 27, 74, 107–8, 124–6

magistrates and judges, 4, 50, 63, 181, 187, 208; Robert Houseman, 203; Angela Neild, 41, 64–7, 191; Richard Wyatt, 70

Malthus, Thomas, and Malthusian views, 43, 76, 257

marriage: abandonment, 77, 134–7, 147, 155–6, 168, 182–3, 197, 200; abusive, 70, 130, 147–8, 196–7; adultery (philandering), 70; bigamy, 134; cohabitation, 121–2, 132–5, 156; divorce, 23–4, 134, 156; parenting (*see* parents and parenting); remarriage, 134; weddings, 56; widowhood (*see* paupers and the poor: widows)

members of Parliament. *See* government: MPs, ministers, and staff

migration. *See* immigrants and immigration

natural justice, 21, 55

New Poor Law (Poor Law Amendment Act, 1834): control, attempt to gain, 6, 91–2, 112; *General Orders*, 102, 113; outdoor relief (*see* workhouses [indoor relief]); parishes, reorganisation of, 3, 15

newspapers and journals: *Daily*

Crawshaw, 185; Jonas Crossley, 190; Henry Goodwin, 106; William Gordon, 86; Thomas Hawkins, 43; Ken Marsland, 131; Colonel McLean, 177; Edward Miles, 141; Donald Munro, 164; Benjamin Nathall, 43; Robert Neil, 111; John Rutherford, 32; William Smart, 227; Alexander Sparrow, 86; James Thompson, 164; John Thorpe, 202; Andrew Wright, 181

– aged. *See* pensions

– agency of, 12, 106, 257

– children, attitudes towards: child benefit (child support) (*see* welfare: child benefit [child support]); illegitimate, 4, 80–2, 104, 122, 180, 212; invented (fake), 90, 158; settlement of, 125; starvation of, 203

– definitions of. *See* fraud: definition and redefinition of

– "deserving," features of: disabled, 111, 233 (*see also* disability); grateful, 4, 14, 244–6; honest, 15, 29, 41, 55, 99; independent (self-reliant), 17, 98, 105, 109, 132, 220; prior contribution, 4, 15–16, 117, 138, 220, 245; sexual restraint, 4, 15

– families, friends, and neighbours of (kin), 71–3, 105–6, 142, 162, 169, 190, 239, 250

– "undeserving," features of: bad language, use of, 56–7; dishonest ("dodgy," "shifty"), 12, 18, 25–9, 34, 41–7, 50, 67–84, 228–33, 253; "dodgy" places, residents of, 82–4; lazy "dossers," "scroungers," "skivers," "workshy," 9–10, 54, 64–5, 86, 105, 116–18, 136, 252; pregnant (sexually incontinent, licentious), 57, 79, 82,

125, 132, 180, 195; ungrateful, 20

– individuals: Mary Ann August, 177; James Bagnes, 203; Henry Beans, 101; Eleanor Beck, 24; James Bennett, 185–6; John Booth, 103; Rachel Boothman, 140; Thomas Bowen, 77; George Bradford, 98; Samuel Bradshaw, 71; Henry Brenner, 127–8; Frances Brizes, 134; Isaac Edwards Bronhealog, 140; Elizabeth Brown, 137; Thomas Brown, 137; Elizabeth Brownlow, 42–3; Phillis Brunskill, 211; Marie Buchan, ix–x; Mary Burns, 191; Ann Candler, 168–9; John Carroll, 86; Mary Chester, 190; George Cleaver, 85; Robert Colson, 56; Percy Cross, 158; Jacob Curchin, 179; Sophia Curchin, 179; Jessie McDonald Datcharn, 128; Robert Davies, 186; Martin Ferguson, 65; Michael Flannagan, 88; Peregrine Ford, 129; Grace Fowler, 105; Catharine Fraser, 112; Alice Geeson, 130; Richard George, 132; Ben Griffiths, 162; Elizabeth Glasby, 80–1; Sarah Goold, 70; Anne Grant, 200; Christopher Grime, 102, 148–9; Ann Gronow, 159; Edward Gronow, 159; Diane Halko, 246; Mrs Charles Hall, 182; Thomas Hardy, 141; Mary Harte, 55; William Haynes, 207; Mary Haywood, 187–8; George Hewins, 193; Mary Hewins, 136–7; Ellen Hodkinson, 180; Hannah Holme, 164; Barbara Ingham, 147–8; James Johnson, 175; John Jones, 140; Isabella Kay, 247; Mary Keating, 208; John Knight,154; Andrea Lawner, 180; William Leeson, 207; Edward Levies, 65; John Lloyd, 65; Emma

Locke, 197; James MacDougall, 79; Barbra MacKay, 74; Jane Mackay, 125; Johanna (Johan) MacKay, 57; "Mary the Black Girl," 93; Kitty Massey, 164; Robert Mawman, 77; Joseph Mayett, 106; Hughina McKay (aka Hughina Neilson), 104; Roderick McKay, 113; Rachel McLean, 177; Angus McPhee, 112; James Miller, 226; Mrs Moon, 212; Sam Murray, 112; James Nelson, 142; James Oakes, 207–8; Sarah O'Hara, 88; Thomas Olden, 209; Christopher Page, 180; Robert Paine, 62; John Pearson, 21–2; Ann Pole, 125; Thomas Pole, 125; Christina Pomfrey, 205–6; Mary Porter, 197; Thomas Potter, 207; Edward Prynn, 107; Joseph Pulford, 129; William Rogers Sr, 137–8, 223; Mrs E. Redford ("Banbury Female Martyr"), 156, 254; Mrs Rhodes, 190; Carl Richards, 35, 18; Henry Rutter, 163; Rachel Scott, 106; James Seel, 103; Edward Shrewsbury, 86; Thomas Smith, 129–30; William Smith, 244; Martha Springer, 134, 212; Abigail Taylor, 124; John Thompson, 71–2; Henry Townsend, 134; Peter Vale, 202; Thomas Venes Jr, 91–2; Jane Vinall, 186; Hannah Wadsworth (Wordsworth), 200; Sarah Wadsworth, 200; Mary Warden, 130; Samuel West, 42; John Whitgrove, 85
– informants on ("snitches"): Joseph Ady, 147; James Betts, 181; Ralph Blackwell, 211–12; Ann Boswell, 201; David Edwards, 159; Leonard Gilbert, 107; Samuel Grundy, 148–9; Matthew Hughes, 165–6; W. Lambrick, 215–16; Thomas Simcox Lea, 207–8; Dr Gregor MacDonald, 57; Colin McKay, 156; Colonel McLean, 177; M.B. Rhys, 65; Charles Spilman, 80–1; Edward Thomas, 159; James Thompson, 164. See also fraud: exposure of (detection, reporting, "snitching")
– widows, 106–7, 135, 190–3, 227; Bagnes, 203; Bainbridge, 134; Brown, 181; Cope, 48; Sarah Doe, 43; Garrett, 212; Elizabeth Haynes, 165–6; Langridge, 102–3; Sarah McBride, 122; Seely, 104; Mary Stafford, 82; Rebecca West, 42; Nancy Williams, 111; Margaret Wilson, 56; Nellie Wilson, 162

pensions: credits, xvi, 24, 237; definitions of, 18; DWP (see government: departments and functions); right to, 249–50; state, creation of, 119; war widows', 103, 122

poetry, 73, 78, 168–9, 251

poverty, causes of, 29; bad weather (winter), 154, *155*, 187–8, 226; definitions of (see fraud, definition and redefinition of); disability (see disability); economic depression (see economic matters: downturns); illness (see illness and injury, mental; illness and injury, physical); widowhood (see paupers and the poor: widows)

prison. See crime: prison

Proby, P.J. 23, 183

racism, 88, 93; Order of the White Seamen's Brotherhood, 91

riots and rioting, 7, 99–100, 214, 231, 253

131, 137, 182, 191, 224, 246–7